H. Capelo, Roberto Ivens, Alfred Elwes

From Benguella to the Territory of Yacca

Description of a Journey into Central and West Africa - Vol. 2

H. Capelo, Roberto Ivens, Alfred Elwes

From Benguella to the Territory of Yacca
Description of a Journey into Central and West Africa - Vol. 2

ISBN/EAN: 9783337127916

Printed in Europe, USA, Canada, Australia, Japan

Cover: Foto ©Andreas Hilbeck / pixelio.de

More available books at **www.hansebooks.com**

FROM BENGUELLA
TO THE
TERRITORY OF YACCA.

Description of a Journey into
CENTRAL AND WEST AFRICA.

COMPRISING NARRATIVES, ADVENTURES, AND IMPORTANT SURVEYS
OF THE SOURCES OF THE RIVERS CUNENE, CUBANGO, LUANDO,
CUANZA, AND CUANGO, AND OF GREAT PART OF
THE COURSE OF THE TWO LATTER;

*Together with the Discovery of the Rivers Hamba, Cauali, Sussa, and
Cugho, and a detailed Account of the Territories of Quiteca
N'bungo, Sosso, Futa, and Yacca.*

BY

H. CAPELLO AND R. IVENS,

Officers of the Royal Portuguese Navy.

EXPEDITION ORGANIZED IN THE YEARS 1877—1880.

TRANSLATED BY

ALFRED ELWES, Ph.D.

WITH MAPS AND NUMEROUS ILLUSTRATIONS.

IN TWO VOLUMES.
VOL. II.

London:
SAMPSON LOW, MARSTON, SEARLE, & RIVINGTON,
CROWN BUILDINGS, 188, FLEET STREET.
1882.

[All rights reserved.]

IN RESPECTFUL REMEMBRANCE

OF

JOSÉ J. DE OLIVEIRA ANCHIETA,

THE ENLIGHTENED, UNTIRING, AND MODEST

NATURALIST AND EXPLORER

TO WHOM

SCIENCE AND HUMANITY

ARE SO DEEPLY INDEBTED

A SPECIAL PAGE OF THIS VOLUME

CONTAINING HIS PORTRAIT

IS DEVOTED BY

THE EXPLORERS.

CONTENTS OF VOL. II.

CHAPTER I.

PAGE

Last day at the fair and meditations under the old sycamores—Desertions and new recruits—General aspect of the country, temperature and effect of humidity—A native court and a cemetery—Sketch of an encampment on the march—Cambolla the *jagga*—Etiquette in the Banza—The sova's hat—Exchange of presents—The banks of the Lui and the baobabs—An excursion towards the Cuango—Difficult roads and dangerous currents—The water-snake and fetish preservatives—Alarm caused by a couple of leeches—The *jagga* of the Bondos and four salt lakes—A sacrifice to science—Native caravans—Proneness of the Africans to trade, and what they owe to it—The *pest of the woods*, and an unpleasant family of ants—Tala-Mogongo; its aspect and vegetation—A lovely prospect and the reflections it awakened 1

CHAPTER II.

Limits of Cassange—Native justice—Reflections upon the African character—The rise and course of the Cambo—The African opium—The insect world—Breaking up of the encampment—Capulca again—Lake Utamba—Deceptive medlars—N'Dala Samba and T'Chica—José do Telhado and mortality of the Europeans in Africa—Cuango and Cuanza—Divisional line of their waters—Cha-Landu and exactions of the petty sovas

—The Ambaquista, distinctive features, habits, importance, fondness for scribbling—Ascent of the morro Bango—Dr. Max Buchner, the German explorer—A queer ecclesiastic—The Lu-calla and Lianzundo cataract—Duque de Bragança and a dinner with Captain A. Silverio 24

CHAPTER III.

On the tramp again—The banks of the Lu-calla and a nice dispute—Catcco, the hunter of wives—The Jinga, its limits and importance—The king, titles and residence—Hierarchical scale—Peculiar mode of bestowal of property—The *ma-lunga* and *quijinga*—The Muco-N'Gola or Mona N'Gola—Strange headdresses and queer pockets—On the summit of the Serra Catanha—A love episode and its unpleasant close—Conjugal relations—An evening discussion and a morning flight—Mineral wealth of the Jinga—Mode of preparing cloth, dwellings, &c.—A storm in the forest, and a further desertion—Den of thieves—A page or two from the diary—A tough cow—Arrival at Cafuchila 48

CHAPTER IV.

The Hungo and its people—Head-dresses—Tobacco and snuff—Ugliness of the women, their indifference to dress—Low estimation in which they are held—The monarch of the Congo—Preparations for departure—Discussions with the natives—Sudden dissolution of a meeting—Abandoned senzalas—A little looting—Lake Tiber—The camp kitchen and an old acquaintance—A siesta disagreeably interrupted—Flight of the caravan—Fallen among thieves—A trial and a singular decision—The forest fired—Woods and vegetation—Quadrumans and reptiles—What explorers have to expect—Discovery of the river Cu-gho—Varieties of trees—Passage of the river and African cunning—A rest in the forest 71

CHAPTER V.

We leave the Cu-gho—Gloomy presentiments—The *mu-chitos* and the desert—An evening of tribulations and a devouring thirst—Trying times of a life in the interior—A Providential interposition—More *mu-chitos* and fresh labour—Caught in the wood—Nervous state of the explorers—All but lost—Scouts sent out in search of succour—Two lines from the diary—A terrible night—Return of José and brief narrative of his adventures—Two solitary hunters—Fresh hopes—Again astray—An apparition of palancas—Night again—Final decision 92

CHAPTER VI.

Opinion of the authors upon laconism in the description of toil and suffering—The night of the 27th May—Apprehensions—Night phantoms—An unexpected discovery—The women of the caravan—A marriage—Famine and plenty next-door neighbours—Having satisfied the body we seek distraction of mind—A wine-party—Quizengamo, an important *quilolo*, visits the encampment—Two pages from the diary—The guides urge us to repair to the Court of the Quianvo—Our own resolve—The Cuango and capricious sinuosities of its course—Frightful effects of dysentery—Putrid fermentation and the failure of food—A dance of the Ma-yacca—Abandoned in the forest—Fever, ulcers, and dysentery—Flight of the guide—The desert—Fragment of the diary—Baffled—Return—The Cugho 113

CHAPTER VII.

The author's experience respecting the importance of the stomach—Brief sketch of the course of the River Cuango—In the Cugho—The land of plenty—*Maluvo* wine and its collection—Lake Aquilonda wiped off the map—The palm and climatologic zones—The Rivers Sussa and Cauali—Vegetation—Sova

Catuma Cangando and indiscreet curiosity of his lady-subjects
—A native song—Strange ceremony among the Ma-hungo—
An interment in the woods—Danje, Luamba, Matamba, and
Pacaça Aquibonda—Caculo-Cabaça—Homicide of a carrier—
The value of life among the negroes—*Vunda*-ia-Ebo and the
last burial—The valleys of the Lu-calla and a story of a
crocodile—A new theory of Cosmogony—The delights of the
table—Passage of the Lu-calla—List of members of the
caravan that reached Duque de Bragança 139

CHAPTER VIII.

Duque de Bragança, its importance and fertility—Dinner-time
again—A Sova god-father—African children and some remarks concerning them—Infants and adults—Explanations
concerning our route—A parallel and the cardinal points—An
alarm—The encampment in flames—Anxious moments—The
papers of the explorers and the ammunition of the expedition
—Carriers and thieves—Things might have been worse—Otubo
and our clumsy assistant—" From sources small what great
events may spring "—The *bi-sonde* and the last night of the
month of July 162

CHAPTER IX.

Final departure from Duque de Bragança—One of José's stories—
The Lu-chilo and the *patrulhas*—The *Ptyelus olivaceus*—Captain Silverio's pets—The *Cosmetornis vexillarius*—José has
another uncle—Samba-Cango, the Hango and the Lu-calla—
Brief notice of the river, conformation of the land and vegetation—The Cariombo and Porto Real—Novel rafts and
ingenious method of propulsion—A visit to Pamba, and a
few remarks thereon—A vegetable giant—The road to Pedras
Negras—José and the basalts—Native silk—Pungo N'Dongo,
its aspect and constitution—Remarkable impressions on the
rocks—Port Hunga and its orange-trees—Philosophical con-

siderations of the explorers—" In the country of eyes, the blind are kings "—The Caballo cascade—The Cuanza, obstacles, fish, cataracts—Brief reflections thereon—Malange, Calundo, and Pungo N'Dongo 179

CHAPTER X.

Return to camp—The *pulex penetrans* and a noteworthy *entozoario*—Variableness of the winds at Pungo N'Dongo—The explorer's staff and the writer's pen—We take leave of Silverio—Cabeto and Cuanza flies—Native lightning-conductors—Capanda and the western vegetation—Brief notice of its ornithology—Sengue and Nhangue-ia-Pepe—Cataracts of the Cuanza—The Sova Dumba—Cassoque—Von Mechow—The Bango and climatological variations—The Cuanza and the Cabulo cataract—Last glance at the interior—The Dondo—Reception of the explorers at that place—A trip on the river—Loanda—Mossamedes—The voyage home 208

CONCLUSION 231
TABLE OF GEOGRAPHICAL OBSERVATIONS . . . 277
HEIGHTS ABOVE THE SEA-LEVEL . . . 282
ADDITIONS TO THE FAUNA 283
FLORA 299
AFRICAN DIALECTS 302
VOCABULARIES 304
INDEX 335

LIST OF ENGRAVINGS.

	PAGE
Domingos'. tender farewell	4
Catraio	5
The Caravan, in a long line, filed off	6
Construction of the Encampment	8
The Jagga Cambolla	11
Plunging into the thick grass	20
Following the steep and broken track	21
Native Box	23
Smoking the fatal Liamba	29
The colossal Lughias	33
A roadside Cemetery	36
An Ambaca Gentleman	41
"I am Dr. Max Buchner"	43
Lianzundo Cataract	45
Nest of the Capata-ieu	47
On the banks of the Lu-calla	49
Jinga Type	53
Cateco, the Guide	59
The Tempest had now reached its height	63
All but lost	67
We found the herd waiting	68
Sharpia Angolensis	70
The Ladies of the Hungo	73

List of Engravings.

	PAGE
Lake Tiber	79
The Holo Type	81
The Court was complete	84
We had to cut our way with the hatchet	87
The Cu-gho Watermen	90
Cynocephalus Porcarius	91
Slowly descending from a height	97
The Mu-chito	99
José and his Companions emerged from the Wood	106
The Palancas	110
Coracias Espatulata	112
Lemba, Mutu's Wife	117
The two Fugitives	121
Yacca Head-dresses	125
The Cuango in Yacca	129
Dances of the Ma-yacca	130
Woman of the Congo	134
The silence of the tomb reigned supreme	135
Qui-vuvi, the Silk-spider	138
Provisions literally showered	142
Curiosity punished	151
A terrible Mishap	155
Cosmetornis Vexillarius (Quimbamba)	161
A Sova Godfather	167
The Peril was intense	174
African Silk	178
The Patrulha of Samba Cango	184
It is a complete system of parallel screws	186
Rocks of Pungo N'Dongo	193
The Caballo Cascade	199
Telphusa Anchietæ, River Cuanza	200
Telphusa Bayonniana, River Cuanza	200
Euprepes Ivensi (new species), River Cuanza	201

List of Engravings.

	PAGE
Chromis Sparramanni (Smith), River Cuanza	201
Dembe (Mormyrus Lhuysi, Steind), River Cuanza	204
Muaca (Hemichromis Angolensis, Steind), River Cuanza	204
Chromis Moss Ambicus (Peters), River Cuanza	204
Highly ornamental frog, River Cuanza	205
River Cuanza Crab	207
Empacaceiro of Quissama	216
The Tipoia of Angola	224
The Voyage home	230

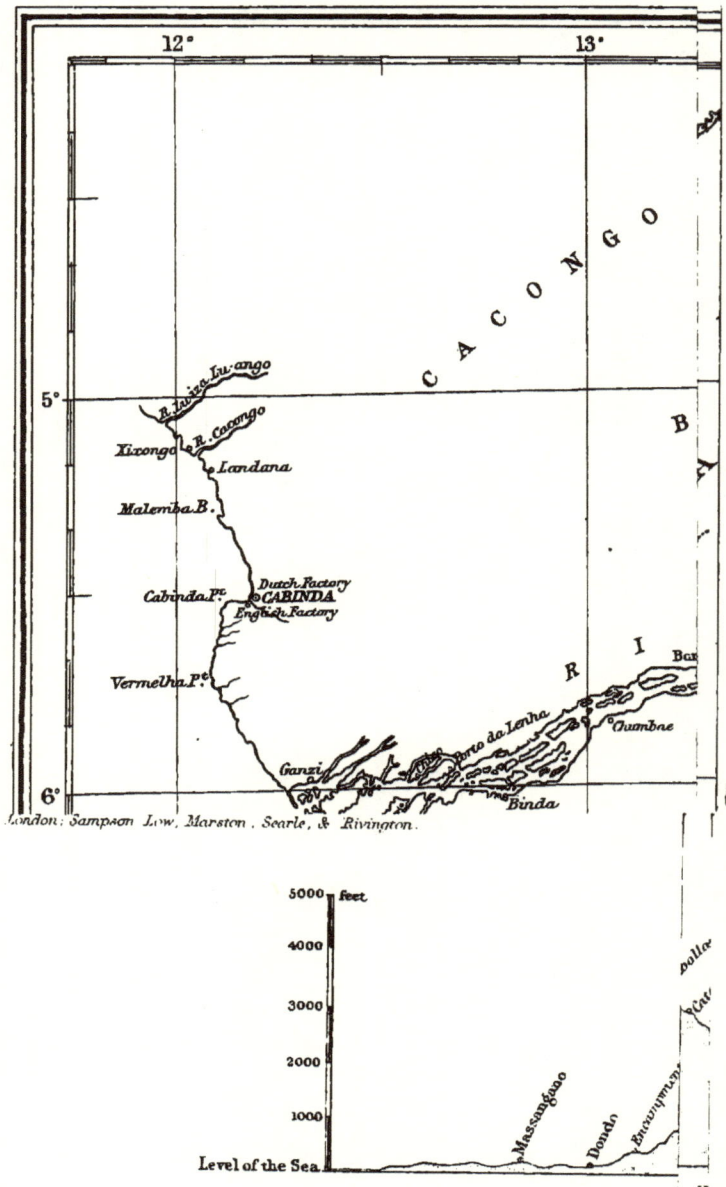

FROM BENGUELLA TO THE TERRITORY OF YACCA.

CHAPTER I.

Last day at the fair and meditations under the old sycamores—Desertions and new recruits—General aspect of the country, temperature and effect of humidity—A native court and a cemetery—Sketch of an encampment on the march—Cambolla the *jagga*—Etiquette in the Banza—The sova's hat—Exchange of presents—The banks of the Lui and the baobabs—An excursion towards the Cuango—Difficult roads and dangerous currents—The water-snake and fetish preservatives—Alarm caused by a couple of leeches—The *jagga* of the Bondos and four salt lakes—A sacrifice to science—Native caravans—Proneness of the Africans to trade, and what they owe to it—The *pest of the woods*, and an unpleasant family of ants—Tala-Mogongo; its aspect and vegetation—A lovely prospect and the reflections it awakened.

WE have before observed that the departure of a caravan for a long journey is always an event of some importance, as the reader would have admitted had he been by our side in Cassange in the afternoon of the 18th day of February in the year of grace 1879.

The ample terrace of our residence was encumbered with the various articles taken from the warehouses by the busy little band of boys. The work began as usual with a great deal more noise than was necessary, accompanied by animated jovial talk, a great display of

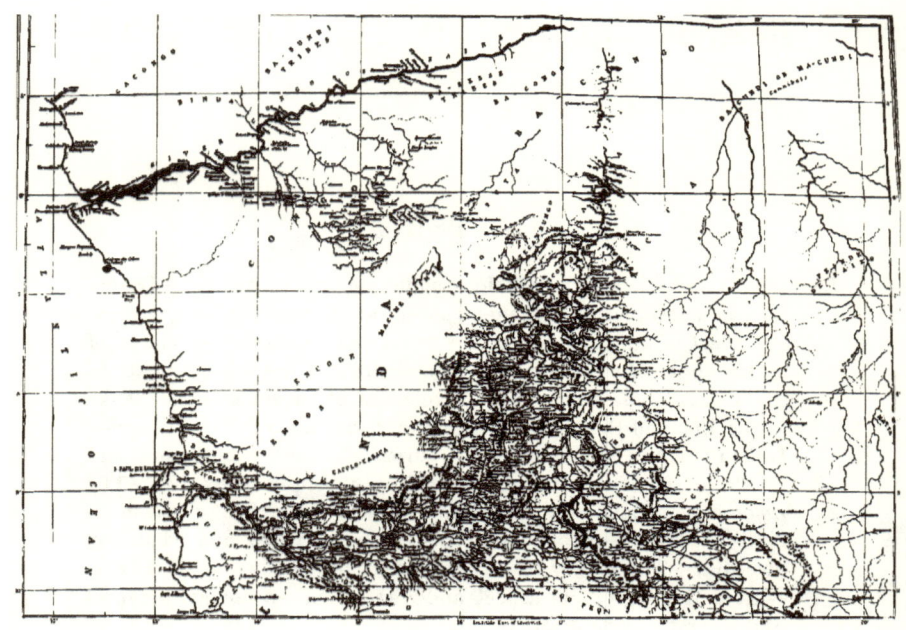

white teeth and sundry jokes from the more lazy of the crew seated on the bales and trunks.

Exchanges of loads, protests against their weight, substitution of muskets, pilferings of ropes and straps, or the loss of a key of an important case, that required to be opened, and which the intelligent carrier, after insane search, in a sudden fit of inspiration, suggested might be *inside*, made up some of the common incidents of the scene.

The sun, as it got high in the heavens, was a signal to knock off work, the goods being then all piled in readiness, and we took our last rest beneath those memorable sycamores.

Each had lighted his pipe and was puffing huge volumes of smoke in silence, his head sunk within the collar of his great-coat, his knees well drawn in and his body arched to the not unnatural position assumed by a man who has only a hard stone to sit upon!

Forty days had we passed in that place, gazing upon the miserable huts, and twice as many plans had we discussed and rejected in the interval. *L'homme propose et Dieu dispose* is a proverb which, however hackneyed, had been found to be only too true in Cassange scores of times.

"Cribbed, cabined, and confined" in that wretched hole, where our goods were stored in semi-picturesque disorder, at one time down with fever, and more often than not under its influence, a constant prey to ticks (*ma-n'cuba*) which had permanently settled about us, there was scarcely any form of annoyance that we had not gone through during our stay.

It has been seen how the excursion to the east was defeated by the Ban-gala; how a previous one to the north was frustrated by fever; how the rains prevented any wanderings in the neighbourhood; and finally, we may add, that interviews with the natives were so bootless and so fatiguing that we at last refused to receive them, owing to the insupportable impudence and pretensions of the petty chiefs.

Although Cassange cannot be reputed the worst of places, owing to the resources which it undoubtedly possesses, it was nevertheless one of those that we left without regret and would willingly have blotted from our memory.

José, our new guide, but recently engaged, had proposed to conduct us by a different road across the Jinga, until we should again fall in with the Cuango; but many of the carriers who took not the slightest interest in such an undertaking and had certainly no ambition to follow it out, deserted in a body and with them went the cabindas who had hitherto stuck by us. The guide, nevertheless, succeeded in getting some five-and-twenty fresh carriers and with them we had resolved to make a start.

The 18th of February had come and gone and at daybreak of the 19th, when in a sound sleep, a voice, issuing from a head popped within our cabin, exclaimed,—

"Senhores, it is five o'clock!"

Springing to our feet we issued the necessary instructions; had a capital breakfast in the dwelling of our good friend Narciso A. Paschoal, whom we beg in this place to thank for many acts of kindness; shook hands and exchanged cordial greetings with acquaintances we had made, and then watched the arranging of our men into marching order.

There were other leave-takings besides our own and some of them even assumed a poetic form. Of this complexion was the tender farewell of Domingos, a carrier, to his beloved Umba, wherein his *n'dengue* (heart) figured very prominently; his improvised song running,

> *Umba-ri-amé muene n'dengue Io-oendè.*
> *Umba-ri-amé muene n'dengue Io-oendè.*
> *Moi N'jinji.*

Or as it was translated to us,

> "Umba, my lady and my heart,
> From thee, N'jinji must depart!"

DOMINGOS' TENDER FAREWELL.

Catraio, our blundering assistant, was spared so painful a ceremony, for the simple reason that his affectionate spouse, for the twentieth time to our knowledge, had run away from him, and now seated on the ground, he sought consolation in his pipe while the bustle and confusion gradually gave place to order, and the caravan, in a long line, the porters duly laden, filed off to the westward.

In this fashion, then, we abandoned Cassange, and struck into the serpentine path which first crosses the undulating plateaux leading to the western mountains, makes its way along the slopes of the latter, traverses the territory of the Ban-gala and Ban-bondo, on the higher ground, and reaches at last the Portuguese station of the Duque de Braganza.

CATRAIO.

The expeditionary corps steered a direct course for the ravine of Tala-Mogongo, about seven days' journey from our point of departure. Crossing numerous rivulets, for the most part affluents of the Lui, some having an impetuous current, running through steep banks of schist others on a low flat bed, frequently inundating the adjacent country and giving birth to tall, stiff grass, ferns, *Papyrus*, *Typhus*, *Nenuphares*, *Victorias*, and *Mariangas*, the homes of numerous frogs, whose croakings were heard at a considerable distance and resembled the cackling of geese, and not a few toads, with a note not unlike the tinkling of grelôts, the caravan reached one of the most picturesque regions in this part of Africa.

What a pity, we thought, that our poets and our painters, who are compelled to see so many things with their mind's eye, cannot be transported hither to enjoy in reality the numerous sights and sounds which this magnificent country possesses in such profusion! What delight these romantic scenes would afford the ardent and

THE CARAVAN, IN A LONG LINE, FILED OFF.

insatiable imagination of the artist and the—but there we stopped, not being quite clear about the delight of the poet under such circumstances. So putting an end to our philosophical considerations, we plunged into the thicket and went on our way.

Under this latitude, the months of February and March are the hottest in the year, the thermometer reaching 87° Fahr. in the shade. The atmosphere so sultry and yet so full of humidity is then perilous in the extreme. When in the heart of the forest, the air, saturated with vapour is almost unbearable, and it is only with an effort that one can breathe at all. Under its influence, the very plants suffer; trunks of stout trees becoming everywhere covered with cryptogamic excrescences in a perfect state of putrefaction. As a natural consequence most metals oxydize with astonishing rapidity, and the barrels of our guns and pistols, our knives, the needles of the compasses and other articles were in a few hours covered with rust. Leather softened, the wood of our instruments warped, paper returned to its original pulp, our goods soaked up damp like so many sponges, to such a degree that it became necessary to open the bales and expose their contents to the sun, to prevent their utter destruction. In man, the effect of this dis-equilibrium of nature is to produce permanent dysentery.

At about noon, on the 25th, we reached the *banza* of the Sova Cambolla, the chief of one of the families in whom the *jaggado*, already referred to, is invested. Only a few moments previously, we had passed a gigantic sycamore under which a Court of so called *Justice* was sitting. An assassin was on his trial, his punishment being the payment of a fine to the family of the victim; and as, on the one hand, there was a *mu-cano*, and on the other a *quituche* in respect of the motives of the crime, the accused was likely to be heavily mulcted.

Leaving the *banza* on the west, we made for a pleasant eminence, which, being crowned with a group of graceful trees, looked a likely place for the construction of our *quilombo*. Loud cries, however, from the natives gave us to understand that the place was a cemetery; and compelled us to seek another site. We had noticed this to be the case so frequently that we determined in future to eschew picturesque localities for the pitching of our camp —at least, in the neighbourhood of villages, for the natives have quite a mania to select the most beautiful spots for the last resting-places of the dead.

Experience soon taught us that the best place for an encampment was in the wood, and as a general rule we erected it there. Such a site had always much in its favour. Material for the erection of the huts and for fuel was ready to the hand; our position was relatively independent, and we were relieved from the visits and inconveniences arising from a residence in the *libatas* of the sovas. On the other hand, we more than once got into hot water with these gentlemen for refusing to take up our quarters in their precincts, but we always found them disposed to yield if we showed sufficient firmness in our own determination. In the present instance having left the *libata*, near which we first thought of camping, half a mile behind us, we came upon some fresh water, and at once gave orders to pile the goods round a large tree.

Then ensued the busy scene that was usual on such occasions. Our men, who were now tolerably expert from long practice, started off in every direction. Some in search of young trees, which were cut down to form the skeletons of our huts. Others lopped off and brought in branches to fill in the interstices and make a first covering of the roof; whilst many more came laden with sheaves of the tall grass, to be used as thatch and as outer coating of the houses.

Work was going on inside as well as out. Three or four of the most expert would arrange the sleeping-places, composed of grass and dry leaves, on which were spread a couple of panther-skins; while Otubo neatly piled upon two or three tree-trunks, set in front of our huts, the whole of the goods, that were then covered with tarpaulins which we carried with us for the purpose.

When the two principal huts were built, the men ran

CONSTRUCTION OF THE ENCAMPMENT.

up their own little wigwams, disposed in a circle about our own, so as to leave our dwellings and the goods in the centre; and in about a couple of hours after our arrival the encampment was complete.

Meanwhile Capulca had been fitting up his camp-kitchen, and having turned out his pans, coffee-pots, knives, tin plates, cups, &c., he set two or three young niggers to work to clean them.

We ourselves were soon engaged in determining by divers observations the geographical co-ordinates with their variations, taking the bearings of the region in which we stood, and registering our meteorological calculations. The entering all these took up our time till about three in the afternoon, the hour generally selected for our principal meal. The little box that held the cups and plates served alternately as our working and our dining-table. Upon it were then placed a couple of plates with knives and forks, and on the ground a large iron pot of *infundi*, a dish of roasted meat, on fortunate days,—smoke-dried fish on others, and not unfrequently nothing whatsoever. Our food was seasoned with Chili pepper or *jindungo* which had the advantage of covering any flavour that the palate would otherwise have found objectionable. A cup of coffee and a pipe to finish off with did wonders towards making us satisfied with our homely fare.

Then would follow the hour for reflection and repose. An indigo sky, a pleasant temperature, a brilliant landscape, and a full stomach invited us to rest upon the springy surface of the grass, growing all about us, leaving to the " gentle zephyrs " the care of fanning us to sleep !

At two o'clock that afternoon we were introduced into the dwelling of the *jagga* Cambolla, a handsome residence, constructed in great part of *marianga*, perfectly interlaced with grass, and surrounded by a stockade.

The macotas, opening and shutting doors, introduced us successively into fresh compartments, till we wished their etiquette at the very deuce. And there was such an air of mystery about the whole proceeding, peeping into corners and nodding of heads as if they expected to find something which they were sure was lying concealed.

Two more compartments, traversed in the same way, brought us to the hall of reception, in the middle of which we found the old chief, seated on a low stool; a large framed, powerfully made man, already in years.

Like many of the other potentates of whom we have spoken he exercises absolute and despotic sway over numerous vassals, whom he treats at his good pleasure, makes war and peace as he thinks fit, takes everything he covets and possesses a variety of other prerogatives which his panegyrists are always dinning in his ear.

He was attired in a long cloth of printed calico, bound with blue, had bangles on his wrists and ankles, wore a bead-necklace, and on his head an enormous hat of a Portuguese infantry soldier of the eighteenth century, and which, driven right down to his ears, gave him a most grotesque appearance.

Regretting, as he informed us, his inability to treat us as he wished, he nevertheless made us a little present of an enormous black ox, which, not only refused to yield to the persuasion of a bullet that was put into him, but took to flight across country *ad perpetuam rei memoriam*.

Presenting him with some cloth in return and one of Cassai's pups, which his Majesty was very anxious to possess, we took leave of Cambolla Cangonga and pursued our way towards the west.

The River Lui.

Before us extended the azure line of the high land, terminating northwards in Mount Bango and the serried heads of the N'guri; and in the south the view was lost in the far horizon, where Bumba, another *jagga* of Cajinga, had his residence. On the south-east appeared a lofty peak, called Cassalla, the summit of which is known only to a few intrepid natives, who, having found water

THE JAGGA CAMBOLLA.

near the top, have converted it into a perfect fortress, held to be impregnable.

Having crossed the Lui, whose banks we found covered with the broad flags of *Arundo phragmites*, green ferns, eschinomenes—a species of sensitive plant—and edemonas, we continued on through inundated plains.

On the last day but one of the month of February, to the north-west of the Lu-ango senzala, the expedition was encamped on the precipitous bank of the Muhamba; a rapid torrent to which the waters from the mountains are drained and rush on to swell the Lui. Here we met our old friends the *baobabs*, those splendid trees we had lost sight of since we left Quillengues. The altitude was shown to be 3321 feet.

The rain at that time was coming down in *avalanches*. So after arranging our meteorological instruments, barometers, and thermometers in the open air, together with the psychrometers to estimate the humidity, we took shelter within our hut and looked disconsolately at the watery picture.

We still obstinately stuck to our idea of travelling north-eastward, in order to see whether we could not elude the Ban-gala and cross the Cuango through Holo. But our guides just as obstinately protested against it, asserting that the attempt would be a certain failure.

"Throughout Cassange," they averred, "the news had spread that the people of the Cuango had forbidden the whites to cross the river. That a short time before, a *t'chindelle* (referring to Otto Schutt) had got into trouble in the Yongo with the Calandula of the Caquilo and the *Banza* Quitumba-Caquipungo; you yourselves, further south, were stopped by the Banza-e-Lunda, and ran great risk of losing all your goods; so that the trying once more to force a way in the teeth of those savages would be to court defeat and probable destruction."

Admitting to a certain extent the force of this reasoning, we nevertheless held that an attempt might still be made by one of us to ascertain the feeling of the natives whilst the others remained in camp, and this being fully discussed and decided on, we at once proceeded to put the plan into execution.

Next morning, therefore, early, the exploring party

set out in the direction of the N'guri range, towering up in the north, and in whose vicinity the *jagga* of the Bondos had his dwelling.

Traversing the little plateau of the Luango, we began ascending and descending the undulating ground and plunging into fresh obstacles with every step. The brawling streams, rushing from the heights through the deep furrows worn in the mountain-side, committed all sorts of vagaries, at one time presenting a narrow but deep rivulet, at another inundating the lower ground, which it converted into marshes, where the water reached our waists.

Issuing from a low-sunken valley, we climbed on to the mountain slope, but had no sooner congratulated ourselves upon the change than we were buried in the thick grass and *papyrus*, and had thus to struggle with the forest and marshy vegetation combined.

These marches up and down, if prolonged to any extent, become somewhat insipid and monotonous, inasmuch as the side of the mountain on the one hand and the vegetation on the other, completely shut out all view, and leave nothing but a peak or two and the sky overhead to relieve the attention.

When crossing the river Bale, with the water to our middle, one of the carriers very nearly lost his life. It was a moment of intense anxiety, which was only relieved by dint of great exertion. The poor fellow stepped into one of those holes of soft mud, which are so frequent in these rivers, and sunk immediately down to his armpits; nothing, in fact, could have saved him if help had not been so near.

The woods we passed through were utterly deserted. Scarce a vestige of the passage of a caravan was discovered; the only evidence being the carbonized trunks of a few trees and a calcined stone or two in the more open ground.

Whilst cutting our way through dense underwood, a perfect labyrinth of canes and brambles, and where almost every tree exposed its complicated net-work of roots to the air, we observed, to our astonishment and alarm, the men who formed our vanguard throw down their loads and rush towards us.

"Uta! Uta!" was the cry. "A snake, senhor, an enormous boa!"

Desirous of ascertaining the truth, we advanced cautiously in the direction they pointed out, and made our way to the trunk of a colossal *Herminiera E.*, lying prone upon the ground, beside the precipitous bank of one of the torrents already referred to. Whilst peering about there suddenly emerged from the grass a gigantic head, followed by an enormous body, which, with a couple of undulations reached the stream and disappeared in the water. This apparition, most probably a water-snake or *Naja*, produced a most disheartening effect upon our men, not one of whom would now venture to ford the river, each saw the dreadful reptile at a different spot, only waiting an opportunity to devour him.

In order to frighten away the beast and destroy any secret and malignant influence it might be supposed to exercise, to the prejudice of our expedition, Master José, or Zé as they called him, here came to the rescue and exorcised the animal by a combined system of fetishism known only to himself. After the lapse of five minutes he came out of the wood, where he had ensconced himself, gave two piercing whistles and then declared the job complete and that we might enter the water without fear. But when half-way across, a sudden dash of the torrent, followed by a piercing shriek, sent all flying—ourselves, we must confess, among the number—while a man in mid-stream screamed out, "I'm lost! I'm dead!"

As, however, in spite of his asseveration he still held his ground, we went to the rescue, and dragged him out, when it was discovered that a couple of leeches had fixed upon his ankle and caused the cries which had so alarmed us.

On the 2nd of March, when passing the base of Mount Catanha, a porter was sent up to the *jagga's* senzala, with the customary present, subsequently following us towards the north-east, in the direction of the territory of the N'ganga N'zumba. That sova was absent, and the information obtained from his subjects entirely dissipated the notion we had conceived of reaching the Cuango in this direction.

"The Ban-gala will not allow you to pass," they all exclaimed; but apart from this, they informed us that the land through which the river Lu-anda ran was all under water; that four salt lakes, the property of N'ganga, also intervened and barred the passage; and that if even these difficulties were got over, the whole of the foot of the slopes beyond was inundated, and the track, for the time being, utterly swallowed up.

By this time our porter had arrived in company of an inhabitant of the senzala, who brought us a basket of *fuba*, by way of compliment, and an enormous bird (hearing probably that we had a taste for ornithology), which was accompanied by the inquiry whether there were any such beyond the *great water*.

It was a large, black palmiped with an immense beak like a toucan; the eyes reminded us of a chameleon, being circular, prominent and movable; the body resembled that of a duck but was much larger.

Unaware whether the creature was an acquaintance of

the naturalists, we evaded a reply, and as the doubt existed in our minds we saw no better mode of solving the problem than to wring its neck in the name of science, and substituting for the internal arrangements bestowed upon it by nature, a little cotton wool, wait quietly for the decision of the masters.

Seeing that there was nothing else to be done, we decided on returning the way we came, besides that the state of our health made such a proceeding advisable.

On the 3rd of the month, not only were we prostrated by fever, but dysentery set in, and the ulceration of the lower part of our legs resisted every treatment that we applied, so that the last days' journeys were a martyrdom.

Travelling again over the same ground, which had not been made easier in the interim, we fell in, upon the third day, with a caravan of Ma-songo, bound for the west with a heavy load of india-rubber and wax, forwarded from Cassange.

It appeared in the shape of a long file of men and boys, for the most part wearing a single rug suspended from a piece of rope round the waist, and in which they tucked their pipes, hatchets, knives and other articles; and as they marched intoning a monotonous song. The boys seemed to be of no little assistance to their elders, who, being laden with packages weighing some ninety pounds, in most cases divided their burthen with the young ones, so that many of these striplings had to carry forty pounds of weight.

The position of a trader in this part of the world is anything but an enviable one. No sooner had we reached the spot than any number of india-rubber balls were offered us for sale, abstracted from the bales by their carriers. As we had no inclination to do business, they dispersed and carried their stolen wares to the neighbouring senzalas where, of course, no end of disputes at once arose. In one instance a fellow wanted to exchange his gun, without a lock, for a new one, making up the difference with wax or india-rubber; in another, a carrier having procured some garapa upon similar terms, his companions managed to abstract and drink half of it, and he could only save the remainder by retiring hastily to the wood, calabash in hand, and consuming it in secret; two or three having clubbed together to purchase tobacco, fell to loggerheads about its division, and so on, making a scene of quarrels, drunkenness, and confusion that was perfectly bewildering.

The Africans, as a rule, dearly love a bargain, and many of them have almost an innate passion for trade. Bin-bundo, Ban-gala, Ba-lunda, Ban-bondo, all alike are traders, and are deemed fitting for it in proportion to their cunning and dishonesty, the latter quality being considered indispensable. Living by trade and for trade, they are to be found wherever goods can be obtained and bartered, and in pursuit of their calling they will plunge into endless controversy, make contracts which they either break or never half fulfil, and spend innumerable days amid interminable talk.

Their fairs or markets are the important centres where the natives display all their dexterity and eloquence, and to which all the great commercial expeditions naturally tend; but they will never lose an opportunity of doing business on the road.

Goods vary greatly in price and facility of sale, according to the countries they pass through, and one may readily guess for what part of the interior a caravan is bound on learning the kind of merchandise with which it is laden.

The natives have everything to gain by trade, and it

may well be said that without it they would be nothing. Commerce, by obliging them to make repeated journeys, carries with it, as a necessary consequence, the establishment of relations and the making of contracts with distant peoples. Compelled to seek out districts where articles can be obtained at the cheapest rate, in order to get the most profit out of them, they acquire a taste for speculation and a clear knowledge of value. Experience has given them considerable expertness, and nature has supplied them with a vast amount of dissimulation as all Europeans who have had any dealings with them know to their cost.

It is really curious to observe the eagerness with which the negro will seek to do a little business. A cloth or handkerchief purchased but a moment before, will be readily exchanged if he see the most trifling profit can be made by the barter. In our own encampment we have had opportunities of observing within the short space of twenty-four hours, a yard of red baize pass into the hands of six successive owners.

The whole of the goods constituting the African trade, south of the equator, are carried upon the heads or shoulders of men, who, collected in caravans, styled *m'bacas* in the south and *quibucas* in the north, and directed by a *quissongo*, march in extended lines across the country. It was one of these we now met, and whose presence has given rise to the foregoing remarks, and which, to our supreme satisfaction, shortly afterwards resumed its way, and left us in peace to construct our own little encampment.

By three o'clock, our huts being built and fires lighted to dry our clothes and prepare our food, we got out the instruments for recording the usual observations, when Catraio (of the " bird of ill-omen " memory, and whose duty it was to take charge of the scientific apparatus) imparted to us the unwelcome intelligence that we might from that date consider ourselves without a ground thermometer, as he had left the iron tube behind him at Cassange in company of a pair of boots! He attributed the forgetfulness to the unsettled state of his mind, owing to the desertion of his spouse, and as there was no help for it we had to admit the excuse. We could not help thinking, however, that if we went on at this rate, we should have very few things left by the time we reached the end of our journey.

Substituting for the first loss an air thermometer, we thought of inflicting condign punishment upon the rascal for the serious inconvenience the second might cause us, when we were relieved from the necessity of doing so by a huge fly, common enough in the thicket, and whose powerful mandibles cause great terror to the natives, which fixed upon the negligent assistant and stung him severely! The insect somewhat resembles the *Capambo* (*Dasypogon Capambo?*) or ox-fly, but is considerably larger. Its sting, which is very venomous, is immediately followed by inflammation and acute pain, that occasion serious inconvenience. Naturalists call it *Synagris cornuta*, but we, among ourselves, dubbed it the *pest of the woods!*

It was on the 7th of March that we again joined company and shook hands on the bank of the Gamba rivulet.

Immediately on our arrival we became sensible of a most horrible stench, which made us suppose that some flesh was about in an advanced stage of decomposition; but we learned upon inquiry that it was due to a visitation of a strange species of black ants, nearly half an inch in length, that had invaded the camp and which emitted the most pestiferous smell as they were destroyed by the men. There was nothing better to be done than to

PLUNGING INTO THE THICK GRASS.

escape the infliction by flight, and on the very day of our arrival we consequently set forth.

Before us rose the vast heights of Tala-Mogongo, with spurs that jut out into the plain like huge promontories, whose precipitous sides, tinged by oxide of iron, have the appearance of titanic walls.

Following the steep and broken track which wound

FOLLOWING THE STEEP AND BROKEN TRACK.

about the flanks of the mountain, now clinging to a mossy trunk, now to a branch that offered a friendly hold, we succeeded in carrying our reduced weight over the asperities that lay between the valley and the practicable heights.

We halted upon a little platform to enjoy the splendid panorama unrolled before our delighted eyes. The inclination of the slope was about 45°, and it was clothed with wood of a dark green colour, so thickly that not a yard of ground was distinguishable. The very trunks of the tamarinds, acacias, and *taculas* were invisible from the wealth of foliage that surrounded them. From the base of this richly-wooded mountain ran on and on, as far as the eye could reach, vast savannas which presented every gradation of green and blue according to the distance from the point of vision, covered at the outset with a labyrinth of tree-trunks, and intersected further on by meandering streams which occasionally glittered as they were caught by the light, and then were lost again. The picture was further adorned by several lofty mountains, such as the Bongo and the serried heads of the Yongo range, that stood out in bold relief against the sky, and the sun had arrived at that point in the heavens when it flooded the whole scene with golden, transparent hues, which had the effect of intensifying, without destroying, the other lovely colours of the landscape!

For half an hour we stood wrapt in wonder and admiration before the lovely prospect, and, as is not unfrequently the case when contemplating similar marvellous works of the beneficent Creator, it brought to us a peace and serenity of mind to which we had long been strangers.

There in the distance lay the mysterious Cuango,— there the lands of the Chinje,—yonder rose the mountains of the Peinde,—all abounding in strange problems, and filled with an unknown people, that we so longed to visit and explore!

And then came the revulsion of feeling born of our

recent trials and disappointments, and almost together we exclaimed,—

"Those infernal Ban-gala!"

But is it in the nature of things we inquired, that so many thousand souls can remain, in an age of civilization like the present, when the spirit of progress is abroad in the world, steeped in ignorance and slavery, a prey to a few wretched tyrants, not a whit more enlightened than themselves, but on whom superstition and fear have bestowed absolute and irresponsible power!

And the answer came, in the strong conviction of our minds, in words as plain as though they had been uttered by a voice,—

"It is but a question of time!"

NATIVE BOX.

CHAPTER II.

Limits of Cassange—Native justice—Reflections upon the African character—The rise and course of the Cambo—The African opium—The insect world—Breaking up of the encampment—Capulca again—Lake Utumba—Deceptive medlars—N'Dala Samba and T'Chiça—José do Telhado and mortality of the Europeans in Africa—Cuango and Cuanza—Divisional line of their waters—Cha-Landu and exactions of the petty sovas—The Ambaquista, distinctive features, habits, importance, fondness for scribbling—Ascent of the morro Bango—Dr. Max Buchner, the German explorer—A queer ecclesiastic—The Lu-calla and Lianzundo cataract—Duque de Bragança and a dinner with Captain A. Silverio.

We were at length out of the territory of the *jaggas* of Cassange, and away from the influence of those importunate Ban-gala and of their terrible climate, for though under the parallel we had now reached there was little to be said in favour of its salubrity, the basin of the Cuango must be considered perfectly pestilential. In spite of this, we more than once, having somewhat recovered from our fatigue, half made up our minds to turn back, and try again, but better counsels prevailed; so definitively turning our backs upon the inhospitable region, we pursued our way.

All our crew expressed a lively sentiment of satisfaction at having escaped out of the clutches of those grasping and cruel tribes amongst which we had struggled so long, and being relieved from the apprehension of another attempt to force a passage through them, the caravan, with Capulca in front, and ourselves bringing up the rear, plunged into the masses of verdure in capital temper. The abundance of low marshy ground and pools of stagnant water makes this part of the country simply calamitous and we did not envy the possessions of N'Dala Quissua, who is the ruler of the district.

We had not traversed more than three miles of the road than we quickened our steps on hearing loud shrieks and cries proceeding from the forest.

Cassai, the hound, on seeing us run, started on ahead and struck into a by-path as if to show us the way. A few minutes brought us to a *quilombo*, outside which a little crowd had gathered. The chief, as we were informed, was not present, and in answer to our inquiries about the shrieks we had heard, we were told with the usual circumlocution that the carriers were amusing themselves with chastising an unfortunate for not paying his debts.

The curious part of the matter was, that he was perfectly innocent, for we learned on rescuing him that an inhabitant of the village to which he belonged had some time before obtained something to eat at the senzala and not paid for it, and that they had seized upon him to settle the score.

His body was in a miserable state from the blows he had received, but when he found himself among friends, he seized a knife and seriously wounded one of his persecutors.

Having, after some trouble, quelled the disturbance, we resumed our journey, taking the late prisoner with us as a guide to the place for which we were bound, situated, as he averred, at no great distance on the road.

It is worthy of remark that we rarely observed among the natives, scars of wounds arising from individual dissensions among them. At the outset we took this as a favourable sign, showing their little tendency towards crimes of violence. With wider experience, however, we considerably modified this opinion, and attributed the fact rather to indifference. The natives, indeed, seldom trouble themselves about others. Personal interest with them is everything, and that satisfied, rightly or wrongly, they care little for aught else. From this indifference to others, rivalry occurs only in special cases. Those games and competitions wherein dexterity is the moving spirit, that love of distinction and thirst for admiration, which in Europe not unfrequently lead to quarrels and disputes are pretty nearly unknown among the natives of Africa. And thus it happens that the chief sources of envy and jealousy being dried up, their consequences disappear. The negro has, besides, a natural horror at the sight of blood, and therefore refrains from committing an assault upon his neighbour, not from any high principle of kindness or compassion, but from timidity and cowardice. When, however, he is brought into contact with civilization, and other interests and stimulants are awakened within him, he too frequently becomes a dangerous assassin. Hence it is that crimes of violence are most frequently committed by those tribes who reside among Europeans, and who are to be found in great commercial marts.

At half-past one on the 8th day of March, 1879, we arrived at a vast cane-bed, pointed out by our guide as the source of the river we were seeking.

Having set up the *abba* on the brink of the marsh, we took observations to determine the longitude and variation, and while chewing a manioc root, and remarking for the hundredth time that it tasted very much like a chestnut, we jotted down the following particulars in our diary :—

The Cambo rises on the slope of Serra Catanha in marshy ground that receives the drainage of the upper plateau, and running northwards between the lands of Quifucussa and Catalla Canjinga, penetrates into the Jinga, and finally empties itself into the Cuango in latitude 7′ 40°, about seven miles below the great cataract of Suco-ia-muquita or Suco-ia-n'bundi,[1] in the territory of the Tembo Aluma, and above two others possessed by the same river. It is the second affluent of the Cuango after the Lui, and is erroneously represented on the old maps, where it is made to run through the low grounds of the Yongo and Holo in a mean direction north-north east.

We were just preparing to make a series of magnetic observations in the interest of science, which nowadays demands so much of the explorer, when the rain quite upset our arrangements, and compelled us to leave the task to future travellers, whom we trust may be blessed by better weather. As to ourselves, we were assailed by a fierce thunder-storm, followed by a deluge of rain, that compelled us to keep indoors, to the unconcealed delight of our followers, who, not in the slightest degree inconvenienced by the clouds of thick smoke that filled the confined space of the huts, passed the pipe round from mouth to mouth in hearty enjoyment of the tobacco, which is very abundant in the country of the Bondos.

As long as they confined their attention to wholesome tobacco it was all very well, but most of them soon abandoned the tobacco-pipe for the *mu-topa*, a horn containing water and a bowl used for the consumption of the fatal *liamba* (*Cannabis sativa*).

The smokers sit round an ample brazier, whence, with small tongs, they draw out a bit of charcoal and place it

---

[1] Suco-ia-n'bundi seems to express a perturbation of sight.

on the top of the bowl containing the liamba. One of them puts the mu-topa to his lips, and takes four or five strong pulls, inhaling the precious smoke, whose effect is to cause a violent fit of coughing, apparently all the more satisfactory if it nearly suffocates him in the process. The instrument is then passed on to his neighbour, who draws it till he remains quite stupefied, his eyes glazed while he breathes as if in a deep sleep. The water in the horn bubbles as the smoke is drawn through it, but the sound is soon lost in the hubbub of voices, each man clamorous for his turn. Meanwhile, those who have already had their pull become, as it were, mad-drunk, throw themselves about, talk and laugh in the most excited fashion, the while the saliva, produced by the inhalation of the burning hemp, runs from their mouths and makes them, with the contortion of their features, dreadful objects to contemplate.

We tried our best over and over again to put a stop to the practice, for the sight of the men disgusted while it pained us; but it was of no use, for they only hid themselves away in the woods and indulged in the deleterious habit in secret.

An entomologist would have been in ecstasies with the variety of specimens to be met with in this region. When the rain was over, thousands of butterflies, adorned with wings of every variety of colour, darted about the wood, and excited our wonder and admiration, and we only wished that the illustrious director of the Museum at Lisbon could have been there to enjoy the spectacle.

At one moment there fluttered past us the *Synagris cornuta*, already spoken of; at another the *macunhapamba* or *Odonata*. On the green stalks of the tall grass we recognized the *mu-curulumbia Mantis*, nearly four inches in length, climbing towards its curious nest, and hard by we saw the still more curious home of the *Capata-iéu*, constructed of small fragments of stick, arranged like a fluted column and fastened securely together by a web. These being burnt, produce an ash reputed of great value for the preservation of the teeth, which may indeed be gathered from the native name, *iéu*,

SMOKING THE FATAL LIAMBA.

signifying a tooth. On the ground the *gongolo* (*Spirostreptus gongolo*) were crawling slowly by the side of *Capricornios*; more than one variety of *Scarabeus* engaged on their laborious task of conveying along enormous balls, formed of matter dropped by herbivorous animals, wherein to preserve their eggs.

The termites, ever hard at work, were reconstructing their habitations. Strange *Arachnidios*, such as the silk-weaving spider, *ma-vuvi* (*Nephita bragantina*) were swinging from spray to spray, fastening them together with their delicate yellow webs. The active and obscure *Xylophages* were mining to the very heart the knotted trunks of ancient trees. Colossal *m'bangarala* (*Cicadas*), in continual motion, perfectly confused us with their peculiar sharp whirr, interrupted every now and then by the still more piercing notes of the *n'gumbe*, a bird that we took to be the *Corythaix paulina*. The wonderful *ma-ribundo* or *ma-libundo* (*Pelopœus spirifex*) whose clay nests might be seen sticking about the beams of the houses, were also among our numerous acquaintance. After depositing in each nest an egg and food for the support of the progeny when it comes out, the parents close it up and abandon it to its fate. Not the least singular peculiarity about the creatures is, the apparent absence of females among them, as all those caught were males. We also saw buzzing about innumerable bees, and certain small honey-producing flies, the latter a perfect scourge of the encampments, which assail the tired traveller in such myriads that he eats flies, drinks flies, sneezes them out of his nose, and coughs them out of his throat, until he is half maddened with the visitation.

At six o'clock, when the sun disappeared, and the earth was immersed in shadow, the insect world retired, and silence fell upon the scene. We then sought the driest place in our little huts, whereon to extend our tired limbs—spread our leopard-skins upon the grass, drew our caps down upon our ears, and invoking divine Morpheus, prayed of him the gift of tranquil sleep. This he was good enough to grant us, and the night passed without any of those disturbing influences which may be interesting to a reader, but are far from pleasant to a weary explorer.

With the first red blush of morn we rose and soon woke up the entire encampment, when once again was repeated the picturesque scene of the starting of the caravan, so full of incident and of a certain wild charm to the traveller who plays his part therein.

After a prolonged performance of stretching of limbs and yawning of huge jaws that are fearful to behold, an incessant chatter, joined to that peculiar sniggering laugh of the negro, accompany the efforts of some of the men to revivify the smouldering embers of the fires, in order to warm the food prepared the night before; while other hands are busy in rolling up the mat-beds, which with joints of meat and bags of fuba compose the baggage of some of the carriers.

The coffee for the chiefs is then set to boil.

The goods, drawn from the heap where they have been piled, are taken out by their respective porters, and secured with their other impedimenta to the *mangos*.

The scene becomes a very lively one; all are at work, or pretending to be so, and a general chorus of voices, in every key, from the deep bass of the stalwart carrier to the faint treble of a puling child, is echoed far and wide.

Meanwhile, the light increases in intensity. Thousands of birds are upon the wing, and gladdened by the sight of day are filling the woods with melody. The mist, which has hitherto hung over the horizon, is now moving upwards and melting in the air, allowing the eye to embrace the outline of the distant hills, from behind which soon grandly rolls the orb of day, which in those latitudes, north or south of the equator, rises approximately at ten minutes past or ten minutes before six.

The hot coffee is taken, to the great comfort of the

inner man; the women with their infants at their backs and baskets on their heads are waiting to fall in; the cook has gathered up his last traps and seen them duly secured; the guide marshals his men who are to act as a vanguard, and at a signal takes the lead; others soon follow; a last look round is given to see that nothing has been left behind, and in a few minutes—of the encampment so recently full of noisy life—there remain but a couple of dozen huts, looking already strangely solitary, and a few heaps of smoking ashes.

Plunging into the woods, with our strength renewed by the night's rest, we make our way, deriving no small assistance from our bill-hooks in widening the path and removing too obtrusive thorns, while we philosophize on the marvels of creation and dilate on the advantage of a bit of adhesive plaster on our corns!

These early morning tramps through the grass and forest land have doubtless a charm of their own, but as certain drawbacks modify every pleasure in this world, so we discover that tall grass laden with water and saturated trees which the slightest wind puts in motion, and thereby creates an artificial rain beneath, may contribute in the end to make a man feel very uncomfortable.

Still we pushed on in good spirits, buoyed up with the hope that we should soon be in the open where the warm sun would dry our clothing and a good meal would fortify our stomachs, when suddenly there broke upon the mind of Capulca a reflection that could not but interest us very deeply; namely, upon what we were to expend the splendid appetite that our morning's march had made wonderfully keen! But one pound of *fuba*, it appeared, was all he could offer for the refreshment of two hungry men, seasoned with as much fresh air as we chose to throw in!

It was really too bad, and the fellow seemed to make quite a virtue of the fact that he had only just thought of it!

Our disappointment was so great that we had scarce eyes or admiration left for the many beauties that met our view as we neared the borders of the forest and got upon clearer ground, so all-engrossing was the subject of an empty stomach with nothing to put into it!

THE COLOSSAL LUGHIAS.

And yet how beautiful were the colossal *lughias*, with their green and tender fruit, and wide-spreading branches, beneath which hundreds of men could find an easy shelter; how charming were the *mu-anza*, covered with the wonderful bark so useful for dyeing leather; how marvellous were the varieties of thorns and underwood, here presenting spongy heads, and there glowing with flowers, as remarkable to the sight as to the smell; but alas! none of these were good to eat, and we were getting so hungry that half their picturesqueness was swallowed up in the great absorbing thought of food.

Cursing the negligence of that very trying individual, Capulca, and envying the philosophy with which our companions in misfortune solaced themselves with their pipes, we drew our belts all the tighter to prevent the emptiness of our stomachs from being too apparent, and still trudged on, the sun, as it made giant strides in the heavens, setting us the example.

Strange as it may appear, our black thoughts were gradually dissipated amid the constant change of scene, and eluding the pangs of hunger, we followed the ill-defined track which edged the forest, now stopping to trim our pipes, now stumbling over the irregularities of the ground.

But these pastimes had not been of many hours duration, when an unexpected disaster overtook us. We had just entered upon an immense slimy plain—a perfect bog indeed, which the guide informed us bore the name of Lake Utumba—when one of us went in up to his knees, and on the other attempting to assist him, both fell flat upon our faces in the slime! Nose, mouth, eyes, and ears, were choked with the sticky mud, and we had the satisfaction, when we could recover our vision, to discover our followers on the broad grin at our disaster.

Our mouths had been thus unexpectedly filled, and *yet* we were unsatisfied; nor did the ghost of a senzala appear to gladden us. At four o'clock, quite fagged out, we were compelled to stop and construct our camp.

No sooner were we installed, than Capulca (that

genius for discoveries) strolled off along the bank of a neighbouring rivulet, the Cu-ji, and ten minutes later came running back radiant with joy, holding up something in his hand. On drawing nearer he showed us, with great glee, a handful of some yellow fruit, not unlike in appearance the European medlar. We seized it with avidity and crammed it into our mouths; and then half a dozen men, proceeding to the tree whence it was taken, gathered and ate a considerable quantity.

At night-fall the fires were lighted, and we soon turned in for our desired rest. About eight o'clock we were startled by sundry sighs and groans, which grew louder as we listened, and mingled with these were other sounds not uncommon on board a passenger-ship when the vessel is lurching heavily.

As we started up to learn the cause, we were conscious of a feeling in the stomach, as if it were bursting, followed by a frightful colic, which made us roll about in pain. The murder was out, we had been half poisoned by the unknown fruit we had so heedlessly devoured; and the cook, the young niggers, and such of the carriers as had partaken of the delusive medlars, were suffering the same pains, and uttering the cries and groans that had so startled us. Fortunately, we were all violently sick, and having got a little sleep after ridding ourselves of our indigestible burthen, we rose up next morning sadder, but wiser men.

We had a gleam of hope ere setting out imparted to us by José, the guide, whose stomach, owing to a fellow-feeling, sympathized with our own. He assured us that before the sun set we should reach the establishments of N'Dala Samba, where he actually possessed an uncle! a revelation and a relation for which we could have embraced him on the spot. Nor did he deceive us with false hopes, for after seven and a half miles' march we entered T'Chiça, and finally reached our destination, pitching our camp close to two farms, where we were enabled at once to purchase provisions.

At length we had something to eat, and there only remained the ceremony of cooking it. In order to mitigate the horrors of expectation, and discipline our appetites, somewhat excited by the previous twenty-four

A ROAD-SIDE CEMETERY.

hours' fast, if we leave out of the account those medlars of painful memory, we sat down and began whittling some sticks, the while José's uncle, to whom we had been presented in due form, told us a few stories, interspersed with episodes of the woods, which, on more accounts than one, we refrain from presenting to our readers.

We were rewarded at last by Capulca's exclamation that "dinner was ready," and great was our emotion to see him draw from the bubbling cauldron two white and well-fed fowls, which he placed upon the board!

In ten minutes nothing was left but the bones, to the great astonishment of José and his respectable relative, who craned their necks in vain to discover if any fragments were left that were worth consuming!

On our recent journey hither we had fallen in pretty frequently with the burial-places of both Portuguese and Africans—a sad reminder of the difficulty of keeping life within the body in these remote districts, where various agents of trading-houses, established in Malange, had taken up their quarters with a view to induce the caravans from the interior to halt for refreshment and secure a little business.

At T'Chiça we visited the tomb of a famous Portuguese trader, José do Telhado, whose reputation for probity is still preserved among the natives. The monument, that is situated in the middle of a little hamlet, is carefully kept up by the last of his old retainers, and was not only strewn with many fragments of articles used by the deceased, but was made pretty by a variety of flowers in bloom.

The mortality in this part of the continent is perfectly frightful. The miasmatic influence of the climate does not appear so intense at all periods of the year, which is intelligible enough; during the rainy season, the elevated temperature not only makes the emanations from the soil far greater, but causes abundant perspiration, excites more thirst, and renders the absorption considerable, and the organism being thus disturbed, violent and dangerous sickness is the result. During our stay in Cassange, three traders, whereof one was an European, were taken off. At Malange, a firm with three partners, and having a branch at Cassange, was also closed, owing to the death of two out of the three associates; and we were forced to come to the sad conclusion, that whatever their desirability as places of trade, they were but little fitted for the well-being or requirements of Europeans in respect of salubrity.

Where we stood we found ourselves on the divisional line of the Cuango and Cuanza basins. On the north, Camicungo pours its waters into the Congo-Zaire, on the east the Camoaxi runs through the Mucari to the Cuanza.

The caravan being duly provisioned, after a visit paid to Sanza, we started in a south-westerly direction.

We were now in the district of Malange, that we intended crossing on our way to the Duque de Bragança, whence it was our resolve to take a fresh departure for the interior.

Impenetrable wood was met at intervals, in great part under water; and in spaces where the ground was cleared, the land was frequently inundated. Traces of game appeared, but no animals were seen; partridges and wood-pigeons were tolerably abundant, but so shy that we could not get a successful shot at them.

Petty sovetas visited us by the dozen, and with one of them, Cha-Landa, we had a serious dispute. Out of mere caprice that gentleman took a fancy to the great-coat one of us was wearing, and after a good deal of beating about the bush, he made application for it through the interpreter. Irritated by our refusal, he blustered to such an extent in the *quilombo*, that we had to show him the outside of it.

No one can conceive the series of petty difficulties and annoyances to which the explorer is subject in these parts. The mere sight of his goods arouses all the cupidity of the miserable little despots, and when they cannot satisfy it by force, they resort to every kind of chicanery. No sooner does a caravan appear at any point, than up spring sovetas, *seculos*, delegates of the latter, relatives of these, and so on, putting forward the most absurd claims; such, for instance, as the taking of a couple of eggs from the wayside, for which they demand whole pieces of cloth in the shape of fine. It often happens that the sova, who appears in the guise of a captain in the army, is merely a private in one of the native regiments raised by the Portuguese government in Africa, who gives himself the airs of a general, at least, is surrounded by a horde of worthless characters, and invariably attended by a sort of secretary or bully, always a finished knave, selected from among the Ambaquistas.

And now that we are upon the subject, we will say a few words about this noted tribe, a sort of African Bohemians, who are to be met with throughout the country from Malange onwards. The Ambaquista is in fact the *âme damnée* of the interior.

One of the surest signs whereby he may be recognized is his general get-up, which is *outré* to the last degree according to his means; another is the mark of the small-pox which he generally bears upon his face; and be it noted, as a peculiarity, that they who are so marked are more cunning than foxes.

Having a profound knowledge of the native character, the Ambaquista makes his way into the senzala, loses little time in captivating the good graces of all its inmates, and principally of its Sova, decides disputes, has the cunning to maintain the opinion of superior understanding with which he is credited, amuses the ruler with singular stories touching the manners and customs of

Europeans, gives him even some notions, however, erroneous, of religion and of worship, and in fact creates himself a position. The circumstance of his being able to write—for a good many of his countrymen have that accomplishment—helps not a little to raise him in the estimation of the ignorant savages, and, as the so-called secretary of the Sova, he is naturally a recipient of all his secrets.

Where the Ambaquista is not attached to the service of any ruler, he makes a tolerable living by wandering about the country with an ink-horn, pens, and paper, packed among the other articles of his little *mu-hamba*, and rarely fails to obtain his two, three, and even sometimes four yards of cloth for the letter he writes at the instigation of the Sova to the authorities, and occasionally from the latter to a native chief. Among themselves, the Ambaquistas have a perfect mania for drawing up protests and memorials. A half-dozen of them, united in council, will indite a protest or two every week.

We heard a little story upon this subject which is amusing in its way, and illustrates very completely both their rage for scribbling and their natural caution not to commit themselves. Five of them having drawn up a very lengthy memorial against one of the Portuguese authorities, were about to sign it, when a grave discussion arose amongst them, owing to the disinclination of each to be the first to affix his name.

The more they debated the question, the more serious it appeared, and they were about to destroy the document in despair, out of the difficulty of finding the x of the problem. Finally, a happy thought illuminated the brain of one of them, and was adopted forthwith as a triumphant way out of the difficulty; and that was to

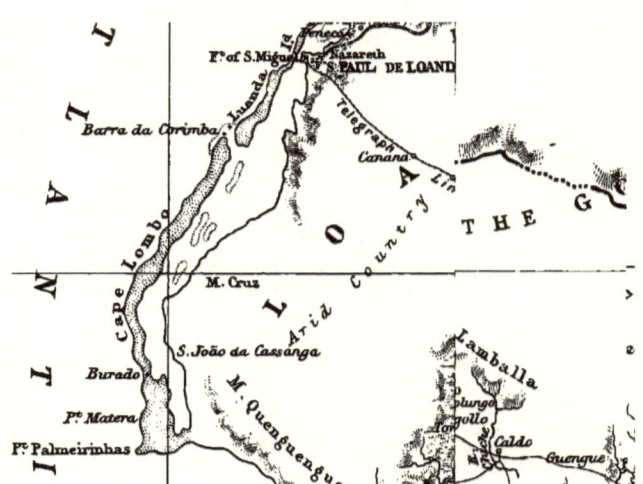

write their names in the circumference of a circle, and therefore without any order of precedence!

The portrait we present to our readers is that of a

AN AMBACA GENTLEMAN.

very superior Ambaquista indeed—a trader and a man of means—a very gentleman of the tribe.

Returning to our narrative, we now found ourselves not far from the town of Malange. To the south of us

rose Mount Bango, near which we pitched our camp, in order to enjoy a short interval of rest, and make the ascent of the mountain to obtain a *tour d'horizon*.

As the density of the underwood was such as to bar our progress, the two first days of our sojourn were employed in cutting a path upwards—a labour wherein our whole caravan was employed, while we ourselves prepared the scientific apparatus we intended to convey to the summit. The ascent was made on the third day, and a very hard task we found it; the chest labouring like the bellows of a forge.

It was a grand spectacle from the top as the mountain rose in solitary grandeur from the plain to a height of nearly 900 feet, and allowed a perfectly uninterrupted view of the verdant savannas through which the Cuanza wound its serpentine course. Further to the northwards was visible another mountain; on the western horizon appeared the lofty peaks of Tungo N'Dongo, not unlike the cupolas of some gigantic edifice; on the north-west the mountains of Ambaca; on the north rose Serra Muhunzo, and on the south lay the town of Malange, all successively marked by the azimuth needle and traced on the paper when the latter descended.

Next morning, the 19th of March, we were seated at the entrance of our hut, sketching the portrait of Master José, the guide, who had put on a large hat, and enveloped himself in a sheet for the occasion, while his uncle, lying on his back with his legs in the air, admiringly looked on; when there suddenly appeared to our astonished eyes an European gentleman, mounted on an ox, and attended by two or three negroes.

As he dismounted, we hastened to meet him, while conjecture was immediately at work to guess the name and calling of the fair man who stood before us. He at once, however, satisfied our mental inquiries by introducing himself.

"I am Dr. Max Buchner, a German explorer, sent on a special mission to the country of the Lunda, where I am to have speech of Muata-Yanvo. Being at Malange completing my staff, and waiting for certain articles I

"I AM DR. MAX BUCHNER."

have to take with me, I heard of your arrival here, and therefore came over with the double object of making your acquaintance and scaling the mountain hard by, an ascent I have promised myself to make ever since my entrance into the country."

Inviting him to breakfast, we soon sat round our improvised table, which was furnished with the best our men could produce, and for the space of a good hour we talked upon every subject imagination could suggest to three men under such circumstances. We dwelt upon the advantages of certain compasses, of the excellent working of certain other theodolites, of direct processes for the determination of the longitude, of the difficulty of transport in the forest, of the most recent news from old Europe, of the broad awakening interest felt by many of her sons for African exploration, of the disastrous influence of the climate of the great continent; of the best mode of warding off its fevers, and other kindred subjects, that made the time fly swiftly and pleasantly.

Dr. Buchner then started with a guide we lent him and made the ascent of the mountain by the track we had cut for ourselves. At four he returned, in a devouring fever, and taking a hasty leave, he retraced his steps the road he had come, and we saw him no more.

We ourselves remained a few days longer in our camp, hard at work during the day and listening to extraordinary stories at night, one of which we record, without, of course vouching for its accuracy.

Some time previous to our arrival a certain celebrated ecclesiastic, whose name, which was not Portuguese, was mentioned to us, made a progress through this part of the country, and played such extraordinary pranks that his fame extended far and wide. The worship that this noble priest endeavoured to set up was that of Bacchus, of a form modelled by himself, and as, instead of young converts, he only met with old *roués* and jealous rivals, he had recourse to the stick! The natives, becoming alarmed at this energetic proselytizer, at last gave him the widest possible berth, so that the congregation of this extraordinary pastor, with a cloth round his head

LIANZUNDO CATARACT.

and a flagon under his arm, got gradually smaller. They called him *N'ganga-ia-puto* (the fetichman of the whites), and at last got so terrified at the stories that were told of his evil powers, that the rumour of his coming was the signal for a general flight. Happily, as *aguardente* grew scarce, the zeal of the missionary cooled, and, as it is presumed, after mature study of the position, he concluded that it was both ridiculous and inglorious to run the risk of the martyrdom of deprivation of alcohol for the stupid and insignificant result of four baptisms and three chrisms, he shook the dust of an ungrateful country off the soles of his feet and travelled coastwise, where it is to be concluded he found a more genial soil and unquestionably more rum.

On resuming our journey we skirted the mountains on our right, and had on our left an immense plain, intersected by several rivulets with marshy banks, where " the fowls of the air and the beasts of the field " might roam with safety, but which was but ill-fitted for the passage of the human foot. We traversed in six days, by the border of the Malange district, the space intervening between our point of departure and the Duque de Bragança, sleeping one night near a little hamlet, where a Sova, in the uniform of a Spanish soldier, worried us almost beyond endurance, at another in the forest; now in the open, and again on the bank of some river.

It was the 28th of March that we sighted for the first time the river Lu-calla, at the residence of Calandula, near the Faba rapids; and on the 29th, having gone a little up stream we came upon the great Lianzundo cataract, a beautiful sheet of foam, ninety-seven feet in depth, with a spring-like vegetation clinging to its steep sides, and at its feet a thicket of orange-trees, which we depict in our engraving.

On the 30th we made the fortress of the Duque, and were cordially received by the Portuguese chefe, Captain A. Silverio, a courteous gentlemen, well advanced in years that had been expended in the service of his country. In the course of three hours our *quilombo* was run up and put into something like order, so that we were enabled to accept in comfort an invitation of the captain's to dinner.

We were much struck on entering the residence, at the novel aspect it presented. A vast verandah, not unlike those of the Arab *tembés*, having been traversed, we reached an inner *pateo* or court, having at one side the kitchen, partly concealed and sheltered by bananas and a paling, about which were cutting half a dozen little niggers, a couple of pigs, a dozen or so fowls, a monkey, a gazelle, and a parrot. The opposite side was taken up with the living-rooms of the establishment, and in one of them, which did duty as drawing and dining-room, appeared the welcome, and, to us, uncommon sight of a long table covered with a white cloth, having dishes containing smoking viands ranged down the centre, and a couple of bottles of wine at each corner!

The succulent food brought to our recollection a subject we had frequently discussed when we had nothing to stay our hunger; and we unanimously concurred, at this joyous moment, that we should not eat merely to live, for that a tender, juicy, delicately-browned beef-steak produced, in its consumption, sensations of the mind as well as the body that were worthy of mature consideration.

We were quite touched when our worthy host uttered the simple compliment, "Will you please be seated?" and the first spoonful of hot soup really did bring tears into our eyes; we recovered courage, however, as we got on, and before half an hour had gone by, found ourselves hob-nobbing with one another with as much ease as if we had been used to that sort of thing all through our adventurous journey.

NEST OF THE CAPATÁ-IEU.

CHAPTER III.

On the tramp again—The banks of the Lu-calla and a nice dispute—Cateco, the hunter of wives—The Jinga, its limits and importance—The king, titles and residence—Hierarchical scale—Peculiar mode of bestowal of property—The *ma-lunga* and *quijinga*—The Muco-N'Gola or Mona N'Gola—Strange head-dresses and queer pockets—On the summit of the Serra Catanha—A love episode and its unpleasant close—Conjugal relations—An evening discussion and a morning flight—Mineral wealth of the Jinga—Mode of preparing cloth, dwellings, &c.—A storm in the forest, and a further desertion—Den of thieves—A page or two from the diary—A tough cow—Arrival at Cafuchila.

TWENTY-FOUR days have elapsed since the memorable dinner recorded in the last chapter, the same scenes being repeated while we waited for the cessation of the rains; sometimes absorbing quinine in larger or smaller doses, at others lying in bed without a sight either of earth or sky.

We had reached the 26th of April, exactly 532 days since we left Benguella for our journey northwards, but in spite of our mishaps our disposition to push onwards remained as strong as ever. We considered our honour and our dignity alike embarked in the solution of the problem we had set ourselves, and, determined to make our constancy overcome the difficulties by which we were beset, we made all preparations for a departure on the first favourable opportunity. The weather alone now stood in our way.

In order again to reach the basin of the Cuango it

ON THE BANKS OF THE LU-CALLA.

was necessary to cross great part of the kingdom of the Jinga—a territory that our informants depicted in the darkest colours, whilst they could scarcely find terms strong enough to portray the exactions and tyranny of the supreme ruler. We were getting, however, quite case-hardened in our scepticism, and resolved to judge for ourselves.

Thus it happened that at daybreak of the 28th of April, 1879, without even waiting for the preparation of the morning meal, we set off for the margin of the river, where a miserable canoe had been placed at our disposal.

The banks of the Lu-calla are almost entirely composed of marsh, so that we had no choice but to be conveyed upon men's shoulders, whereof several brawny ones were at once offered for our accommodation. As these offers came from the natives of the district, and additional hands are always welcome, we gladly accepted their proposal, our guide promising them a couple of yards of cloth each by way of remuneration, with which they appeared to be perfectly satisfied.

When, however, we were about half way through, the cunning rogues struck for higher wages, and vowed they would go no further!

In Europe, where contracting parties have reason to be discontented with the working of a contract, it is a usual thing to have recourse to arbitration to settle the dispute; but as that was not the custom in Africa, and the fellows threatened to let us down in the mud and deep water unless their demands were complied with, we were forced to put our indignation and sense of the justice of our case in our pockets until we felt firm ground under our feet again.

We were then near the residence of the Sova *Zundo-ia*-Faco, into which we entered with a rush, followed by the mutinous Jingas. We found that chief, whom we immediately recognized by the possession of a battered old hat, squatted on the ground in the open air, adorning the sides of a rough kind of bench of his own manufacture, his Majesty having, apparently, a turn for carpentry.

Having coolly appropriated the bench for our own use, we sat down on it, in order to plead our cause, leaving the Sova the choice of the ground, and for two mortal hours we discussed the question of our agreement with the men, which terminated in our being compelled to give them three yards each instead of two.

On the 30th of April we had run up our *quilombo* near the dwelling of the *Canda*-ia-Legho, when a man introduced himself as one willing to act as a guide.

As we were examining him from head to foot, he quietly seated himself, and began to relate his story. Having the "gift of the gab," and being as well versed in gesticulation as a Neapolitan, he had uttered in ten minutes quite enough to fill some volumes, and had thrown his arms and legs about like the sails of a mill in a heavy gale, during the whole of which performance we remained perfectly quiescent, partly from a feeling of politeness, but more through not understanding a twentieth part of what he said.

When he had finished, our interpreter gave us a brief summary of his discourse. According to his own account he was a proficient in the highways and by-ways of the district, was well acquainted with sovas in general and with a good many in particular; was one of the most disinterested members of his profession (that of a hunter), which he had adopted from inclination, and whence sprang many advantages, the chief among which being the ready acquirement of many wives culled from various countries, all of whom were passionately fond of him, and lived in perfect harmony with each other.

As we regarded his sour aspect and wrinkled skin, we could not but think that some of these African dames must be rather easily contented.

He went on to say that having got tired of one of these same spouses, with whom he had been living through the rains, he had resolved to go northwards for a little change of air, and in order to see another of his wives whom he had not set eyes on for upwards of a twelvemonth.

Well, we thought, if the possession of a number of wives can be considered in this country as a guarantee of respectability, here is a respectable man *par excellence*. A nephew of our visitor who stood by seemed almost to divine our meditations, for as we made them he gravely nodded his head in the affirmative.

"As you know the country so well," we remarked, oblige us by saying which you consider the best road to the territory of the Hungo."

"By taking this direction," he answered, pointing to the west-north-west, "and passing by the Serra Catanha, a man would find himself in very uncomfortable quarters, as it is the district of the Quibungo Quiassama—a terrible tyrant. On the north-east he would find an even worse character in Tembo Aluma; so I should advise as the most reasonable step, to proceed directly to the king's court."

"The king's court!" The words raised our suspicions that it was another attempt to impose upon us. Still, we let it go; and having engaged his services, we dismissed him for the night with the words:—

"We shall start northwards on the morrow, so, at break of day, be in readiness, here."

A couple of "*calungas*" exchanged between us put an end to the interview, and he had scarcely retired than we found ourselves face to face with the sova of the district, one of the most silent of his class we ever met with. As we had just as little to say to him, we made him a present of six yards, and then, retiring to our huts, we posted up our notes and went to bed, passing in a sound sleep the last hours of the month of April—the spring time of the dear old country.

We were now in the very heart of the Jinga (a queen of which country figures in the sonnets of Bocage), nowadays a mere reflex of its former grandeur; it is divided into three provinces, Sussa, Danje, and Dongo, and has recently received an acquisition of territory in the shape of the Matamba lands. Its boundaries are the Cuango on the east, and the Lu-calla on the west; while on the north it is limited by Hungo, and on the south by Holo. Its commercial importance is almost nil.

The Jinga, like all old and decaying nations, is allowing itself to drift along the downward path which leads to utter ruin and annihilation. The autocrat of the Jinga bears the title of king, a designation which struck us as rather pretentious, seeing that he differs but little in appearance or intellect from the commonest carrier. The monarchs of the country are always styled N'golas Quilluanjes Quissambas, though they have their own special names, that of the reigning king being Calunga N'Dombo Acambo. He resides in a senzala pompously styled a "court," surrounded by many vassals, dukes, counts, marquises, and what not, whom he uses for his own pleasure and advantage.

The Jinga is divided, not into fiefs, as there are no direct lords, but a large number of estates frequently held for life, and which as they fall in are bestowed by the monarch upon whomsoever he thinks fit. He is governed in his choice by considerations which will appear in the hasty sketch we append of the complicated hierarchical-social scale of the government.

The first dignitaries in the order of their rank are the *vundas* (a species of duke); the second the *candas* (a sort of count), followed by *quilluanjes, zundos, dambis, capelles, catecos, n'gola-n'boles* (a kind of secretary), *matomuzumos*, &c., who occupy the estates above referred

JINGA TYPE.

to, surrounded by their slaves, and form the royal suite.

Whenever one of these personages dies, his nearest of kin does not, on account of his relationship, succeed him, since such an arrangement would not suit his Majesty's views. Various wealthy, ambitious individuals are sure to step in and make lumping offers for the vacant property, which is, in fact, put up to a species of auction, with this difference, that the matter is held pending sometimes as long as six months, in order that the competitors may continue pouring their valuable stores into the king's warehouses, there to await his decision, and, it is needless to say, are charged pretty heavy warehousage in the shape of exactions.

When the matter is finally settled the successful man is *undado* (invested or sworn-in), and receives a *ma-lunga*[1] (bracelet), and the *qui-jinga* or *ca-jinga* (cap), with the declaration of *vunda* or *canda*, and he may then in his turn select his subalterns, or as it is politely termed may appoint *m'pembas* of *ma-tomuzumo n'gola-n'bole*, &c. A personage so invested need only doff his *qui-jinga* in presence of the king, to whom he always does obeisance, by touching the ground with his lips and clapping the palms of his hands together. He may also put the prefix of *calunga* or noble to his name, just as the monarch himself uses the term of *mueniche*. Finally, repairing to his estate, he becomes lord of all it contains.

The Jingas style themselves Muco-N'Gola, or Mona-N'Gola. In shape, they are well-formed but slender, very dark in colour and of a uniform tint. They affect a great variety of hair-dressing, the favourite form being a great bunch on the top of the head, adorned with bands, braids, plumes of feathers, spiral strips of brass, plates of the same metal, beads, &c.

We were considerably amused with their pockets, which, owing to the monstrous size of their *coiffures* they arrange on the tops of their heads with the opening behind! Into this they thrust every small article the

---

[1] We should have thought, as there is only *one*, that *qui-lunga* would have been the more correct expression; as, however, we never heard it so used, we give it as we found it.

hollow will contain, the woolly texture of the hair aiding considerably to keep it in. Their dexterity in putting away anything that was given to them was such that it appeared on our first acquaintance with these people very like sleight of hand, for we saw the upward movement of the arm to the back of the head, and noted the hand come back empty; and as politeness would not allow us to go round to see what had become of it, we at last procured an answer to the enigma from our own people.

At noon, on the 2nd of May, under a blazing sun, we arrived pretty well fagged on the slope of the Serra Catanha, where, under the shade of a leafy acacia, we spent nearly an hour in philosophical meditation, drying our garments, drenched with perspiration, and munching manioc root.

From the summit of the mount we had a fine view of the extensive plains of the kingdom of the Jinga, commencing by the Province of Dongo. Senzalas, scattered about in every direction, represented the estates above alluded to, and whereof some *canda* or *vunda*, with a few dozen slaves as attendants, was the lord and master. In the distance, on the banks of the Hamba, rose the pretended court, surrounded by the dwellings of the king's retinue, while numerous flocks and herds gave animation to the green hills.

While engaged in the contemplation of this beautiful scene we were startled by a tremendous hubbub in the direction of the senzala and at once hurried hither to learn the cause.

We might have guessed as much. Don Juan was at his old tricks again, and we could not help thinking that if he only showed in the field of danger a tenth part of the boldness which distinguished him in the paths of love, he would have made a famous hero.

And yet—to look at him—he was one of the most unlikely beings to command success in those same paths that the eye could well light upon; it was his consummate impudence and vanity that spurred him on, and made him frequently successful where a handsome but a modest, retiring man would not have had the ghost of a chance.

He was short, thin, bow-legged, prematurely aged by excesses of all kinds; bore on his scraggy neck a huge head with a sinister-looking face, to which two ill-shaped, yellow, furtive and cunning eyes occasionally lent an expression of revolting ugliness—certainly not removed by a pair of lips of enormous thickness, which only parted to show his broken and irregular teeth. This is no exaggerated portrait of Capulca, whom we pompously styled our *chef*, and who, in spite of these physical defects, was the most terrible lady-killer it was ever our fate to fall in with.

On the present occasion, time hanging rather heavily on his hands—for our meals were not of that extensive character to occupy very much of his attention—he conceived that it would be an agreeable pastime to bandy soft speeches with some of the lady inhabitants of the district, and actually persuaded one of them to take a stroll with him in the fields. Whether at her invitation or not, it matters little, he accompanied her back to her dwelling, and was just entering the doorway when he almost flattened his nose against the master of the house and husband of the lady, who at once, pouncing upon him, called for assistance and had him secured. That was Act the First.

In Act the Second we find him roaring for mercy under the infliction of a dozen lashes or so, well laid on by one of the government delegates; and when he was let loose more dead than alive, the scene was closed by his having to pay a thumping fine to the fair one's *sposo*.

It is somewhat in this fashion that most of their amorous delinquencies are punished—the lash being spared where the woman is at fault, but vigorously applied if the misdemeanant be a man. This was summary justice, we thought, with a vengeance; yet somehow it commended itself in many ways to our judgment, when we compared it with some of the long and tedious processes with which we had become familiar in old Europe.

The native system, however, in treating offences against the marriage laws cannot always be approved, as the following instances will show: A lady, becoming tired of daily intercourse with her lord, clandestinely quits his roof and finds a home with a more congenial companion. The husband, in order to remove any difficulties that such a proceeding might involve, seeks out the new protector, and in the most business-like way demands an indemnity, which the latter invariably pays. Should he be averse to keep the frail one, he pays something more, in accordance with an amicable arrangement between the parties, and in this case the husband takes back his wife without any disturbance of his equanimity; indeed, the *gentlemanly* way in which the whole affair is conducted is beyond all praise.

That incorrigible rascal, Capulca, elected the former course, and in spite of his sore back, after he had paid his fine he coolly requested that the caravan might be augmented by an additional member, in the shape of his new spouse!

Abandoning at length the shade of the friendly acacia, where, in addition to our cook's escapade we had a few words with Catcco, our new guide, who had, by accident or design, mistaken his road, we camped on the edge of the Serra at no great distance from the residence of the noble *Canda*-ria-Massango. A little further in advance was the dwelling of another of these lordlings, called *Canda*-ria-Canzella, a perfect bully of a fellow, hopelessly given up to drunkenness.

This latter came to the *quilombo* to visit us, at the very time we had another visitor from Duque de Bragança, a trader there of the name of Figueiredo. This gentleman had come over to explore the neighbourhood in our company, but the whole of the day till nightfall was taken up with a hot discussion between himself and the petty chief, the subject being a lady of whom Mr. Figueiredo had been deprived.

After worrying us to the limits of our patience, one of the disputants got dead drunk and the other went to bed; nor did we wait to hear the result of the contention, which was certain to be renewed next day, for having snatched an hour or two of sleep, at three in the morning, before it was light, we quitted the place, leaving plaintiff and defendant in the arms of Morpheus.

We trudged along the lofty heights of the Serra Catanha, whose eastern flank, the work doubtless of some convulsion of nature, was seamed by steep precipices, exhibiting here and there huge blocks of sandstone and granite, fantastically shaped in the semblance of turreted castles and frowning fortresses.

The region is evidently rich in minerals. Silver appears to be exceedingly abundant, as various of the dignitaries who called upon us wore bracelets and anklets, and carried large batons of that metal. We could get, however, no reliable information concerning the mines whence the metal was obtained, or respecting the process employed in the working.

Tacula is perhaps one of the most important staples of the trade of the country, if we might judge by the quantity of people we saw collecting this wood and heaping it in piles. It is employed for various purposes, such as staining the hair and body, but more particularly for dyeing cloth. The natives of the Jinga are

CATECO, THE GUIDE.

accustomed to use it very much for this latter purpose, the natives asserting that it preserves the fabric and keeps it cleaner. They moreover make an infusion of *tacula*, dust, and oil, steep cloth therein for some days, and then expose it to the sun. The result is a species of oil-cloth, which may be useful in keeping out water, but it stinks abominably.

The dwellings of the Jingas were unlike any we had yet seen. In shape they were elliptical, the sides being of grass thickly interwoven, with the door at one of the ends of the larger axis, sheltered by a porch with trellis-work. They were not wanting in picturesqueness, and some of them were neat and pretty.

To the north of the road we were pursuing, lay the territory of Matamba, and on the east the Dongo, whose extreme limit, just visible in the distance, was marked by an irregular blue line. Our guide Cateco steered his course unhesitatingly through the territory. His gait was almost as regular as that of an automaton, his step firm and assured as a hunter's should be, and with his long gun over his shoulder, he climbed mountains or strode down into valleys, crossed ravines or forded brooks with the same equanimity, merely stopping at a place where two paths diverged to exclaim,—

"*N'gila mumo, n'gana*" (This way, gentlemen), or perhaps, to save himself the necessity of uttering even this brief explanation, he would simply block the road we were *not* to take by bending a bough across it, or placing a bramble at the commencement of the track.

Having thus travelled northward for some distance we arrived, tired and panting, at a village belonging to the *Canda*-ria-Lumbombo, where we raised our huts and spent the rest of the day in scientific labours. Next morning, however, the 4th of May, by daybreak, we were again upon the road, making for the lands of the *Zundo*-ia-Cassungo.

The weather, which had been fresh and clear since our entry into the territory of the Daujo, became suddenly overcast and threatening. A suffocating heat made the

earth crack in every direction, and the first drops of rain
that fell were immediately dried up. Large masses of
cloud, rolling quickly up from the south-east, portended
a storm near at hand. Not a leaf stirred; the motion-
less trees, white with dust, seemed anxiously waiting
and looking for the water that was to put fresh vigour
into their drooping sprays.

Within a few paces of us, in the ravines which bordered
our path to the westward, lay the sources of the river
Hamba, a large affluent of the Cambo, visited by us for
the first time. Crossing to the left side by a rude bridge,
we suddenly came to a halt through an unforeseen circumstance that occasioned us fresh embarrassment. We
were first attracted by loud shouts in the rear, and
hastening back to inquire the cause learned from José,
one of our guides, that seven of the carriers had deserted
with their guns, and left their loads in the middle of the
path to take care of themselves! José assured us he
had made every possible effort to dissuade them from
their purpose, but without effect, the only answer they
deigned to make to his persuasions and arguments being
" *tund'enu* " (We are off), and off they went.

It was not easy to arrive at a clear explanation of such
conduct. Fear, perhaps, had something to do with it,
the apprehension of going further northwards into a
region which they felt convinced was peopled by cannibals;
but there were evidently additional motives in the shape
of disputes and quarrels with other members of the
caravan, and something besides which they did not
choose to reveal to José.

Their defection could not have been worse timed, for
at that moment the storm burst over us and the rain
began to fall as it only does come down in this country.
We immediately called a council beneath the shelter of

an acacia, as we really for the moment did not know what better to do. Caught as we were, perfectly unprepared, the men standing about looking like so many sheep, dripping with water, the thunder-claps, so loud and incessant that we could with difficulty hear ourselves speak, and the groaning of the trees as they bent beneath the tempest of wind and rain, rarely did we feel so utterly non-plussed as on that occasion.

As the goods lay out in the open, our first care was to get them round us, to which end the guide went off with some of the men, and this being done we did our best to distribute them over every working member of the caravan. After a deal of chopping and changing, grumbling and persuasions, we succeeded, after half an hour's hard work, in settling the matter to our minds, and valiantly trudged off through the forest, though we were wet to the skin. It need scarcely be said that we did *not* wish every kind of felicity might befall the fugitives; indeed, I am afraid we mentally consigned them to very uncomfortable quarters—a sentence which, though it did them no harm, was a miserable kind of balsam to our own feelings.

In the laying on of this "flattering unction," we were heartily assisted by the carriers who had to bear the increased burthen caused by the flight of their fellows, and even Capulca, whose antecedents might have taught him to be silent upon such a subject, broke in with,—

"Oh! let them alone, senhors, before the sun sets, they will find out their mistake. It is ill joking with the sovas of the Jinga, and what with their *vundas* and *candas* and *catecos*, our friends will have a lively time of it. For my part, I wouldn't take a dozen steps away from the caravan, for all the goods in the world! Only a few days ago—"

THE TEMPEST HAD NOW REACHED ITS HEIGHT.

As this commencement threatened to have a long yarn at the end of it, we requested him to fall into his place. With the temperature at 86°, and a tropical rain falling, one is but little disposed to listen to long stories.

The tempest had now reached its height, and we had no other resource than to pack ourselves into the smallest compass, so as to present the least possible surface to the elements and as we crouched under the trees let the water as it poured down the napes of our necks find an exit at our boots! These frightful storms are bad enough to bear when the traveller has taken certain precautions against them, but when they catch him unawares they are simply atrocious. The sheets of rain, by converting the soil into paste, obliterate every vestige of the track, while the water considerably increases the weight the men have to carry. The clouds are so dense, and so completely shut out the sky, that within the forest it becomes black night, with all the horrors attending the hours of darkness; the flashes of lightning, as they partially illuminate the scene, give to the gaunt trunks of the trees the appearance of the bars of some gigantic cage, in which the dripping, miserable wayfarer is caught without the chance of an escape, while to the rolling of the thunder is added the soughing of the wind, the crash of breaking branches, the swishing of the rain, and other nameless unintelligible sounds that a lively imagination or a superstitious mind converts so easily into the groanings and repinings of uneasy spirits!

A tempest, fortunately, does not endure for ever, and it is short in proportion to its violence. So after a time the clouds broke; a patch or two of blue sky became visible through the rents, a ray of sun shot through another aperture and widened the breach thus made, till the forest was illuminated with the golden haze and the sun-light glistened in every raindrop and puddle; the black masses of vapour rolled away, the earth steamed beneath the glowing heat, and one began to wonder at the fancies which an hour ago held the mind enthralled.

Giving ourselves a shake or two as a dog does on issuing from the water, we resumed our journey, camping at two o'clock near the senzala of the chief *Zundo*-ia-Cassungo, at the base of Serra Catucua.

The 5th of May broke serene and beautiful, and we set out in good spirits for a long march. That amiable disposition was not, however, destined to last long, for Cateco, who had views of his own, guided us through paths and by-ways which seemed to lead to the habitations of every acquaintance he possessed in the neighbourhood. We found them to be perfect dens of thieves, where our patience was put to the severest test, and our means were diminished to an alarming degree.

Innumerable *vundas*, all of them grasping rascals, wanted cloth, beads, *aguardente*, on the largest scale and on little or no pretext whatsoever. First there was a certain *Vunda*-ia-Navina, then an impudent Cambaxe, further on a *Vunda*-ia-Buta, at a few dozen paces in advance a *Vunda*-ia-N'gola-Quilluanje, a little while afterwards a *Vunda*-ia-Miquenha; a very horde of cringing or hectoring nobles, whose capacity for swallowing every thing that they could beg or worry out of us was infinite.

Boiling with rage, we encamped near a small river, the Quimbaxe, apprehensive of going any further that day, lest we should be utterly despoiled. Another reason was, the extreme interest attaching to the country round, which we found it impossible to examine or survey whilst our minds were worried with resisting extortion and paying tolls.

Happily, an apprenticeship of many months engenders

a certain practical scientific experience, and the traveller who is accustomed to note the orography of the lands he is passing through, the direction of the mountain chains and their ramifications, the sources of streams and rivers, &c., acquires a rapidity of glance and observation that enables him considerably to abridge the labours of the field. Thus it is, that with a couple of extreme latitudes and longitudes, two opposite azimuths and a *tour* halfway, he has no difficulty in committing to paper the rivers whose courses he falls in with, the direction of their sources, their sinuosities, and the bearing of the serras—a sketch which a subsequent careful examination in his hut enables him to complete to his satisfaction.

We extract from the diary the notes of the two following days, the 6th and 7th of May, for being jotted down at the time they will serve better than any narrative to enlighten our readers upon what an explorer has frequently to endure upon his march.

PORTUGUESE-AFRICAN EXPEDITION.

May 6, 1879.   Page 510.
Aneroid 2272 ft. (uncorrd.)   Temperature 82° Fahr.

2.10 P.M. Camped near the River Candanje, to the N.W. of a lofty peak of Serra Catucua, 245° true (Lu-ache and Cambo, rivers), 76° true, in parallel 8° 22′ S. ☉ mer. = 72·06 ; azimuth rect. 150° true.

To-day's journey infernal ; broken, frightful ground, through two ravines, Catucua on the W. and Temo on the E. forming the basin of the Hamba. Scaled and descended eight steep mounts, of not less than 1000 feet, which half-killed us with fatigue.

Our guide, who knows the country, tells us that between here and the Cuango the ground will get gradually worse; and that the next twenty-five days' march will be nothing but ups and downs, the mountains and valleys covered with lofty vegetation.

From this point we see the Hamba, which by a narrow curve opens out to the N.E through rocky banks.

To the W. of the camp mountains and valleys intercept the view.

*   *   *   *   *   *   *   *

We have just visited two graves close by, respecting which we heard a story somewhat in the style of the fable of the two crickets that managed to devour each other.

A couple of natives had started from the coast together, in order to sell their goods : on their return they camped near this spot to divide the proceeds.

As, however, they disagreed in the process, from words they came to blows, and in the end killed one another.

They seem also to have buried each other besides, for an eye-witness, who saw them lying dead in the evening, found only their toes sticking out of the earth at sunrise next day !

We should have liked to question that witness as to whether he had covered up their toes !

* * * * * * * *

PORTUGUESE-AFRICAN EXPEDITION.

May 7, 1879. Page 511.
Aneroid 2275 ft. Temperature 80¼° Fahr.

Broke up camp at 7.30 a.m.

Fresh labour and difficulties. These marches are very trying to the men, who have already had eighteen months of it in the interior.

The road to-day was along a track which, in the space of a quarter of an hour, led us north, south, and east.

Covered with huge flints, it was a perfect ankle-trap, with vegetation in between, that made the passage of a heavily-laden man all but impossible.

The carriers, cut, bruised, and exhausted, refused to go any further. Poor fellows ! we pitied them from our hearts, with their seventy pounds' weight to carry !

The path led us from Candanje to *Calunga*-Mudille; thence to *Calunga*-N'bondo, and finally to *Calunga*-Mutomba, where we are now camped ; the entire road running along the edge of the great precipice lying on our left.

* * * * * * * *

We closed the events of the day just recorded (the 7th of May) by a hot discussion with the Sova, *Calunga-*N'bondo, who in the most *delicate* and *polite* manner wanted to force upon us one of his oxen. As we refused to accede to such an arrangement, which we knew would be a dear bargain, that rascally Cateco determined to second his intentions, and on the 8th at daybreak, starting at the head of the caravan, by previous agreement with the too generous chief, he guided us by a path which turned out to be a *cul-de-sac*, and left us in a deep river, called the Mucuna, and took to his heels!

After searching about for a path in vain, we had to retrace our steps, and found ourselves at length almost at the spot we had started from.

ALL BUT LOST.

We managed to catch our guide, and on the following day took a northerly direction, but got on so slowly that on arriving at Mahabo we found the herd waiting for us that we might select one of the animals.

Then ensued a discussion that lasted hours. The Sova did not want to *sell*, but to *give* us a beast, only, by way of preliminary; he himself wanted a present of sixteen pieces of cloth!

We came to an arrangement at last, the high contracting party letting us have a fat cow, but which turned out to be so old and tough that we could scarce get our teeth into the meat when it was cooked.

We were informed that this was one of the wealthiest

WE FOUND THE HERD WAITING.

Sovas of the Jinga, an assertion we readily believed, judging from his extensive herds of cattle. We could not help observing, however, that all his wealth failed to secure him respect, for the animal having been brought down and quartered, all the natives who had been engaged in the occupation, took up their little bundles, and turning their backs upon the great man, sneaked quietly off.

It is a noteworthy circumstance that the possession of this world's goods does not of itself insure superiority among these people : it merely secures to their owner the advantage of satisfying his inclinations. That feeling of respect, which in the old country is shown towards the great capitalist, seems to be quite unknown here. This is due, probably, to the fact that some of the wealthiest Sovas are the most exacting, and will stoop to the meanest actions to increase their store.

The real *aristocracy* of the country, if we may use such a term in connexion with these savages, is the hunter whose prowess is indicated by the number of skin rings bound about his weapon—each ring showing an animal brought down—or the warrior who has distinguished himself in battle, or the man who has dared to penetrate into a region till then unknown. These hold the highest place in public esteem, and are not unfrequently selected for important offices at court.

Sick of all the petty annoyances to which we had lately been subjected, we longed for a quiet spot where we could find rest, and shouldering our dismembered old cow, we set off in search of such a desideratum. We did not, however, find one to our mind till the 16th of the month, when, having gone over some fearful ground, we sighted, near the bank of the Cu-ilo, a river for the first time marked down, the residence of Cafuchila, one of the principal Sovas of the Hungo, whom Cateco specially recommended to us.

On a nearer approach, we were informed that the ruler himself did not reside there, but only a sister. Still, as it was of small interest to us whether it were a sister or a brother, we encamped in due course.

But if we were indifferent to the subject, others did not take the same view of our proceeding, as the reader will learn in the next chapter. We will merely observe, on closing this, that two hours after our arrival we learned that it was not a sister who lived there after all, but the Sova himself who had just departed this life; then they told us that the Sova was not dead, but had decamped; and finally this was again corrected by the assertion that the chief had gone on a journey!

"Anyway, what does it matter to us?" we exclaimed, "whether the man be dead, run away, or travelling?"

"But," explained Cateco, "they want to go and fetch him."

"Let them go, and good luck go with them."

It turned out to be *bad* luck for us; and little did we dream when planting our huts in that longed-for spot, that we should be the poorer by twenty pieces of cloth ere we got quit of it!

SHARPIA ANGOLENSIS.

CHAPTER IV.

The Hungo and its people—Head-dresses—Tobacco and snuff—Ugliness of the women, their indifference to dress—Low estimation in which they are held—The monarch of the Congo—Preparations for departure—Discussions with the natives—Sudden dissolution of a meeting—Abandoned senzalas—A little looting—Lake Tiber—The camp kitchen and an old acquaintance—A siesta disagreeably interrupted—Flight of the caravan—Fallen among thieves—A trial and a singular decision—The forest fired—Woods and vegetation—Quadrumans and reptiles—What explorers have to expect—Discovery of the river Cu-gho—Varieties of trees—Passage of the river and African cunning—A rest in the forest.

WE are now in the territory of the Hungo, and have as yet said nothing of the aspect and customs of its inhabitants, for the simple reason that as the data had to be culled from the notes of our diary, we have only at present reached the point where we can properly speak of them.

The natives of this part of the continent, who are called *ma-hungo*, have a special type, very different to that which distinguishes the people further south. From the moment of our entry into Matamba, we began to remark that difference principally observable in the colour of the skin and the mode of dressing the hair. To the jet black of the Jinga had succeeded the mahogany hue of the Ma-hungo; and in place of the trim bands and plaits of the former, we found a far more simple style adopted in the Matamba. The Ma-hungo men do not plait their hair at all, but either leave the wool alone, or, shaving portion of the head, adorn the sides with blue glass beads or other more common ones.

Their dress is a simple cloth suspended from the girdle, with a brass bracelet on the wrist; they carry a musket whereof the metal is kept clean and well-polished, and occasionally a curved sabre of the old huzzar fashion, with metal sheath.

They cut away the two front teeth to the gum, and sometimes the two lower ones also, which gives them a most repulsive appearance. In their mode of life they are barbarous to a high degree. They anoint and disfigure their bodies with oil and clay, and they carry with them in consequence a *bouquet*, that is perceptible at several yards' distance.

Both men and women smoke incessantly. *Nicotiana tabacum* with a large lance-shaped leaf abounds, together with another quality having a round leaf (*N. rustica* or *vulgaris?*) that is sold by the leaf or in small conical piles in which it is packed. Their most inveterate vice, however, is that of snuff-taking, which all more or less indulge in. They use for the purpose cylindrical boxes, wherein they put the dried or toasted leaf, that is pounded with a small wooden pestle, and they add pepper to it to give the mixture a more pungent flavour. Their mode of taking it is peculiar: thrusting into the box a stalk of the massambala with part of the ear attached, as if it were a spoon, they fill the little cavity with snuff, carry it to the nostrils, and inhale it with a powerful sniff. The operation so far is the mere indulgence of a vice; but with most of them it does not stop there, for the operator, introducing the little spoon for a second time into the box, smears all the upper lip with the powder, which sticks there readily enough through the

THE LADIES OF THE JIUNGO.

Page 73.

running from the nose, and this done, he or she seems very proud of the disgusting result.

We said he or she, for the ladies indulge in this habit quite as frequently as their lords, and the effect may be imagined when, their mouths and noses plastered over with the yellow powder, they open their lips and display their toothless jaws!

As we are upon the subject of the gentler sex, we will add a few more words about these degenerate daughters of Eve. The women of the Hungo are, in general, far uglier than the men, and their savage appearance is in harmony only with the soil on which they live. The mahogany colour of the skin, not uniformly tinted, but often patched and spotty, is not by any means so agreeable to the eye as the shiny jet of the natives further south. As one meets them abroad *en grande toilette* (that is to say as bare as the palm of one's hand) with a layer of clay upon their heads to keep down the woolly hair, a pipe in the mouth, a snuff-box dangling from the girdle, powerful limbs (many of them are five feet nine inches in height) a basket suspended by a narrow leather thong from their foreheads, and hanging down the back,—a feeling of pity is mingled with the disgust which the sight of them occasions.

They seem to have the most sovereign contempt for any sort of clothing, if we except a little scrap of baize, which they wear like an apron, only behind instead of before. Thirty times to one they rejected the cloth we offered them, taking beads in preference, to adorn the flat tresses that surround their head, and which represent the labour of months—perfect nests, wherein the parasites must lead a quiet, peaceful life, and multiply undisturbed. If by any chance they did accept a piece of cloth, they gave it to their husband, or wrapped their child in it, or made any use of it rather than to cover their own nakedness.

They appear to be held in esteem merely as beasts of burthen; and if we had any doubt concerning the existence of love, as a sentiment, among the tribes further south, we can have no hesitation in affirming that not a scintilla of it is to be found here. Everything is absolutely practical. A man appreciates his cows far more than he does his wives, and will make sacrifices to recover the former if stolen or strayed, but as to the latter, they may disappear without any hue or cry being made after them.

The dances to which we have more than once referred in the course of our narrative are practised here, but all their grotesqueness has disappeared, and left nothing but the obscenity, in which the women take the most active part.

Their dwellings are filthily dirty; and their clay utensils are clumsily made; nor do the other articles with which they adorn the interior of their huts, and that are familiar to the reader, display any greater taste or skill. There are mortars, drums, benches, stools, bows, lances, canes, wooden platters, oars, fetishes, calibashes, cartouch-boxes, powder-horns, bracelets, pipes, knives, marimbas, and other things which the Ma-hungo, like their congeners, manufacture for their use, but they are rude and unfinished.

The supreme authority acknowledged by this people, who are indubitably of a different origin from those in the south, is the King of the Congo, residing in the north at St. Salvador, one of the three monarchs of whom they have any notion; the other two being the King of Portugal, and the King of the Jinga.

In the afternoon of the third day of our sojourn in Cafuchila, the guide, Cateco, appeared before us and inquired in a queer sort of way whether we still intended to start next morning as we proposed.

"*Olé!*" was our reply. "Of course we shall leave; the Sova does not appear; only his sister is at home, and we have no idea of taking root in this place."

Turning on his heels with an insolent air, he walked off towards the village, as if to make the necessary arrangements, but hours flew by and he did not return to the *quilombo*.

The night passed over quietly enough, and with the first blush of day we began to get all the goods ready for departure, and sent for Cateco; but he was not to be found; the rascal was hiding for some purpose of his own, and we had once again to leave without a guide.

No sooner had we commenced our march than we began to understand the position of matters, for in almost every direction we heard the confused sounds of large bodies of men, followed shortly after by the beating of the war-drums, and the appearance in the neighbouring woods of many armed natives. We were surrounded, that was clear; and according to their notions we had committed some crime, of which we were profoundly ignorant, but which we were expected to pay for.

In the course of a few moments there issued from the grove on the left three warriors in company of the traitor Cateco, with feathers stuck into their heads and making threatening gestures.

Our first impulse was to rush upon the fellow and give him what he well merited—a thoroughly good thrashing. But the rascal, as if divining our intention, no sooner saw us approach than he took to flight, his long, thin legs and arms, and lanky body, surmounted by his plumed head, giving him the appearance of an African flamingo. His companions had some difficulty to catch him for the intended conference, and when they did the whole four returned; then one of them, after a short silence, and in a harsh voice, gave vent to the following pithy discourse:—

"Muene Puto! The Ma-hungo are wrath with you. The sister of Cafuchila, now in charge of the state, has been deceived by you, as you said you would await the Sova. Did she not send you one of her macotas to hear from your own lips that you would await the coming of the Sova who is now two suns' journey distant?"

"She did," we replied.

"Did you not say that you would wait?"

"We did."

"Is she not the lady of these lands?"

"She may be so."

"Did she not give you flour for your daily food?"

"Well, not exactly give, she sold it us."

"Anyway, you cannot quit this place because you have not *two tongues!* Either stop or go back: if you do otherwise, you must pay."

It being now our innings, we posed in a proper attitude, and putting José, our interpreter, in front of us, uttered in a measured way the following words:—

"Macotas! We came here to pay a visit to the Sova; we did not find him, for which *our heart is much afflicted*, and therefore we are about to pursue our onward journey. We never dreamed of possessing *two tongues*, a monstrosity which only an error of nature could produce. We are good and loyal friends" (José could make nothing of the loyal, so he substituted *fat*, which no doubt answered the purpose just as well), "what reason, therefore, have you to act as you are doing? Does it not appear to you treachery towards the whites? If you were in the country of the whites, think you we should act as you are doing? It is not our intention to flee from the Sova, and as a proof of our friendship we have here a present to offer him."

At this point we thought matters were looking a little brighter, when the trio interrupted us with,—

"What is your present?"

"A piece of gingham, half a piece of cotton, and six handkerchiefs," we replied, trying to look as grave as judges.

"*Eh-eh!*" exclaimed the three rogues together, "Cafuchila is a great Muene, he governs all this land; he is greater than Tembo Aluma, greater than Quinbungo Quiassama; only the Mani-Congo is greater than he. He allows no one to pass without permission. *Eh-eh!* wait one day longer and he will be here. He has not seen the whites; he wishes to talk to them and drink *aguardente* with them; wait, wait two days longer and he will come."

What is the use, we argued between ourselves, of continuing all this palaver? we shall be talking here all night, and yet leave off where we began. But at this moment a diversion was afforded by that inimitable Cateco, who addressing us in an insolent kind of way said,—

"And have you nothing else to offer us?"

This was too much for our patience, so we answered,—

"Yes; we have a stick" . . . . seizing a good stout one, ready at hand.

The action, which was perfectly unmistakable, broke up the meeting, the false guide and the three doughty warriors incontinently taking to their heels.

Giving at once orders to march, we plunged into the vast campaign country to the north, the echoes for some time repeating the tumming of the drums; these, however, grew fainter as we advanced, and at length were lost altogether to the ear.

A couple of miles further on brought us to some plantations of manioc, pepper, pumpkins, and other products, and we shortly after descried a couple of senzalas in the woods.

Although furnished with the ordinary utensils and articles of savage life, they were totally deserted of inhabitants. By the ashes of the fires that were still warm and the general disorder perceptible about the huts it was evident that their inmates had recently taken to flight. This is no uncommon thing in the interior of Africa, where the first beating of the war-drum will frequently cause a senzala to be abandoned.

That cunning Capulca, having satisfied himself that there really was nobody about, plucked up courage to make a recognisance and returned with a staff and a dozen maniocs that he had looted. His example was soon followed by others; one appropriated a very good skin; another picked up a pan; a third, some other article; and we ourselves secured a little fetish, quieting our conscience for the theft under the pretext that it was done in the interest of science and for the gratification of European curiosity. Lighting our pipes at a smouldering fire we quitted the spot and resumed our way.

Still keeping a northerly course, by an open track, we fell in with another deserted hamlet, through which we marched in triumph, and two miles further on, descending an abrupt slope, we came, at half-past eleven, upon a lovely lake surrounded by high ground, the name of which, as we subsequently learned, was the Tiber.

Its banks, cut into a variety of fantastic creeks and mimic bays, thickly clothed with verdure, offered a most enchanting prospect, the contemplation of which soon banished from our minds the annoyances of the early morning; for having now become habituated to the life of the woods we could give ourselves up to the enjoyment of any novelty that came in our way with the same light-heartedness as any of the natives—our companions.

The water, whose limpidity left that of its namesake in old Rome far in the shade, faithfully reflected the image of the steep and richly varied banks and the azure vault

LAKE TIBER.

above; not a sound disturbed the holy stillness: not a ruffle broke the mirror-like surface of the lovely basin; and we might have fancied ourselves suddenly transported by some kindly genius to this enchanting spot as if to show us of what Nature was capable in her happy moods in the interior of savage Africa.

The magic of such a scene was susceptible, we thought,

of being heightened if contemplated under the most favourable material circumstances, that is to say, under the influence of a hearty breakfast; so rousing Capulca from his pleasant occupation of munching one of his stolen maniocs, we gave orders for the preparation of the meal.

Making for the nearest tree, and arranging close to it three large stones (our invariable camp fireplace), our chef divested himself of his cap, boots, and pipe; and kneeling down to attend to the fire, his cook's knife in its sheath stuck out behind him, he bore so extraordinary a resemblance to a baboon with a stiff tail, that we could not refrain from laughter at the sight!

Pending the preparation of the meal, we set ourselves to gather small shells in order to enlarge the conchological acquirements of the naturalists, and when breakfast was ready we eagerly attacked the invariable fowl. It was an old acquaintance, or at least must have been very near of kin to many hundreds of equally lanky, stringy creatures upon which it had been our fate to banquet for many a long month. While carefully picking its bones, we discussed—as we had often done before—the tooth-resisting power of this species of biped in Africa, and when the herculean task was over, we lay back on the grass, our heads supported in our hands, disposed for a comfortable siesta.

It did not last long; nothing pleasant in this world ever does; for while watching amused, with half-closed eyes, the young niggers licking the plates as they gathered them up, and swallowing any scraps (they must have been very few) we had inadvertently let fall, we saw a sudden movement of alarm among them, and with the warning cry of "The Ma-hungo!" ringing in our ears, we sprang to our feet.

The cry had roused the whole caravan, the men seizing their guns. On looking round we were convinced of the presence of the enemy, for they clustered on the neighbouring hills and showed their heads above the grass, all apparently armed with guns and assagais.

"They are back again," was the universal exclamation, "and we shan't get by; they mean to rob us!"

"Well; if they try, we must defend ourselves," was our response.

And giving orders to march, we filed along the edge of the broken ground, in the midst of a roar of voices from the savages, which the echoes repeated in the strangest sounds.

It was a frightfully trying march up that mountain side, under a burning sun, our only track the irregular furrows made by the waters, everywhere strewn with sharp, flinty stones. On reaching the summit we discovered at the base the upturned faces and shining bodies of our pursuers.

THE HOLO TYPE.

The women of our caravan were in terrible trouble, for what with heavy loads upon their heads and their infants at their backs they could with difficulty get along, and we deemed it prudent to bring up the rear to prevent the laggards being seized and carried off by the natives.

The mountain was succeeded by a plateau, in crossing which we came upon the important track called the Holo, that runs westward to Ambriz, passing through Dembo Naboangongo. We at once struck into it, followed closely by the horde of barbarians, who pursued us with cries and threats, stopping when we stopped, and moving on when we moved. This convinced us of the inefficacy of any attempt at negotiation.

At times they would conceal themselves, and the joy of our crew was great. It was always, however, short-lived, for heads would pop up again in the most unexpected places, as if the wretches had burrowed through the earth like moles.

Four anxious hours were spent in this manner, hours that seemed weeks in length, and we were uncertain as at the outset, about what we had better do : for we stood unsupported, in a savage, desert country, with comparatively few resources, and surrounded by a hostile people. At this moment a murmur, as of some important discovery, came from the vanguard, and we ourselves observed, as we commenced the descent of the high ground, that we were in the neighbourhood of a senzala. We at once decided upon camping there; and on reaching a convenient spot the loads were willingly lowered and piled, and the men set to work to procure materials for the huts. On seeing this, the Ma-hungo closed up on all sides and completely surrounded us.

Suddenly there issued from the senzala an old noble, recognizable by his *cajinga*, who came towards us. As he approached, we were so little prepossessed by his general appearance, his enormous mouth, hanging lips, wrinkled skin, flattened nose and blear eyes, that we could not help muttering, "Another thief!"

Little wotting of the unfavourable effect he had produced upon us, he addressed us with the words,—

"I am the chief of this senzala. Who are you? Whence

do you come? And who are these people surrounding you?"

At first we hesitated about making him our confidant, but on second thoughts, seeing the not too favourable eye he cast upon the Ma-hungo, we thought it better to give him some explanation. Upon our hint, therefore, the *muzumbo* furnished him with a brief narrative of the events of the day, the persecution to which we had been forced to submit, and the absurd pretensions of the Ma-hungo, who claimed twenty pieces of cloth in payment of an offence that was either imaginary or that we had never committed.

"Fear nothing," said the ugly old chief, after listening to this story: "I will decide everything."

And in a rage, real or pretended, turning to our pursuers, he began to rate them soundly, interspersing his discourse with such gentle epithets as "thieves, rogues, and villains," so that our hearts, as well as those of the whole caravan, were gladdened within us at this evident leaning to our side. Before this untoward affair, however, was terminated, we were forced to alter our opinion, and to confess that the hoary old Jinga was a more cunning rogue than all the rest put together, as he was sharp enough to swindle both parties alike.

Deeming that at his advanced age a vertical position could not be particularly comfortable, we found him a small bench to sit down on, and when he had taken his place beside ourselves, our people and the Ma-hungo gathered round and the Court was complete.

The interpreter José, on our behalf, opened the case, and bitterly complained of the annoyances to which we had been subjected; and when he had done our adversaries, by their mouth-piece, made answer. This was followed by reply and rejoinder, till one would have thought the gates of some lunatic asylum had been suddenly opened and the inmates had broken loose.

The old judge listened, but appeared to be in no sort

THE COURT WAS COMPLETE.

of hurry to pass sentence, meanwhile night was approaching, and he knew the natives would not stop there after dark. This evidently was his policy; he wanted to gain time, so as to force them to modify their claims. As the sun neared the horizon their demands were already reduced to fifteen pieces ; as it was setting they dropped down to twelve ; and when its last rays disappeared they had fallen to ten.

"Ten be it," we exclaimed : admitting to ourselves that the good man had done us this much service in reducing the claim of these wretches to one-half.

A bale having been opened, and the ten pieces counted out, the natives took possession, and at once marched off, to our intense satisfaction. Imagine, however, our astonishment and disgust when, on the retirement of the band of thieves, the arch-thief, our African Daniel, holding out his hand, said, in a snuffling tone,—

"*Bin-delle,* now hand over the other ten pieces to me ! "

And we had to do it, iniquitous as we considered the arrangement ; and thus were brought to a close an absurd adventure and a singular trial, the first in the country in which we flattered ourselves we should obtain justice.

So disgusted were we with the events of the last few hours that we had almost made up our minds to resume our march at night, but this idea was abandoned as soon as formed, for not only was the darkness at our place of encampment complete, but before us, at some four to six miles distance, the northern horizon in an arc of 100° suddenly wore the appearance of an ocean of fire.

The flames lent to the hills and mountains on that side a weird appearance, fitted to daunt the boldest heart; and very shortly afterwards, while regarding the fearful spectacle, flames broke out to the south, the work, doubtless, of our recent adversaries, who, on retiring, had amiably fired the woods to interpose a barrier to our further progress ! We stood, in fact, in a perfect circle of fire, and never did we pass a more anxious night !

How truly did we not then recognize the truth of Stanley's descriptions! How vast is the difference between the inhabitants of the middle basin of the Congo, into which Europeans rarely penetrate, and the comparatively gentle peoples of the south—the Quiocos, the Ganguellas, and the Songos! How much savagery and ill-faith are centred in these monsters, for they are men only in form! And the more we reflected upon the subject, the more serious it presented itself to our minds, for was it likely that matters would improve as we went on? From what side were we likely to find protection, when everything that bore a human shape was our enemy, whose sole aim was to bring about our ruin?

A delicious morning dissipated many of the gloomy reflections born of night and of the horrors that surrounded us. On starting, we plunged into the woods, the few natives that appeared fleeing in terror at our approach, and shortly afterwards, descending a steep incline, found ourselves at the bottom of the valley. There the gigantic fig-trees, *m'pafu* (Elemi) and immense palms, connected by a network of the spiral stems of the *Calamus florus*, and other creepers, formed an almost impenetrable jungle, inhabited by troops of monkeys of revolting aspect, among which we recognized the *Cynocephalus porcarius*.

A river with marshy banks then completely intercepted our path, and as there was not the ghost of a bridge, we were compelled to wade across with the water up to our waists.

Continuing our way over hill and dale, keeping a steady northerly course, at one time through a marsh, at another by a piece of woodland, we came, by chance, at four o'clock in the afternoon, when we were despairing of such *good luck*, upon a little village named Mucole

WE HAD TO CUT OUR WAY WITH THE HATCHET.

Quipanzo, where we were at once the victims of a swindle; for having engaged a guide there and given him six yards of cloth for his services, the fellow decamped, and we had to go on without him.

The ground was so frightfully rough and broken that, unable to continue longer in a northerly direction, we diverged to the eastward, a course that we pursued for a couple of days, one of us suffering from fever, the other from rheumatism. The path was encumbered with a profuse growth, called by the natives *mu-chito*, a perfect dedalus, for which the Hungo is celebrated. We had literally to cut our way with the hatchet and the sickle, and whole hours were passed with immense labour to open up a mile of road.

Many a day was spent during this journey in the midst of such labyrinths, where the foot of man had probably never before trodden, which the native carefully avoids, and whose only inmates are monkeys and baboons or some frightful reptiles, which find a home in the hollow trunk of an ancient tree or about the network of roots that are as much above the ground as under.

These are true thorns in the sides of an explorer, and when he meets them he is bound to put out all his energy, so that he may, by his example, prevent the demoralization of those who follow him. For as they struggle through pestilential bogs or almost impenetrable woods, stumbling here, sinking there, laying down their loads to take up their hatchets, they would infallibly drop beneath their fatigues and deprivations were they not encouraged by the words and activity of their leaders, to whom they look up, so to speak, for inspiration.

In the midst of all our worries, labour, sickness, and torment, a gleam of pleasure was at length afforded us, not, it is true, unmixed and unalloyed, but that still, to a certain extent, compensated us for much of the suffering of the last few days.

On the 23rd of May, while descending an easy slope, we observed at the foot, and extending for a considerable distance over the lower ground, a thick growth of reeds and osiers that hinted at the presence of a large river. Our conjecture was a true one, and when we reached the bottom we found a vast stream of water which the inhabitants of a neighbouring senzala informed us was called the Cu-gho, an affluent of the Cuango, which we at once marked down upon our map, and to which, a little later on, we were enabled to assign a length of 100 miles.

It springs, according to our informants, in the northwest, amid the territory of Macume-N'jimbo, in a spacious lake, and along it lies a track which, *viâ* Quizau Malunga, connects the interior with the coast.

In front of us, on the north-north-west, extended the district of Quicongo, rugged, mountainous, full of lakes, lying at the bottom of deep valleys; on the west-north-west lay the lands of Quiteca N'bungo; and to the north of the latter appeared the territory of Futa, where nestled the Ba-congo tribes.

How savage was the aspect of the whole scene! Accustomed as we were by this time to the interior of Africa, it somehow seemed to us that this region was unlike anything we had yet beheld in it. The soil, the air, the inhabitants, all seemed different. The vegetation, mainly, imprints upon it a distinct character. Palms predominate. There are, for instance, the *Elais*, the *Hyphœne*, the *Borassus*, a species of *Chamœrops* (the fan-palm), the leafy *Raphias*, whence is extracted the *Maluvo*, of which we shall have more to say. Species of hemps begin to appear in families which are generally herbaceous near the tropics,

Malvaceas, more especially, among which figure the *Adansonia* and *Eriodendron anf.;* and even various *Rubiaceas,* show symptoms of this transformation.

We found in this district numerous species of *Nymphaceas,* together with *Euphorbiaceas* and *Acantaceas;* precisely the contrary to the *Fugeras* and *Orchideas epidendres,* which, rare throughout the continent, almost disappear in these latitudes.

The gigantic *Burseraceas,* producing the Elemi balsam, to which we have already alluded, under the names of *m'pafu* or *m'bafu,* are quite common. Down their enormous trunks runs the white resin which, evaporating in part, forms drops that stand out like the gutterings of huge wax tapers. In close proximity to the former are the colossal *Landolphias,* whence is obtained the india-rubber, a gum that is very abundant in the Hungo.

We rested on the 23rd of May near the *libata* Cambamba, and started off again on the 24th for Mangongo, with a view to crossing the river. This operation, that constitutes one of the most difficult problems in Africa, when the traveller has to employ the native boats, was very nearly in our case bringing about a serious conflict.

At the outset the natives hid their canoes; then they would accept none of our offers; a little later they averred we should not cross the river at all, and only yielded at last under reiterated persuasion. And we had to bear all this when we were consumed with fever!

The passage at length began; but when they had carried half our party over and had thus divided the expedition, they struck, and would do no more work!

" What is the matter ? " we inquired.

" We don't intend to take over any more."

" For what reason ? "

"Because four pieces are too little."

"But a bargain's a bargain. You agreed to the terms, which are your own."

"You must give us two more pieces, otherwise you may stop where you are."

In a moment of nervous excitement we seized our gun and raised it to our shoulder with a view to fire at the

THE CU-GHO WATERMEN.

impudent swindlers. But our better judgment prevailed and prevented an act which might have been attended with very serious consequences.

We therefore had recourse to diplomacy; spoke them mildly, while we were boiling over with rage; and after a promise of increased pay, and three mortal hours passed in discussion and persuasion, got over safely to the other side, missing, however, at the last moment, when the fellows were all gone, a she-goat that had formed part of the last boat-load.

Late as it was—four o'clock in the afternoon—and sick, worn out, and trembling with pain and excitement, we were bound to go further on in search of a convenient place to pitch our camp; which, after marching in a north-north-west direction, we thought we found in the midst of a thicket, and worked till nightfall at our huts.

Judging from the musty smell that soon saluted our nostrils, we must have selected—if not the actual lairs—the immediate neighbourhood of the haunts of wild beasts; but we were so thoroughly done up that at that moment we cared but little where we lay our heads, so that we obtained rest. This blessed resource was happily not denied us; and thus at the extreme limit of the Hungo we slept profoundly.

CYNOCEPHALUS PORCARIUS.

CHAPTER V.

We leave the Cu-gho—Gloomy presentiments—The *mu-chitos* and the desert—An evening of tribulations and a devouring thirst—Trying times of a life in the interior—A Providential interposition—More *mu-chitos* and fresh labour—Caught in the wood—Nervous state of the explorers—All but lost—Scouts sent out in search of succour—Two lines from the diary—A terrible night—Return of José and brief narrative of his adventures—Two solitary hunters—Fresh hopes—Again astray—An apparition of palancas—Night again—Final decision.

WITH our proximity to Yacca commenced the most trying portion of our whole journey. So long as we remained on the Cu-gho we remarked, and the guide confirmed our observation, that the natives appeared more and more anxious about the road we intended to pursue, whispering among themselves that in such-or-such a direction not a living soul was to be found, and that the only known track, that of Cha-Massango, lay along the river's course. We had, however, got so accustomed to the assertion that certain territory was a desert while we found it everywhere peopled, that we paid little heed to their apprehensions, and resolved to continue on.

On the 25th of May, therefore, having risen in the dark and whilst the woods were still echoing with the mournful cries of the monkeys and the more painful ones of the jackals, we were seated by the fire waiting for day, which an inexplicable presentiment seemed to tell us would be one of trial. The blessed light of morning soon appeared, and brought with it the energy which naturally comes to the man whose mind is prepared for a great struggle.

"Wake up! Wake up!" was the cry, and the men unrolled themselves from their mats and busied themselves with preparations for departure.

No one said a word; we ourselves, as glum as our followers, waited till all was ready, and the silence that had fallen upon the entire camp was in singular contrast to the hilarity and chatter which usually attended our setting out.

Our first care was to discover a path, and as our guide after a little search found a goat track, we struck into it and filed off in a north-easterly direction.

For the first hour we picked our way amid the crags which formed the steep bank on the left side of the Cugho, stopping occasionally to listen for the slightest sound that indicated the existence of humanity. Not a murmur, however, met our ear, and not a vestige of a living thing caught the eye as we descended the bare declivity, plunged amid some ragged palms, and reached at the bottom a deep ravine, almost concealed by the abundant vegetation, where every vestige of a path had disappeared.

Face to face with this new obstacle, we groped about till we found an opening into which, stooping our heads, it was so low, we unhesitatingly dived. The hard sandstone was here succeeded by a spongy soil, that soon became a slough covered with leaves, osiers, and sprays of the *Metroxilon*, through which water was perceptible. We were evidently in the channel of a little river.

In lieu of the radiant light of the sun we had a semi-darkness which scarcely enabled us to pick our way, and the light boughs of wavy trees were replaced by giant trunks with overhanging branches scarcely less gigantic.

The forest, ever increasing in density, became at last all but impenetrable, so that we had to make a dozen trials ere we could force a passage. At half-past nine, all but disheartened, and yet apprehensive of stopping where we were, we came to a halt and sent scouts out in different directions, with orders to communicate their position by shouts and cries. The reports of several guns from the north made us start in that direction, and after tracking our way through the underwood we got out of the maze and reached our companions.

It was then ten o'clock. The sun, that was high in the heavens, darted his full beams upon the neighbouring plain, covered with a new kind of low and yellow grass, which we got through without much difficulty; but before three quarters of an hour had elapsed we found ourselves engulfed in another thicket of colossal *muchito*, which covered for some few leagues the entire basin of a broad river called the Cuviji.

It is difficult to conceive the dangers that beset a traveller in these woods. The black and shifting soil, formed by the accumulations of centuries of *débris* of the vegetable world, the humidity below retained by the imperviousness of the subjacent bed of clay, the tepid vapours of the soil rising like a thick cloud between the tree-trunks, the water dropping from the upper leaves, the suffocating heat, the sudden chill, the overpowering smell of decayed vegetation, mingled with the pungent odours of other living plants, constitute a sum of elements that the pen attempts in vain to describe.

Pushing on through this wonderfully beautiful but still fearful forest, with many a hard struggle by the way, the caravan, as before, came at length to the end, and emerged into the open. The prospect before us was a rugged bit of country, exhibiting various bare, circular mounts and deep, green valleys, of which our past experience made us doubtful, but not the slightest indication of a track to show that it had been traversed by man.

We stood, in fact, in a perfect desert, and a very short halt under the burning sun produced a thirst which it was difficult to satisfy. The men sought for water everywhere, but not the smallest brooklet was discoverable in dale or valley.

At 4.30 p.m. we found ourselves on the summit of a lofty mount, dropping with fatigue, burnt by the sun, and fainting with thirst. A magnificent panorama of hills and conical rocks, disconnected and without order, was presented to our view, and as we regarded it, our hearts sank within us, for we readily comprehended that as there were no river-beds, the water which fell from the clouds and formed little lakes in the hollows became speedily dried up. Nevertheless, we despatched half a score of men in different directions to search once more for the precious liquid, but they returned one after the other without success.

The position was a most critical one, for evening would soon be upon us, and yet, what was to be done? Anyway, remaining there was useless; so putting our trust in Providence we resumed our wearisome journey, ourselves taking the lead by way of setting an example to our half-demoralized caravan.

But as we trudged along, uncomfortable ideas rose up in our minds, and found expression in the half-muttered words, What if the reports of the dwellers by the Cu-gho should be correct, and the territory on which we are entering be indeed a desert, devoid of water, bare of people, with no resources to support animal life, and the further penetration into which will involve destruction, by starvation and thirst!

Shaking off with difficulty these gloomy reflections, and clinging to the hope engendered of former experience, we kept sturdily on our way. As ill-luck would have it, two of the carriers, overcome with fatigue and thirst, set down their loads after we had got over a couple of miles, and declared they could go no further, so we had to carry the guns of our immediate attendants, and make them assist in conveying the goods.

It was then half-past five in the afternoon, and our anxiety had reached its culminating-point. In front, some of the strongest and boldest of our party eagerly pressed on, in the hope of being the first to slake their burning thirst, but it was labour in vain, mountain, plain, and valley alike showed by their sterility that no water was there.

The sun was already hidden behind a bank of cloud, a mantle, as it were, waiting to enwrap the god of day as he sank towards the western horizon, and his disappearance lent a most melancholy aspect to the arid district. Day was about to close, and heaven only knew what was to become of us after thirty hours' thirst! Most assuredly, by the following morning, not one among our men would be capable of taking a step under a load weighing seventy pounds.

But that was not the worst; our discomfort was deep enough, but a lower depth was looming in the distance. Without water, how were we to cook our *infundi*? And how, therefore, should we manage if we suffered from hunger and thirst combined?

In the depressed condition of our minds, what wonder if we should ask ourselves whether the barbarians of

Losing Heart.

Central Africa were worthy of the sacrifices we and others made on their behalf? when all our labour, care, anxieties and suffering were to be met by ingratitude!

But we had brief space for these or any reflections. The lads of the party who had borne up so bravely began to give way, and first one and then another slipped to the ground with his burthen, and cried, "We can do no

SLOWLY DESCENDING FROM A HEIGHT.

more. Let us go back, senhors, let us go back. There was water on the road we came from, there is nothing ahead of us but rocks and stones."

We spoke to them kindly and encouragingly, though our words scarce found an echo in our own hearts. We urged them to take a little rest and then try again; assured them that their fatigue and trouble would soon end, and that water and food would shortly be at their disposal. And as we uttered the promise, the report of a gun and then another from the front broke upon our ear, and was repeated from the rocks around, as if a dozen muskets had been fired. A frenzied excitement at the signal succeeded the depression that was akin to despair. Hoarse cries came from the cracking lips which a moment before seemed incapable of proffering a word. Arms, baggage, everything that encumbered the motion of the limbs, were for the time abandoned, and the long file of carriers just then slowly descending from a height appeared to be animated with a feverish life, and rushed downwards eager to see the origin of the preconcerted signal.

Before us ran a vast river which one of the lads, Fortuna, happily named, had just before discovered. Like madmen we dashed into the stream, buried our faces in the limpid water, drank it as a dog might do, little reflecting, and for the moment little caring that everything we then possessed of means was strown upon the rugged way!

When we had come to our senses we began to think of our encampment, and while part of the men in far different spirits returned to the place where they had left the baggage which they gradually collected, others filled their calabashes with water and made preparations for the evening meal. They were all, however, much too tired to construct the usual huts, so we determined to take our rest in the open. Never was rest more needed; and under the brilliant stars which twinkled in the vast canopy of heaven we composed ourselves to sleep.

By midnight the south-east wind that had been blowing, moderated, and the moon, as she rose, looked down

THE MU-CHITO.

Page 99.

peacefully upon our handful of men, lying in easy attitudes about the smouldering camp fires, in happy forgetfulness of the trying adventures of the day. Ere we dropped off, we heard, mingled with the rush of the Fortuna between its dark green banks, other strange sounds due to the various quadrumen, as they chased each other amid the boughs of the trees, or to the night-birds shrieking as they flew by.

On the 26th, at daybreak, well provided with water, having despatched what remained of some dried meat, we started along the high ground in an easterly direction, in search this time of food, for we felt convinced that along the river we should fall upon the Cuango (of which we conceived the Fortuna was an affluent) and the human habitations we sought. Unfortunately, we were perfectly wrong in our conjectures, and at about four miles from our starting-place, we discovered, immediately beneath our feet, a ravine, into which we descended.

But on reaching the bottom we found a dense thicket of trees and our old enemy, the *mu-chito*, where we lost ourselves for a couple of hours. On emerging from it between the river and a lofty bank on the south side, we kept along the ridge till we met with another thick wood, where we soon found that we were completely surrounded by water and plants.

The caravan floundered about the high and stubborn grass in search of some opening whereby they might issue from the trap—but for a long time unsuccessfully. At length, fancying we saw a sort of track through the dense vegetation, we followed it, but to our dismay soon observed, by unmistakable signs, that it was a path made by hippopotami, and all our care had to be devoted to the task of not running against the monsters.

As we stayed our steps for awhile, the silence was profound. The river, choked with rushes and canes, seemed to run in every direction, or to divide itself into numerous branches, and while one of them appeared to flow eastward, another decidedly ran towards the north. Making our way to the margin, we found matters even worse; the treacherous soil gave way beneath our weight and we sank up to our knees, so that we were obliged to lend a hand to help the vanguard out.

Dead-tired and depressed in spirits, we felt ready to succumb beneath the weight of such gigantic difficulties, unknowing what to do or what to advise, and our spirits were not raised by the questions we overheard our companions put to each other.

"Where is it we are going to? How shall we ever get through this desert country—without food—without a path—where wild beasts may meet us at every turn?"

How indeed! we began to ask ourselves; and is it not a species of insanity to go further? The only other course open is to turn back, but then, what becomes of our labour and our mission?

Torn by these conflicting emotions—the feeling of the quasi-impossibility of advancing pulling us in one direction, while our duty and our pride were urging us in another—we still went on till we were ready to drop.

The life of the woods, which is generally miserable enough, becomes aggravated in all its worst features as the traveller plunges deeper into this great continent. The huge obstacles and constant privations not merely weaken and wear out his body, but at the end of some months' marching they produce a state of irritability, and nervous excitement closely allied to derangement. An extraordinary change in individual character soon becomes apparent. The extravagance of gesture, precipitation in every act, abruptness in issuing orders, baseless fears, and a desire to rush along the road, as though pursued by some phantom, all are evidence of the change that is being wrought, and are symptoms of the malady known here as African spleen.

The ideas which at such times rise up in the mind are, as a matter of course, closely connected with the objects of the explorer. A plan that he may have conceived becomes a pivot upon which turn all the labours of the brain; by day, during whole hours of abstraction, he figures to himself endless streams, colossal lakes, new tracks, and strange habitations; by night his dreams are still of Africa, but mingled with them, the extravagances and monstrosities proper to a state of semi-consciousness.

How often when in that half-sleeping, half-waking condition have we not beheld the Cuango, coursing through a vast plain, and finally debouching into the Congo-Zaire! How often have we not dwelt on the awful beauty of that region, and wandered through the vast basin of the immense river, noting the huge plain, here covered by many feet of water, there clothed with a dense vegetation exhaling miasma and death under a blinding, scorching sun! We could even trace the course of the numerous rivers that flowed into the all-absorbing stream; the Cuango, the Lu-angue, the Cassai, the Moaza-N'gombe, converging to one receptacle, where their waters intermingled! In that same half-dreamy state we found ourselves gathering information from native sources, passing through scenes of the most extravagant character, yet bearing an impress of such vivid reality, that when we were broad awake, we tried, but tried in vain to dismiss them from our mind. The map of Africa was stereotyped upon our brain, and not even the pitchy darkness of our hut could shut it from our view!

Did these strange vagaries, these fixed prepossessions portend the dawn of madness? Was the brain yielding to the pressure put upon it, while the body was weakened by fever, privations, and fatigues? It was a fearful fear, and as, from this lapse of time, we look back upon those terrible days and try to realize all the dread apprehensions that we then suffered, a feeling of infinite pity and compassion for the suffering mortals comes over us, as though for men who were other than ourselves!

Amid the straits to which we were now reduced, there was one great and overpowering necessity which demanded instant attention, that of procuring food; so abandoning the margin of the river, we cut a path with the hatchet through the forest which clothed the mountain side, in order to reach the summit and obtain a view of the surrounding country, and when we did so we saw the folly of our recent struggles, and obtained an explanation of the imaginary branches of the river we had been pursuing. The forest extended as far as the eye could reach, and in the open ground we distinctly observed two rivers, one to the north, the other to the south of the mountain, and whose waters met at some distance beyond its foot; the smaller one, the Fortuna, our recent discovery, which flowed into the Cu-gho; and the point where we stood, was the *massango*, or confluence of the streams.

With the knowledge thus acquired, there remained no doubt upon our minds that we must retrace our steps, as a forward motion was simply impossible. As we continued our observations, we remarked in the far distance, eastward, what we took to be smoke, but no sign of a human dwelling. The country was utterly deserted, and our stomachs, in consequence of the disappointment, began to protest energetically against the neglect to which they were subjected.

It was then three o'clock in the afternoon, so calling a council we resolved upon a plan which we proceeded forthwith to put into execution. Fortuna, the lucky (for we had reached a stage when such superstitious trifles were not ignored), accompanied by a couple of companions, was ordered to proceed in an easterly direction, and he was furnished with a gun wherewith to signal in case of a discovery and defend himself and party against attack. Somma, an intelligent and active *mu-sumbi*, with three or four more, was instructed to make his way to the south in search of game or anything else in the shape of food, while José, the guide, was desired to go northwards, to see if he could meet with the habitations of man. We ourselves were meanwhile to keep watch and ward with the reserves over our goods, and wait for tidings from the scouts.

When they had departed we set to work to construct an encampment and scour the neighbourhood in search of edible roots. As the quest was perfectly unsuccessful, we were fain to content ourselves with cold water, and such scraps of flour as we could gather from the sack after it was turned inside out like a glove. Then we entered in our diary the laconic phrases which we literally transcribe :—

PORTUGUESE-AFRICAN EXPEDITION.

May 26th, 1879. Page 542.
Aneroid 2349 ft. Temperature 84° Fahr.

An awful day. Camped on a mount near the confluence of the Cu-gho and Fortuna, completely cleared out of provisions. Very down and glumpy. Country deserted. Not a soul yet met with. Hungry, feverish, and sick. Horary for longitude :

$\odot$ at $2^h = 53, 31$. $H = 1^h. 50^m. 28^s. 30^t$. Azith. $= 369,9$.

$\female$ mer. $= 67,97$.

What next? We must wait.

It was the only thing to do, so we did it with resignation while counting the minutes and listening to catch the slightest sound. But in the immense solitude there reigned a sepulchral silence which we ourselves scarcely ventured to break.

Meanwhile the sun ran his imperturbable course; passed through the stages from brilliant yellow to deep orange, and nearing the horizon irradiated the patches of cloud which floated beneath the azure vault of heaven, shot a few grand rays through a rent in the dense vapour, and then, in disappearing, carried with him our last lingering hopes!

"Nothing," we murmured sadly to each other; "otherwise they would have returned."

Night fell, and brought with it increased depression. Extensive fires in the east and the moon which then rose seemed to augment the solemnity of the prospect.

Hours passed over when we were aroused by the report of a gun; it was Somma with his party; and shortly after another report warned us of the arrival of Fortuna. They brought us, unluckily, no comfort; they had found no cultivation, no track, not a vestige of a human thing. The forest, they said, was all around us, but they had sought in vain for a path which could hint of its ever being traversed.

In José, now, lay the sole hope that was left us, and our readers may believe that we did so with intense anxiety. His route had been northwards, and in that direction we looked and watched.

As early as four in the morning we were on the lookout; we had tried to sleep, but in vain; we had been listening the night through. The morning breeze as it fanned our fevered temples was an immense relief; but we were faint and sick for want of sustenance.

The sun reappeared and lit up all the landscape; but

to us it brought little relief, as we regarded the worn and haggard looks of our companions in misfortune. As for ourselves, wrapped in our great-coats, seated on the ground and our backs supported by the open trunks, we wound up our chronometers and recorded the readings of the thermometers, and having thus performed our duty towards science, restored the instruments to their places and once more gazed out upon the country.

There was nothing new in it; there was no change from the day before; the same valleys and the same woodland met our eyes, and the same silence reigned over all.

As time sped on, it became urgent upon us we knew to take some resolution, to make some effort unless we intended to wait, with arms folded, for the approach of death by starvation. But what was that resolution, what that effort to be? To return? we were far from any inhabited place; by the road we had come it would take us two long days, and how were they to be got through, fasting, while we had already fasted so long? To go forward? whither? amid the frightful obstacles we beheld from our point of observation? And José? could we, ought we to abandon him? A thousand times, no! Remain we must, and to remain we resolved; further determining to use our efforts to draw fish from the river and to scour the woods in search of game.

The idea was no sooner uttered than it was seized upon with avidity, and once again did the encampment display a semblance of motion. Anything that could serve for a net was hastily rummaged out; lead was cut into little pieces to make small shot for birds; some of the hands set to work to manufacture snares, and parties were in the very act of setting out for the river, when from the forest, in a north-west direction, the report of a couple of guns turned us for the moment into statues!

"It is José!" was the universal cry.

And as we looked we saw José and his companions emerge from the wood, with a firm and elastic step which was in strong contrast with our own weakness,

JOSÉ AND HIS COMPANIONS EMERGED FROM THE WOOD.

bearing upon their heads what we felt was to restore us to new life!

It is impossible to describe the wild joy which took possession of our whole band at the sight. As the men rushed towards the new arrivals, eager to relieve them of their load, they cried,—

"Is it food you are bringing us?"

And José raised aloft a string of *bagres* from the river, drew from his belt a root of manioc which he flourished in the air, and pointed to the packages carried by his attendants, in eloquent but silent answer to the eager queries.

José's expedition, as subsequently related to us, may be summed up in few words.

When he and his party left us the evening before, he made his way through the neighbouring woods, and coming out upon the river, considerably higher up than we had met it, they found to their satisfaction that they could ford it, which they at once proceeded to do. Having reached the other side, they observed what appeared to be a goat-track, into which they at once struck, and marching along it, uninterruptedly, they came, to the surprise of the guide, upon a solitary hut, all but buried in the high grass. On entering they found themselves in presence of a couple of hunters, who had taken up their residence in that spot in order to pursue their avocation. The men were intelligent and friendly, and José had no difficulty in bartering a piece of cloth and a bag of beads for some thirty *bagres*, a parcel of manioc roots, about eight pounds of flour, and a couple of *bindas* of *maluvo;* he, moreover, drew from them a promise to act as our guides upon the road. He would have returned that very night, but learning that the forest was not particularly safe during the hours of darkness, owing to the wild beasts by which it was infested, he discreetly waited till the next morning before making the return journey.

Whilst our worthy guide was doling out his news, we were in like manner distributing the provisions he had brought, and though the banquet was not a luxurious one, still manioc root and dried fish to a man who has been next door to starvation are not by any means to be despised. Heartily thanking José for his good service, which we promised duly to reward on reaching the coast, we resolved to lose no time in pursuing the path he had discovered; and so soon as the wants of nature were satisfied, we got ourselves into marching order and broke up our camp.

Our course was north-westerly, and following in the footsteps of the guide, we arrived, after about an hour's march, at the point where the Fortuna was fordable, and which river, as José informed us, was called by the natives Unguiji, and came from a far distance and had its rise in a lake.

On reaching the other side we began climbing in an oblique direction a rugged mount, which made us perspire at every pore, till the caravan at length sighted the hut spoken of by José, and that had been prudently erected beside a running brook. It was then 11.30 a.m. of the 27th May, 1879.

We did not consider it of good augury that, on our arrival at the hut, its two inmates should take to flight and conceal themselves in the wood, but this was what they did on catching the first glimpse of our people, and it required all José's powers of persuasion to induce them to return. When they did so we endeavoured to persuade them to guide us to some inhabited spot, on the bank of the Cuango which, after an infinity of trouble and tempting promises, they agreed to do, and took the lead of the caravan for the purpose.

Unencumbered by any stores of provisions we rapidly skirted the forest and crossing an arid, granite mount, we descended on to the picturesque margin of the river Mapemba, where we halted ten minutes for a rest. On resuming our march we scaled the lofty bank on the opposite side and found on the top a vast plain, destitute of trees, through which wound a sort of track.

Our guides here said they could go no further, and that we had only to follow the path to find ourselves at the Cuango. Little agreeable as the announcement was to our mind—for recent experience had made us suspicious and doubtful—there was no help for it but to let them go, more particularly as being paid beforehand we had no means of detaining them. On separating, therefore, we pursued our way, but after the lapse of about an hour, all indication of a track having disappeared, we lost ourselves completely in the high grass!

Some of our readers may perhaps argue,—

"But in the centre of a plain, with compass in hand, it surely must be easy to reach any determinate point."

To which we will make answer, that until tried, few can tell how difficult it is to follow a right line where there is no visible point in the distance; and this was exactly our case, for owing to the high grass and cistus that surrounded us, all view was completely shut out.

Groping about, therefore, amid these obstacles, our course was very far from being a straight one; the sun blazed down upon our heads; fatigue began to weigh our limbs, and there loomed upon our minds the probability of a renewal of our sufferings from hunger, thirst, and anxiety.

The Cuango lay, to a certainty, in an east-north-east direction, and to that point we endeavoured to steer, so putting in the vanguard three of our stoutest hands, to cut away the grass and weeds that blocked the way, we followed slowly on.

Ill-luck appeared to pursue us upon this terrible journey and with cruel irony placed food, so to speak, within our reach only to snatch it away. As we plodded along, one of the carriers reported that he had seen upon the left various dark, moving objects which he took to be *palancas*.

We at once started in search, working round to leeward of the spot, so as to prevent their getting scent of us. In a few minutes we came in sight of them and could observe their beautiful heads peering between the grass.

THE PALANCAS.

They were large female antelopes, hornless, with long necks, elegant in shape, with very light and lustrous skin, having the appearance at first sight of a herd of wild asses. On our nearer approach, something caused them to take the alarm; and hesitating for a moment in restless attitude, they darted away with all speed.

We let fly a couple of barrels at the nearest, but missed; and to our immense annoyance and the surprise and disappointment of the whole caravan, they got off scot-free! We followed them up for some distance, but we might as well have chased the wind, for not another shot was afforded us! One of us succeeded in getting a hasty sketch, tolerably approximate to the truth, but that was the only record afforded us of their apparition.

This last misfortune seemed to deprive our crew of what little courage was left them. Ten hours, which appeared as many months in length, had elapsed since we left the banks of the river Fortuna, and still there was no evidence of human habitation. Surely, we thought, one more day of such suffering will decide our fate, and the caravan, already demoralized, must perish of inanition. The very Ban-sumbi, the most robust of our men, were sinking beneath the strain put upon them, and we expected at any moment they would throw down their loads and refuse to carry them further. The young niggers hobbled along, bent like old men; the women, in most instances overladen with their infants, the perspiration pouring from them as they walked, took every opportunity of stopping by the way, more willing to resign themselves to their fate, if it brought them rest, than to go on seeking for what they deemed undiscoverable. We ourselves, though carrying no load, did not suffer less than any of our people. A general debility had taken possession of our entire organism, rendering it difficult for us to stand upright, owing to the indescribable pains in the back and loins.

It was mainly in the ascents that these inconveniences and troubles were experienced, every hill-side becoming a calvary, upon which we expected to faint and die. Our temples on these occasions beat like sledge-hammers, our eyes were veiled with mist, and the rapid action of the heart produced a feeling as of suffocation.

The sun was rapidly declining; the heat diminished,

but in the same proportion our hunger and thirst increased, and yet the further we went, the more distant still appeared our chances of alleviation.

Knowing, however, from cruel experience, the danger of stopping, and determined in our own minds that we would not turn back, we still crawled on, conscious that we must advance till we found water, or drop by the way.

The main body skirted a gentle declivity, while parties were despatched to the right and left to search in every hollow; and we then had another climb. Night was falling as we reached the edge of a steep and bare descent, and discovered about a mile to the westward the windings of a great river. At the foot of the hill on which we stood we observed an extensive valley covered with grass, intersected by irregular lines of darker vegetation that hinted at the passage of several brooklets.

"We will stop here!" the men exclaimed as with one voice; nor did we proffer a word in opposition to the general will. Besides that it would have been useless, we felt ourselves that we could no further go. It was then seven in the evening.

CORACIAS ESPATULATA.

CHAPTER VI.

Opinion of the authors upon laconism in the description of toil and suffering—The night of the 27th May—Apprehensions—Night phantoms—An unexpected discovery—The women of the caravan—A marriage—Famine and plenty next-door neighbours—Having satisfied the body we seek distraction of mind—A wine-party—Quizengamo, an important *quilolo*, visits the encampment—Two pages from the diary—The guides urge us to repair to the Court of the Quianvo—Our own resolve—The Cuango and capricious sinuosities of its course—Frightful effects of dysentery—Putrid fermentation and the failure of food—A dance of the Ma-yacca—Abandoned in the forest—Fever, ulcers, and dysentery—Flight of the guide—The desert—Fragment of the diary—Baffled—Return—The Cugho.

To the man who has never had the misfortune to pass entire days of hunger and thirst, with the temperature at 86° of Fahrenheit; who has never experienced the dire sensations of intense fever, aggravated by the anguish of dysentery, the terrible itching caused by parasites, and which the flannel vest renders almost unbearable; to the man again who never felt the excruciating suffering caused by scorbutic wounds in the legs and feet, making the pressure of the boot a martyrdom; our dwelling to such length upon these subjects may appear perhaps both troublesome and undignified. We consider, however, that such a judgment is not a fair one, inasmuch as no traveller is capable on his return to Europe and in the quiet repose of his own study, to set down faithfully, after the lapse of months, what he suffered in those inhospitable regions, or give a just measure of the physical and moral tribulations which at the time oppressed his miserable existence. He may retain a faint recollection of them, but hesitating between his diary and his wish to say the exact truth, he is likely to suppress a great deal that we consider it proper to lay before the world for the behoof of future explorers.

Stanley, that active and indefatigable genius, was conscious of this truth when in the Zinga on the 10th of June, 1877, he wrote :—

"The details of the tortures I suffered cannot be described, but they are indelibly engraved in the depths of a heart which feels all the bitterness of the pains which wrung it."

It must have been a heavy load of suffering that induced a man, usually so laconic, to pen those lines; they owed their origin to countless struggles, to the pangs of hunger and thirst, to consuming fever and the loss of faithful companions; yet many readers probably passed over that simple paragraph without a second thought. In justice to him and others we intend to be less brief, and in the present chapter to give a faithful record of our vicissitudes and reflections.

It was on the 27th of May that the caravan, whereof we were the chiefs, found itself on the left bank of a certain river, without shelter, pinched by hunger, full of bodily ailments, seated on a bare mount, in a narrow circle, surrounding a fire as half starved as ourselves.

The thought of the morrow was in the minds of all. Ten times that day had we lost ourselves in our wanderings, and we knew too well that the continuance of such a course must, in the end, be fatal to some, if not to all. As we scanned the horizon we put the question to ourselves, "How long can this continue?"

In the far distance we discovered, aided by the pale light of the moon, certain high land, on the summit of which we perceived fires. Could they be senzalas, or were they the fires of wanderers like ourselves? none could say; this, however, was certain, that not a sound came to our ears indicative of human beings. The whole country lay in profound repose, only interrupted in the depth of night by a troop of wolves hovering and howling about us. Other black, shadowy forms, the more fearful from being undefined, were creeping stealthily in the valley below, so that our guns, upon the cock, were kept constantly pointed in that direction.

A slow fever was undermining our remaining strength, and a terrible insomnia had taken possession of us both. Our heated imagination passed in review a multitude of scenes, of thoughts, of disjointed ideas, which ebbed and flowed in an uninterrupted stream. On inquiring of each other, we found the experience was mutual, so drawing our coats, which were stiffened by the cold mist of night, closer around us we tried to sleep. A vain endeavour truly; and at three quarters past four in the morning, we were witnesses, against our will, to day breaking in the east.

So soon as the light permitted, a careful survey was made of the surroundings, the result being, that we were near the bank of the river Cuango, posted on an abrupt mount which bordered it on the western side; that the stream ran, in a broad sheet, through banks clothed with dark green foliage, forming an edging to the tall wavy grass; that on the heights beyond the further bank white patches were discernible which by the glass appeared to be human dwellings; that northwards, the land was broken and uneven to the last degree, and that behind the hills in that direction white smoke was rising into the air.

As the watch marked the hour of five, we organized a party to go to the river to procure water, and despatched another up the stream to make a reconnoissance, whilst we ourselves to occupy the time till their return endeavoured to take the bearings of the surrounding country.

We had not, however, been long engaged at the work before we saw two of the party rush back again through the grass and make their way up the ascent uttering loud cries. They were mere lads, though one of them, Lianda, was quick-witted and expert, who informed us in a breathless state that they had, immediately after setting out, discovered an immense encampment inhabited by fishermen, where the abundance of good things was such that, to use the young fellow's own expression: "There were so many calabashes of *maluvo* that all of us put together would not be so many."

The effect of this announcement may readily be conceived, and we lost no time, after recovering from our surprise, in setting out for the favoured spot.

In a tortuous line we descended the rugged slope, placing the women of the caravan in front, who, with their infants at their backs, intoned, as they went, a mournful song, meant by its simple words to be one of thankfulness. All honour to the sex and all honour to these not unworthy members of it! On fortunate days they were the first at work, and by their handiness and cheerfulness they gave to the camp what life and gaiety it could ever boast of; and on the sad and trying ones, the fewest complaints came from them, whilst their patience and endurance were beyond all praise. How often, when fighting with a host of obstacles, has not the sight of them, plodding on in silence, encouraged us as men to even greater efforts; and how often too did we not behold a like effect being wrought among their untutored companions, and a respect engendered that at the outset was unknown!

We did our very best to foster this respect by the rigorous rules we laid down where the sex was concerned. All quarrels and domestic difficulties were referred to us for solution, and woe betide the husband who dared to lay a finger upon his wife or steal a cloth from her to barter it away! Scores of times Capulca discovered this to his

LEMBA, MUTU'S WIFE.

cost, for though a gallant gay Lothario among strange ladies he was a very Othello to his own Desdemona. But for every blow he administered to her back, he got a dozen on his own, most religiously paid, for in matters of this kind we made it a point of honour never to be in his debt.

The garments they wore were delivered to them at set times; we treated both them and their children when sick, and if, by any sad chance, one of them became a widow, we were careful at once to keep her apart till we could find her a second husband.

While on this point we may mention that when in the Quioco poor Filippe died, Lemba, his wife, was separated in this manner, and on the following day, ranging in a line those unmarried men who cared to enter the lists, we made her come to the front with ourselves that she might make her choice. It was curious to observe the eagerness with which the candidates followed her eyes; for it is no light thing to be the object on which a woman's choice shall fall amid a bevy of competitors! At the outset they were all on the broad grin, for they looked upon the affair as a capital joke, but on observing the serious air with which we presided at the ceremonial they composed their countenances and anxiously awaited the young widow's decision. And when it came and her choice was really made, the only countenance that displayed hilarity was that of the chosen youth who bore the name of Mutu. Summoning him from the group, we inquired:—

"Does this woman please you?"

To which he answered, "She does."

"Would you like to live with her?"

"I should."

"Be it so: now listen. Henceforth she shall be your companion and your wife; you will live with her and have your rations apart; you will be responsible for her acts, and if you do not immediately repair her transgressions, you will be punished; remember, you must not lay a finger upon her, but live in peace." And thus were married Mutu and Lemba!

To resume our narrative; the sun shone full upon our faces, as though to congratulate us on our good fortune, and obliquely illuminating the landscape, still in part concealed by morning mist, gave it an aspect of juvenile beauty and a sense of serenity that were consoling to the awakening spirits.

Breaking away from the grass, we crossed the little thickets that were scattered in every direction over the plain, and at length came out in the neighbourhood of the hamlet.

It consisted of half a dozen huts or sheds perfectly well built; a palisade, formed by a species of bamboo split in half, formed the enclosure within which they nestled, while various fireplaces served for the cooking of fish. Our first glance also showed us *bindas* of palm wine, bundles of manioc and slices of meat hanging within the dwellings, and several persons moving about. On the right there was a larger number busy in assisting at or witnessing some occupation, which we shortly discovered to be the dismemberment of an enormous buffalo, lying on the ground, that had been killed the day before.

At our unexpected arrival, all occupations, both indoors and out, were immediately suspended, and the natives, half in alarm, half in curiosity, regarded us, open-mouthed; while we, staring with equal interest, but with no sort of fear upon the colossal ruminant, exclaimed,—

"We have been near starving in the midst of plenty!"

Five minutes after this moving spectacle met our eyes, we were squatting down with our knees almost on a level with our chins, in a little circle, having José in the middle, busily engaged in making purchases the while he replied to our eager interrogations.

"Who are these people?"

"Ma-yacca."

"Who governs them?"

"The Quianvo or Muene Puto Cassongo."

"Where does he live?"

"Over there!" pointing northwards.

"Is he powerful?"

"He is indeed."

These scraps of information, with others obtained in the same way, we entered in our diary, interrupting that occupation from time to time to give instructions about the longed-for meal to Capulca, who, meanwhile, having recovered his usual loquacity never had his mouth shut for a moment.

Two delightful hours did we spend over his labours, taking whatever was ready, and eagerly waiting for more, washing the whole down with copious draughts of *maluvo;* until having eaten and drunk to repletion we took a long and welcome siesta.

Having ordered the construction of the encampment and fed and rested the body, we sought a little distraction for the mind, so as to dissipate somewhat the dark clouds which still hung over it, and with this view we took a stroll to a neighbouring village.

On our penetrating into the neighbouring wood, we startled a couple of young women, who, in the costume of Mother Eve before the fall, fled at our approach, leaving their baskets behind them. Their head-dresses amused us mightily, being terminated at top with two high peaks, and as they first started from the grass we could not help likening them (meaning no disrespect) to a couple of she-asses.

Having gratified our curiosity by a peep into the fugitives' baskets, we pursued our way, when Master José suddenly stopped, pointed up to some fruit hanging from a tree, and clapping his hands to his abdomen

A Wine Party.

went through the performance of a person suffering from colic.

"There it is!" he exclaimed; "don't you remember it?"

After a cursory examination we had no difficulty in recognizing the fruit, for it was no other than the medlars of painful memory that had punished us so severely in the Bondos!

Continuing our path, after this meeting with a former

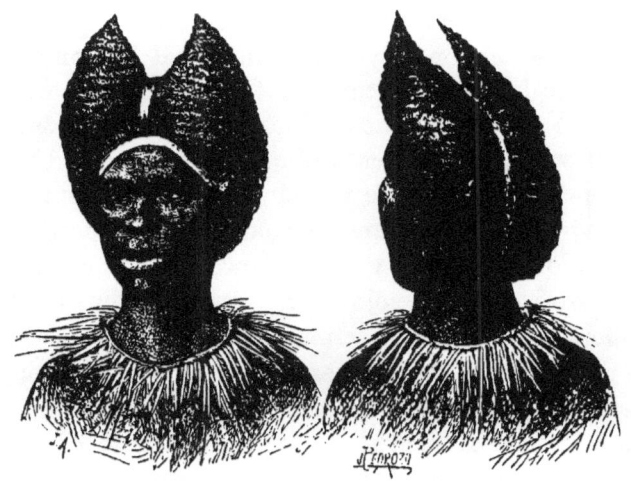

THE TWO FUGITIVES.

acquaintance, puffing and blowing beneath a sun hot enough to fry eggs, we at length reached the senzala, constructed on a piece of cleared ground.

We arrived at a time of high festival, at least we found the principal inhabitants engaged in a drinking-bout, seated around enormous *ganzas* or calabashes. At sight of us, however, they started up in half alarm, a feeling which we did our best to allay by inquiring in a friendly manner what they had in the *bindas*.

"*Maluvo, N'gana*" (wine, senhor), was the reply.

And as *maluvo* is not by any means to be treated with contempt, we determined to do as the rest did, and sat down to have a share. Seeing a whispering but warm discussion going on between some of the party we were curious to learn the cause, which we managed to gather by the aid of our guide.

It appeared that one of the elders of the group had been entertaining his hearers with wonderful stories about the whites, and they were discussing his last assertion that "we were amphibious; could live just as well in the water as on dry land; and that he once had a friend who had lived near the 'great water' and used to see the whites swim over it from their own country."

As it would have been difficult to undeceive them, we left the care of doing so to our attendants, and turning the conversation into another channel procured all the information we could gather concerning the country in which we were then sojourning, its abundance of food products and other important particulars.

Whilst so engaged a messenger arrived in hot haste from our *quilombo* with the news that an important Sova had just arrived there for the purpose of paying a visit to the whites. Hastily, therefore, concluding our business with our new acquaintance by the barter of some yards of cloth and some beads for *inhame*, eggs, and fowls, we started off to receive our new visitor.

On our return to camp we found our companions standing in attitudes of profound respect about a group of natives, in the centre of whom was the great chief. We have no intention to inflict upon our readers another description of a reception which in no important particular differed from a score that had preceded it; but will merely mention that our visitor was one of the first *quilolos* of the Quianvo, called Quizengamo, residing on the other bank of the river near the Mussala brook; that he was enveloped in a species of *mabella* mat, had no very attractive physiognomy, and wore his hair in what appeared to us a ridiculous fashion for a man, namely drawn up from the back and sides on to the top of the head and there secured.

We transcribe from the pages of our diary the results of our interview, which lasted three hours and a half, together with some further particulars we gleaned from other sources:

PORTUGUESE-AFRICAN EXPEDITION.

May 28th, 1879.   Page 603
  LEFT BANK OF THE RIVER CUANGO.
    Aneroid 2376 ft. (not cor$^{d.}$)   Temperature 000°.
        Lat. 7° 20′ 57″ per. ☉ mer. = 67,75.
    Azimuth angles (station in encampment).
        2° E. (Senz. 0′ 5″—Cuango 0′ 8″).
        52° 5′ (lofty mount a 6′ 0″ ?).
        91° 0′ (mount b 1′ 0″).
        107° 0′ (mount c 2′ 1″).
        127° 5′ (mount d 2′ 1″).
        165° 0′ (azimuth rect. of encampment).
        241° 0′ (mount e 1′ 6″).
     River—up, mean 109° 0′; down 0°

First *quilolo* of the Quianvo paid us a visit this day.

* * * * * * *

The interpreters assured us that the Ma-yacca were, for the greater part, slaves of the Lunda established there.

The history of their origin is similar to that of the Ma-quioco, with this difference, that instead of descending from one woman, they appear to have descended from two. These histories are of course more or less fabulous, and must be received with the utmost caution.

The aspect of the Ma-yacca is not so distinct as that of the peoples further south. Mainly of a pacific disposition, as far at least as could be judged from those with whom we came into contact, they are extremely savage and suspicious. Their head-dresses are quaint and very diversified, some arranging the hair so as to give it the appearance of a hat or cap, others braiding it in long tresses, which they wind round the head; some again drawing it all from the nape of the neck on to the top of the head, but no one fashion so predominating as to give it a preponderance over the others.

They go nearly naked or scantily clothed in *mabella*, owing to the scarcity of any manufactured cotton. Their dwellings, which are geometrically well built of *marianga* interlaced with grass, have from a distance, a picturesque appearance.

They give but little attention to agriculture, but a great deal to fishing, and are poor breeders of cattle or sheep. One good reason for the latter deficiency may be found in the circumstance that the Ma-yacca as we were informed by Quizengamo are not permitted to breed cattle at all, and only on rare occasions goats and sheep. That the sovereign retains such breeding as a prerogative of his own, and that the man who dared to infringe such a law would infallibly lose his head, for with the system of fetichism so prevalent, his act would of a certainty be discovered and denounced. Our informant assured us we should find proofs of this in the circumstance that our eyes would not light upon a single ox on the left bank of the Cuango. This extraordinary monopoly, the cause of which we vainly endeavoured to fathom, has not been satisfactorily explained.

The men devote a good deal of attention to the chase, hunting *palancas*, many of which are of enormous size, and whose horns they showed us, other antelopes and gazelles, all of which are very abundant in this part of the country.

The territory on both banks of the river Cuango is subdivided into many districts bearing special names which are apt to puzzle the traveller.

On the west, for instance, the lands of Quiteca-N'bungo, Macume-N'jimbo, and Futa, already spoken of, are inhabited by the Ma-sosso, who bestow various names upon them, according to the special district; and this is also the case with the territory of Yacca on the east.

The supreme chief of the Ma-yacca is the Mequianvo, Quianvo, or Muene Puto Cassongo. His residence is under parallel 6° 30', near a rivulet called N'ganga, and about four hours' journey from the Cuango, where he has a port.

The stories told us on the spot respecting the *quilolos* were so diverse and contradictory, that we considered them doubtful after a careful process of sifting. Some asserted that the Quianvo was more powerful than the Muata of the Lunda, inasmuch as on the death of the Yanvo the former appointed his successor. Others not only denied this, but affirmed that the former was but a vassal of the Yanvo. The interpreters on the other hand said that it was all false alike, inasmuch as the potentates did not even know each other. This last assertion we considered was going too far, though we could not learn that they had ever met.

The Quianvo is a man of medium stature, strongly built. On his days of reception, he makes his appearance enveloped in a cloth, his head adorned with a broad fillet embroidered with beads, and fastened behind, on the upper edge of which are stitched several red parrot's feathers. His wrists and arms are adorned with bangles.

He imbibes large quantities of *maluvo*, and feeds on small game, such as gazelles, &c.

He keeps up commercial relations with the coast (Ambriz) by a direct path, a prolongation of the river, by the aid of the Ma-sosso, who when they come in search of india-rubber and ivory cross his territory on their way to the Muata Compana and Muene Congo Tubinge.

YACCA HEAD-DRESSES.

This latter Sova appears to be an important personage. He has his residence on the banks of the Muluia and has a great river as a frontier, said to be called Baccari. His states border on the vast region occupied by the Ba-cundi, or Ma-cundi, ferocious cannibals, who occupy, as we were informed, the north-eastern district, and whom they invariably spoke of with a shudder.

They possess, finally, a large river, like the Cu-ango, which flows into the sea.

As we were the first whites who had ever appeared in the dominions of the Muene Puto Cassongo, Quizengamo was very anxious that we should go and pay our court to him.

When he had left, a native of Sosso was presented to us, and we drew from him a few more particulars to add to our previous notes.

This man told us that he knew the Congo-Zaire, that he lived on the road to San Salvador, at N'cusso, a place at no great distance from the villages of the Mambo Assamba and Malungo Ateca. He finally offered to act as our guide.

In the chain of mountains of the Zombo lie the sources of the Luquiche, the last affluent of the Cuango, on the left bank. At two days' journey up the stream from its mouth, numerous rocks obstruct the passage of the river at a point called Quicunji, and still further up is the embouchure of the Quilo Quiasosso. He maintained that there was no possible road along the Cuango, it being all a desert, and he asserted that the said river "*mona-calunga,*" that is to say, flowed into the sea.

He also spoke of a meeting of the waters of the Cu-engo and the Cuango, and further on of those of the Cassai and other rivers of which he spoke in accents almost of horror, saying that they were enormous and constantly overflowing.

He recounted that two years before, he was passing through that very district, at the *massango* or point of confluence, when he saw a *mun-delle* (white man) in an *oáto-iá-puto* or European canoe. This, no doubt, was Stanley.

He certified to the existence of the great lake, and of the famous dwarfs; and concluded by stating that it would take six months to reach the meeting of the waters !

The foregoing having been entered at page 603 and following ones of the diary, we closed the book, very tired with the labour of gathering and recording the notes, so as we were by that time dripping with perspiration, we went and sat in our shirt-sleeves under a rude porch we had constructed to our hut, and with a calabash of *maluvo* between us, were soon at our old work, weaving plans.

In the opinion of the natives it was a matter of necessity that we should cross the river and repair to the residence of the Quianvo, by the only known track, and along which we could alone obtain means of subsistence; but as this was the old story, we did not seem at all inclined to seek that monarch's presence. We considered that our means, in the shape of goods, were already at quite low enough an ebb without running the risk of reducing them still further.

"What is the use?" ran the current of our remarks between ourselves. "It will be only rousing up another thief. And who knows whether he may not take it into his head to seize and strip us altogether? In case too of the necessity of beating a hasty retreat, how could we cross the river, without canoes, and pursue our journey westward?"

These considerations had such weight with us, and appeared to be dictated by such plain common sense, that we determined in our high intelligence to go our own course, that is to say, continue along the bank of the river under the guidance of our Sosso man.

"Our aim," we argued, "is to study the Cuango and not to visit rulers. If we do so, we shall have to set against a problematical good and the gratification of our curiosity, a certain delay, and a diminution of our substance; whilst the state of our health is not just now of that robust kind that we can afford to take any liberties with it."

Thus resolved, we spent the rest of the afternoon in laying in stores and had a good, sound night's rest.

On the 29th of May, at cock-crow, everything was ready in the *quilombo*. Day was ushered in by one of those delicious mornings of which our poets generally can have the very faintest notion, seeing their little or no inclination to undertake a journey to the great continent.

The dense veil of vapour, as it gradually thinned and dissipated under the gentlest of south-east breezes, the herald of approaching day, laden with delicious perfumes, gave to view the scattered mounts, some grey and craggy, others covered with leafy vegetation, and as the first rays of the sun began to tinge their summits, the effects of colour, light, and shade were simply magical.

The hills, obscure till then, became suddenly clothed in every variety of green; the intermediate plains looked, with the half dispersed mist, like fairy lakes, and the distant serras seemed to reflect the deepening azure of the skies.

All nature smiled; the earth, the firmament assumed at each moment an increasing loveliness; the former from its myriads of flowers, the latter by the presence of the radiant star of day.

Flecks of gilded cloud gave a fresh charm to the picture, and whilst the eye gratefully embraced these exquisite creations of the Supreme, the ear drank in with no less delight the murmuring sound of waters, the whisper of the breeze among the leaves and grass, and the hymns of praise of thousands of awakening birds.

A soothing emotion stole over our hearts as we gazed upon the spectacle, so frequently renewed yet never tiring; and the arduous labour we had still to overcome ere reaching what we could consider our ultimate goal, appeared easier of accomplishment when resumed under such auspices.

We did not, it is true, foresee the terrible privations that were yet in store for us, and with which we were to struggle for bare existence; for had it been possible to peep but a little way into the future, souls far stouter than our own must have revolted, and refused to make this final plunge.

Again passing by Cha-cala, the senzala we had visited with José, we directed our march to west-north-west on account of a great bend in the Cuango, and were followed for some distance by a few natives. The soil on which we trod was firm and hard but would evidently be soft

THE CUANGO IN YACCA.

enough in the rainy season. Here and there we passed a thin plantation where the manioc was poor and scarcely reached the waist. A little further on the river, being barred by a high rocky bank, again resumed its northerly course, and the caravan was compelled to climb over a steep mount, from whose summit we observed the windings of the stream.

At 11.30 a.m. we were at Mafungo, where by means of a small canoe we sounded the depth of the river and discovered eight feet of water. Thence, the stream, again turning to the westward, overflowed its banks, while various little sandy aits, more than one adorned with a group of hippopotami, appeared in the centre of the river bed.

Another lofty mount barred the way, which it was necessary for us to scale, but as it was not possible to do so just then we camped at a senzala called Lobenda, reserving the ascent till next day. The heat was suffocating; and the temperature stood at 88° Fahr., without the slightest breeze to cool our tired limbs. Dysentery among other ailments began about this time to appear, with alarming symptoms, and a permanent fever was burning our very entrails.

After a little excursion to the river, where we saw a good many hippopotami, and making the necessary surveys, we returned to the encampment, where another annoyance awaited us. The evening before we had purchased a good number of fresh bagres, which we endeavoured to pickle with a little *maluvo* vinegar, after frying them in palm oil, in the hope of preserving them for some days. What then was our disgust when Capulca opened the basket in which they were kept and showed them to us literally covered with maggots! In twenty-four hours the whole had become decomposed;

and not the fish only, but the buffalo beef which had been distributed among the men, so that we were compelled to throw it all away! We were thus deprived of food, and it was only with difficulty that we could prevail upon the natives to sell us a lean fowl to add to another, equally meagre, in our possession.

As evening fell, while looking at the natives dancing

DANCES OF THE MA-YACCA.

in the open, one of us became disabled by fever, and the other was not long in following suit. We had, therefore, to retire when the fun was at its loudest; and as the stomach refused to retain the lean fowl after we had it cooked, we got no dinner.

Meanwhile, the dancing and uproar continued a long time afterwards. The performers had the most ferocious appearance. The men with feathers and antelope horns stuck into their hair, and bunches of grass about their ankles brandished their assagais under the direction of a leader, a very Hercules of a fellow with a rough beard and cannibal aspect, and formed a semicircle whereof the other half was composed of women.

The latter, with their hair tied in a top knot, their bodies bedaubed with vermilion and wearing a species of short kilt made of straw, kept clapping their hands and twisting their bodies into grotesque and obscene attitudes; when the one in the front row came forward and meeting the man opposite her went through a performance of which the least said the better, and the two then took up their places in the centre; they were followed in due course by another couple, and so on, each pair, not unnaturally, endeavouring to outvie those who had gone before, in singularity.

The noise they made was something horrible to men troubled like ourselves. To the beating of drums and the clapping of hands, were added the discordant shrieks of the women and hoarse cries of the men, and ever and anon the ears were startled by the blast of a long horn which some strong-winded performer was blowing greatly to his own satisfaction and presumably to that of the assembled company.

Meanwhile, our dysentery would not stop, and next day we had to undergo the torture of a forced march, under a leaden sky.

Our idea, somewhat modified, was to keep along the Cuango or reach the port of the Quianvo. On our arrival there, it not being our intention to visit that potentate, we proposed taking a westward course by the track leading to the country of our guide. It did not appear, however, that our plan was to the latter's taste, for when we were about to make the ascent the rascal gave us the slip, and hid himself in the dense *mu-chito,* so that it cost us no end of trouble to ferret him out of it. Having, after immense fatigue, got to the top, we took an hour's rest, while gazing upon the river below, where our glasses showed the hippopotami sunning themselves on the little sandy islands that were scattered over the stream.

Resuming our journey with immense difficulty, for the drain upon us from fever and dysentery made us fearfully weak, we observed numerous tracks through the grass made by herds of buffaloes, and it behoved us to be specially careful and on the alert to avoid being run down by the ferocious beasts. Little disposed as we were to make the effort, we felt that we must, ere the day was out, reach the river Macolo, on whose bank there was a small senzala, the only spot where there was a chance of obtaining provisions.

We reached that place at four in the afternoon in a state almost as impossible to conceive as it is to describe. Fever, ulcers, dysentery, all were trying us at once, and our limbs would scarce support us from actual fatigue. The heat too, was most oppressive, for at five o'clock p.m. the thermometer marked 83° Fahr., and the perspiration had wetted us through. Our poor dog seemed to suffer as much as ourselves, and stretched out at her full length, her tongue hanging from her mouth, she looked a picture of utter fatigue and helplessness.

A troop of natives, who surrounded us, made matters ten times worse with their exactions and begging, and it was with infinite difficulty with such interruptions that we succeeded in purchasing some flour, manioc roots, beans, a couple of miserable goats, a few fowls, and a quantity of fish.

Our guide now again gave us trouble. He insisted

upon our crossing the river at that point, and proceeding to the court of the Quianvo. "There are no people to the north," he argued, "the road lies the other way, no track is to be found northwards for many days."

"But there is a track, so let us go to it. Is it not the same that leads to your country?"

"Yes; but what you have paid me is too little; give me another piece, otherwise I shall turn back."

Measuring him fixedly with our eyes, *procellosi oculi*, and from which, judging by our feelings, we are sure that no particularly friendly rays were darting, we felt our hands convulsively clutch our staff, the while we were sorely tempted to give the fellow a good drubbing; suppressing, however, the temptation under a mental promise that the punishment was only reserved, we acceded to his modest demand, and on the 4th of June, at daybreak, started on our venture, after a fresh altercation with the fellow, who insisted upon receiving his extra piece in advance.

Making for the high ground, we reached the top in about half an hour, whence we had an extensive prospect of the circumjacent country. For many miles round the aspect of the territory is singularly uniform. The lofty mounts which throw out spurs in various directions are all of them bare at the summit, while the valleys at their feet are full of a dense, leafy vegetation. These eminences are so extremely numerous that they impart an extraordinarily rugged aspect to the scene. The bed of the river owing to this cause is wonderfully tortuous, in the distance we observed the broad sheet of water which, receiving the brilliant rays of the sun, meandered through the plain in a silver streak, its capricious curves running at one time north-north-west, and a moment afterwards to the south-east. Further on, the banks seemed steep and rocky, mount after mount rose abruptly from its margins, and confined the stream within a narrow valley.

To the east-north-east the needle gave us successively the culminating points of azure mountains which we saw extending in a line from north to south. The undulations of the ground, on our side of the river running right across our path, made our march, at times, so slow and

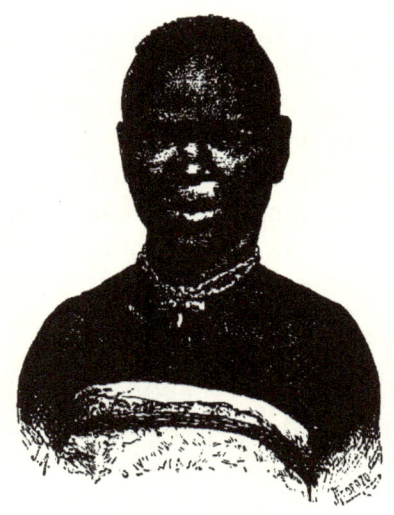

WOMAN OF THE CONGO.

painful that we got over barely a mile an hour. The sun, too, had heated the rocky ground to such a degree, that our men could not press it with their feet after eleven o'clock in the day.

Our guide pointed out to us the direction of the residence of the Quianvo, which we marked to the north-east. More to the north there rose into the air a lofty and arid mountain, which we were informed was the point where the Cuilo disembogued into the Cuango in the

THE SILENCE OF THE TOMB REIGNED SUPREME.

midst of rocks and stones. The sombre-looking region to the north-west was the country of the Ba-congo.

We were compelled to halt until the great heat had somewhat subsided. At the bottom of a ravine we plunged into a dark wood and found, as we hoped, a little water in the low, marshy ground. We there set up our camp, but had not done so more than about ten minutes when we heard an uproar amongst our fellows, occasioned by the desertion of our guide! A little before, the rascal seemed quite satisfied and resolved to act faithfully by us, and then, without alleging the slightest reason, he shouldered his gun and was off, leaving us in a position that can only be faintly conceived!

It is useless to tire the reader with the details of our misery between the 4th and 11th of June, the day on which we got back to the bank of the Cugho on the north-west. Suffice it that the narrative would be a tissue of suffering from hunger, thirst, fever, and struggles experienced in a region whereof the tracing on the map will give a faint idea.

That which, however, the map cannot reproduce is the melancholy aspect of that vast tract of uninhabited country, shunned by man for more than one reason, whereof the absolute want of water is the chief. What frightful solitudes they were! What sadness, which sunk into the soul, weighed upon the entire territory! The silence of the tomb reigned supreme upon those rocks and hollows, whose gloomy and naked aspect, made more terrible by the blinding light of the equatorial sun, seemed to bar all relief to the many ills under which we were sinking! No occasional scraps of green, no clouds to temper the intensity of the sky, offered any relief in the midst of that awful desert, where the silence was appalling, the immovability of every blade of burnt grass was insufferable, where the heat was suffocating, and where the valleys but echoed to the groans and laments of our exhausted crew!

The further we advanced northwards, the more were all our evils aggravated. The solitude became if possible more solemn and more awful. It might have been the chosen region of grim death himself, but that the occasional presence of a wild beast showed that some of nature's creatures at least paid it a passing visit.

It was on the 9th of June that we attained the extreme point marked upon the map, and which appears thus recorded in the diary:—

PORTUGUESE-AFRICAN EXPEDITION.

June 8th, 1879.   Page 608.

  LEFT BANK OF THE RIVER CUANGO.
    Aneroid 2394 ft. (not corr.)   Temperature 80° Fahr.

Desert still continues.

At midday upon a rocky hill. ☉ mer. 60° 15′ 29″

To-day's march a fac-simile of the five preceding ones. Not a soul in sight.

Since sunrise we have drifted literally at the mercy of the ground.

We can go no further. We turn back to-day. Ten men suffering with dysentery.

No appearance of the guide's track. Little water, and rations at the lowest ebb. Quianvo (senzala bearing 179° true.)

Cuango visible in the distance. We mark an extraordinary bare mountain bearing 335° true N.E., and imagine it must be the same that is near the Cuilo.

Great conflagrations to the N.W.

Heat intense. Fever at night-fall, dysentery permanent.

A cursed territory is this of Yacca!

Turning our faces southwards, partly over the same ground, our troubles crowded upon us, as the extracts from the diary will show:—

PORTUGUESE-AFRICAN EXPEDITION.

June 10th, 1879.   Page 609.

  Near YANGA GALAMO.
    Aneroid 2346 ft. (corr.)   Temperature 89° Fahr.

What a day has this been! The longest march we have yet made in Africa, covering twenty-five miles.

Having left the foot of the Huamo, we came at 10.30 upon several lakes, lying under colossal mountains.

As we had very little to eat, we resolved to go on.

Unhappy wretches that we were, we only plunged into an immense desert—savage, awful—through which we trudged west and south.

It was six o'clock in the evening when by chance we reached a lake. This part of the country abounds in them, but rivers there are none.

Frightful dysentery. One of us seriously ill.

No appearance of the Cugho; it must, of course, be a long way off yet.

What shall we possibly do here, if our remaining modicum of flour gives out? This is Africa with a vengeance! Lately we have not seen a head of game.

It is 9.30 p.m., and the heat is still great. Fires in the distance to the northwards. The Cuango lies behind us, with the remainder unexplored. What will they say of us at home? So near to a solution of the problem and obliged to give it up? Patience! Patience! It is all that is left us. So farewell to our hopes! May those who come after us be more successful!

The caravan was encamped on the margin of a lake when the above lines were written. It was ten at night; and thousands of stars were twinkling in the firmament; But there was no sleep for us; that dreadful *insomnia*, our companion in suffering, forbade forgetfulness.

The gloomiest thoughts had taken possession of our mind, and stretched at full length, one within, groaning with fever, the other without, we were each a prey to them.

At midnight the moon appeared, it seemed to us a yellow blotch upon a dark ground, like a tinsel ornament upon a funeral pall. A painful and inexplicable sentiment pervaded the soul, the heart seemed overflowing, and at length tears filled our eyes! Moments like these can scarce be realized by him who reads of such journeys in his cosy chair.

Poor explorer! Moved by the simple interest of science, he sets aside his ease, his family, his health, and risks his very life in these distant lands, and yet he alone can appreciate the strange influence exerted upon the mind by this tropical nature, so beautiful, so grand and yet so awful. Feeling it all, he for the most part conceals it within his heart of hearts, apprehensive that in Europe, the flippant sarcasm of his critics may fall upon his enthusiasm or upon a too truthful record of his fears, his labours, and his sufferings!

It was on the 11th of June that we resumed our march, and the day appeared an age, so full was it of toil and anxiety. But we were not forsaken by Providence, although our rebellious spirits seemed inclined to think so, for as evening was approaching, to our great joy we discovered, on climbing another weary height, some human habitations on the banks of a river, and we knew that that river was the Cugho.

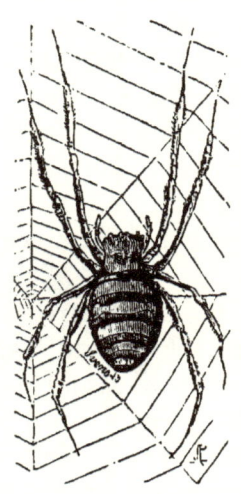

QUI-VUVI, THE SILK SPIDER.

CHAPTER VII.

The author's experience respecting the importance of the stomach—Brief sketch of the course of the River Cuango—In the Cugho—The land of plenty—*Maluvo* wine and its collection—Lake Aquilonda wiped off the map—The palm and climatologic zones—The Rivers Sussa and Cauali—Vegetation—Sova Catumba Cangando and indiscreet curiosity of his lady-subjects—A native song—Strange ceremony among the Ma-hungo—An interment in the woods—Danje, Luamba, Matamba, and Pacaça Aquibonda—Caculo-Cabaça—Homicide of a carrier—The value of life among the negroes—*Vunda*-ia-Ebo and the last burial—The valleys of the Lu-calla and a story of a crocodile—A new theory of Cosmogony—The delights of the table—Passage of the Lu-calla—List of members of the caravan that reached Duque de Bragança.

AMONG the facts that are most susceptible of originating great consolation upon this our little planet, there figures indubitably one which, although by some placed only in the second class, should, from our point of view, be held to hold a high rank in the first.

We refer to the pleasure experienced by the man who, having a perfectly empty stomach and who has felt for long hours the slow torture of hunger, unexpectedly comes upon the means of filling the cavity.

However sublime and poetical the scenes through which a man may be passing, and however intellectually superior the sensations transmitted to his soul through the medium of the eyes and ears, they count as nothing if the digestive organs are left out of calculation. An empty stomach is of that exacting nature that it will admit of no considerations beyond its own exigencies. So that, though it may be a machine independent of the spirit and the will, it cannot be said that the converse is equally correct.

Great ideas do not precisely spring from a full stomach, but they are formed when it is full; and if unaccompanied by that very commonplace circumstance, the grandest conceptions soon dwindle and perish. We will not too vigorously adhere to the Latin phrase *Fruges consumere nati*, but without food man does nothing at all.

So it happened that, struggling as we had been for more than a month with the difficulty of regular sustenance, and during the latter days with the actual outposts of starvation, a profound change had come over the chiefs of the expedition, noticeable more particularly in indifference to assume the initiative. In both alike the will had become bent, the energy half extinguished, the ideas scattered and confused, and a huge spectre had been evoked which was ever present to our weakened nerves, the spectre of gaunt and griping famine!

We were no longer capable of thinking, that is to say, in a regular and consecutive manner; we let matters simply drift, and saw with perfect indifference things which at a later period would have evoked our anger, our compassion, or our active interference.

This being the cost,—what was the gain that could be set against it? We had succeeded in acquiring for geographical science at least this knowledge, namely, that the Cuango is a river, like many others on this vast continent, less capable of being turned to account than was generally supposed, so far as its navigableness is concerned.

From parallel 11° 30', approximately, where its sources are to be found, up to 5° 05' at the Quicunji cascade, the river has a sinuous course of 580 geographic miles, and a total fall, between its extreme points, of about three feet four inches per mile.

Rocks, stones, rapids, and cataracts interrupt the stream and twelve of the points at which they do so are known to us, namely,—the first at parallel 10° 17′, to the east of Muene-songo; the second at 10° 25′, near the Camba rivulet; the third at 10° 08′, Caxita rocks; the fourth at 10° 05′, the Louisa falls; the fifth at 10° 05′, a cataract a little above port Muhungo; the sixth at 9° 20′, Zamba; the seventh at 19° 19′, Tuaza; the eighth at 9°, cataract Cunga-ria-Cunga; the ninth at 7° 42′, Suco-ia-Muquita or Suco-ia-n'bundi; the tenth at 7° 38′, just below the Camba; the eleventh at 7° 35′, in the midst of numerous islands; and the twelfth at 5° 05′, the Quicunji waterfall, which is only passable after the heavy rains.

The greatest navigable tract, therefore, is that space which lies between the cataract at 7° 35′ and Quicunji, or about 190 geographic miles. The river there is of variable width, never less than seventy-six yards and a half, and from five to twenty feet in depth.

The current loses a little of its speed in the upper section, where the stream in the summer season has a fall of about three feet two inches per mile. We think it well to mention that our longitudes being strictly correct, as the record, partly chronometric, was compared both on departure and arrival at the Portugese station of Duque de Bragança, and the latter again at the terminus on the coast, it appears to us that the point of affluence of the Cuango (or Ibari-N'Kutu) as marked upon the maps, just above Stanley Pool, is erroneously placed considerably to the eastward. It is indeed difficult to conceive such a lay of the land as would allow two water-courses, of the importance of the Cuango and Congo-Zaire running almost parallel to each other and in opposite directions! Any way, we shall shortly have a solution of this doubt concerning the longitudes, inasmuch as that intelligent explorer, M. de Brazza will, in due course, bring over to Europe the results of his investigations.

PROVISIONS LITERALLY SHOWERED.

Having arrived at the margin of the river which some time before we had crossed lower down, we entered upon a new and more smiling period of existence. No sooner had we pitched our camp than natives flocked in from all sides, so that in an hour we found ourselves in a position to restore much of our lost flesh and animation. Provisions literally showered! Beads and pieces of cloth were transmuted into poultry, pigs, sheep, flour and any number of calabashes of *maluvo*. The cries, chatter, and discussions of human beings, were mixed up with the hoarse grunting of a dying porker, the bleating of a sheep, and the remonstrances of fowls in the hands of their executioners.

Standing in the centre of a group, our redoubted *chef* by our side, we presided over successive auctions, disputing with one, arguing with another, and at length yielding to not too exorbitant demands. And when the sun of the 11th of June gave us a parting glance, he left us in a state of satisfaction to which we had long been strangers.

We had each eaten and drunk for four, and only when we were full, considered it necessary to gather up and store the surplus, to prevent our stomachs being again subjected to the starving rations of the past. Our men, on the other hand, like veritable children, forgetful of the sadness of many previous days, gave themselves up to pleasure, and extraordinary to relate, kept up their dance as long as their calabashes of *maluvo* retained a drop of the precious liquid, but ere that moment arrived, we had dropped off into a profound sleep.

It was the eve of the birthday of one of us. On the 12th of June, he completed his twenty-ninth year, and he boasted that he was the youngest explorer who had ventured into African wilds. In honour of the event we determined to remain in our present site for at least that day, and amuse ourselves with a visit to the river, where crocodiles and hippopotami abounded.

The leisure thus obtained will allow us to give some account of the celebrated *maluvo* or palm-wine whereof mention has, of late, so frequently been made.

The palm-wine, which is found in this part of Africa

from parallel 7° northwards, but not south of that point, saving near the coast and in small quantities, is an agreeable drink, the flavour of which remotely reminds one of muscatel, and, when newly obtained from the plant, is extremely sparkling and aromatic. After about twenty-four hours ascetic fermentation sets in, and it becomes very acrid and intoxicating. This is the stage at which the natives appreciate it most.

It is extracted from two different plants, the *Elais Guineensis* and *Raphia*, of which we have already spoken, a true dwarf palm. In the first place, the natives climb the tree, and making an incision near the base of the branch which sustains the new fruit, they fix a calabash at the spot, to receive the sap, and replace the receptacle as it gets full; in the second instance, they effect a cutting near the nerve of the leaves (which are used as supports for the coast palanquin), and there insert a calabash, with a spout, to collect the juice. The liquid extracted from the latter is relatively more agreeable, aromatic, and abundant than the former.

Amid the dense *mu-chito*, with which we had such terrible struggles, we met with the plants in abundance; in fact they might be called perfect vineyards. No native will dare touch another's calabash when collecting the sap, and an infringement of this rule would be likely to lead to serious consequences. A certain regularity is observed both in making the wine and in preserving the portion of forest that produces it. The calabashes used for its collection are placed at sunset and daybreak. We observed the natives in the early morning engaged at the work of gathering in the first *crop* and again in the evening, so as to have it fresh or at a certain degree of fermentation, according to the taste of consumers. The quantity must represent many thousands of quarts per senzala, if we could judge by the quantities we saw consumed at the places where we stopped.

The river Cugho describes, from the point where we were now sojourning, a curve eastwards something like the letter U. Its bed is excessively tortuous, and the banks are high. Lakes[1] in considerable numbers were pointed out to us in different directions, and amongst them one to the north-west, in the territory of Macume N'jimbo, whence, as it was stated, the river derived its source.

We remained long under the impression that the celebrated Aquilonda, which we had been seeking since our arrival in Yacca, must be somewhere in this neighbourhood, and we made constant inquiries among the natives as to its whereabouts, but without success. Unlike, therefore, almost all the explorers that have lately been in Africa (and who, if they were not the actual discoverers of lakes did at least survey and define some that were but little known, as for instance, Stanley the Victoria, Cameron the Tanganika, Serpa Pinto the Carri-Carri), we were forced, to our regret, to *strike out* one which had been bothering us for a very long time. The natives only stared when we talked about this great lake Aquilonda, and they looked even more astonished when the subject of the celebrated river Barbela was broached, which we described as a drainage canal of the lake in question.

[1] The lakes observed by us in these parallels, as well as those of which we procured information, do not, as at first sight might be imagined, constitute large pools in the midst of extensive plains, so as to lead one to suppose that the ten marked between the basins of the Cuango and Cugho are the mere remnants of a vast lake partly dried up. They are, on the contrary, small basins of two, three, and four miles in extent, confined by lofty mounts, whose surplus waters in the rainy season escape through little ravines into the lower ground, and soon get evaporated.

"Nothing, nothing, senhor; there's no such a thing," was their invariable remark.

After mature reflection, therefore, we have come to the conclusion that this great lake must be a chimera evolved from the brain of some imaginative missionary (perhaps a capuchin friar), who, being in the Congo and hearing some of the natives of the Zombo or Sosso talk about the Cuango and other great rivers to the eastward, and dilate upon the existence of similar waters in the direction of the Lunda, conceived a vague notion about huge lakes, so without more ado jotted one down upon his parchment map under the Latin designation of *Aquæ Lunda* vulgarized as time went on into Aquelunda and Aquilonda.

Ten miles above our camp the Cugho receives an affluent on its right bank, called Cauali which, rising in the Danje, runs a course of not less than 100 miles, and receives the drainage waters of the eastern side of the Finde plateau.

The Cugho, which forms a perfect barrier to the desert lands of the north, is dotted all along its right bank by numerous senzalas of Ma-hungo, of whom we have already spoken, an extremely superstitious and ignorant people, whose occupations are fishing and hunting in the surrounding district. To these tribes belonged sundry of the hunters we fell in with in the forests.

A fact that is worth recording here is a confirmation of the special character of climatologic zones with regard to the flora, the latitude and altitude exerting upon it their well-known influence. The palm, like the baobab, keeps within its own perfectly defined limits; and thus the *Raphia*, whence the *maluvo* is derived, and which is so profusely met with in the north, disappears as if by enchantment south of parallel 8°. Northwards, the *Raphia* is everywhere visible, but not a vestige of it appears below the line we have defined. It is just possible that this arrangement does not penetrate into the heart of the continent, or into the Lunda, but if so, it will be due to the lower level of that country.

Having spent the 12th of June in rest, to the alleviation of the febrile condition from which we were continually suffering, and having dispensed the necessary medicaments, namely, chlorate of potash to two scurvy patients, diluted nitrate of silver to another with ophthalmia, quinine, camphor, and adhesive plaster to fourteen with wounds, and sulphate of magnesia to a score who did not like to be left out of the good things, orders were given to pack up and make ready for a fresh start.

The time had arrived for us to abandon the northern districts, for neither our strength nor our resources would permit us to venture there again. Instead, however, of making our way directly to Ambriz by the Finde and Lu-oje, we decided to follow a south-south-west track, and having examined the basin of the Lu-calla, to proceed afterwards to the Cuanza, the course of which we were desirous of surveying.

On the 13th, as soon as daylight appeared in the camp, the sick and the sound alike turned out, and our carriers, with their loads of sixty pounds apiece, nerved themselves for their work in a most praiseworthy manner.

The country at first was level enough but it soon assumed its broken character. In the distance, to north-north-west, we distinguished notable masses of darker vegetation. These were the banks of the Cauali piloting its waters northwards. To the south-east a dense barrier also indicated the course of a winding river. This was the Susso, which, parallel to the former, conveys the waters of Matamba by the Cugho, into the Cuango. We therefore followed the divisorial line of the waters of the two rivers, steering our course by the compass.

Numerous lakes, in every respect similar in character to those already described, lay to east and west of our track, whence we were enabled to draw our supplies of water.

We were now under the full influence of the south-east gales. On every high and exposed spot of ground the impetuous wind buffeted the caravan, and at times threatened to sweep it away. White fleecy clouds scudded rapidly along in the direction of the ocean, and the sky itself wore the appearance of the sea.

From the Sussa affluents, on the elevated plateau, we passed on to those of the Cauali, descending a. rough region, and then came upon an infinity of small rivulets, furrowing the ground in every direction, and which of themselves made the march a very toilsome one. Small hamlets hove frequently in sight, whose inhabitants, in little troops, having nothing else to do, followed us for hours.

The vegetation wore a characteristic aspect, different to that observable more to the eastward. Trees with slender trunks sprang from the bottoms of the valleys in search of light, and then threw out their upper branches in the shape of umbrella heads, whose lustrous and strangely-shaped leaves sheltered from the sun's beams many a broad patch of ground. Among them was one of unusual dimensions, elegant in shape, covered with brilliant red flowers, which at times constitute perfect zones of the forest, and perfectly resemble the *Spathodea campanulata*. The air was full of winged seeds like down, yielded to the violent wind by colossal *Eriodendron*, in such quantities that the ground was literally carpeted with the soft, satiny wool.

We found immense quantities of sugar-cane, from three to three and a half inches in diameter, on the banks of rivulets near human dwellings. Maize would appear to grow here all the year round, for we saw some already in ear, and other plants just springing, so that we were able to get it fresh and roast it to make bread. Whole plantations of tobacco and abundance of cotton were visible in the clearer ground, the latter apparently being represented by more than one species.

Near the village of Quimana we for the second time met with the track running from the Holo to the coast, and which leads to the great *pambo* or cross-road to the south-east of Encoge (N'Hoje); there, subdividing, one path runs directly to Ambriz, and the other to Bembe, along the river M'briche as far as the Ambrizette, where the latter river disembogues.

After a lapse of four days we encamped at Songanhe for the purpose of laying in stores and receiving a visit from the Sova, Catuma Cangando, whose place we had left behind. He turned out to be a fierce-looking old fellow, with a rough beard, wrapped in an immense cloth of striped chintz.

The day we spent in the village was one of confusion from morning till night, and at least for six hours it might be said that the white men were "on view." Nothing would induce the natives to clear out; and as for the ladies, their interest was unbounded! and when they were tired of staring at us, they would go and look at the outsides of the goods, then pay a visit to the kitchen and come back and stare again at us—a performance that went on for hours.

We expected from one moment to another that they would want us to strip, in order to satisfy themselves whether our bodies were covered with the same long hair as our faces. But they obtained their knowledge without solicitation in this wise: One of us, tired of being made a show of, had gone into his hut, and drawing the curtain over the entrance, had got into his india-rubber bath for a wash and refresher. He had not, however, been disporting himself there, like another Neptune, for more than five minutes, when some damsels, moved by curiosity, drew aside the curtain to peep in. They did so, however, so clumsily, that down came the curtain in their hands and . . . . . there was a tableau! The bather shouted out like one possessed, and no wonder under the circumstances; and the spectators, at the apparition of what may have seemed to them a white monster, ran off screaming, the women and children expressing as much alarm as if they had beheld a crocodile. Even the Sova took the alarm and seemed inclined to join his subjects in their flight! The situation was certainly an uncomfortable if a comic one, and there was something also in it to wound the amour-propre of the principal performer in the comedy; for however little he might pride himself upon his personal charms, the fact of his being an object of terror, from which women and men alike fled in dire fear was, to say the least of it, sad and humiliating.

Having recovered, however, from this vexation, we decided upon having our dinner in spite of our company, and then spent the rest of the afternoon in entertaining our visitors, exhibiting our arms, firing them off, and otherwise amusing them till, seeing the men by numerous signs, such as opening their mouths and putting their fingers into their throats, and pointing to the pits of their stomachs, give evidence of the cravings of hunger, we dismissed the untiring dames to their homes and domestic affairs, of which they had been so long neglectful.

Departure from the Village.   151

Early in the morning of the 17th we were again astir, and on starting took a south-south-westerly course. The little village, as we left it, had already begun to assume

CURIOSITY PUNISHED.

its wonted melancholy air, the men retired, and the women, who were the last to go, looked with longing eyes at all the wealth that they had been permitted to glance at, and which was now slipping away from them for ever.

"We are off to the *calunga*" (the sea), was the cry of our joyous band, and then they struck up an improvised song, the sense of which is embodied in the following lines :—

> Good-bye, Cuango, woods adieu,
> We're going, other scenes to brave ;
> The whites are eager now to view
> Their *oátos*[2] floating on the wave.
> *Eh-Eh-é! Eh-Eh-é!*

Mounting a lofty hill we came upon the territory of the important Sova Catuma Caimba, and observed in quick succession a number of hamlets dotted about. Quitanguca, Cabenda-Candambo, Mucole-Maiale, Funda-Imbi, Petro, and Quicanga were all so many resting-places where there was a lot of gossip and many a calabash of the country ale to be emptied while it was enacting, and which, as Capulca expressed it, "enabled them to go on their way with a contented *heart!*"—we presume he meant a contented *stomach*.

We have referred on a former occasion to the ceremony attending the expectoration of the Sova, and along this road we found it assume another shape. When the great man, after a long speech at his receptions, clears his throat, one of his subjects rushes forward and kneeling in front of the chief joins his hands and then opens them like a book to receive the precious contribution. His Majesty then going through an elaborate preparatory performance, opens his august lips and spits into the open palms of the man who may not inappropriately be called the royal spittoon; which individual, after the operation, rubs his hands over his naked body and then dries them by wiping them under his arm-pits!

[2] *Oátos*, European boats.

As we were passing near the senzala of another ruler, N'gana N'zendo, we met in the wood with a multitude of men and women who were making a horrible noise by cries and clapping of hands. On coming nearer we perceived upon the ground in their midst the corpse of an old man stretched upon the ground. A tall fellow with feathers in his hair, seated on a stool, was directing the chant by beating time with his palms. Hard by, some men were engaged in digging a grave, whilst others with small baskets were preparing one of their usual "remedies," or in other words a last meal for the defunct. As soon as they caught sight of us, moved by the more novel excitement, they abandoned their funeral rites, and came flocking about the caravan; but as we had no desire to interrupt their ceremony, we quickly passed on.

A few miles further, at the senzala of Munda, we descended a steep slope and entered the basin of the river Cauali, whose sources we shortly after crossed. We were then in the lands of the Danje. On the west lay Luamba,[3] on the east Matamba and Pacaça Aquibonda. At no great distance to the north-east were the sources of the river Sussa, to which we have already referred; to the south those of the Lu-ando, and to the west those of the Lu-calla in the territory of the *Calunga*-Canjimbo, the limit of the States of the Mutemo Ambuilla (Dembo).

This region, of great interest from a hydrographic point of view, was explored by us as closely as possible in order to define the distribution of the waters. From

---

[3] The lands of Luamba constitute a district which at the present time is almost independent of the Jinga. They are governed by a powerful Sova, *Vunda*-ia-Vunda N'gola (meaning the greatest among the *Vundas* of N'gola) generally known as *Calungo*-Luamba, who holds but little intercourse with the King of the Jinga.

the highest ground in the neighbourhood we sighted the mountainous territory of the celebrated Dembos, whose eastern tribes are known under the name of Caculo-Cabaça.

While passing the Camaxe rivulet, an affluent of the river Danje, an untoward event occurred which caused us much regret and sorrow. On descending in a long file the slope which led down to the rivulet in question, we heard just ahead of us the report of a gun, followed by a cry. Turning sharply round, we saw the man who was nearest to us and just behind suddenly drop his load and fall to the ground with a heavy thud. We ran up at once, and on a couple of his companions raising him we observed blood oozing from a wound in the abdomen. The poor fellow had been shot by a ball which, missing us, who were in front of him, found its way into his body.

It was an accident, but yet a culpable one, as it was caused by a neglect of express instructions. Over and over again we had urged upon our crew never to have their guns loaded with ball upon the march; they would do it in spite of us. It happened that on that day Quissongo, an old man, either from a desire to kill game or out of some timidity which urged him to the act, loaded his gun by the sly, and while passing some trees that impeded his way, he turned round to shift his load; on stooping, a bough caught the cock, the gun went off, and as the barrel was pointed our way, the result was what we have described. A poor woman with her infant at her back was almost like ourselves in the direct line of fire, and it was a marvel how she or we escaped.

Fording the rivulet, we hastened to the neighbouring senzala of the *Vunda*-ia-Buta in order to perform an indispensable operation. The projectile had entered at the base of the abdominal region, and passing through the intestines had lodged in the left buttock, very near the surface. Our first care was to make an incision, and after sounding, try and extract the ball. Unhappily it escaped us and slipped back into the interior. All our efforts to lay hold of it were useless, and we felt that every hope of saving the poor fellow was gone. There remained

A TERRIBLE MISHAP.

nothing but to dress the two wounds and wait the consequences.

The man never uttered a complaint, or seemed to regard his involuntary assassin with the slightest feeling of anger. A look of melancholy resignation sat upon his features; and, strange to relate, the unhappy fellow had more than once uttered a presentiment that he should die in the woods. In the Cuango he had been brought to the brink of the grave by dysentery; from this he had recovered—to fall a victim to an accident when drawing near the close of his labours! When the operation was performed, we despatched José to the village to pay our compliments to the Sova, and present him with a piece of six yards of gingham.

Half an hour afterwards he returned with the ruler's reply :—" The Sova is satisfied with his present. He is very glad to see the whites in his country, and intends shortly to pay them a visit. Only" . . . and there José stopped.

" Only what ? " we inquired, for we were certain that some imposition remained behind.

" Only," continued José, in a hesitating tone, aware that he was about to communicate something unpleasant ; " only, the Sova added that the whites had committed a crime in his territory ; they had killed a man, and must pay; because, he said, if he were in the whites' country and killed any one, they would certainly make him pay for the deed."

This message, delivered aloud, in presence of the poor wounded man, struck us as so brutally inhuman that our first thought was to lay a stick about the guide's shoulders to teach him better manners, and not, in the hearing of a sufferer, talk of him as if he were already defunct. Calling to mind, however the effect of such a chastisement on another guide in the Quissongo, we prudently held our hand, and coldly inquired,—

" What does the Sova ask for the pretended crime?"

" He wants four yards of cloth."

Human life we thought is cheap enough in this part of the world. Four yards! why this very chief would ask more to bury him!

On the 26th of June, pursuing a southerly route, we came upon the course of the Lu-ando, which we determined, and on the 27th pulled up at the *Vunda*-ia-Ebo, the limit of the lands of the *Vunda*-ia-Cassanda, where our companion breathed his last sigh, and where we interred him. This made the sixth of our losses, and his grave was the fifth we had dug in the interior, as our first death occurred at Benguella.

Thanks to Providence the most difficult part of our task was over, and by the Divine mercy we ourselves were as yet spared. It is true that the climate as we got nearer the seaboard did not improve, but after so many vicissitudes we trusted that we were not to succumb when we were so near the term of our mission; and in reflections of this nature, with the sound of the mattocks ringing in our ears, the evening of the 27th of June closed in.

On the 28th, while the inhabitants of the neighbouring senzalas were still snoring, we turned out of our poor huts to pursue our journey for the fiftieth time, marching along the basin of the Lu-ando, which we had first to wade across with the water to our necks. Beyond extended the verdant valleys intersected by the waters of the Lucalla, the scene animated by groups of senzalas, and numerous herds of cattle, through which we pursued our peaceful way; admiring the calm beauty of the scene and contemplating the sort of steak yonder stately ox would yield.

Coming upon the track which had been made by the passage of many caravans, we struck into it, and for half an hour or so had nothing but the tall grass for prospect. Beside us marched José, who chattered about all sorts of things—he was a famous story-teller—and amongst others related the history of a crocodile of the

Cuanza (a *personal* acquaintance) which he asserted, was so old that he had had time to devour more than a hundred persons. A small forest grew out of his back, and when at length he was killed, there were found in his inside not only such "unconsidered trifles" as bracelets, hatchets, benches, and what not, but a powerful fetish, to which this wonderful crocodile owed the advantage of selecting his victims!

Capulca, who was listening to the story, here put in his word, and said that he knew of a special remedy, viz., that of a certain herb which, on being well chewed and thrown into the river, was sufficient " to do the business" of every crocodile that ever swam in it, and he only wondered it was not used; and then flying off at a tangent, he gave us a dissertation upon a novel cosmogony, which made the firmament composed of stone and the stars of mica (or according to his phrase, of "that stuff that sparkles"), and much more to the same effect, when there suddenly came in view on the south-western horizon a long row of houses.

It was Duque de Bragança, the outpost we had left some months before.

As we approached it all the incidents that had occurred in the interim came rushing on our minds with a fidelity that made them appear as if they were the events of yesterday. The torrid heats, the desert lands through which we had so painfully plodded, the agonizing pains that acute fever had inflicted upon us, the incessant fears that haunted us, the resolution to give up our further march northward, the hunger and thirst wherewith we were alike assailed, all returned in consecutive order to our memory at sight of the fortress which had witnessed our departure.

Happier thoughts, however, soon banished these sad

and gloomy ones. We recalled to mind the charming little dinner of our old friend Silverio, and the recollection of those delicious fowls and appendages made us quicken our march and infused fresh vigour into our limbs.

We are afraid our readers will accuse us of dwelling far too often and with most undignified unction upon our victuals; but really they must bear in mind the great inconvenience attending bad food in long journeys in the interior of Africa, an inconvenience only surpassed by having nothing to eat at all, before they condemn us too severely; and as we candidly confess that we are not as indifferent to these matters as, shall we say an Anglo-Saxon? we could not help feeling a stir within our inmost depths at the proximity to a well-served and civilized table.

But we were still at some distance from the desired goal, and our impatience made it appear to recede from us the nearer we approached. How different, we thought, to this toilsome march, where José and his companions are puffing and perspiring beneath their loads, may be the approach to the little town within the course of time, when the voice of a railway porter on the arrival of a train, shall echo from the neighbouring rocks, " *Vunda*-ia-Cassanda, fifteen minutes for refreshments ! "

The idea amused us, and we even discussed the best spot for the erection of the station of our imaginary line, when we at length reached the bank of the Lu-calla. We had given notice of our approach, and found old Silverio waiting our arrival with an ancient canoe; it was good enough not to founder on its way, but to convey in safety to the opposite shore the whole of our caravan, composed at that time of the following individuals :—

NAMES.	BIRTHPLACE.
Capulca, cook	Benguella.
Catraio, assistant	,,
Filippe, servant	,,
Mupei, servant	Mulondo.
Capenda, servant	Peinde.
Quissongo	Bihé.
Master José, guide	Luanda.
José (the elder)	,,
Son of the Quissongo	Bihé.
Liando	Lunda.
José	,,
Otubo	Tunda and Celli.
Jimbo	,,
Quimbundo	,,
Capuia	,,
Quimbundo (lad)	,,
Ganga	,,
Gando	,,
Somma	,,
Fortuna	,,
Muto	,,
N'jila	,,
Jamba	,,
Quissongo	,,
Quingando	,,
Capolo	,,
N'gila (lad)	,,
Gumbe	,,
N'jâmba (the elder)	,,
Sabi	,,
Bonga	,,
Calumbo	,,
Gando (old)	,,
Quiêu	,,
Cassauda	Cassunge.
Domingos (N'jinji)	,,
Canguia	,,
Cambuta	,,
Narciso (old)	,,

NAMES.	BIRTHPLACE.
Tamby	Cassange.
Mangumbala (boy)	,,
Autonio	,,
Joaquim	,,
Chico	,,
Antonio (Undalla)	,,
Quitumba (old)	,,
Bembe	Caconda.
Lemba	Luanda.
Quissongo's wife	Bihé.
Capulca's wife	Sambo.
Catraio's wife	Dombe.

Having reached the further bank without accident, we made at once, in high good-humour, for our former encampment, whilst Silverio gave the necessary orders for the coveted dinner.

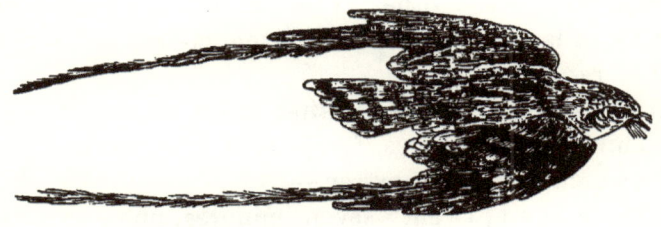

COSMETORNIS VEXILLARIUS (QUIMBAMBA).

CHAPTER VIII.

Duque de Bragança, its importance and fertility—Dinner-time again—A Sova god-father—African children and some remarks concerning them—Infants and adults—Explanations concerning our route—A parallel and the cardinal points—An alarm—The encampment in flames—Anxious moments—The papers of the explorers and the ammunition of the expedition—Carriers and thieves—Things might have been worse—Otubo and our clumsy assistant—" From sources small what great events may spring "—The bi-sonde and the last night of the month of July.

"ONE, two, three . . . now," cried one of us, while, drawn up in a vast circle, half the population of the Duque observed the remarkable proceedings, making their own comments the while.

One of the chiefs of the expedition was determining the horary by the height of the sun, having the *abba* in position; while the other explorer, squatting down near a trunk, was counting by the chronometer the seconds as they ran.

The observer was shortly after heard to exclaim,—

" Thirty-three degrees, forty-three hundredths."

To which came the answer,—

" Three hours, twenty-seven minutes, one second and no thirds." This was followed on the other side by,—

" Azimuth, three hundred and fifty-nine, and five-tenths, north by east; day 30th of June, 1879."

Then, gathering up the instruments, the crowd dispersed, retiring in groups and explaining what they had seen in their own way; one man, whom we overheard, saying,—

" They're looking through that tube to see the countries they're going to."

It was consoling, after so many vicissitudes, to find ourselves in a peaceful and hospitable country, into which we seemed to have been whisked by some friendly enchanter, and where the delights of idleness and the table of friend Silverio were likely, between them, to detain us for some time.

Duque de Bragança is the most north-easterly of all the Portuguese strongholds. In a geographical position determined by the following co-ordinates, viz., latitude 8° 57′ 16″ S., longitude 16° 10′ 00″ E. of Greenwich, height 3478 ft., it presents in the way of declination, inclination, and horizontal component respectively the figures 18° 50′, 34° 58′, and 6,85.

Seated on a treeless plateau, near the right bank of the river Lu-calla, the chief place of the district is composed of an ample fortress made of bricks, with loopholes, parapets, and a fosse in bad order; it is surrounded by a couple of dozen dwellings, or thereabouts, among which figures as the most remarkable, the residence of the chefe, situated on the eastern side.

Its establishment dates from the time that the Government despatched an expedition to this part of the continent for the purpose of repressing the excesses of the native Jingas, who, in their incursions, threatened the district of Ambaca. Its commercial dealings are almost nil. A few sacks of *ginguba*, some calabashes of oil and bundles of *tacula* are exchanged in the course of the year, but as to any trading-houses of mark, we looked for them in vain.

It may, however, be suggested that probably with a

little effort and with less military preponderance the territory might be turned into a vast agricultural district, as we saw growing tobacco, cotton, and *ginguba*, and further north, in the Danje, the sugar-cane of a colossal size and splendid appearance, as well as other products.

The district of the Duque, far from the centre of Government, with some fifty to sixty outposts, was considered, when not the seat of active operations, as was recently the case against the Caculo-Cabaças, a mediocre field of *exploitation* by certain military officers who, moved by a spirit of cupidity and utterly oblivious of the dignity of their cloth, committed the most unheard of extortions, both in the recovery of the tithes (now happily abolished) and in their demands on the small Jinga proprietors. We were informed that not so very long ago an unfortunate Sova received an intimation, through a mere private of mobiles, for the payment of a certain fine in the shape of cattle. As he refused to accede to the claim, a detachment, swollen by a little army of volunteers, was sent off under the command of a subaltern, who, in a single raid, carried off one hundred and eighty head of cattle composing the Sova's fortune. The consequence was the retreat of the despoiled chief into the Jinga, where he had been preceded by others, similarly situated, and the whole district became depopulated and ruined.

This digression is, however, apart from our mission, which has nothing to do with subjects of this nature; we merely mention the circumstance here because it has given rise to what we hold to be unjust and painful accusations against the Portuguese central Government, which was most probably ignorant of the whole affair.

The lands now under review are of great fertility; the climate is to a certain extent salubrious, and would be more so but for the too great proximity to the river, whose banks, that are frequently inundated, constitute hot-beds of infection; on the other hand cases of decisive fever, that are so common on the sea-board, are far less prevalent here. At the period of our sojourn, a fresh south-easterly wind drove across the clear blue sky a few flecks of white cloud, and cooled the temperature during the hours of its greatest elevation.

The inhabitants of the district are a mixture of Jingas, Ambaquistas, and a few natives of the Bondo, who with the soldiers of Loanda have become leavened into one mass, and constitute the existing families who devote their time to the cultivation of small farms, whence they derive their daily sustenance.

We had jotted down the foregoing remarks on a fresh page of our diary (for, thank heaven, our paper, at least, never failed us), when we were interrupted by a message from the chefe that "Dinner was served."

It seemed as if it were always dinner-time in this hospitable establishment; indeed, so bent did our kind host appear upon making us forget the many times we had gone without such a meal, that we were compelled to take no end of walking exercise to do justice to the good fare.

The repast was like many joyous ones at which we have assisted. Each played his part in a very praiseworthy manner, and the conversation was gay or sober, grave or joyous as the subject varied, now turning upon the comparative merits of Yacca and the Duque, now interrupted by a burst of laughter at some witty or humorous remark.

"Nothing can well be worse than a life in those lovely woods!" exclaimed one, as he inhaled the savoury steam which issued from a dish of pirão, flanked by an equally steaming fowl that had just been placed upon the table; and then continued in a sententious tone, "If Adam were as hard set in his paradise as we frequently were in ours, he must have been rather glad than otherwise to be driven out of it."

While enjoying ourselves and chatting in this fashion there walked into the room the strangest of figures, a tall, bony African, wrapped in an ample gingham cloth, wearing on his head so monstrous a military hat that the one which adorned the brow of the *august Jagga*, Cambollo-Cangonga, would have sunk into insignificance by comparison.

The sight of this apparition made us suspend operations and sit back in our chairs with surprise, when our worthy amphytrion gave us the key to the enigma.

"It is my godfather,"[1] he explained, "whom the baptism of a daughter has connected with our family."

Continuing our inspection of the visitor with more interest after this announcement, we ascertained that within that variegated covering stood a Sova, whose name, as we also learned, was *Vunda*-ia-T'chirimbimbi who, with a most gracious smile, took off his huge hat and shook us both by the hand.

We could not remove our eyes from him; we had seen a good many Sovas, but we had never beheld a Sova godfather before. He sat down with us to table, and clinked glasses in the most natural manner possible, so that, after mentally drawing a comparison between this well-behaved individual and the many savage specimens of the genus "native" we had met with on

---

[1] I have used the word *godfather* in order to retain the authors' pleasant witticism, although the degree of relationship conferred by the Portuguese title *compadre*, and which is equally applicable to the man who acts as sponsor and the man whose child is held at the baptismal font, is unknown to us.—A. E.

our travels, one of us could not help exclaiming to our host,—

"Eureka! the way to civilize Africa is to turn all the Sovas into godfathers!"

Our attention had been so taken up with the new-comer we did not at first observe that with him had entered at least a dozen young *gamins* (whether the offspring of

A SOVA GODFATHER.

T'chirimbimbi or otherwise we did not know) until the hubbub the urchins made prevented the possibility of our ignoring them any longer. The visitation reminded us that we had not hitherto made any special mention of *young Africa*, and we therefore took the earliest opportunity of repairing the omission by entering in our diary that very evening the following few particulars concerning them.

African children are, beyond all compare, more intelligent and more agreeable than African adults. Little fellows of five years old often do such clever things and display such an amount of reasoning power as to cause both wonder and admiration. Gaiety and fun are inherent to them, and in this particular they are quite on a par with their European compeers. Quite the reverse of eastern children, so taciturn and melancholy, with that yellow skin which gives them an air of biliousness and suffering; the little nigger, with his glossy black hide and disproportioned stomach, runs, jumps, and exercises his lungs from sunrise to sunset.

Receiving no spiritual training at the hands of an ascetic, who oftentimes fills the imagination of a child with stupid, senseless fears, the youth knows neither fear nor superstition; even as regards the fetishism prevalent amongst them, he apprehends little more of it beyond the tiny horn or rag which the mother hangs round his neck to preserve him from death.

But in proportion as he passes from the state of childhood to that of adolescence, these characteristics become modified; he loses his candour, and becomes sly, distrustful, covetous, and above all, stupid.

Whether it be that in the later days, having his mind bent on the mere satisfaction of material necessities, the negro does not exercise his intelligence and that from such apathetic state arises a *quasi* atrophy or brutishness, or otherwise, we cannot say, but the fact is undoubted, that the adult is more stupid than the child, and the old man is stupider still. It is probable that the outrageous habits of alcohol-drinking and hemp-smoking have much to do with bringing about this result.

With the mulatto the above remarks do not so well apply; the men do not become so brutified, and when young they more nearly resemble the Orientals. They are dull as children, less intelligent and expert. They do not gambol and play like the little black fellows, and if by chance a mulatto child should appear among a troop of young niggers, he is always ill at ease, and as if apprehensive of their companionship.

When the mulatto comes to man's estate, if a superior education do not dissipate his deep prejudices, he seems always bent beneath the weight of an incurable disappointment. He looks upon the least ambiguous phrase as a slur upon his own person, and every joke an insult. He considers himself, without reasonable cause, to belong to an inferior race. He takes for granted that he is despised, and, thrown upon himself, seeks out the elements of active, intellectual labour, which furnish perhaps a means to preserve his mental faculties.

But nothing of all this belongs to the negro; as a youngster he is gay and happy as a bird; as an adult he is emphatically what the French call *bête*. He is not a bad fellow in the main, and whatever really evil and vicious tendencies he may have, as a rule, only come out late in life.

Having thus recorded our judgment upon the blacks, little and big, a judgment which, as being formulated during the digestion of our dinner of the 30th, may perhaps be disputed by those who have greater experience than ourselves, we began to put things in order with a view to a speedy departure from Duque de Bragança.

As it is not impossible that some among our readers, moved by a not unnatural curiosity, may inquire, "How is it that these men who have more than once put forward as a motive for separations, and special marches, their desire to enlarge the area of their labours, should have returned to Duque, where they had already been, instead of selecting another route on their way to the Cuanza?"

To which, with all respect for the opinion insinuated in the question, we beg leave to reply,—

When in March, 1879, we arrived at the district of the Duque we found ourselves lightened of a good part of our belongings, inasmuch as the calculation we made in Cassange to reach parallel 5°, travelling directly northwards by the east bank of the Cuango, was not applicable to our altered circumstances, under which, although journeying westward, we had still to go over about as much ground to reach the 5th parallel. It became, consequently, a matter of moment to make up at least the void in our expenditure caused by our journey from the Cuango to the Duque. Having requisitioned the authorities, we waited and waited, but as no goods appeared and the season was rapidly advancing, we determined to go on without them—in order not to remain for an indefinite period at the station—and use all possible economy upon the road. But when we reached the territory of Yacca our apprehensions began to be confirmed, for though we had obtained a few goods from Sr. Figueiredo (whose name has been previously mentioned), the only person in the place who had any to dispose of, we saw our resources melting away to such an extent that we had the prospect before us of absolute penury, joined to the sickness from which ourselves and followers were suffering. It was this state of things which prevented our visiting Muene Puto Cassongo, from the fear that we should be unable to fee him in proportion to his expectations; and it also had much to do with putting a stopper to our further journey northwards till we reached the Zombo track. There was consequently no choice but to return to the Duque de Bragança, where we knew resources might be had; and our itinerary southwards along the Cauali, became therefore subordinate to the position in which we stood and which these explanations, we trust, have made clear.

The month of July found us recovered in health and spirits, and we were only waiting for the 19th to pass over, in order to witness on that day a partial eclipse of the sun, and convey the results of the observations to Europe.

The goods were received, and those carriers of the interior, designated in the previous chapter under the description of Cassange, were paid and discharged as being no longer required. We then busied ourselves with packing our merchandise in a convenient form so as to be enabled to take a fresh departure at the earliest hour. Events, however, were preparing that were to add another instance to the many presented by this changeable world that the best matured plans may from one moment to another be upset, and that the man who boasts of affluence at one minute may the next be reduced almost to beggary.

The 24th of July, a magnificent day, the anniversary in the capital of our dear country of the advent of liberty, passed over, and evening came on in all her beauty. The national flag flying over the fortress, the soldiers in their best uniforms, gave to the little place an air of gala, showing that though far from the metropolis, and distant from the country which has covered with her glorious standard millions of square miles of the globe, her children in her remote colonies were participating in the just gaiety of their brethren in Europe.

We were in our usual place, our legs under the chefe's table, sipping our coffee, and doing our best to drum into the thick head of a black *pseudo*-captain of the *garde-mobile* the definition of a parallel, so as to make him understand that though we had not been to the mouth of the Zaire we had reached the parallel of the mouth. The unhappy man was one of those beings who are incapable of comprehending the axiomatic principle: *the whole is greater than any of its parts*, for the simple reason that there were *foxes who had tails bigger than their bodies*, and he therefore exclaimed in an angry tone, as if he thought we were poking fun at him,—

"It's of no use your telling me that; how could you be at the Zaire if you weren't there? It's all a mistake;" and he added by way of argument, "It once happened to me to have to march south—here he pointed to the east—and I marched on and on till I found myself at last due north! That must have been, of course, the way with you, and that was how you made the mistake."

With most exemplary patience we answered equally *of course* that it was not so; nor indeed was such a thing at all probable with men like ourselves, who were sailors to boot, and that if he had only had by him some one who knew how to box the compass he would have been enabled to discern that it was owing to his confused notion of the cardinal points that he made that remarkable journey.

Any further discussion of the subject was cut short by loud shouts for help, and an alarm sounded by the bugles of the detachment, which made us spring to our feet in hot haste, and rush to the door where the cry of "Fire! fire!" was resounding on all sides.

Confused masses of people were rushing across the

little piazza in the direction of our camp, screaming as if they were possessed. We meanwhile stood irresolute, looking first at Silverio, then at the captain, as if either of them could give any explanation of the uproar; when we heard several of our carriers shouting our own names.

Rushing out, we were horror-struck after going a few paces to find that it was our own encampment in flames! Waves of furious fire, fanned by a strong south-easter were igniting one after another and eagerly devouring the dry wooden huts with their grass roofs, till there appeared a sea of angry, roaring, crackling flame, from which flew into the darkness of night showers of brilliant sparks.

Our trouble was extreme; and as we rushed panting to the spot, we figured to ourselves the loss of all our labours, and the destruction of charts, maps, diaries, instruments, everything which we held almost as dearly as our lives. We had but one thought and one cry, and in a voice broken by exertion and emotion we exclaimed, "Save the books!"

Who shall say what we suffered at that supreme moment! How can we convey to our readers the terror and the affliction of two poor men who beheld, as it were, the annihilation within a few minutes of time of the hopes and aspirations of twenty-four months of toilsome effort, and who had often been sustained and saved solely by the smiling prospect of a distant commendation of their labours, which was now to be snatched from their grasp!

In a fit almost of despair we dashed into the burning enclosure, where the suffocating heat and frightful vibration of the air made breathing all but impossible.

We made our way to our own huts to find them two bare skeletons dropping piece by piece beneath the action of the expiring flames; the others were already heaps of ashes, and the destructive element had broken through the outer palisade and was seeking fresh material to devour.

At a short distance from the scene of ruin lay a confused heap of trunks, cases, bales and parcels, some partially burnt, others just catching fire, conveyed thither in haste and thrown pell-mell to save them, if possible, from destruction.

The peril was intense. From all points loaded arms went off as they came in contact with the flames; explosive balls blew up in our immediate vicinity, and cases of ammunition flying into splinters threatened the lives of all around.

Amid the heap of baggage we were each endeavouring to discover our respective trunks that could not at first be found, and whereof one was afterwards extracted from the ashes with some of the books that had been a prey to the flames.

It was whilst we were thus engaged that we perceived dodging in and out the smoke and fire various black figures whose movements struck us as suspicious; for when we approached they disappeared into the darkness. Capulca it was who explained the mystery, and which was of a nature to confirm the opinion we had formed from experience of how little trust was to be placed in the men of the interior. Whilst we, with half a dozen faithful followers, were striving our very utmost to save the papers and scientific material of the expedition, Otubo, instead of keeping watch over the scattered goods, was abstracting pieces of cloth and everything else he could lay hands on, and removing them with the aid of a handful of his Ban-sumbi comrades and a few scamps of the place to the neighbouring wood!

THE PERIL WAS INTENSE.

Enraged beyond measure at this shameful spoliation, we gave chase after him in order to inflict a severe thrashing on his black hide, when, to our astonishment, we came full butt against another marauder, in the shape of our captain of the *cardinal points*, who, after appropriating a piece of valuable cloth in the *south*, was scuttling off with it to the *north*, when he was stopped by an equally honest gentleman who disputed possession of the property. They both took to their heels before we could lay hands on them, and left us to the pleasant reflection that we were in a perfect colony of rascals.

Returning to the scene of the disaster, we continued to order the removal of the remnant of our property to the residence of the chefe, Captain Silverio, who, suffering from rheumatism, was unable to give any active assistance.

It was eleven o'clock before the whole of this painful episode was at an end and darkness fell upon the scene. We stood alone and sad at heart, on the spot which a few hours before represented our *quilombo*. The place was nothing now but a field of smoking ashes, from which rose the distorted carcasses of one or two of the huts, mere black poles exhibiting here and there a patch of smouldering fire. Scattered about and borne hither and thither by the wind, were fragments of half-consumed paper, which we feared might be portions of maps, drawings, or important data procured, we only knew, with how much toil! Daylight alone could tell us the extent of our loss; and as soon as it appeared we set to work to draw up something like a list of our late possessions.

By one of those accidents, which we are too apt under such circumstances to describe as providential, we, who were accustomed after our labours of the day simply to collect our papers and place them on top of a trunk, so as to have them ready to our hand for night-work, had, on this particular occasion, replaced the greater part *within* the box. Still, a good many, that we wanted for constant use, were left outside; such as the register of meteorological observations (of one of whose leaves we exhibit in this volume a *fac-simile*), sketch-books (in which great ravage was made), a manuscript book of co-ordinates, and other similar records.

We discovered that of the goods we had recently purchased some of the bales were burnt at the ends and others had disappeared altogether. Beads and similar articles were dispersed and lost, guns were carbonized, our own body-clothing so diminished and despoiled, that all that was left us were the things which we actually had on, and an ancient hat with the crown stove in. We could not help thinking as we looked at each other in broad daylight, with our disordered beards, our hands and faces grimed with ashes, our unkempt hair, part hanging in elfin locks, the other standing on end beneath our helmets, that we looked amazingly like those doubtful cavaliers who, if met by a traveller on the highway, would cause him involuntarily to seek the handle of his revolver, to be prepared for all emergencies.

It was only after a day visit to our late camp that we appreciated to the full the extent of our misfortune. Catching Otubo, on our arrival, we administered to him at once a sound thrashing, and succeeded in making him disclose the places where he had hidden away the stolen property, which amounted to the trifle of twenty odd pieces; besides smaller articles. We then set about hunting among the ashes and picking up the fragments of paper, many of which had travelled a mile away from the scene of the conflagration.

How frightfully destructive an element fire can be

was never brought so closely home to us before. Our meteorological observatory was in ruins; and as we raked among the ashes we brought to light the remains of an aneroid; a watch black and half melted; thermometers tubeless; remnants of gaiters; heels and soles of boots, whereof the upper leathers had disappeared; the crowns of helmets twisted out of shape; and, sad to tell, a poor eagle that we kept chained in a crib, in order to convey it to Europe, lying roasted at the foot of the pole which had held it prisoner!

Having raked about and searched till we were convinced that no more remained to be done, we returned to the residence in order by the aid of the fragments of the last diaries to replace as far as possible what had been lost, and try and discover the cause of the fire. For this we had not very far to look, and though we cursed the stupidity to which it was due, it was a remote consolation to find that no malice dictated it.

Catraio, that most clumsy and ill-starred assistant, having set up the observatory in the open air, conjectured, from a peculiar whispering sound that issued from one of the huts, and from a bite or two on his own proper person, that a band of warrior ants was making an attack on the *quilombo* in that direction.

Wishing to ascertain the fact, he suddenly bethought him of the observatory lantern, and taking out the candle it contained, he lighted it at the kitchen fire, and proceeded to make his search.

He was quite correct in his premises; there were the *bi-sonde* sure enough, and the first he trod upon bit him so sharply that he dropped the candle and fled. In falling the flame caught the dry grass, and the wind fanning it, set the whole place in a blaze, producing the results we have above related.

During the whole of the 25th of the month the expedition was in course of re-organization. If our resources were of the meagrest before the fire, it may easily be judged how scanty they were after it. One result of our altered circumstances was the abandonment of an idea we had formed to go back to the *Calunga* Luamba, proceed to the sources of the Bengo, in the territory of Calandula, and thence make our way to Ambaca.

At five in the afternoon we held a council, at which it was resolved to leave on the 1st of August by the direct route, and take with us our good friend Silverio, who, having sent in his resignation of the office of chefe, was enabled, by the arrival of his substitute, to carry out a long contemplated plan of shifting his residence to the Pedras (rocks) of Pungo N'dongo, where a convenient little house was ready to receive him with the modest retiring allowance of some forty-five dollars.

With the last stroke of midnight, which terminated the month of July, followed by the *alerta!* of the sentinels on the fortress, that was echoed and re-echoed in the stillness from the neighbouring heights, we retired to rest; prepared at daybreak to be once more upon the road.

AFRICAN SILK.

CHAPTER IX.

Final departure from Duque de Bragança—One of José's stories—The Lu-chilo and the *patrulhas*—The *Ptyelus olivaceus*—Captain Silverio's pets—The *Cosmetornis vexillarius*—José has another uncle—Samba-Cango, the Hango and the Lu-calla—Brief notice of the river, conformation of the land and vegetation—The Cariombo and Porto Real—Novel rafts and ingenious method of propulsion—A visit to Pamba, and a few remarks thereon—A vegetable giant—The road to Pedras Negras—José and the basalts—Native silk—Pungo N'Dongo, its aspect and constitution—Remarkable impressions on the rocks—Port Hunga and its orange trees—Philosophical considerations of the explorers—"In the country of eyes, the blind are kings"—The Caballo cascade—The Cuanza, obstacles, fish, cataracts—Brief reflections thereon—Malange, Calundo, and Pungo N'Dongo.

BEFORE quitting the fortress for good, it became a matter of necessity to overhaul the whole of the packages that constitute a traveller's baggage in Africa, and more especially those relative to the commissariat, the defective organization of which causes on the road the most serious inconvenience. Although therefore the old captain, with the patience of Job and the will of a giant, was doing his best to get things into trim, we were just as busy ourselves in removing goods from one place to another, changing porters, securing trunks, and abandoning our temporary camp.

Meanwhile all sorts of discussions were going on in the caravan. Now it was a sheep that no man could be found willing to carry, at another it was the *tipoia* of

Sr. Silverio that "stopped the way;" then the kitchen utensils could not be persuaded to stow themselves or to be stowed away in the *mu-hamba* set apart for them, because that incorrigible Capulca, wishing to travel *light*, had stuffed into it his cursed jack-boots and a lot of masquerade rubbish, rejected by a carrier on the ground that it was no part of his business to convey them; and finally the division of an ox's hide to be cut up for sandals for the men, led to as much noise and confusion as if the animal to which it belonged had gone mad and was running a muck amongst them.

When matters had a little calmed down, we gave a last glance round, and to the order of "raise your packs" started in front of the caravan.

Passing through the plantations that surrounded the stronghold, we descended the incline, at bottom of which ran the Quimbaxe rivulet, and then began to climb the hill which rose from the opposite bank.

The commencement of the journey presented no incident worthy of special mention, unless we can rank as important the infliction of a dozen blows of a stick upon the broad back of Otubo, who at the last moment was found drunk, with his load, in a little hut where a couple of his lady acquaintances were endeavouring to conceal him.

We were favoured with lovely weather. The glorious sun was gilding the tops of the trees beneath which we were passing, their branches so interlaced that they formed a natural harbour, wherein thousands of birds had their homes, and fluttered, and chirped, and sung in notes as varied as their plumage.

Master José, who was prattling at our side in his usual lively fashion, pointed out to us a couple of graves wherein were interred the victims of a double assassination, committed by an amiable chefe of the fortress who was accustomed to get rid of people who were distasteful to him by sending them into the forest to cut wood, and then ordering them to be quietly shot and buried. By José's description we fancied it must have been the same gentleman who perpetrated that little pleasantry of the cattle-lifting, to which we have before alluded! These are some of the delights of a subaltern military administration!

A march of an hour and a half brought us to the river Lu-chilo, a clear, limpid stream, which furnishes water to the Duque, and on whose right bank was a *patrulha*[1] where the tracks diverged. Steering our course for Ambaca, we continued in a south-westerly direction, and set up our first camp at a hamlet called Cassanje.

Whilst we were resting beneath the shade of a sycamore and getting wetted, almost before we were aware of it, by the incessant droppings of the *Ptyelus Olivaceus*, we were spectators of what we considered to be a great waste of energy and breath on the part of our travelling companion, Captain Silverio. The old gentleman, who was passionately fond of animals, was engaged in catching a cat and saving a monkey.

Like most persons who possess this mania he was singularly unfortunate in his pets, and was in constant trouble either about their health or mourning over their untimely ends. " I am not quite sure," we have heard him say, " whether in my wish to be kind I am not really cruel, for I never catch anything on the road in order to make a pet of it, but it is sure to die by the way."

[1] These *patrulhas* are military stations scattered about the province, where two or three mobiles are kept on guard. They serve to protect the roads and afford a refuge for travellers.

He was quite right in the latter part of his remark on the present occasion, for the little monkey got a sunstroke and fell into the water as we were crossing the river, and though we dragged it out alive, it succumbed a short time after, in spite of our best medical skill to save it.

As to the cat, in a fit of feline ire at being enclosed in a sack, and bumped against every tree the carrier who had it on his back came near, he managed to make a hole at the bottom of his prison while he was *en route*, and by the speed of his flight gave no one a chance of catching him again.

Our excellent friend, afflicted at the loss of his two fresh acquisitions was, for a time quite inconsolable; he shed tears over the loss of the monkey, and got into such a rage with the carrier who had unwittingly let his prisoner escape, that, but for his rheumatism, which stiffened his joints and prevented his moving with any activity, the delinquent would have been heartily thrashed. He was, however, on the alert, and kept out of the way.

After all, the fondness entertained by the old gentleman for animals was, after a moment's reflection, perfectly intelligible. Condemned as he had been for years to a life in the interior, surrounded by natives whose habits and inclinations were alike distasteful to him, he had acquired a love for dumb creatures which not only returned his affection but often displayed a nobility of character to which the negroes were utter strangers.

The evening of that day was spent in endeavouring to catch a specimen or two of a night-bird which, with the disappearance of the sun began fluttering about in every direction and wore a very peculiar appearance owing to a long feather at the end of each wing. It is known to naturalists under the name of *Cosmetornis vexillarius*, whilst the natives of those parts call it the *quimbamba*. It is asserted by some that these feathers, like the tail of the *Viduas paradiseas* appear at a certain fixed period, after which they are no longer seen—but this is denied by others. The family of the *Caprimulgidæ* has many representatives here, such as the *Huicumbamba*, *Caprimulgos Shelleyi*, and others.

As it grew dark, we were obliged to give up our amusement, which had resulted in nothing, and return to the *patrulha*, where we sat round a candle and passed a couple of hours listening to the captain's stories, when we separated for the night.

With the first peep of day, refreshed and invigorated by a sound sleep, we were up and on the march, sniffing with satisfaction the sweet morning air, redolent of perfume.

José, who was chattering as usual, informed us that in Ambaca he had *another uncle !* The information recalled vividly to our minds a former occasion when the possession of such a relative, by our worthy guide, gave him, in our eyes, so respectable a character. We could not now refrain from observing that he seemed to have extensive connexions. "Immense," was his answer, and for a whole hour, as we jogged along, he gave an uninterrupted history of his parents and grandparents, his uncles, aunts, and cousins, about whom, it must be confessed, we felt so little interest that for the greater part of the time we heard him talking, but could not for the life of us have repeated afterwards any of the information conveyed.

Our second halting-place was at the *patrulha* of Samba Cango, where we were edified by the perusal of a notice from the commandant of the division (for by this high-sounding name, we know not why, the subalterns of the chefes are styled), affixed to the wall, the orthography and construction of which document would have puzzled a philologist.

On leaving this spot we travelled west-south-west into the heart of the Hango, skirting the sides of the Papa

THE PATRULHA OF SAMBA CANGO.

Serras. In proportion as we approached Ambaca the Lucalla increased in size and volume of water. It was no longer the rivulet of the territory of *Vunda*-ia-Ebo, but a powerful stream winding in and out the broken ground. The tortuous course of the river appeared strewed with rocks and stones, with small rapids and other impediments which took from it all its value.

We afterwards came upon a constant succession of valleys, some bare, others clothed with verdure, disposed perpendicularly to the line we were pursuing, and thus contrasting remarkably with the formations on the opposite bank where the lofty Serra Vunji rose in sight.

Resting by the wayside for half an hour or so, we went on again, and covered during the day a good twelve miles, bivouacking at last in Bulo Jango. To the north-west an extensive serra formed the horizon. Westward we observed blue hills promiscuously dotted about. Vegetation seemed to be on the wane. The red sand-stone was prevalent all about us, and not a senzala was visible.

Bondo-ia-Quilesso was met with further on, and it was about that spot that we saw many of our old friends the baobabs, those giants of the vegetable kingdom known at Angola under the name of *imbundeiros*, and whose grotesque shapes have no parallel in the African flora.

Our march now became trying and uncomfortable. Steep hills, covered with scrub and stones, crossed our path, and left us no alternative but to surmount them, and the difficulty of ascending them was only matched by the trouble of getting down on the other side. Further on we had to wade across the river Cariombo, which at the fording-place divides into three separate branches, all of which empty their waters into the Lucalla, at the point where the latter river turns southwards.

On the 8th of August we arrived at Porto Real, which has nothing grand about it but its name; indeed, its resources were at so low an ebb, that we had some difficulty at first in procuring a boat. The canoes, or rather rafts, we subsequently saw amused us mightily, while they excited our admiration at the ingenuity displayed by the natives in overcoming the difficulties by which they are beset. As there is no timber for the construction of a decent-sized vessel—seeing that the savannas of Ambaca are so bare of wood that the people are obliged to use grass for the cooking of their food—the aborigines make up bundles of *mabu,* whence they remove the flowery top, dry them by long exposure to the sun, and then fasten them together so that the whole pile assumes the shape of an isosceles triangle, and somewhat resembles the *m'badji* canoes observed by Schweinfurth among the Bornus.

Launching this structure into the water, they use neither paddles nor oars to move it, but a young nigger sprawls on his stomach on each *quarter* of the vessel and employs his legs that are dangling in the water to propel the skiff along. It is a complete system of parallel screws, and by either working together or separately, to starboard or port, the desired direction is obtained. Long practice has, of course, given them such experience in pilotage that they steer for the point to which they are bound with a nicety.

After our men and baggage were got over, we stayed behind for some little time to watch the evolutions of the mariners in mid-stream, and were delighted at the dexterity they displayed. What astonished us most was to learn, that though the river is full of crocodiles, there was no instance of one of the *screws* having fallen a prey to their voracious jaws. This must have been due (or at least they *said* so) to the fetishes they carried about them, consisting generally of a seed or tooth or horn hung round the neck!

Having taken careful note of this clever contrivance as worthy of imitation in the interior, and promising to

IT IS A COMPLETE SYSTEM OF PARALLEL SCREWS.

Page 196.

make use of it in any future explorations thither, we left the port for Praça Velha, formerly the residence of the chefe of the district, and as being far better situated than the present one was, as a matter *of course*, set aside, in order that it might not prove an exception to the old and invariable Portuguese custom of selecting the very worst spot for a permanent station. We believe there is scarce a Lusitanian, if he had to choose between Cintra and Trafraria to pitch his tent, but would select the latter, on the ground of its being readier to hand or more convenient, or any other excuse whereby to make the worse appear the better reason.

On the following day we recrossed the Lu-calla, having decided upon paying a visit to Ambaca, the chief seat of the district, which we had left some five miles to the westward. Being desirous to make some surveys of the river ere the sun got too high in the heavens, we started so early in the morning that the *Scops leucotis* and *Athene perlata* (species of screech owls), had not yet gone to rest, but were occasionally making the welkin hideous with their lugubrious cries the while they sat ensconced in the hollow of the trees.

None can imagine our disappointment on reaching our destination to find that it was a miserable village consisting of a single street with three houses (if they even deserved that name) and a dozen and a half wigwams. Crossing a bare piece of country we entered the precincts to find a few groups of negroes, who, squatted on the ground at a place pompously called the market, exposed to the sun and to a myriad of flies, two quarters of an ox, a few potatoes, and a little flour.

This tumble-down and most desolate station, seated on sandstone and amid cracked masses of schistus, from which it derives something like stability, and having about it a singular air of distrust and gloom, boasts on one side of some little plantations of *giuguba* and tobacco, which are dispersed over a slope that inclines northwards, and extend to the edge of a narrow valley intersected by the Pamba rivulet. Behind it, like giant sentinels, a score or so of mounts rise from the lower ground, their bald granitic heads giving one a fever only to look at them. A roasting sun blazing in a cloudless sky, and half a dozen Europeans of cadaverous aspect, their heads wrapped in linen and their legs full of ulcers, complete the unattractive picture. Every soul one meets in Ambaca is in mourning, as though death were so wide-spread that none can escape the exhibition of such semblance of woe.

Most persons are aware that Ambaca is the country of those industrious gentlemen of whom we have before spoken under the denomination of Ambaquistas. It is undoubted that in no other part of the province could one be so easily bamboozled as in that *holy* city; and though we ourselves, owing to our being thoroughly forewarned, escaped fleecing on the present occasion, we had been so frequently deceived before that the very name of Ambaquista made us feel ill at ease.

It is asserted that Ambaca was once upon a time thickly populated, that it had wealth, occupation, and movement. Judging from present appearances, it is difficult to believe that it was so; but we were informed that the persecutions and grasping of the authorities little by little drove people away to seek their living under more secure auspices. That which gives a semblance of truth to the assertion about the former prosperity of Ambaca is the incontestable fact that from remote times the district was considered one of the most profitable to a *zealous* administrator, and that a good deal of competition for its possession went on among gentlemen who were moved by a feeling to be *useful*.

The aspect of affairs at the present time is simply this, that Ambaca is worth nothing at all, because all she ever had has been squeezed out of her, and it would be difficult indeed for any place to retain importance when her wealthiest sons have been driven away, and those who are left are systematically despoiled. And thus it is that although the soil is well fitted for certain crops the land lies fallow for want of cultivation. The chief products of the district are *ginguba* and tobacco, but the fields are so few and scattered that it is easy to foresee even they may be abandoned unless a more favourable tide should set into the place. It is, however, no part of our mission to attempt to lay before our readers an economic-administrative plan for the reorganization of the districts of the Portuguese Western Province in Africa; so leaving that most arduous task to wiser heads than ours we will resume our own special narrative.

After remaining in the suburbs a sufficient length of time to fix three stations of the *abba*, take the bearings of the land, and examine the site for the terminus of the line called the Ambaca railway—existing at present only in the fervent imagination of African agriculturists and merchants, and in certain big folios which special archives conceal from profane eyes—we returned to the residence of the official who was doing duty in the absence of the chefe, in order to rest from our fatigues and restore our exhausted strength by the ordinary process of meat and drink. Breakfast over, we took leave, wishing the inhabitants of Ambaca better health and a little less heat, and turning our faces eastward we retraced our steps to the encampment.

On our road thither we observed one of the extraordinary baobabs already referred to, and which was of such monstrous shape that it seemed as if nature had produced it in a fit of spleen. The stupendous trunk of this goliath struck us as so remarkable that we not only walked round but measured it, and found the circumference to be no less than fifteen fathoms, while its roots were visible at thirty paces from the stem, making it a perfect voyage to circumnavigate it completely!

We again crossed the river on one of the novel rafts and rested on the other bank long enough to make the sketch we present to our readers, regretting that our want of skill as draughtsmen has prevented us exhibiting a more finished picture.

It was the 8th of August that we resumed our journey bound for Pedras Negras or the Black Rocks. Scaling and descending mounts and ravines, and traversing woods in the fresh morning air under the guidance of José, our whole attention was given to the search for basalts. It had become a sort of mania with us, since we had declared that there was a basaltic stratum in the Serra Hengue, to discover a fragment, no matter where, so that we might fall back upon volcanic action to explain the crags of Pungo N'Dongo, which, however, we are no more capable of doing now than we did then. Considering our geological investigations fruitless, and tired of hearing José, for the twentieth time, inquire, " Is it this ? " as he pointed out the most unlikely rocks, we gave the matter up, and contented ourselves with admiring Nature, who there unrolls before the delighted eyes a majestic panorama that Dr. Livingstone had admired before ourselves. Nor was music wanting to lend a charm to the landscape, for the overhanging boughs were peopled with feathered songsters that kept up a continual concert.

Being somewhat tired, we thought how delightful it

would be to enjoy all these lovely views while being conveyed in the palanquin; so summoning the bearers we put our sketch and note-book in our pockets and reclined ourselves at ease in the *tapoia*. It was an unfortunate mistake as it turned out, for the swinging motion was so conducive to slumber, that having half closed our eyes in order to enjoy the illusive feeling that we were travelling in a dream, they were soon shut up entirely, and for two good hours we were fast asleep.

When we awoke, so great was the change in the aspect of things that we might well believe we were still dreaming. We were in a bare rocky country, whereon the sun was blazing, as an African sun is wont to do. Birds, trees, fresh zephyrs and basaltic piles had all vanished! Of the lovely landscape on which we had closed our eyes only the faintest recollection was left, and of the topography of the country not a trace.

" Hola! Stop! Stop!"

And jumping out by way of relieving our consciences, we fell foul of our bearers.

" How the d——l could you let us sleep like this? How many mountains have we crossed, and have we passed any rivers?"

And with our note-book on our knees, listening and scribbling, we paid our devoirs to science by guessing at the curves and irregularities of the country we had been carried through.

We were then on the banks of the river Heleji, where separate the roads to Pungo N'Dongo by the Lungue and to Malange *viâ* Calundo. Striking into the track on the right, we soon reached a *patrulha*, where we had a good night's rest, which enabled us to go on again with fresh spirit next morning on our journey southward.

We were then just entering the inner limit of the

mountainous region. On our right and left, before and behind us, we beheld nothing but serras, peaks, mounts, and chains of lofty hills, confusedly mixed up together and extending as far as the eye could reach in every direction. The road became more and more solitary— anything in the shape of a dwelling being a rarity. Feathered game, however, was not wanting, and from time to time a wood-pigeon or a partridge would rapidly cross our line of march without any one attempting to bring it down, so great a difference does it make when a man has his bellyful and when he is on the point of starvation.

For the first time we perceived some singular cocoons, of the shape of slices cut out of a cheese, having within, curious to relate, more than one chrysalis, as we easily conjectured by the rattle when shaking them. The outer cover, in capital condition, was made of a substance in every respect analogous to silk, and very probably as useful; it is certainly as unknown in Europe as is that of the *qui-vuvi* spider we have before alluded to, and which we met with very abundantly.

The path led us by rapid curves through extensive woods, at one time leading us across a brook with a sandy bottom, at another through a torrent with almost perpendicular sides, hugging the flanks of the serras Catenda, Cachinje and Quilulo, until it brought us out into a long and open plain where the most singular prospect met our eye.

Upon ground of no great elevation, and still here and there obscured by the morning vapour, rose in groups, without any order, enormous cliffs of various shapes, from the column to the sphere, jumbled all up together, and extending for some leagues eastward till they were lost in the horizon.

Assuming as they did the strangest shapes, these rocks, seen at a distance along the track we were pursuing, looked wonderfully like a huge castle, with turrets and embrasures, which only giant architects could have conceived and erected. These were the famous Pungo N'Dongo rocks (commonly known as the Black Stones) where the Government of Portugal has

ROCKS OF PUNGO N'DONGO.

established the head-quarters of a district. As we approached them their aspect underwent a change, increasing rapidly with their nearness in grandeur and sublimity.

Rising majestically as they did in the middle of the plain to which we have alluded, they appeared to defend the vast *enceinte* they enclosed, both from indiscreet eyes and from the vegetation that stopped at their foot, satisfied with bestowing upon the region a contribution of fresh water which welled from out their flanks and went gurgling, in the shape of many rills, to seek the lower ground.

Having for some time contemplated these gigantic cliffs, we pursued the track which led up to an entrance on the north-north-west and conducted us by a narrow gully between their perpendicular sides. From an analysis we made, we came to the conclusion that the Pungo N'Dongo rocks are exclusively formed of a hard and tough conglomerate, wherein figures clayey schist, mixed with gneiss, porphyry, a little mica and a species of basalt, although as regards the latter we speak with a certain reserve, owing to the doubt existing in our minds.

Lying precisely under latitude 9° 40′, they crop up again eastward under the name of Guingas, some twenty-five miles distant; and further on still, where they bear the name of the Quitoche stones, near the point where the River Lombe disembogues into the Cuanza.

The first idea suggested to the mind of him who ascends any of these rocks (for they are almost all accessible to a good climber), and who, observing their arrangement, tries to explain by the existence, throughout the conglomerate, of flints perfectly entire, the indubitable action of water, is, that formerly the bed of the river Cuanza flowed over these stones, and that a volcanic convulsion, by upheaving them, drove the course of the river some miles to the southward. What tended more especially to confirm this opinion in our minds, was the discovery, in a rock near the slope of one of the peaks, of the impressions of human feet mixed with those of a quadruped, probably a dog, of which we took a sketch to make the matter clearer. In one of these imprints we recognized perfectly, by the more decided marks of the toes, that the person, in walking over damp and pasty ground, had slipped in planting his foot and thereby caused an unnaturally long impression. There were other smaller ones, apparently those of a woman or youth, all quite distinct, and concerning which no doubt whatsoever could exist.

"What a pity," we exclaimed, "that we cannot convey this rock to Europe! What a mine would it not be to our men of science!"

Within the shelter of these singular rocks, and in the vacant spaces left between them, the town has been erected, exhibiting the most tortuous conceivable streets, due to the capricious position of the huge stones. Orange and other fruit-trees spring from every fissure; and the inhabitants among other peculiarities have to put up with a shorter day than people living beyond the influence of the rocks, as, in consequence of their great height, the sun rises later and sets much earlier than elsewhere. Cold and limpid water, accumulated during the rains in the cavities of the rock, flows in little runnels through the place; we heard it asserted that it was a fruitful source of scurvy, but we do not guarantee the truth of the assertion nor do we lend it any credence.

In one of the narrow streets, we found near an enclosure an enormous baobab, around which clings many a tradition; as in former times, beneath its spreading branches were held the councils of the court of the Jinga, at the period when her celebrated queen had her residence there.

On the western side some ruins were pointed out to us as marking the former habitation of the Portuguese Minister, José de Seabra da Silva, whom the chances of political life, in the time of Sebastião José de Carvalho e

Mello, drove from his high-backed morocco chair to the mats and *mabellas* of an African couch!

We made the ascent of one of the peaks, wandered all over the town, dined with a party of friends, where, for the first time, we heard of our late companion, Serpa Pinto's arrival safe and sound in the beginning of the year at Durban, and having decided upon dissipating in our native country, the ill-founded prejudice entertained by our compatriots respecting the Pedras Negras (to whom we recommend Pungo N'Dongo as one of the healthiest places in the province), we took measures, without loss of time, to pursue our labours, by making a survey of the Cuanza.

On the 27th of August, leaving among the rocks and stones the idleness of many days, we turned our backs upon our late encampment and steered a course south by south-east, bound for Port Hunga. Our marches, however, were no longer the straightforward, business-like affairs of former times. Regular food, *aguardente*, and numerous caravans on their way to the coast, distracted the men's attention and made them averse to anything like hard work. The *Calunga*, the "great-water," was in their thoughts, and they not only voted the Cuanza a bore, but feigned to consider it a very poor specimen of a river.

Master José, who had begun to be alarmed at our insatiable and inconvenient curiosity, pretended to hold everything of light account, convinced in his own mind that if he showed us, say one cataract, we should at once want to see two. He therefore frequently tried to throw us off any scent, by interminable talk, stopping constantly on the road " to point a moral or adorn a tale."

At four in the afternoon we reached Port Hunga, and were received at a charming country house, surrounded by an orange plantation, whose golden fruit shone temptingly in the warm sun.

Having received a visit from the old Sova who, owing as he stated, to a powerful fetish, had been suddenly struck blind; we passed the following day in the depths of a thick grove, talking and ruminating on a variety of subjects.

Our task would soon be at an end. We were day by day drawing nearer to the civilized world, and the circumstance, agreeable as it undoubtedly was on many accounts, did not nevertheless fill us with entire satisfaction. In spite of the sadness which belonged to our old mode of life—notwithstanding its perils and its sufferings, its anxieties and its labours, it had somehow taken a hold on our affections. There was a charm about its primitive character, its entire freedom, its utter absence of conventionality. The simple hut, the murmurings of the wood, the voices of our men engaged upon their various vocations in the camp—all these things, as they trooped through our minds, left an impression of regret when coupled with the thought that we should see and hear them no more!

Man cannot live for many months together in any place or form without becoming, to a certain extent, accustomed to it, and without feeling a certain pang when his connexion therewith is severed. What he has to suffer in the interior of the vast continent of Africa may at times appal him, as our record will have shown, and yet, perhaps not one beheld his return without a sigh as he contemplated the vast gulf that lay between a life replete with action and novelty, and the monotonous routine of existence hanging about the *macadam* of Europe.

We had learned, however, sufficient philosophy to endure with a shrug what we could not remedy, so pulling down the branch of an orange-tree which was just within our reach, we plucked some of its tempting fruit and quenched our sentimental feelings in its delicious juice; then turning to our old friend Silverio who, lying on his back, and immersed in those deep considerations which always suggest the idea of the circle that has its centre everywhere and its circumference nowhere, and which we call the infinite, we challenged him to a game known as the "Chinese," and that consists in guessing whether the sections of the fruit about to be opened are odd or even. As he always lost he got no orange, as he was too lazy to rouse up to pick one for himself.

It was on the 29th of the month, at about eleven o'clock, that the expedition reached a point just below the great rapids of Mutula, near the residence of the Sova N'Gola Quituche; and still continuing along the bank of the Cuanza, we fell in with another blind ruler, who gave precisely the same reason for his affliction as the previous unfortunate, viz., that a fetish first deprived him of one eye, and then another did the same cruel office by the remaining optic! As it appeared that only the Sovas suffered from blindness in this part of the world, the old French saying, *Dans le pays des aveugles les borgnes sont rois*, came into our minds and made us paraphrase it into, "In the country of eyes, the blind are kings."

Resuming our course at a right angle, for the river, barred by the rocks, ran here directly southwards, we sat down to a quiet contemplation of the rapids,

"In that oblivion of mundane things,
Which ... soon was banish'd by the insects' stings."

Unfortunately for us it was so. The place was infested with the young of those small flies we have once before alluded to as making honey like the bees,

THE CABALLO CASCADE.

and which, on smelling us out, swooped down in their thousands, eager for the attack. It would appear that they had a strong preference for white flesh (perhaps on account of its being less odoriferous and more juicy), and on their arrival they settled so thickly upon Silverio and ourselves that they covered us completely. We swept them off by dozens at a time, but these were replaced by hundreds, so that acknowledging our weakness before the enemy we took to flight.

We tramped along in tolerable disorder after our defeat, for the space of an hour, when we reached the senzala Candumbo and found the direct path leading from Pungo N'dongo to Malange. To the east, in a broad curve, we observed the river suddenly widen, and then form one of the most remarkable cascades we had met with in the course of our journey. It bears the name of Caballo, and has a very formidable aspect. Parallel lines of rocks, equi-distant from each other, and each line at a lower level than the one above, constitute a gigantic staircase, occupying the whole breadth of the stream; the water tumbling successively from one step to the other, and forming so many small cascades, which, at a distance, look like one vast sheet of foam. Above the falls there are two islands covered with trees, and called by the natives *qui-colo* (Quiangolo) and *qui-colo* (Caquilla).

We encamped right in front of them, after clearing away the dense and lofty grasses, partly beaten down by the hippopotami, which at night-time invade the low-lying banks; and after completing a sketch of the cascade, we proceeded to record in the diary the following particulars.

The river Cuanza, as far as we have surveyed it, does not lose the character of a valueless watercourse, full of obstacles, and difficult to cross from one bank to the other. Between Port Hunga and the point where we are now sojourning there are no fewer than six cascades

TELPHUSA ANCHIETAE, RIVER CUANZA.
(*Phot. from nature.*)

and rapids; and hence upwards there are many more, and of a more important character.

TELPHUSA BAYONIANNA, RIVER CUANZA.
(*Phot. from nature.*)

From an average breadth of forty-four yards, it widens out westward along the foot of a high mountain range called Quiambella, which borders it on the south.

On quitting the plateaux of the Songo, those monotonous and immense savannas, the river runs almost perpendicu-

EUPREPES IVENSI (NEW SPECIES), RIVER CUANZA.
(*Phot. from nature.*)

larly to the broken ground, and by a succession of leaps, as it were, makes its way to the sea. Mount Catenha, and

CHROMIS SPARRAMANNI (SMITH), RIVER CUANZA.
(*Phot. from nature.*)

on the north-north-west the Quitoeta, are the two great barriers which curb the waters of the plateau, and drive them into the Lucalla and Cuanza, the two large channels by which the drainage is performed. It is extremely rich in fish, crustaceans, and reptiles, whereof we exhibit a few specimens obtained higher up the stream; among them figuring the *Muntalandonga, Euprepes Ivensi* (a new species) which, though found in the Luando, is likewise an inhabitant of the Cuanza. We procured also specimens of a frog, of two or three crabs, whereof there are many, of some reptiles, and of fish of various kinds that make their home in the river, as may be seen by the engravings in this chapter, photographed after we returned to Europe from the specimens we had preserved in spirit.

Enormous *bagres* are taken out of the Cuanza and the marginal lakes, and after being dried or smoked they are despatched to the Songo and other districts, and constitute a not unimportant native trade. We heard mention when on the spot of the celebrated mermaid (*Manatus senegalensis*) having been seen beyond the rapids. We never, however, ourselves set eyes on one at any point whatsoever; the natives showed us what they called a skin of one of these creatures, and told us stories about them, but little worthy of credit.

Hippopotami may be heard blowing all along the banks of the river, and numerous crocodiles may be seen warming themselves in the sun, on the little sandy islands, and disappearing at the slightest unusual noise.

Both the ornithological and entomological fauna would offer a wide field for study, which a naturalist fresh to the work might turn to good account, but which we, in our position, found it impossible to pursue. And so it is in many other branches. The explorer at the outset is feverishly impatient to see everything, to note down everything—rushes from geography to meteorology, and thence to the natural sciences—is in a constant flutter of excitement, and bewildered with his theodolite, his scalpel, his presses for plants, and his paper for maps and plans. Then comes the more sober stage. He first throws over the insects, then the birds, gives plants the go-by, and as he nears the end of the journey sticks to geography alone.

For a couple of days we still continued our course by the river, halting on the 31st of August at 11.30 a.m. at Quibinda, where we encamped in order to perform our necessary labours. About seven miles from that point up stream there is a cascade called Quitaxe, and eight miles higher up still the river falls in the shape of an important cataract, the Condo, well known to our merchants who are accustomed to make pleasure-parties from Malange to visit the grand spectacle.

We here deem it opportune to insert a digression, suggested by our last remark about the little trips of our countrymen residing at Malange, with a view to put public opinion right upon a point about which there appears to be considerable uncertainty. We mean the discovery of the cataracts of the Cuanza, which is attributed to every foreign explorer who falls in with them. Dr. Livingstone, for instance, on crossing from the Upper Zambese to the Dondo fancied that he discovered there, as by enchantment, the Cabulo cataract, situated almost within a stone's throw of Cambambe, but which had been familiar to us from time immemorial; and quite recently another traveller who reached the Condo, announced to Europe that he presented it with a novelty *till then unknown!*

Now a simple inspection of the map of Angola, bearing the name of the Marquis de Sá da Bandeira, will suffice to show the mistakes which the best of geographers may sometimes commit, where they pin their faith to the

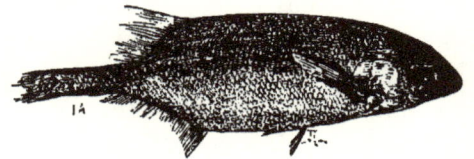

DEMBE (MORMYRUS LHUYSI, STEIND), RIVER CUANZA.
(*Phot. from nature.*)

ordinarily available maps; but the last assertion we allude to is so gross that it requires no comment.

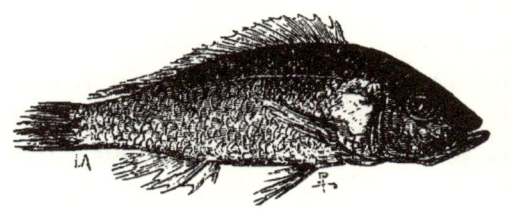

MUACA (HEMICHROMIS ANGOLENSIS, STEIND), RIVER CUANZA.
(*Phot. from nature.*)

Having thus had our say, we will leave the cataracts of the Cuanza, *which we did not discover*, and pursue our journey.

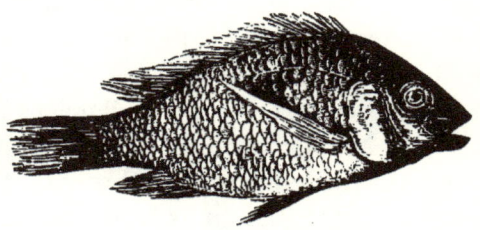

CHROMIS MOSSAMBICUS (PETERS), RIVER CUANZA.
(*Phot. from nature.*)

With the first blush of morn of the 1st day of September we were astir, almost as early as the birds, and set out in a north-north-east direction by the track running to Malange in order to connect our surveys with those made near the same spot before we started for the north.

It will be comprehended that such a connexion was highly important, inasmuch as now, after a lapse of some months, we were about to return to a point where the chronometer would determine a longitude, and therefore on making a second observation we should obtain the *mean* of our marches with the utmost exactness, and the bearings of the entire region in respect of

HIGHLY ORNAMENTAL FROG, RIVER CUANZA.
(*Phot. from nature.*)

Malange, which would in turn be corrected when we reached the coast. We must add, to the honour of Mr. Dent of London, that his chronometer (one of the best we ever met with) reached that spot with a variation of only 2.5 miles! A circumstance upon which we lay some stress, and consider of very great advantage, was the constant attention we paid to our marches, because from time to time, halting for two, three, and four days, at elevations on the first and last, we were enabled to record those marches to a nicety. To tell the truth, we never discovered any differences, and the chronometer, which on entering Benguella showed 4ˢ 30ᵗ, indicated after perfect acclimatization 7ˢ 30ᵗ, and so continued till we reached the coast.

It will be readily estimated how invaluable such an instrument must be in the interior, more especially if we bear in mind that the largest stream of water surveyed by us—the Cuango—ran due north and south, and that a great part of its projection was made with the chronometer, inasmuch as the plane-table or theodolite could not possibly be carried with us for 700 miles through forests and savannas, over mountains, and across streams.

The general process adopted by us for the tracing of the maps always had for a basis the constant determination of the geographical co-ordinates, for the greatest possible number of stations, and then by successive *tours d'horizon* we succeeded, by means of crossings, in embracing a zone of road of twenty, thirty, and even more miles. Availing ourselves of the three great resources of navigation—latitude, longitude, and azimuth—we employed them always as a primary element of all our labours, and we completed them afterwards either by the theodolite or by the plane-table in the narrower and more important regions.

The chronometer, therefore, was one of the most useful instruments, and on that account we used every care for its preservation; and we hold it to be absolutely necessary in the interior where it can be combined with the satellites of Jupiter for great arcs of longitude. Unfortunate, however, would be the explorer who should attempt to determine positions consecutively by the satellites of that planet! In a very short time errors on one side or the other would be sure to create confusion that could with difficulty be escaped, and could only be avoided by putting the watch on one side.

One chronometer, at least, is an indispensable adjunct, and the explorer who goes to Africa without one, will soon find it simply impossible to do his work, or he must restrict himself to small portions of ground, of which he can make precise maps, with correct sections and level curves, things after all of little benefit to African geography in the present day.

Passing the rest of the day on the Lombe at Caballo, receiving visits, making presents, and listening to long-winded stories, we closed the diary without recording in it anything of note, and slept such a sleep as had rarely been granted us—full nine hours off the reel.

On the 2nd of September we were near Malange at the Lombe do Motta, having half resolved to make a trip to Cacol-Calombo to see some grottoes, but an attack of fever upset the plan, and on the following day we started for Pungo N'Dongo by the Calundo track, anxious to bring our journey to an end, inasmuch as our people were much reduced in strength and showed less and less inclination to obey orders.

Many caravans crossed us on the road, and were the means of still further retarding our progress, but finally, on the 8th of the month, we once more arrived in camp, having terminated our journey without any incident of moment.

RIVER CUANZA CRAB.

CHAPTER X.

Return to camp—The *pulex penetrans* and a noteworthy *entozoario*—Variableness of the winds at Pungo N'Dongo—The explorer's staff and the writer's pen—We take leave of Silverio—Cabeto and Cuanza flies—Native lightning-conductors—Capanda and the western vegetation—Brief notice of its ornithology—Sengue and Nhangue-ia-Pepe—Cataracts of the Cuanza—The Sova Dumba—Cassoque—Von Mechow—The Bango and climatological variations—The Cuanza and the Cabulo cataract—Last glance at the interior—The Dondo—Reception of the explorers at that place—A trip on the river—Loanda—Mossamedes—The voyage home.

On our return to Pungo N'Dongo we again took up our quarters in our former camp in order to give the caravan the few days' rest required before pursuing our survey of the river and then marching in the direction of the coast.

Among the most important districts of the interior, we had already visited Malange, Duque de Bragança, Ambaca, and Pungo N'Dongo; we had yet, therefore, to see Cazengo, Golungo, Icollo or Zenza, and Dondo. As, however, the last mentioned was upon the bank of the river, we decided to proceed to it at once, and subsequently visit the others if our strength or circumstances should allow.

We therefore spent some days in perfect repose; feeding, talking, some strolling about, others paying visits; a few trying to avoid the clutches of Satan by placing themselves, through the medium of baptism, under the safeguard of Holy Mother Church (this was more especially the case among the girls); and finally many in seeking to cure maladies from which they were still suffering, or that had appeared with a change in their mode of existence.

Since our departure from Duque de Bragança we had been attacked by a new scourge, and a pertinacious, villanous one it was, unknown to us in the interior, and which we suppose afflicted us now so that we might conclude, with a perfect *connaissance de cause*, the history of those miseries which the climate, ants, flies and mosquitoes had so brilliantly begun.

This was the infernal Brazilian flea (*Pulex penetrans*), wherewith the whole of this part of the country is thickly peopled, and which, penetrating into any wounds or sores, particularly about the toes or fingers, produce an inflammation that has to be very promptly attended to (more especially where a negro is concerned) if it be desired to avoid the loss of a limb!

Cases of amputated legs are common among the blacks, who have allowed themselves to become a prey to these vile insects, and with whom at last, any treatment short of amputation is impossible, through the affected part being literally swarmed with the vermin.

When attacked about the feet—the toes are usually first affected—the poor fellows would go hobbling about the *quilombo*, a misery to themselves and a danger to all about them, so that we were forced to look sharply after the sufferers in order to effect a speedy cure, ere they became disabled altogether.

Another disgusting insect (a sort of *entozoario*) likewise made its appearance at this time, and was no less pernicious than the former although somewhat more rare. Burrowing into the muscles of the legs (as in the instance we witnessed) it there deposits its eggs, whence issue short, round maggots, for all the world like those observed in certain fruit, and which, in obedience to their instincts, commit the most frightful ravages. Multiplying with extraordinary facility, as is always the case with the lowest forms of the animal kingdom, it may readily be supposed that in a longer or shorter space of time the limb so attacked would, if no remedy were used to check the evil, be in the very gravest peril.

We do not remember any instances of quadrupeds suffering from this last-mentioned insect; but the flea attacks pigs and dogs very severely; our own faithful hound being one of the sufferers and requiring constant care and attention on account of the deplorable state to which her paws were reduced by the visitation. It seems that goats are the only small quadrupeds that are free from these disgusting vermin, all our informants agreeing in the assurance that there was no instance of one of these animals being attacked.

The temperature during the last few days had sensibly risen, more especially during the frequent intervals of calm that are prevalent in Pungo N'Dongo. The cliffs are situated in a zone where the winds are liable to constant variation. The regularity of the breezes of the interior, blowing from the south-east or north-west, according to the period of the year, is unknown here, and it is too distant from the coast to be influenced by the sea-breezes. The wind, therefore, constantly shifting from south-east to south-west, and at times to north-west, causes in the interim besides the calm, an insufferable heat, that is enough to knock over any one exposed to its action.

On the afternoon of the 13th of September we were seated at the entrance of our little *tembé*, with Master

José on our right, busy with his needle, the lads in front, engaged in arranging their respective packs, and on our left Capulca, in the act of giving the last culinary touches to a roast leg of mutton, the scent from which we were sniffing preparatory to making its nearer acquaintance. One more step, as it were, and we should be at the ocean, our element, whereon as boys we had spent some of our happiest hours. A few more miles and this helmet and these gaiters would cease to have a *raison d'être*. The long staff, which was seldom out of our hands, would have to be thrown aside for the insignificantly small steel pen; we should have to exchange for the prattle of José a lot of scribbling on our own account whereby to transmit to the public the impressions of our journey; and at the thought we both turned pale!

It had never been our ambition to lay before the reading world our sayings or our doings; if we had ever pondered on the subject at all, it appeared to us a task above our strength to put our remarks into an intelligible shape, fit for the perusal of men of science—and we feared that our attempts to do so must fail. Even now we feel very great diffidence as to whether what we offer will be acceptable in their sight, but we have plunged in too deeply to recede, and we must accept the fiat of our critics, whatever it may be.

To the bustle of evening succeeded the calm ease of night, which in turn gave place to the renewed activity of morning. To the west of Pedras Negras the track runs directly towards the sea, taking Capanda by the way. But as we deemed it of moment to connect our present surveys with those already made on the Cuanza, we decided upon travelling anew to the southward, that we might reach the river.

It was on the 14th of September, at daybreak, with

all preparations made that we bade adieu to our good friend and companion Captain Silverio, to whom the familiar intercourse of several months had strongly attached us.

"Farewell," he said, in a faltering tone; "Europe is waiting for you, and will know how to recompense your sufferings and appreciate your services. You have richly earned your rest, and may you enjoy it to the full. As to me, I am an old fellow, and can never hope to see you again; the only rest that I am likely to find is in the grave, to which I am hastening."

Dear, kind old man! Please God, your gloomy presentiments will not be speedily verified, but in the company of your wife and child you too will find a graceful repose, most truly deserved after your laborious life!

According to José's assurance we were not likely to be much harassed on the road. We might study and survey the river at our ease, and yet, under his guidance, reach Dondo by the 23rd or 24th of September.

Encouraged by the promise, we moved off in single file to the left of the stones, passing an hour at Caughi, a sort of fortified villa, the property of an old gentleman, who possessed considerable influence in the neighbourhood. We found it abandoned, owing to dissensions among his sons, and pretty well reduced to a mass of ruins.

Following the track that continued to wind through gloomy forests, we camped at noon on the bank of the Cuanza opposite a place called Cabeto, and near a little waterfall. But we had scarcely sat down when we were besieged in due form; and we say it advisedly, never did we suffer so much from the attacks of our old enemies, the flies, before. It was impossible to rest, to write, to do anything in fact but use strong language!

Strong *measures* were not a bit of use, and although with a towel round our head and another in our hand, we sacrificed myriads to our fury, myriads more filled up the gaps and renewed the fight with increased energy. Smoke had no sort of effect upon the wretches, and it was only with the appearance of night that the combat subsided, and we could get a few hours of absolutely necessary rest.

We would not give the creatures a chance to re-commence hostilities next morning, for we abandoned the field before they were up, and pursued our way, remarking how the mountains drew away from the river, while the stream, widening at this point, gave to view a portion of its course, and then soon after became involved among the rocks and shoals of a most broken and irregular bed.

Sanza Manda stood upon our path, where enormous crumbling barges indicated the spot at which in former times the gangs of slaves brought from beyond the river were received, to be subsequently transhipped according to instructions.

We here noticed for the first time stuck into the roofs of the huts branches of the *n'dui*, known to science by the name of *Decamera tonantis*, and that the natives place there to serve as lightning conductors. It is not impossible that the wood, which is very hard and a good conductor, might be of service if properly arranged; but stuck up as we saw it, often in the shape of a fork, unpointed and ineffectually connected with the cupola of the building, it required a large amount of faith to attach any importance to the contrivance. We fancy, indeed, that it derived its value in the eyes of the natives much more from fetishism than from science, and that like the bottles thrust into the thatch, which attracted our notice on former occasions, it was used for the purpose of scaring away evil influences.

Returning to Capanda, as we observed that it was almost impracticable to continue further along the bank of the river in that direction, we crossed that splendid chain of granite mountains, among which it is averred there exist trachytes or volcanic rocks that would, if visible, be of the utmost interest to geologists.

The land then gradually subsided, vegetation became less dense, grass more abundant, and from the midst of it sprang samples of the baobab (that reminded one of giant bottles of champagne), exotic palms, and colossal *Eriodendron*, with a straight trunk, partly covered by the branches of the *n'burututo* (*Cochlospermum angolensis*) displaying their yellow flowers, *Erithrinas* with red berries, and other plants, peopled with birds, some of which had adorned the branches with rows of pendent nests, whereof one bough, as we counted, had no fewer than forty-seven!

Among the feathered tribe most worthy of mention figures the *n'gunguachito*, a sort of toucan, known as the *Bucorax caffer* (Boc.), or the wood-turkey, more bulky than its compeer in Europe, with a long beak, crimson feathers on the fore part of the neck, and a long tail. The more lofty trees were full of these birds, each perching, or flying with its mate, like the turtle-doves. They are difficult to shoot, owing to the height at which they perch and their having a sentinel always on the look-out, who gives a warning *cô cô*, at the first glimpse of danger, as a signal for them to clear out.

There is another bird, a very interesting one, somewhat similar to the European cuckoo, called the *Scopus umbretta* (Gmelin) and nick-named the kidnapper. We were informed that it never made a nest for itself, but when it required one, priced about till it found a residence to its mind, which was then and there appropriated.

Finally, we met with the *Buphaga erythrorrhyncha* (Stanley) or *Tanagra erythrorrhyncha*, which feeds on the vermin engendered on the hide of cows and oxen, where it may be seen busily engaged, and subsequently abstracting for the service rendered the hair it requires for the formation of its nest.

Many other birds known by the names of *bigodes*, *freiras*, and *viuvas* (moustaches, nuns, and widows) are seen flying in abundance, and the catching and conveying them to the coast for sale constitute an important trade.

The number of caravans we saw upon our track, both coming and going, was very remarkable. Scarcely an hour ever intervened without our meeting with, or being passed by, dozens of negroes well laden. Oil seemed to be the staple article they carried; but there was a good deal of india-rubber, some ivory, and a lot of *ginguba* done up in sacks.

The long marches made by some of these negroes in the interior, more especially by those engaged in the post-office service, are really worthy of note. With a gun over the shoulder, and a *mu-canda* on a stick, they bowl along at a swinging pace, and cover their forty miles a day. A porter, a sort of *empacaceiro*, assured us that he had gone on one special occasion from Pungo N'Dongo to Loanda, in the space of *three days*, and had returned to his point of departure within the same time!

While we are on the subject of *empacaceiros*, we beg to present to our readers the portrait of one from Quissama, and add a few words by way of dissipating the strange idea that has been formed of these men in the old country. People there have conceived the notion, and some have set it down in writing, that the *empacaceiros* constituted in former days a sort of secret association, organized to put an end to cannibalism. We could learn nothing at Angola, in answer to our inquiries, that corroborated this in any way. As to themselves they have no conception of such a thing. From the outset they

EMPACACEIRO OF QUISSAMA.

appear to have been hunters of the *m'pacaça* or buffalo, whence they derive their name, and from their bold habits of life were of powerful assistance in all journeys into the interior. On this account they were employed in the post-office service, and as guides to caravans, until, little by little, a quantity of them became enrolled by the Portuguese Government into a corps, employed in the services above alluded to.

Of late years they have become dispersed, and curious to relate it is in the Quissama, where cannibalism is far from unknown at the present day, that *empacaceiros* are still to be found. The long lazzarina gun shows by the skin rings which adorn its barrel the number of animals it has laid low. Wrapped in a wretched cloth, they carry about them all articles that are required in the wood, and ornament their heads either with a bunch of feathers or two or three horns, which give them a devil-may-care appearance. And in this guise, or merely armed with an assagai, the *empacaceiro* will wander alone through forests and savannas, feeding on roots, sleeping in the trees, doing battle with beasts of prey, and not unfrequently a prisoner for days together on the summit of some tall baobab, where he has sought a refuge from inundations or the incursions of buffaloes.

Among the caravans to which we have alluded was one composed of Ban-gala men, at the hands of whose connexions we had experienced that peculiar reception alluded to in the first volume when we attempted to cross the Cuango, and of whom, in consequence, we had retained so vivid a recollection.

Being encamped near us, we took the opportunity of renewing our acquaintance, for we found them as quiet as lambs under present circumstances and that they had, or pretended to have, no knowledge of what had occurred on that occasion. They had come, they said, from the Lubuco or Luba territory, about which we made sundry inquiries. We were disappointed, however, in getting anything out of them. They were either mute as fishes or dealt only in monosyllables. What we particularly wanted to learn was information respecting the great lake of Quifanjimbo, whether it had any canoes and whether the tribes that resided on its borders were dwarfs. To all our inquiries they answered *yes*, although we made a sketch of one so as to make our meaning more intelligible. Like most negroes, however, they had no comprehension whatever of drawing, and as to perspective, it was of course an unknown art. They were so little able to recognize a figure when put before them in black and white, that they turned the paper about in every direction, and seemed to understand it just as well upside down as in any other position. Where a mere bust was concerned they did not seem to recognize that it belonged to a human figure at all, and we had not paper enough to make a cartoon of life-size, to see whether that would have been more intelligible to their understanding.

This circumstance convinced us of the impossibility of untutored men seizing an idea for which their minds had not been previously prepared. And yet they themselves executed a few rude works of art that must of necessity have required a certain study and reflection. They carved on their weapons and on many of their instruments figures of animals and of men, and in the latter case marked with precision the characteristics of the black race; so that one was at a loss to comprehend how it was that they could make a doll to serve as a fetish and yet could not recognize a delineation of that same doll executed by more skilful hands and approximating much nearer to the human form.

These caravans, when upon the march, offer to the eyes of the curious traveller an infinity of strange articles that are well worthy his attention, and more especially those referable to personal adornment. All negroes, with very few exceptions, are fond of ornament, and the head receives a great deal of attention at their hands. The Ban-gala push this mania to an excess. The long tresses of their hair are intertwined with beads, shells, and bands or plates of metal, and are otherwise converted into structures that occupy entire weeks in their fabrication. On the other hand, when once done, they remain untouched for months, being merely anointed in the interval with abundance of palm oil!

Feathers and skins are indispensable articles of their attire, although the material they use to set off their charms appears to be matter of little moment. Stones, shells, brass and iron equally serve their turn, and copper wire, or a human tooth is alike turned to account. The rage for adornment does not spare their flesh. Some pierce their ears, others the membrane of the nose; while another will drive a red-hot iron through the cartilage in order to introduce a piece of carved wood into the orifice, which seems to produce no other effect than to interfere with natural cleanliness and make the breathing difficult. Tattooing or branding the body is also coming into use amongst them, the process being borrowed from the Luba and even further to the north-east, where the practice appears to be common.

At the close of our interview with these people, from whom we had derived so little satisfactory information, they retired to a neighbouring thicket, where they had established their *quilombo*, and spent the remainder of the evening and great part of the night round their fires smoking their eternal pipes. As to eating, that was an operation we did not see one of them perform.

It is remarkable how these men can, during journeys of such duration, bear up against the fatigue of long marches, under heavy loads, with little or no food! They will go dozens of leagues with the utmost indifference, with a manioc root in their girdle, and sometimes not even that, getting a drink here, a smoke there, and occasionally a handful of flour. It is difficult to exaggerate the miserable existence of many of the natives on these perilous journeys, where, in case of illness or accident, they are liable to be abandoned to their fate. In the very caravan to which we have alluded there was a sad confirmation of this remark. Two brothers had started with it together for the Luba; but one of them, suffering from ulcers and dysentery, was compelled to give up the journey, so the brother and his companions divided his load among them, and left the unfortunate on the road-side, either to perish or be made a slave by the first party who fell in with him.

On the 15th we halted at the Sengue, where the Cuanza has two cascades, Quissaquina Caboco and *mupa* Palanca, in the midst of arid land, whose very aspect made one hot; on the 16th we were at Muta, and next day arrived after many a stiff climb over rocky hills at Nhangue-ia-Pêpe, where we camped near a senzala surrounded by masses of euphorbias, intending on the 18th to visit the cataract in the neighbourhood.

On our way thither we found a perfect forest of mahogany trees, and the appearance of the falls, when we reached them, struck us as very fine. The narrow defile through which the Cuanza rushes, widens at that spot, as if to allow the escape of the river, which may be there about a hundred feet across. The water, falling to a depth of twenty-five to thirty feet, dashes wildly over the stones that intercept its passage, in a westerly direction, though the stream is shortly turned aside by the projecting foot of a mount, from which escaping it enters a gorge formed by the Serra Cassasio in the district of the N'hongos. We contemplated the cataract from the precipitous bank on the right of the river, which was so lofty that it was with difficulty we could distinguish a man engaged in fishing on the brink.

It is scarcely necessary to add, after the foregoing description, that the river is not navigable, and that from this spot to the Dondo it could not be under any circumstances on account of the formidable obstacles presented by its bed.

Having taken the bearings and made the other necessary surveys, we returned to our camp, more dead than alive from fever. The state of bodily weakness to which we were both reduced was becoming grave. During the last few days we could eat little or nothing, and as a general rule, fever intervened almost immediately after our principal meal at three o'clock, which prevented the food remaining on the stomach. The consequence was, we became weaker and weaker, and it was evident that the moment had arrived to terminate an undertaking that our strength would no longer enable us to carry on.

Pursuing our journey, we met with a most serious obstacle between the stations of Pungo N'Dongo and Dondo, and which will, as we fancy, give the engineers of the railroad it is proposed to construct no end of trouble. It takes the shape of certain lofty serras standing at right angles to the track and completely barring it from north to south. Even the black *engineer* (if we may so call him), who is wonderfully acute in avoiding difficulties in the formation of his paths, had no alternative here but to cross the mountains in a direct line, so as to gain the western side.

On reaching Danje-ia-Menha, we again camped, for we were suffering so badly from fever that we could go no further. But this was not the worst of our complaints. Our scorbutic sores had increased to such a pitch that it was perfect torture to walk at all. Our gums, which were highly inflamed and spongy, bled freely at intervals ; a painful feeling of utter fatigue had taken possession of us, and our legs would scarce support our bodies though they were many pounds lighter than when in a state of health. Nor could we conceal from ourselves that our mental faculties were weakening with the weakness of the body, so that the calculation of the simplest latitude caused us hours of depression. It was, in fact, the advent of anæmia with that infinity of symptoms nowadays more or less known, and which are the reverse of pleasant to experience.

Having devoted the remainder of the day to treating our complicated maladies, we lay down to rest, though we rose again with Phœbus on the 20th September, and with the aid of our staves hobbled forth once more upon the road.

We had just crossed one or two little rivulets and left behind us a group of huts called Cassoque, when we sighted, coming towards us, a numerous caravan, which we judged from such loads as sealed cases, new trunks, and articles of a similar character, to be headed by an European. The vanguard, on being questioned, confirmed our suspicion, and in a few minutes, on turning a corner, we came in sight of a couple of white men, one of whom appeared to be the chief.

He was a man of medium stature, strongly built, of a florid complexion, with a fair beard, wearing a light coat and a broad-brimmed hat.

His manner was so frank that, although we suspected he might be one of those proud and taciturn sons of Great Britain, we ventured to break the silence as we met, and therefore saluted him with the customary " good morning."

From his reply we soon discovered that our language was not very familiar to him; still, by dint of patience and pauses in between we managed to comprehend each other.

We then learned that it was Von Mechow, the German explorer, coming from Loanda and proceeding to Malange, where he intended organizing a caravan, and, by the aid of a boat he had with him, descending the Cuango to its embouchure in the Zaire, and making a complete survey of the river. The conveyance of his baggage and boat had given the illustrious traveller no little trouble owing to the want of capable carriers and men who were willing to render him any assistance. His own determination had, however, carried him through, and in the best possible spirits he was disposed to seek Fortune's favours.

Having in few words narrated to him some of the difficulties we had encountered, and which Von Mechow did not appear to appreciate to their full extent, and referred to the Jinga, its inhabitants, our sufferings in the interior from fever, thirst, and what not, we gave each other a hearty shake by the hand and parted—he, fresh for the fray; we retiring, full of wounds, but not entirely defeated, from the field.

We next camped at Bungo and had another night of fever. We found our elevation to be 915 feet, so that we should very shortly reach the sea-level.

How great was the difference in the temperature, in the pressure, and in the air we breathed! The fresh south-easter of the high table-land, which made the vault of heaven clear as a bell, seemed to cut us through. Now, there was a heavy, murky atmosphere announcing the proximity of the ocean, by the accumulation of vapour which the sea-breeze gathered along the extensive territory of the littoral.

Night fell, the mountains that surrounded us, and that had passed through a variety of tints with declining day, now wore another aspect beneath a moon in her first quarter. We were ill at ease; compelled to abstain almost entirely from food owing to the state of the stomach

THE TIPOIA OF ANGOLA.

and mouth, whilst the fever was rampant in us. It was the last time that, wrapped in our leopards' skins, we slept after the manner of the woods and wilds; for we were on the threshold of civilization.

With the dawn of day we resumed our journey, but this time we were compelled to have recourse to the *tipoia*. Our track hugged the southern slope of the serra Lucna, and ran over very broken ground, interrupted by ravines; small streams ran murmuring through them on their tortuous way to the Cuanza, which in a mountainous region tumbles near Cambambe in the shape of the Cabulo cataract, the last obstacle it meets with in its long and boisterous course ere reaching the ocean.

Resting for some minutes under the shade of one of the baobabs, we cast a glance back upon those eastern lands we were now leaving, and then once more took to the road.

On quitting the wood we observed with some emotion first one, then two, and subsequently many telegraphic poles, the symbols of progress, whereby we were again to be brought within the pale of civilization.

Passing the *Pambos*, a point where many roads meet, and where a considerable number of natives were met together in a permanent *quitanda* or fair, we sighted, at half-past eleven, the silver line of the Cuanza, which meandered through the extensive plateau and glistened in the sun. It was the same river we had met with so near its place of birth, at that time, narrow, comparatively sluggish, with sandy banks, and which, gradually absorbing a host of minor streams as it ran on, now appeared before us, so broad and so majestic.

Through the openings of the broken ground we caught sight of the dull old town of Dondo, set in a thicket of palms and cocoa-trees, and then we knew our mission was at an end.

Finally, at mid-day, on the slope of a hill, we came to a halt to receive and salute the European gentleman who had there come out to meet us. It was Duarte Silva, an officer of the Portuguese army, one of the distinguished and indefatigable members of the important commission sent by the Government to Africa, to carry out certain special public works, who had perceived us from his villa, and hastened to bid us welcome.

The news of our arrival soon spread, and many other friends and acquaintances were shortly about us, eager with congratulations, invitations, and offers of service, and with whom we subsequently passed many agreeable hours.

Within a day or two of our settling down, the commercial corporation of Dondo gave us a banquet, where we had the pleasure to be presented to each individual member of that body, who with great courtesy and kindness showered us with favours and praise.

We would fain, ere our return, have abandoned the course of the Cuanza, and travelled northwards to the valley of the Bengo, continuing our route subsequently by land to the capital of the province. But, by the advice of our friend, we gave up the project, seeing that the state of our health was not such as to make it prudent to attempt any fresh adventures—and determined to make the best of our way to the sea.[1]

---

[1] During our voyage we made all the observations in our power respecting the river.

The basin of the Cuanza is an immense plain of loose and muddy soil, formed by the action of the waters, of extreme fertility, whose power of producing sugar-cane, owing to that cause and to the amount of disposable labour, would be almost unlimitable if the difficulty of the pestilent climate could only be got over.

The whole of the region is intersected by watercourses, and abounds with lakes, which, from their position, do not allow any effective drainage, and therefore help to form permanent marshes.

The traveller therefore who traverses the river's banks, finds that after the efforts of years but one plantation, at the spot known as Bom Jesus, and a couple of dozen paltry senzalas, where the natives are constantly struggling against the influence of the climate, have survived the ordeal.

The Cuanza is so important a highway into the interior that it ought under no circumstances to be disregarded, as we are under the

Embarked. 227

On the 11th of October, therefore, we embarked on board the steamer *Silva Americano*, on the route to Cunga, and we take this opportunity of thanking her commander, Antonio de Sousa, for the consideration and kindness he showed us on the voyage.

From Cunga, a larger steamer conveyed us to Loanda,[2] at which port we arrived on the 13th of October, 1879, and where we met, at the hands of H.E. Counsellor Vasco Guedes de Carvalho e Menezes, the then Governor-General, the most friendly reception and the most delicate attentions.

---

impression that with very modest resources and by means of a careful survey of its waters, it might at all seasons be made perfectly navigable by steamers of the draught and tonnage of the *Silva Americano*.

At four or five points it is at the present time more or less impeded; but if these places can be got over by the natives by floating their canoes through side channels, it is clear that the work of drainage must be of the simplest kind, since a man with a shovel is capable alone of removing in great part the obstacles presented.

The bar ought certainly to be made the subject of a speedy and special survey, for should it be much longer delayed, the difficulty that may now be surmounted, may become in future all but impossible to vanquish.

[2] The city of St. Paul da Assumpção de Loanda, built on the northern slope of the high land which terminates at the sea by Mount St. Miguel, is composed of one high and another lower portion, bearing respectively the names of *upper and lower town*.

The native quarters are at the back of the city, as for instance the Sanga-n'dombe and N'gombota, and there are numerous farms which are styled *musseques*.

The internal population does not exceed 9000 souls, divided into 3500 male adults and 3000 women; of children there are 1200 males and 1300 females.

The European population represents at most 1100, whereof two-thirds are convicts.

The *musseques* contain 2000 inhabitants, and the suburbs and island 2350; so that the gross population amounts to some 13,350, all told.

Our journey, therefore, from the capital until our return to the coast, had lasted exactly 729 days!

At Loanda we were received, with the whole of our caravan, in the house of Sr. Manuel Raphael Gorjão, Inspector-General of the public works of Angola, of whose noble hospitality we cannot say too much. To the efforts and activity of that gentleman are due all the improvements that the province at this time enjoys, improvements which reveal the broad intelligence of that able official, who, estimating with a just sense the necessities of the country, has succeeded, by dint of hard labour, in securing to the province, within the short space of three years, an extensive telegraphic line, an ample establishment admirably mounted, a hospital, meteorological stations, and a technical school; has definitely surveyed a line of railway over a space of 156 miles, and opened into the interior a considerable number of roads, among which we may mention that of Cacuaco, another from Dondo to Caculo, a surprising piece of engineering, and another again to Biballa.

Many pleasant days were passed in his residence, marked by a genial conviviality that we shall not readily forget.

A banquet was also given to us by the Trade Association of Loanda, at which H.E. the Governor and the entire commercial body were present, and where we were flattered by further commendations of our toils and fatigues.

We must not forget in the enumeration of persons from whom we received untiring attention, our excellent friends, José Bernardino, the then Secretary-General Joaquim Salles Ferreira, Francisco Salles Ferreira, Guilherme Gomes Coelho, Miguel Tobin, the worthy representative of the Banco Ultramarino, José Maria do

Prado, J. Newton, Dr. Oliveira, Dr. Lopes, Miranda Henriques, Urbano de Castro, and many others.

Having decided upon making a trip to Mossamedes, where a more genial climate would assist us in the task of arranging our notes and re-establishing our health, we started with the least possible delay on board the steamer *Zaire*, commanded by Pedro de Almeida Tito, who received us with the same kindness as heretofore.

On the very eve of our departure, we were delighted at the appearance of our old friend Avelino Fernandes, with whom Stanley, Serpa Pinto, and ourselves, passed such a pleasant time prior to setting out upon our journey. He was a charming young fellow, full of life, intelligence, and high spirits, and greatly inclined to works of exploration. He had been, it appears, most active on our behalf, and learning that we were beset with difficulties in the interior, he had actually formed a plan of starting to our assistance, and was only deterred on more favourable news coming to hand. He had that moment arrived from Vivi, where he had been with Stanley, admiring the herculean work undertaken by that man of iron temperament, and had started off at once to see us on hearing of our return.

We spent a couple of months at Mossamedes in company of the intelligent band of young men who were at that time fulfilling important offices in connexion with the public works, and from whom we received so many proofs of friendship that it would be impossible to find words wherewith to thank them.

We now began to breathe more freely. The splendid climate of Mossamedes, the succulent food, prepared in the European fashion, soon restored our exhausted frame, which regular and moderate work considerably assisted.

It was now time, we thought, to turn our steps homewards, and towards the end of January, having taken our last farewells, we repaired on board the steamer *Benguella*, under the command of our esteemed friend, Captain José Roberto Franco.

We have thus laid before our readers the particulars of the two years' campaign in Africa we had the honour to direct, and we trust they will pardon our boldness in having done so under the exaggerated form of two volumes in octavo. We ought perhaps here, properly, to bring our long story to a close, but loth to part company with those whose indulgence has led them thus far, we venture to add a few more words in the shape of a conclusion.

THE VOYAGE HOME.

CONCLUSION.

We deem it advisable, by way of conclusion to the present work, to exhibit in the shape of a summary the most important particulars of our surveys and experience, believing that they will be more useful in that form to persons whom they interest than if found scattered through the volumes. As, however, the limits imposed to the work and a just apprehension of becoming tedious will not permit of too great prolixity, we will touch as lightly upon the chief topics as a clear intelligence of facts will allow.

Beginning with the subject of geology we may remark that the physical configuration of the African continent, and more especially of the portion south of the equator, is nowadays too well known to require minute description. It may be summed up in these few words: a depressed central basin surrounded by a vast circle of high land, gradually descending to the sea, and rent by deep ravines, through which rush huge watercourses, engendered in the interior, till they overflow and seek the lower level fronting the ocean.

From a very general geological point of view we may define the regions running from the littoral to the interior in the following order, viz., lime-stone, sand-stone, and granite. But on going more minutely into the subject, we shall find that these distinctions are not very exact; inasmuch as the component parts frequently run into each other and change places, while precise lines of demarcation are wanting.

The geological formation on the western coast at the points observed by us between Loanda and Mossamedes, and even further to the north, exhibits generally near the sea a belt of tertiary deposits, with abundant masses of sulphate of lime and sand-stone, from which they are separated by beds of white chalk alternating with primary rocks, for the most part gneiss, abounding in quartz, mica, hornblende, granite, and granulated porphyry.

Towards the south, large tracts of feldspar become visible.

At Mossamedes, whole mountains are composed of sulphate of lime; while carbonate of lime, accumulated in shells, is very frequent. Both rock salt and nitrate of potash are found in stratification.

Along the Mocambe chain, we were informed, there exists a basaltic line of great length. From that point the shifting soil may be said to commence, extremely abundant in sand, constituting true *saharas*, as in the parallel of Tiger Bay.

In the transition from the lower zone towards the interior, for instance at Dondo, vast tracts of schist rock, in perfect laminæ, compose the soil; and sand-stone, reddened by oxyde of iron, is visible in every direction. Proceeding further into the interior we find, in a perfectly mountainous region, the ground to be composed of granite-quartzy rock, extremely hard and compact; this is the case throughout the belt crossed on the way and up to Pungo N'Dongo, the surface soil being formed by the disintegration of the granite itself.

These geological characteristics will naturally be repeated to the south and north in identical parallel regions, with variations in the high table-land, where we meet occasionally with hard and tough red sandtone, and rocks of feldspar, as in the basin of the Lucalla.

Our information respecting mines is of a varied character. In the earlier portion of our work we made reference to them in connexion with the Dombe. Southwards, at Mossamedes, we found carbonate and sulphate of copper in small quantity in the layers of chalk, to which they impart a green colour. We have reason to believe from what was told us that asphalt also exists there, and that coal is obtainable in the Dondo, and at Oeiras in the north ; still, as some kind of bitumen might have been mistaken for the genuine article, we will not guarantee the correctness of the assertion.

Little can be said on the score of the precious metals. Mica appears in the interior to have deluded many into the belief that they possessed the secret of a silver-mine. Thus, for instance, the natives referred to one existing on the left bank of the Lucalla, near the Banza Dalango, which people from Malange had endeavoured to visit. In the Jinga silver appears to be abundant. It has been stated also that indications of this metal have been observed near Cambambe ; but to none of these reports could we apply the test of proof.

We can, however, say with absolute certainty that iron and copper are to be found all over the continent; the first of good quality, and the latter not inferior to the American. This the natives make use of, and speak of the mines at Catanga and Garanganja in high terms of praise.

The three zones or belts to which we are now referring, are very unequally provided with trees, and may be classified as follows : the mangrove, the baobab, and the acacia; the last belonging to the interior, is generally considered the most salubrious, and where it grows the marshy influence is less sensibly felt, and the European consequently beneath its shade finds greater security.

Almost all travellers speak with favour of the superiority of the mountainous zone. The great watercourses which furrow it, flowing rapidly from their spring-heads to precipitate themselves into the region below, do not anywhere stagnate or spread over the neighbouring lands, so that, except in rare instances, marshes are unknown. In this vast tract of country the ground rises to a considerable height, under parallel 11°, and thence gradually descends either to the north or south. It is a true rib which crosses the continent from east to west, and constitutes the divisional line of the waters of the two great rivers, the Zambese, and the Congo-Zaire; and it is in our opinion the most fitting place of residence for Europeans south of the equator, that is to say between it and the tropic; which is proved not only by the distribution of plants but by the people who inhabit it.

A fact worthy of special note on this subject is, that whether we regard them from a physical or intellectual point of view, the tribes appear distributed in a gradually descending scale north, south, and west, towards the coast. If, for instance, we take the Ganguellas and the Ma-quioco as the starting-point for this simile, we shall find that the peoples as they approximate to the sea, such as the Ba-cuisso and Ba-cuando, are relatively inferior to those of the higher regions. If, on the other hand, we travel northwards, we shall observe in the Jinga, the Ma-hungo and the Ma-yacca the same sensible difference. And an identical rule holds good if we turn our steps southwards, inasmuch as the Hottentots and Betjuans are held to be the very lowest types of the negro race.

It does not appear to us easy to find an explanation of this phenomenon. The altitude and nature of the soil have, of course, much to do with it, but we fancy that the special influence lies in their distance from the commercial centres, which compels them to become travellers. The tribes that at the present day occupy the countries of the great continent we traversed, appear for the most part to have derived their origin from remote quarters and different sources, the types becoming accentuated, later on, through purely local circumstances.

If, for the time being, we set aside the peoples of the sea-coast, we shall observe in the men of the interior, Bihéno, Ganguella, Quioco, &c., certain general features which may be roughly delineated as follows: a well-developed frame, prominent bones, powerful muscles, more especially in the upper part of the body, a pronounced curvature of the vertebral column, immediately above the pelvis, dolichocephalus skull, flat at the sides, forehead arched, teeth oblique, more in the upper jaw, the colour of the skin varying from black to dark bronze.

In the north the type appeared to us to differ considerably from that above defined, generally of a jet black colour, the natives of those regions and the Jingas more especially have not the same physical development as the eastern tribes; they are more slender, and there is a less pronounced obtrusion of the upper jaw, bringing the facial angle nearer to 75°.

With little activity and love of investigation, the Jingas, through having lived near the sea, and finding great part of their necessities supplied without labour, appear to have acquired a nature in harmony with their position, and show no inclination for long journeys or large operations.

Bearing in mind the foregoing circumstances and the fact of the people in the south-east, principally, referring in their legends to a migration from the north, we are compelled to admit that at remote periods Central Africa was the field of a great evolution, wherein the countries under review were invaded. As, however (to repeat what we have before hinted), on the arrival of the Cassange tribes, the Jingas were established on the littoral, it must at once be inferred that the latter (Muco-N'gola or Mona-N'gola) invaded Angola, establishing the seat of their government at Loanda,[1] long before the time that the Tembos dreamed of directing their steps thither.

To this fact must be added another very remarkable one. The Jingas assert that they subjugated the Congo when they settled down in the country. If this be the case a kingdom of the Congo must have been already in existence.[2]

[1] Loanda or Lu-anda signifies no doubt "a lower part," this designation having been adopted because at the outset the Court of Angola (N'gola) was at Quiassamba on the sandy island which lies opposite the higher land where, at the present day, exists the city of St. Paulo.

Its long shape might perhaps have given rise to the name of *Dongo* (a native boat), which the monarchs of N'gola subsequently retained for the district wherein they almost always reside.

In Pedras Negras this term is met with as designating the royal dwellings, and at the present time in the Jinga the site occupied by the king is still the district of the Dongo.

[2] Bastian informs us that "prior to the formation of the kingdom of the Congo the banks of the Zaire were peopled by independent tribes of the *Ba-t'cheno* (?) or *Ma-t'cheno* (?) conquered and united by a chief named *Nimia Luco-em* (?) the first king of that country, who erected the *Banza*-ia-Congo" (Ambassi), but this is an incorrect designation, as is properly observed by the estimable secretary of the Geographical Society, and eminent publicist Sr. Luciano Cordeiro, in his "*Hydrography of Africa*," as it comes from *M'baje-ia-mucanu*.

Conclusion.

We thus obtain three distinct invasions, which may be styled that of the Congos, that of the Bondos (comprising all those who speak the *Bunda* language), issuing probably from the Yacca or more to the eastward, and that of the Tembos, comprising the Ban-gala, Ma-quioco, Ma-songo, perhaps the bin-bundo, drawn from the region of the lakes, designated " Nano," on the coast. We may assign as the date of this last invasion the 16th century; the others being of an earlier period.

The Bondos being established as we have described, it is natural that from their position on the ocean, where they were engaged in fishing, they should have extended further down the coast, in the direction of Benguella and Mossamedes, with a view to enlarging the area of their piscatory excursions.

But among the tribes that are now collected there, fresh variations appear, which plunge the observer into serious difficulties. The Ba-cuisso, Ba-cuando and

---

Are the *Ma-t'cheno* then the aborigines of that part? That is the question.

The word *Luco-em* is likewise a strange one; when analyzed we find the first part almost always bestowed upon special individuals, such as in the Lunda, the celebrated woman of whom we have made mention as *Luco-quessa*, and the Maskers of the woods, *Luco-iche* which we have written *Muquiche* and others.

A constant comparison of these peculiar terms is extremely advisable, in order if possible to obtain the thread which can guide us through our labyrinth.

In the case above alluded to *Luco-em* must have been the first who was entitled *Muene Congo*, which, through corruption, became at a later period, *Mani-Congo*.

And if *Congo* in the language of Angola signifies debtor or tributary, and *iche* or *xi* expresses property, we shall obtain a confirmation of the fact that the *congos* were tributaries of Angola, and therefore even at the present day the monarch of the last-mentioned territory is designated *Muen-iche* or owner of the land.

Ba-ximba, have a perfectly different aspect, approximating in character to that of the Hottentot. The trapezoidal conformation of face, the prominence of the zygomatic brow, and the angularity of form, all point to the influence of the southern people on the inhabitants of this territory, so as to induce the belief that they are a mixture of Bondos and the southern tribes.

To sum up, therefore, we shall have, for the numerous tribes now coming under the denomination (not a very correct one) of negroes, between Senegal and the south, the following divisions,—

In the north the tribes of the Ogowai basin, the Ba-congo, of whose settlement we can say but little, and who probably are connected with the peoples belonging to the basin of the Niger.

Then come the Ban-bondo who occupy the kingdom of Angola, and who have migrated from the north-north-east, possibly from the Upper Zaire, where, at the present day, we meet with the Ma-yacca, Ma-cundi, &c.[3]

[3] It does not appear to us that the Ma-yacca were totally unknown in Europe.

In the *Annual Report* of the Jesuits (Guinea) of 1602-1605, we read, "The invaders who, during the first half of the sixteenth century infested the territory of the west, styled themselves *Yaccas* in the Congo, *Jingas* in Angola, *Gallas* in Ethiopia, and *Sumbas* in Guinea."

We must, therefore, infer from this that there was already a notion of the inhabitants of Yacca, and consequently our idea of supposing them to be the ancestors of the *Bondos* or *Bundas*, that is to say from their using the *Bunda*, *Qui-n'bunda* or *Lu-n'bunda* language, a designation whereby we must after all distinguish the whole of the dialects of the territory of Angola and in a certain way connecting them with the Accas, has some show of reason on its side. By attentively following the studies of Schweinfurt (a veritable master upon such subjects) we have been induced to assimilate the Ban-bondo to the Niam-niam, in physical conformation and disposition, colour, &c, so that we have become all but convinced of the relationship existing between these peoples, otherwise so distinct.

These again are followed by the tribes of the Ma-quioco, Ban-gala, Ma-songo, and perhaps the Ganguella, whom we will comprise under the name of Ba-lunda, since they themselves claim such origin (known, as we have mentioned, as Ba-nano), and who reside in the countries we have already indicated.

Finally, on the south-south-west, and part of the sea-coast, all those tribes whom we include under the designation of N'hembas, Ban-cumbi, Ban-ximba, Ba-cuisso, Ba-cuando, &c.[4]

The foregoing is our opinion upon the subject, which has no pretension to be a profound study of the ethnological connexion of the tribes of Central and West Africa; it is a theory submitted with all due deference, and which can be set aside or modified by those who bring more knowledge and experience to bear upon the subject than we can lay claim to.

Having thus described the tribes of this part of Africa in a general and cursory review, we will now enter a little more into detail, so as to bring them as closely as possible within the knowledge of our readers. And to begin, we will remark that the life of the African is simple and primitive, and his social condition very gross.

Of a thousand senzalas, or thereabouts, we visited, we found almost the same identical features in the con-

---

[4] The Ba-nhaneca and the Ban-cumbi occupy approximately the region comprised between the river Cunene and the slopes of the plateau to the west.

On the south they are bounded by the Ban-ximba; on the east by the Ban-cutuba (N'hembas people) on the west by the Ba-cuisso (nomads) and the Ba-cubale; and on the north by the whole of the tribes which we indicate by the name of Ba-nano.

Catuba appears to refer to the special arrangement of the waist-cloths pendent from the girdle.

struction of the dwellings: the same mode of roofing, covering, and arranging them. Either stakes or canes driven firmly into the ground, the interstices filled in with grass or clay—sometimes both—a thatched roof, with two or three inner divisions, presenting, as a whole, some a conical shape, others a regular square pyramid, and others again a long ellipsis.

The house is, for the most part, the property of one only. The chief almost always relegates the huts of all the inhabitants of the village to a station behind his own dwelling, and surrounds the whole with a palisade, or occasionally leaves it completely open. Within a short distance, the villagers have their fields and plantations, whence they derive their daily bread, and frequently about the palisade such plants as bananas, stramonium, and others, are encouraged to grow.

Their laws and the organization of their states always present a difficult problem, upon which we shall only lightly touch.

Emigration, conflicts, and instability of living being constant, social order varies according to circumstances; the connexions of to-day are altered to-morrow, the chief of yesterday yields to the conqueror of to-day, so that we fancied we frequently discovered in one and the same people different organic principles.

As to the rest, the elements of their legislation (if we may use such a term) do not appear to have been based on the organic principle of the family, or if they were we believe that they were not adapted, properly speaking, to an isolated family but to a group of many. It was not the Patriarch who, laying down rules for his children, created the first element of law, but the chief who, taking measures for defence, or conquering in turn, established certain precedents which he imposed

Conclusion. 241

upon those he deemed his vassals. For this reason, in the states of West Africa, the will of the chief rules supreme, he being the principal creator of the law which is, in consequence, as variable as that will.

It will be inferred from this that personal liberty is purely problematical in that part of the world; none is less free than the savage whose daily life is regulated by the strangest dispositions and privileges which the chief dictates and imposes, but never allows to be called in question. Absolute and supreme law dwells in the ruler or chief of his village; and to him therefore belongs the judicial and administrative power which he alters at his good pleasure, listening at most to the opinion of certain of his principal vassals (macotas), who generally seek to learn the tendencies of the monarch in order to support them. And thus, the settlement of all disputes concerning the division of land (the source of the primitive legislation of Europe for the security of property) appertains to him only, so that jurisprudence is reduced to this—the chief's word and passive obedience.

Social order and the observance of determined precepts depend so much upon the will of the chief, that disorganization almost inevitably ensues at his death. Directly a district loses its head, the people, left to themselves, at once step over the barriers by which they were confined. Confusion, controversy, and tumult, are the result of such a position, which the consciousness of unexpected liberty increases even more. The strong oppress the weak, commit extortions, attack property, pilfer right and left, till complete anarchy ensues—a state of things which many do their best to prolong; and it is only through the predominance of some strong will—some bolder and more ambitious spirit among them—that they are prevailed once again to assume a semblance of order.

We never met with one single law touching upon political prerogatives, or the most elementary notion of an assembly; not even the elective right (put in force on the occasion of a ruler's death) is perfectly regulated, but is subject to circumstances such as we have described when speaking of the Ban-gala, among whom at the present time a *Jagga* cannot be elected because one of the pretenders to the dignity has abstracted the case containing the insignia of command.

Certain rules and usages are observed, it is true, but what is a remarkable fact, instead of respecting the private interest of each individual, or the common good, they turn, for the most part, upon matters of pure ceremonial, and to follies of this kind the officials devote themselves with an amount of seriousness that it is difficult to conceive. Salutations, the formalities attending receptions, visits to the chief, and such puerilities, appear exclusively to occupy their minds, and for the regulations of which special rules are drawn up and adopted. On the other hand, the inheritance of a son, the right to bequeath property, the possession of a wife, are matters that are left to govern themselves, and remain, of course, at the mercy of the purest accident.

Even their relations with strangers are dictated by circumstances, and it is only in extraordinary cases that one can suspect that such a thing as a law exists (and what a law it is when discovered!). For instance: should a white man come into a place, take food and not pay for it, or pay what is deemed too little, the first passer-by, however innocent, will have to pay for him!

As the customs among Africans[5] are regulated by precedent (to which time gives all its force), it is natural to suppose that some rudiments of law must have been

---

[5] We, of course, refer to those with whom we had dealings.

engendered, but it is an unquestionable fact that the progress of the natives has been simply nil, influenced doubtless by the imperfect or unknown organization of the family.

With respect to religious matters we have, on a former occasion, viz., in Chapter IV., of the first volume, made mention of what we deemed to be the views of the savages on the great continent, restricted to fetishes involving terror, and false or no notions concerning the Divinity. We will therefore merely add the following:—

Not considering fetishism as a form of religion, and in the absence of such worship as is bestowed upon material substances, we persist in maintaining that the negro possesses none. It must not, however, be assumed that we dispute the existence of religion among the African natives, merely from the simple fact of our not assimilating that which we saw there to what we ourselves know upon the subject; but because not a single evidence or act hinted to us in any manner whatsoever a tendency that way.

If, however, to constitute a theogony it is sufficient to have the simplest sentiment of fear (thus implicating in a certain indirect way the consciousness that man entertains of something superior to himself), then we believe all humanity has a religion. This, however, is not the fact, as Sir John Lubbock very justly observes, for " we cannot admit as proof of the existence of religion the fear of a child in the dark," to which we will add, or the terror of a man who, in the obscurity of night approaches the graves of his fellows.

By the acquisition of a fetish, the negro supposes that he possesses a resource, but to which he attaches no particular notion, and from which, at most, he derives the satisfaction of possessing an object having a preservative influence against some unforeseen evil. The said object, in fact, does not imply the idea of any connexion with a superior Being, whose good graces the fetish might have the power to attain, but a mere material means, invested with formula more or less magical, to counterbalance actions in struggling with which he might, if unaided, prove impotent. It is concentrated magic, the complete reverse of religion.

And not only does religion not exist, but we have arrived at the conviction that the sentiments which its influence awakens and fortifies, are extremely rare. For is not religion—apart from the fact of putting man in relation with the Divinity—the true moral law, the cardinal point whereby conscience begins to steer its course along the tracks of good and of evil, a perfect scale whereon are marked the sentiments, as they grow in the just measure of man's progress therein?

Be this as it may, we feel perfectly satisfied that those idyllic tales of certain travellers who conceived natives possessed of refined sentiments, and who have put on record how a *mu-rotze* or young girl refused in marriage a man whom she did not love, had no foundation out of their own lively, creative fancy.

Let us consider for a moment whether the negress does or can love in the lofty sense of that word. If she loved—if she had the consciousness of that sublime sentiment which opens to us on earth the gates of heaven—she would manifest it in her actions, and by its aid attain to some belief, some religious faith, inasmuch as her very felicity would help her to comprehend that there must be something better and purer above this material mundane life. But who is capable of inspiring her with such a feeling in the brutalized state of slavery in which she lives? Her husband! Most certainly not. He simply encircles her with an iron girdle of obligations and despicable labour, compels her to live in the dirt, like his dog, and toil and travail for his pleasure: she, on her part, dares not touch or even look at him without permission; she may not eat at the same table, far less from the same dish as he, and must not accept liquor from his hand. In a word, the wretched wife is compelled to absent herself from the conjugal roof at determinate periods of each month; and at the sublimest moments of her existence, that is to say, when she is about to become a mother, she must remove far away, and give birth to her offspring as remote as possible from the man out of whom some of these self-same travellers have tried to make a tender and feeling husband after the fashion of Europe. Triply bound down, therefore, as she is, to materialism, how is it to be supposed that she can soar to the transcendental regions of ideality?

On these and other grounds, therefore, we retain our conviction, that every attempt to attribute to the negro a notion concerning the Creator, modelled after the manner of our own conceptions on the subject, is illusory; for the negro has no such notion. The very puppets he makes, wherein many persons pretend to discover an idol which, modified and developed, might signify the idea of the Supreme, never go beyond fetishes—things not to be confounded with the idol—inasmuch as the idol is adored, it personifies, so to speak, a principle, and has—if we may venture to say so—a direct action which is implored; whilst the fetish, on the contrary, possesses nothing of the sort, or at least must be considered perfectly passive.

Many authors, nevertheless, maintain that it is so, and among them our illustrious compatriot, Sr. A. F. Nogueira, who in his fine work entitled *A raça negra*, "The Negro Race," observes that the Ba-nhaneca and Ban-cumbi designate by the name of Huco or Suco, according to the dialects, an invisible God, who sees, hears, and knows, what they think and say.

With all respect for the authoritative opinion of that gentleman, we venture to submit that such an idea is due simply to the contact of civilization, and which, to a certain extent, he demonstrates in the following period:

" They yield to him no worship or adoration whatsoever, but . . . . ."

If we admit with Sir John Lubbock that fetishism allows of no temples or idols—and in our humble opinion no worship either—let us examine the first step taken on the road to religion and we shall see in totemism the commencement of adoration, which shamanism developes by ecstasies, and idolatry completes by a worship. Henceforth, all religious progresses up to the superior formulas have those manifestations inherent in them. How is it possible then that the Ban-cumbi, who have so transcendent an idea of the Supreme Being, to all appearance, indeed, absolutely formulated on our own, should omit to worship him, when they have attained to so high a degree of perfectibility touching the idea of the supernatural? For a very simple reason; that such an idea does not belong to them, but has been plagiarized and ingrafted on an ill-prepared stock, and is consequently worthless. They have heard speak of something which they had a difficulty in comprehending, and gave to it a name, just as they have bestowed upon the sea the title of *calunga* or *lunga*, (long) of whose length they had no notion, and precisely as the Ma-quioco had their *N'gana N'zambi*,[6] of which they knew just as little.

[6] It must always be borne in mind that *N'zambi* or *N'zamba* in Lun'-bundo signifies an elephant, and therefore the object of such a designation would appear to be to impart an idea of greatness, a quality im-

The negro is very far removed from this superior state, and it will be a difficult task to detach him from the brutal superstitions which generally torment him and any circumstance aggravates—such as night, for example, when the imagination, more accessible to terrors, magnifies the ideas of the day. As to the creation and prayers he is a total stranger, even the principle of good and evil requires among many tribes attentive study ere we can definitely establish it. Nor should the assertion excite surprise, inasmuch as an acquaintance therewith involves the notions of justice and injustice, and therefore of conscience.

With respect to the latter we agree, if not entirely, at least very nearly, with Captain Burton who, speaking of East Africa, says,—

"Conscience does not exist .... and repentance expresses regret for missed opportunities of mortal crime. Robbery constitutes an honourable man: murder—the more atrocious the midnight crime the better—makes the hero."

On the West Coast this is far from being strictly true, nor do we wish to insinuate that the African has a decided propensity for crime, as we have mentioned in the early pages of this volume, but after committing it he does not feel what we call repentance because, as it would appear, he is ignorant of the iniquity of his act.

The moral sentiment among the natives is at present in embryo, which may be gathered from the facility whereby crime is commuted by a money payment. Among almost all the tribes with which we came into contact, the assassin who had property might condone his

pressed upon them, and which they have expressed by the term appropriated to that animal, the largest that they knew.

crime by indemnifying the family of his victim with a certain sum, and would thenceforth be free to repeat the offence.

Another circumstance which proves the unconsciousness of evil-doing, is the unconcern wherewith a native in obedience to orders will commit a wicked act. Thus we have seen a negro, when commanded by his chief, perpetrate one, two, or three murders (as for instance the *Muene Cutapa* in the Lunda) with the utmost indifference and without any evidence of remorse. It is a mere question of education.

We shall not feel surprised if these lines should fall like a bombshell upon the conviction of many notable thinkers upon this subject. We grieve as we set down the fact, but although we respect the opinions of others, we think it only right, and in accordance with our duty, to give the results of our own observation, which, after all, many may perhaps repute to be false. And we deem it advisable again to mention, that our remarks refer to the peoples of the interior who are far removed from European contact, such as the Ma-coco, Ma-yacca, and Ma-hungo; and not to the tribes on the littoral, whence, we fancy, travellers have taken back to Europe particulars of not too veracious a character.

Turning now to the question of language we must admit at the very outset that it is so vague and obscure that we hardly know how to tackle it. Both the ethnology and language of Africa constitute studies, that are, so to speak, unknown, and the pronouncing any opinion upon them entails the risk of setting out with a blunder. Confining ourselves, therefore, to a rough sketch, and in order to give our readers a just idea of the alarm which an incursion into such a dominion may reasonably inspire, we append a list of a few of the tongues spoken on the great continent to the south of the Equator, beginning to the north of the Zaire.

We there find the Ashantee, Dahomey, Joruba, Benga, Ueta, Onfué, Onglo, Fanti, Insubu, Dualla, Diquelé, Nupé, Ibo, Efique, Maxi, Evé, Otji, Acra, Baza, Cru, Crebo, Vei, Susu, and Mandé of the Ma-n'dinga, Timné, &c., &c.

In the Gaboon territory, there are the M'pongué and the Ocandé, together with the Fiote to the south in the Luango and Cacongo.

On the banks of the Zaire we come upon the Lu-congo, and in the south the Lu-n'bundo or Qui-n'bundo, the Luherero, the Qui-cobale, Lu-camba, Lun-cumbi, Lunhaneca, and the Lun-gambué, spoken on the banks of the Cunene, Ovampo, &c. Then on the west coast, downwards, we have the Nama and Cora (Hottentot dialects), the language of the Bosjemans, which towards the east becomes transformed into the Oεu, Tonga, Zulu, Tebele, Batosleta, Sechuana, with their dialects the Serolong, Sesuto, and Sechlapi, which further on give place to the Tequezo and Kaffir between Zululand and the Zambese, and finally, the Ma-cua and the idioms of Tete and Senna.

North of the Nyassa appear the well-known Qui-suahéli, Qui-niamezi, Qui-nica, together with the Qui-camba, Qui-iao, Qui-cuio, and many others.

This startling list shows how hard a nut the subject is to crack; and we, with our limited knowledge, know not too well how to go about it. Nevertheless, we venture to put forward a few considerations.

The circumstance which most tends to engender the variableness of a language is no doubt that of its not being a written tongue. The least modulation or change in tone may effect great modifications of words, and as a consequence favour their corruption. An alteration in the habits of a tribe will suffice, in our opinion, to introduce a change. A migration from a flat to a mountainous country, for instance, would induce individuals who, up to that time, through living in the valley, took no note of distance and had no occasion to raise the voice, to lengthen the sound of certain syllables, singing their phrases, so to speak, in order to be heard from one height to another, without the labour of drawing nearer. Again, the dwelling near great watercourses, cataracts, &c., would produce similar results, so that a language that abounded in certain regions, in soft and flowing terminations might, in another, end in hard finals. This is the case with the languages of equatorial Africa; and hence we believe we have the origin of that infinity of dialects spoken by the southern tribes.

According to the able opinion of R. Hartmann there exists incontestably an intimate connexion among all the African tongues. Under shelter of the dictum of that illustrious philologist, we likewise are free to declare that with respect to those that are known to ourselves, a similar relation exists, and that the Lu-lundo, Lun-n'bundo, Lun-cumbi, Lu-nhaneca, Tebele, and Kaffir, represent dialects of one and the same mother-tongue, as may readily be ascertained by an examination of their vocabularies. A simple examination of the numerals among the different peoples of Southern Africa will suffice to confirm this assertion, and if the reader will only compare the lists of words we append to this work with those supplied by Serpa Pinto and Cameron, he will admit the truth of the remark.

If, for example, we take the particulars furnished by the latter traveller we shall see that the Rua[1] dialect,

---

[1] Styled *Qui*-rua, the syllable *qui* prefixed to the name of the district referring to the language there spoken.

although at first sight very different, expresses the figure 4 by the term *tuána;* this, the Ban-cumbi make *cuána;* the Bin-bundo *uána;* the Ban-bondo *bicuána;* the figure 5, styled by the first, *tutano,* becomes respectively *táno* and *bitáno.* The numeral 10 exhibits an extraordinary similitude, the Qui-rua calling it *di-cumi,* the Lun-cumbi designating it *ecumi,* the Quin-bundo *li-cumi,* and the Lun-bundo *cumi.*

This rapid analysis will suffice to make good the truth of our assertion, which a comparison of the terms will render more evident.

The African languages are generally poor, imperfect, complicated by most varied signs, which of themselves complete a phrase through the non-existence of correlative ideas. Thus it happens that a speaker not to the manner born, finds a want of many generic terms; for *trees* he discovers no other word than *woods*, and has no equivalent whatsoever whereby to express certain qualities. We have given one example of this in the present volume, where the interpreter, halting upon a corresponding word for *loyal,* substituted *fat !* Words representing abstract ideas are rare, and are generalized by means of the infinitives, to have, to see, to run, &c. Where *sex* is concerned they add to the designation the word man or woman; thus a cock and a hen in Quin-bundo are respectively expressed by *ossanja-olume* and *ossanja-occai,* meaning a man-fowl and a woman-fowl. From this peculiarity sprang those long-winded speeches which tried our patience so severely, and the unconscionable delay in replying to the simplest question.

One curious fact is worth noticing, namely that the savages show little or no tendency to contradiction. We do not say that among themselves, on their own ground, they do not contradict each other, but they never displayed such inclination towards ourselves. With us, it was *yes* to everything, and it at last became so annoying that we restricted as much as possible our inquiries; for it must be allowed that it is a little trying after building up a fabric with an hour's careful labour to find the whole edifice toppled over through your informants answering affirmatively to questions of an exactly opposite character to those whereby the building was in the first instance constructed. We suppose that as the inquiries in no way interested them they got bored, and answered by that monosyllable, unless it were done out of a desire to please or to mislead us.

All ideas respecting time, distance, number, and quantity, are very confused in their minds, and occasionally they take a form very puzzling to a European. For instance, we once asked,—

"How long will it take to go from here to the point where the Cuango enters the Zaire?"

And the question, after an extensive preamble, brought this reply,—

"You will have to wear out two pairs of sandals?"

The same confusion was observable in many of our transactions. On one occasion we purchased an ox for fifty-four yards of cloth, and wanted to pay for it in pieces of stuff in this way,—

1 entire	18 yards.
1 broken	15 ,,
1 broken	16 ,,
An additional 5 yards . .	5 ,,
Total	54 yards.

This arrangement, however, would not suit them at all; they insisted that the whole lot should consist of cuttings of nine yards each (half-pieces) the sum therefore made up as follows,—

```
Complete   .  .  9+9
Broken  .  .  .  9+6+3
Broken  .  .  .  9+7+2
                 ─────────
                 27+22+5=54
```

We have already pointed out that in the dialects that were known to us, the singular and plural were formed by proper prefixes, that for the human race they were put before the name of the territory, viz., *mu* or *mun* in the singular; *ba*, *bin* or *ban* in the plural; and for inanimate objects, *qui* or *t'chi* in the singular, and *ma* or *man* in the plural.

The prefix *t'chi* may also be used; and it forms its plural in *bi*, if applied to appellatives, thus, we should say,—

leaf, *t'chi-sapa*—leaves, *bi-sapa*.
white-man, *t'chin-delle*—white-men *bin-delle*.

In the Lunda language many appellatives form their singular in *mu* and their plural in *a*, as for instance,—

woman, *mu-caje*—women, *a-caje*;

and even in the Lu-lunda we find the respective formations of *e* and *mu*; for example,—

friend, *e-camba*—friends, *mu-camba*.

There are many substantives among the Lu-nano dialects which have another form of plural, for instance,—

wolf, *n'bungo*—wolves, *djin-bungo*.
crocodile, *n'gando*—crocodiles, *djin-gando*.
pig, *n'gulo*—pigs, *djin-gulo*.
bee, *n'hique*—bees, *dji-n'hique*.

Then there is the particle *no*, forming the radical of people, with *ba* as designative; *lu* expresses tongue, and *tu* meat.

The prefix *ca*, frequently met with, appears to be used in the sense of diminishing or making lower; and therefore the Ban-gala, wishing to cast a slur on us, said in lieu of *Muene-puto*, *Ca-puto;* and the Muata-Yanvo, when speaking of a Lunda tribe he has subjected, will style them *Ca-lunda*.

We cannot within the limits of this work dilate at greater length upon the subject of language, the study of which, as yet exceedingly backward, requires very persistent labour; the hints we have thrown out may, however, be of some service to those who have resolved to make a plunge into the difficult labyrinth.

Having thus given a rapid sketch of the African tribes, of their distribution over the territory we visited, of their laws, religious belief or unbelief, and finally of their idioms, we will now add a few words concerning their nutriment.

It may be absolutely affirmed that the staple of their food or the base of it in the countries referred to, is represented by the four following articles, which vary according to the different regions: viz, Manioc (*Manihot aipi*), better known as *Jatropha manihot;* Massambala, varieties of the *Sorghum;* Massango, scientifically called *Penisetum typhoideum* (now belonging to the genus *Penicillaria*) whereof there exist two varieties, the smooth and the barbed, due probably to culture; and Maize or Indian Corn (*Zea Mais*), which is found there also in abundance. All these articles form bread after being reduced to flour.

Unfortunately for the native he has no mill, so that he is obliged to resort to the simple process of the pestle and mortar, the only one he knows to produce the result he requires. This method, however, almost always involves the infusion of the root or tubercle to be pulverized for a longer or shorter time, and exposure to the sun. As a natural consequence fermentation ensues, and with it the necessary variations, so that all the African flours are heavy, indigestible, very disagreeable at the outset to the European palate, and never swelling sufficiently to make a tolerable bread. To this the native adds whatever else is attainable by way of relish in the shape of meat, fish, and vegetables; a very small quantity of the latter being sufficient to provoke the consumption of some pounds of the bread.

Ginguba is likewise of great service to them, and whole tribes support themselves upon it. The Jinga, the Mahungo and the Ma-yacca consume extraordinary quantities, without even the appliance of fire, and just as they pull it out of the earth. Besides this, there are indigenous and exotic fruits, too many to enumerate, from the *Vitis heraclifolia* to the banana, as also the varieties of *inhame* (a species of yam) tubercles of the *helmia*, potatoes, and other less known roots which they devour greedily. And finally a bit of sugar-cane and a calabash of sour milk or mead complete the list of articles consumed.

A vegetable diet is almost exclusively the rule throughout the continent. It is only under extraordinary circumstances that an ox or sheep is killed for consumption, and then the native, very like a child, dances about the victim and gives loose to transports of joy at the unusual treat. We have frequently seen our men in camp, upon the slaughter of an ox eagerly hack it to pieces, screeching with delight the while, and not leave even the contents of its intestines unconsumed! On such occasions the scenes which took place about the smoking pipkins were really extraordinary, ending in a general *batuque* or dance, such as we have elsewhere described.

Bearing the deprivation of food for an incredibly long time, the native will content himself with a few grains of *Arachis;* but when the time comes to satisfy his appetite, he is with difficulty satiated. He will take in pound after pound of flour, until his belly shines with its distension and appears ready to burst. This is most particularly the case with the aged; and with them, as emptiness in turn supervenes, the abdominal skin, through want of elasticity, forms into huge wrinkles, imparting to the body a very unpleasant and, indeed, repulsive appearance.

The African generally, we are sorry to say it, has a decided propensity to drunkenness. Whether it be that we are to look for the cause of this vice in the scarcity of strong liquors, and the impossibility of resisting them when they come to hand, or that by their abuse the negro finds a distraction from his monotonous and miserable existence, we cannot say, but it is incontestable that when he gets hold of the liquor he drinks himself blind drunk.

Although the potions they brew are sufficiently inebriating—of course taken in large quantities—the natives prefer European spirit for such a purpose, as they find in its effects a difference that we will try to explain.

At first sight we might imagine that the preference for the latter was based on the fact of its being so much more powerful and producing its effects with less labour; but this is not the reason; the cause of the preference, as they explain it, is that they get *lively* drunk upon *aguardente*, but *sadly* drunk upon mead!

We were enabled when in Quioco, to confirm this opinion out of our own experience, as regards the mead. We happened to pay a morning visit to a certain Sova before we had broken our fast, and were in a manner compelled to drink a great deal more of the stuff than was good for us; and on our return to the *quilombo*, we found that we were partially intoxicated, and that the visitation took a different form to what it does through alcohol in Europe. Not only could we not stand properly on our legs, but there was a sensation in the brain of utter wretchedness, a constant beating of the temples, a violent headache, and vomiting—in fact, all the sensations belonging rather to the poisoning by tobacco, than the cerebral disturbance produced by alcohol. This being the case it is not suprising if a special distinction should be drawn by the natives between their own drink and that of the Europeans, as the latter produces in them sensations so different to those they can obtain from hydromel or other home-made liquor.

Referring again to their food, we would remark that the Africans do not seem to eat so much for the pleasure of eating as for actual support. All their dishes are flavourless, and are proper only for the simplest palates, being very far removed indeed from what we consider palatable. They are not averse to putrefaction. On the other hand our condiments, scents, and aromas, affect their nervous system with most disagreeable sensations, if we may judge by the wry faces they make over them. A fruit of any kind that is very sweet and has anything like a turpentine taste about it pleases them infinitely more than another which, from its delicate flavour, commends itself to our fancy. There are certain fruits that are highly esteemed among them, and which to us are just as repugnant, such for instance as a variety of the *Carica papaya*, the scent of which resembles nothing closer than that arising from the fecal residues of the canine race! Others again are insipid and odourless, and are devoured with as much gusto as some of us would display on consuming a *charlotte russe*.

The African native having been thus sketched from a material point of view, let us now consider him from a more general and philosophical one.

What has the black done and what is he good for? His history is as ancient as that of the white man. Wheresoever the latter has had to struggle with the rigours of an elevated temperature and a burning sun we have seen the former by his side, devoted to the most arduous labour, living in the midst of misery, and constituting an individuality which, being the product of far different circumstances, appears as variable as they, and as difficult to emphasize. His physical and moral value depends upon the direction given by those in authority over him; and to them belongs the duty of placing him on a relative scale of vice or virtue, and modifying the propensities inherent to his nature.

As, however, the object has always been to make capital out of him, the negro, at the mercy of the master (who had no other object in view), without an opinion, without a standard, without a family or a household god, gave himself up, as an infallible consequence, to all those ignoble passions to which a low and unaided nature is susceptible. From his tenderest years he began to nourish a hatred for those who had enslaved him—to long for things beyond his reach—to brood over some scheme of vengeance; and under such circumstances he became converted into what we have seen and heard tell of, an anomalous creature, without any defined, and much less any properly ordered sentiments and qualities.

It is not he, certainly, who should bear the blame, but those who brought him to that pass. Merchants, traders, middle-men and agents alike, turned the poor wretch to account, without ever dreaming of granting him any recompense; and from the very first day they found the negro incapable of wrestling with them intellectually, they ostracised him from the community, and on the score of his inferiority, excused themselves from considering him as a brother. We do not hesitate to proclaim aloud, based upon our present knowledge of the negro, that to slavery, but above all to the contempt entertained by civilized man for the black race, is due the unfortunate creature's precarious moral position. To this unhappy, this fatal hatred of race we owe it that Portuguese, English, French, Dutch, and subjects of other nationalities, have, at the mere contact of the negro, completely changed all their preconceived sentiments of pity, devotion, and love; and, strange to say, the more northerly the European race, the greater and more unyielding the hatred.

Speke, in his "Sources of the Nile," exclaims, "I do not deem the negro in Africa capable of raising himself from the inferiority in which he lives."

But what reasons can be adduced in favour of such an assertion? Is it the fact of such relative social inferiority? But how is the native ever to rise out of it while he is persecuted on all sides by the white man?

From time immemorial Egypt has been the point whence issued all the misery that found its way into the interior. The blacks, fleeing in terror, became gradually surrounded, till scarce a resource was left them; and who shall say whether those vast invasions, much spoken of in the interior, all proceeding from the north, Jaggas, Bondos, and Tembos, were not the natural consequence of such persecution; and whether the immense tribes, seeing themselves beaten in that direction, did not migrate towards the south? In their flight the negroes plunged into the wild and desert country, where their whole attention was taken up with a struggle against the asperities of nature, and yet, in the midst of these difficulties they succeeded in doing not a little.

But even here they were not relieved from slavery; and the devastations, murders, and scenes of refined cruelty to which the traffic gave rise, constitute in our mind an efficient reason to prevent any tendency towards progress.

But we have arrived at a period when things are taking a different turn, and have yet to see the result when the incubus is entirely removed. The traffic is officially proscribed by all civilized nations, and as a consequence the African is on the road to a complete transformation. It is true that in the centre and north-eastern disticts of the great continent slavery still exists, and travellers can point to thousands of victims to the practice in those unhappy lands. The origin lies, however, in the baneful influence of the Arab race, the true pest of Africa, against which we in Europe should unite in a permanent crusade.

The state of the negro in the Portuguese colonies (those with which we are best acquainted in Africa) after the great and generous act of the emancipation of the slaves—which greatly modified the mode of being of social life—and the conditions of labour, have undergone a vast change. Morality has made an immense gain; justice and equity, being able to act untrammeled, have curbed the maleficent instincts of perverse natures, and interposed a shield between them and the oppressed; and where in former days the poor, untutored negro worked beneath the lash of an ignorant colonist, he now finds a man who knows how to appreciate the value of free labour and to draw from it advantages superior to those previously obtained. Ideas, more in consonance with the true principles of honesty, are spreading far and wide, and a happier future is visible to every unprejudiced eye.

The African cannot be supposed as yet to thoroughly comprehend the infallible transformation that is being wrought on his behalf, inasmuch as from time immemorial the black has been a slave without the opportunity of proving that he was susceptible of becoming a free man, the head of a family, and an honest worker; but we shall shortly see him under just and well-pondered incentives pursuing (perhaps more speedily than any of us suppose) the track that leads to perfectibility.

It is necessary, however, as Cameron observes, not to forget that our state of advancement is the fruit of ages of labour, and to expect the African to attain to it in a couple of decades, implies an absurdity. The education of the native must be effected by successive gradations, and it would be a grave error to impose upon him our customs of to-day, without giving him any previous preparation. To presume that a negro is the equal of a white man, or to insinuate to him that he is so, is a crime; as Serpa Pinto very justly remarks in the paragraphs from his recent work, which we transcribe:—

"Some of these missionaries," he says (vol. ii. p. 302), "with little knowledge and narrow intellect, commence by instilling into the natives, hour by hour, from the sacred pulpit, whence should only be heard the accents of truth, that they are the equals of the white man, that they are on a level with the civilized; when they ought rather to say to them, in the tones of persuasion and authority, 'Between you and the European there is a wide gulf which I have come to teach you to bridge over. Regenerate yourselves; quit your habits of brutish sloth; labour and pray; abandon crime and practise the virtue which I will show you; cast off your ignorance and learn;—and then, but not till then, can you stand on the same level as the white man: then, and then only, will you be his equal.'"

* * * * * *

"To tell the ignorant savage that he is the equal of the civilized man is a falsehood—it is a crime. It is to be wanting in all those duties which were imposed upon the teacher when he set out for Africa. It is to be a traitor to his sacred mission."

We may further add, to compel the black man to conform to the habits and mode of life of the European, and force him to such conversion on the spot, appears to us most certainly an error. It is, however, lamentable that the growing industry of many nations will not admit that it is so; moved simply by its own interests, it does not or will not see that the forcing itself into Africa under pretext of acting for the good of the native tends to no other object than the gain of the individual trader, and the discovery of markets where he can dispose of his products, though it involves the compelling a man who yesterday was covered with a cloth and stuck feathers in his hair to mount a chimney-pot hat and imprison his arms in a ridiculous frock coat!

In religious matters the utmost care that is used would be but little; special interests already begin to show themselves in the religious fervour with which the missions are invading Africa. We can foresee, and we venture to point out to the Governments concerned, that the progress of the African native towards civilization is likely to receive a severe check from this cause. The nations of Europe are despatching missions from all quarters with a view to make converts. On the other hand the Arabs, armed with the Koran, are bent upon the same errand and making no inconsiderable progress. What with these numerous sects and forms, each claiming to be the expositor of the only true faith, to the exclusion of all others, the poor negro, already oppressed by his chief, dazed with the recollections of the fetishism of his fathers, harassed by the missionaries who overwhelm him with Bibles and Korans, will shortly not know which way to turn for comfort or repose. If, from free America, the Mormons should take it into their heads to come over to Africa, with a like object of proselytism, the confusion will be such that only its equal could be found beneath the growing walls of Babel of old!

It therefore strikes us, that the only way out of the difficulty is the establishment of an international Catholic association, which would, by means of a general plan having identical bases, administer spiritual bread to the natives of the dark continent. We are fully aware of the obstacles that would have to be overcome in procuring anything like concerted action among nations whose forms of faith are so widely apart, but that problem, which we do not ourselves attempt to solve, should prove the primary care of the spiritual association. A movement of this nature, once recognized by all the nations who have undertaken in Africa so noble a task, would enjoy such aid and protection as would bear down any mere sectarian attempts and mainly frustrate the efforts of the representatives of Yatreb's famous prophet.

One of the first duties devolving upon the society would be a study of the native dialects and the translation of the Bible and prayer-books into those idioms. To begin the conversion of the negro by first teaching him Dutch or German appears to us so extraordinary that we must perforce consider the method a useless waste of time. Nothing is so painful to a people as to be compelled to abandon the language of their fathers, and now that Arabic has a tendency to spread over the continent, such a system as the one we suggest would deal it a heavy blow. This should be followed by a general plan of social organization, having the family for a basis, mutual aid and remunerative labour.

The native should then be taught to fashion and use a plough, to extract iron from the earth by the most profitable means and to combine it with carbon in order to produce steel. Care should be taken to give him the first notions of a mill, to reveal to him the mode of turning to account the immense water-power at his disposal, to point out to him the advantages of cultivating the ground—these, and such as these, should be the objects of missions in those benighted lands.

From the very first day that the negro sets eyes upon the missionary, he should behold in him, not the *n'ganga* or fetishman, dressed in a black gown—which may very well be dispensed with—and dealing in more or less mysterious formula, but a superior guide, a kindly man, an upright judge, from whose actions only good and happiness should flow on his behalf. For such a post we ought infallibly to seek a master—not one who would attempt by overstrained mysticism to teach the native the road to heaven—but one who could place him in a position to overcome the difficulties of some primary industry on earth. The missionaries should therefore be themselves educated in the practical and utilitarian methods of the applied arts, to the exclusion of a like proportion of apocalyptical and wearisome theological study. Commerce would become gradually developed, in proportion as necessities arose; labour grown into a habit, would exercise its moralizing influence; from the sacrifices made thereto would spring a knowledge of value and of economy, together with the conviction that by its influence a well-being was acquired which further perseverance would make greater. Other natural results would follow, such as the desire to possess, and the wish to leave those possessions to natural successors, and thereby secure the comfort of those whom a purer life had taught the negro to hold in affection. By such a course of education what would a negro become? We answer, a being like ourselves; and we believe that most experienced persons, who have devoted their attention to the subject, will give the same reply.

The future of the great continent will depend upon many kinds of exploration, among which mining will doubtless take the lead; and this will be followed, as a natural consequence, by agriculture. The rich and varied native productions of the vegetable kingdom, and the facility of acclimatizing exotics, will undoubtedly soon induce the colonizer to devote attention to a soil whence can be drawn such inexhaustible treasures.

It is in fact marvellous to note the accumulation and variety of articles, chiefly vegetable, of those fertile lands. The imagination is bewildered with the sight of the multitude of gigantic trees, shrubs, and plants, that are little if at all known. It would occupy many pages to enumerate with anything like minuteness the wealth of the productive soil.

Setting aside for the present the trade in ivory—which, to a certain extent, is on the decline, although perhaps the richest of the whole and which, as regards the Portuguese colony, is specially carried on by the roads connecting Cassange with the Lunda, the Bihé with the Catanga and Lua, and along the Cubango to Bucusso—our narrative will show the interest that should attach to a methodical exploration of the vast territories in the interior of the continent.

On leaving the littoral, we find in the vegetable kingdom the sugar-cane, which grows in the valleys of the great rivers, such as the Cuanza, the Cu-vo, the Lu-oje, &c., and even in more elevated positions, where water is abundant, for instance in the Dombe and elsewhere. Even at the present day it produces *aguardente* in sufficient quantity to supply the necessities of the native, and might, by great development, furnish all the markets of Europe with sugar. The *broca*, and more recently another worm not less destructive, have, it is true, attacked the plantations and destroyed great part of the cane. Careful study would, however, as a natural consequence, discover some process of a kind to prevent the destructiveness of these insects.

Alongside the cane we have those noteworthy palms such as the *Elaïs guinensis*, the pulp of whose fruit yields, after lengthened steeping, a thick, red oil, of tolerable flavour before it gets rancid, called palm-oil, and the stone of which produces an empyreumatic oil that finds a ready sale in Europe.

Moreover, we find the *hyphœne* and *borassus* with leaves that are employed in the manufacture of hats and other articles. The *Adansonias*, whose inner shell fibres form the *licomte*, greatly used at the present day in the making of cloth and paper. The *palmachristi*, adapted for medicinal purposes. The *aloe*, which grows profusely. *Tobacco*, found everywhere, that of Ambaca having a fine aroma. *Hemp* is not less frequent. *Cotton* in abundance, and of various qualities, grows throughout the Province. Then we have *coffee*, already appreciated in our markets, and covering the whole of the mountainous region; the best being obtainable at Cazengo. *Ginguba*, yielding much oil, and whereof the stores on the high table-land of Ambaca and in the eastern territories appear inexhaustible. *Pepper* is met with everywhere. *Rice*, from the quantities we observed in the Bihé growing on the high land, must be cultivated on a large scale. *Maize* grows very freely, whether in Callengues, Caconda, or Duque de Bragança. *Sorgho* is widely spread in the interior, and constitutes generally in those parts the food of the native. Nor is the *massango*, upon which the Ganguellas and Maquioco are mainly supported, less abundant.

Among other products we have the *Elemi balsam*, in extraordinary quantities; *Copal gum*, the trees producing which are found both upon the coast and in the interior in extensive woods; *india-rubber*, produced from colossal climbers ruthlessly cut down by the natives to extract the sap; *dragon's blood*, the working of which has already been attempted; *tacula*, that is permanently collected in the Jinga; and many others too numerous for our work.

In the animal kingdom we must mention *ivory*, alluded to elsewhere, as represented by the tusks of the elephant and sea-horse, eagerly sought for throughout the continent, and *rhinoceros horns*.

There is abundance of bees' *wax*, obtained mainly from the Ganguellas; of *silk* both of the spider and the hanging cocoons already referred to in this volume; and of *marabout* and *ostrich feathers* which find their way into most markets. There are *ox-hides* in plenty: and the skins of such wild animals as lions, panthers, leopards, and other smaller creatures are pretty readily obtainable.

Of minerals, whereof mention has more than once been made, we discover *iron* in the specular or hematite form. *Sulphur* in the chalks; *copper* in all the mountainous regions and in the interior, appearing to be run in the form of a cross; *coal*, discoverable in one or two places;

gold in the Lombije and other parts; *silver* in the Jinga (Dallango), Cambambe, &c.; and *rock salt* in many territories of the continent.

These simple data will suffice to give a rough idea of the wealth of this vast continent, which, under European guidance, should show a prosperity in the future that will not yield the palm even to America.

Its colonization, however, is a great problem, and will require very serious study. The life of the European in tropical Africa, if not at the present time impossible, is, to say the least of it, full of perils and difficulties. The main object, therefore, at the outset must be to endeavour to modify the circumstances which now beset him; to establish populous centres; to create the necessary means for his existence; and in a word to render the African territory salubrious.

The immediate measures which present themselves for such a purpose are two, viz., to connect by roads, conveniently disposed, certain points of the interior with the coast; and to direct the waters of the great rivers, so as to drain the marshes and the low-lying grounds, and thereby modify that vegetative force—which is the origin of all the unhealthiness—to the advantage of the loftier regions, whose vegetation would, in such case, become more highly developed.

The numerous cataracts of the African rivers though causing in many places an obstacle to navigation, nevertheless facilitate the distribution of the waters. To conduct those waters from the river-heads, by a combined system of irrigation, to properly selected and salubrious sites; to use them as an element of life to the vegetable kingdom and as a potent motive power for thousands of mills and factories; to drain them wheresoever necessary, and never allow them to stagnate; in fine, to control and direct the waters of the continent should be the civilizer's first care on behalf of those most fertile lands in the more elevated regions.

It may be objected that so vast a problem can only be solved in the course of thousands of years, and that the best course to pursue is to be satisfied with things as they are. But to this we will reply, that, though the hints we have thrown out never contemplated a speedy solution, they represent ideas which might be at once initiated, by way of showing the direction that the herculean labour should take, more especially in regard to roads and the establishment of colonies.

It will have been gathered from several passages in these volumes that a residence on the high ground is best adapted for the preservation of health, and we will add here, that if a European has a chance of living at a height of 3000 feet, he ought not to pitch his tent at 300. It is true that the more lofty territory is at the present time relatively more bare ; but inasmuch as all the great rivers take their rise in the elevated ground, with such a soil, under the influence of sun and water, all apprehensions as to the risk of labour and capital being expended unprofitably may be cast to the winds.

On account of its special orographic character and peculiar climatic circumstances, Africa offers a great contrast to the continents in the northern hemisphere. Her great cities, her vast marts, her commercial emporiums, will infallibly have to be established in the interior, and the more so where approaching the equatorial region. It is on the lofty savannas of the Quioco, on the mountains of Quillengues, on the plateau of the Huilla, noted for their salubrity, that we shall see successively planted the earliest colonies, if it be desired to live and progress under the influence of the climate of the great continent.

On the coast the miserable little *Comptoir* must still exist, isolated in the midst of arid lands, under the direction of some native or sickly European, but for the mere purpose of attending to the transit, depositing merchandise and produce, and superintending their landing and shipment. No earthly good can ever come of a residence on that sterile threshold, where the stoutest labourer, with the best of wills, must sicken and die, yielding to the earth his own spoils in lieu of himself reaping any permanent advantage. No; the road lies inwards and upwards. On the high table-land where the fresh breezes blow; where the European can breathe freely, and where he will live for months together in a temperature containing so little variation that were it not from constant watching of the thermometer the figures would appear incredible, as the following tables will show :—

Days	January.				February.			
	Latitude S.	Longitude E. Greenwich	Altitudes	Temperature	Latitude S.	Longitude E. Greenwich	Altitudes	Temperature
	° ′	° ′	ft.		° ′	° ′	ft.	
1	—	—	—	—	13.44	15.02	5387	69
2	—	—	—	—	,,	,,	,,	,,
3	—	—	—	—	,,	,,	,,	,,
4	—	—	—	—	,,	,,	,,	,,
5	—	—	—	—	,,	,,	,,	70
6	—	—	—	—	,,	,,	,,	,,
7	—	—	—	—	,,	,,	,,	,,
8[1]	13.44	15.02	5387	69	,,	,,	,,	,,
9	,,	,,	,,	,,	,,	,,	,,	,,
10	,,	,,	,,	,,	,,	,,	,,	71
11	,,	,,	,,	,,	,,	,,	,,	,,
12	,,	,,	,,	,,	,,	,,	,,	—
13	,,	,,	,,	,,	,,	,,	,,	—
14	,,	,,	,,	,,	13.41[2]	15.18	5157	72
15	,,	,,	,,	,,	13.40	15.21	5347	,,
16	,,	,,	,,	,,	13.39	15.24	5095	71
17	,,	,,	,,	,,	13.37	15.26	5285	,,
18	,,	,,	,,	,,	13.33	15.32	,,	72
19	,,	,,	,,	,,	13.29	15.38	5216	71
20	,,	,,	,,	,,	13.25	15.43	5157	—
21	,,	,,	,,	,,	13.21	15.49	5151	71
22	,,	,,	,,	,,	13.19	15.54	5338	—
23	,,	,,	,,	,,	13.15	15.59	5575	69
24	,,	,,	,,	,,	13.08	16.03	5610	,,
25	,,	,,	,,	,,	13.02	16.08	5430	,,
26	,,	,,	,,	,,	12.58	16.13	5338	70
27	,,	,,	,,	,,	12.53	16.20	5568	,,
28	,,	,,	,,	—	,,	,,	,,	,,
29	,,	,,	,,	,,	—	—	—	—
30	,,	,,	,,	,,	—	—	—	—
31	,,	,,	,,	,,	—	—	—	—

[1] In Caconda.   [2] On the journey.

Days	March.				April.			
	Latitude S.	Longitude E. Greenwich	Altitudes	Temperature	Latitude S.	Longitude E. Greenwich	Altitudes	Temperature
	° ′	° ′	ft.		° ′	° ′	ft.	
1	12.48	16.27	5610	69	12.22	16.50	5161	—
2	12.14	16.31	5443	,,	,,	,,	,,	69
3	12.39	16.34	5397	—	,,	,,	,,	,,
4	12.37	16.37	5337	,,	,,	,,	,,	70
5	12.31	16.41	5291	,,	,,	,,	,,	,,
6	12.28	16.43	5421	,,	,,	,,	,,	,,
7	12.26	,,	,,	—	,,	,,	,,	,,
8[1]	12.22	16.50	5161	—	,,	,,	,,	72
9	,,	,,	,,	,,	,,	,,	,,	,,
10	,,	,,	,,	,,	,,	,,	,,	,,
11	,,	,,	,,	,,	,,	,,	,,	,,
12	,,	,,	,,	,,	,,	,,	,,	,,
13	,,	,,	,,	,,	,,	,,	,,	,,
14	,,	,,	,,	,,	,,	,,	,,	,,
15	,,	,,	,,	—	,,	,,	,,	,,
16	,,	,,	5157	70	,,	,,	,,	,,
17	,,	,,	5161	,,	,,	,,	,,	—
18	,,	,,	,,	,,	,,	,,	,,	74
19	,,	,,	,,	,,	,,	,,	,,	,,
20	,,	,,	,,	,,	,,	,,	,,	72
21	,,	,,	,,	,,	,,	,,	,,	,,
22	,,	,,	,,	,,	,,	,,	,,	,,
23	,,	,,	,,	71	,,	,,	,,	,,
24	,,	,,	,,	,,	,,	,,	,,	71
25	,,	,,	,,	70	,,	,,	,,	72
26	,,	,,	,,	,,	,,	,,	,,	,,
27	,,	,,	,,	69	,,	,,	,,	—
28	,,	,,	,,	,,	,,	,,	,,	,,
29	,,	,,	,,	70	,,	,,	,,	—
30	,,	,,	,,	,,	,,	,,	,,	71
31	,,	,,	,,	,,	—	—	—	—

[1] On the journey.

Conclusion.

Days	May.				June.			
	Latitude S.	Longitude E. Greenwich	Altitudes	Temperature	Latitude S.	Longitude E. Greenwich	Altitudes	Temperature
	° ′	° ′	ft.		° ′	° ′	ft.	
1	12.22	16.50	5161	71	11.53	17.38	3770	68
2	,,	,,	,,	72	,,	,,	,,	,,
3	,,	,,	,,	,,	,,	,,	,,	,,
4	,,	,,	,,	—	,,	,,	,,	,,
5	,,	,,	,,	71	,,	,,	,,	,,
6	,,	,,	,,	70	11.49[1]	17.42	3740	,,
7	,,	,,	,,	,,	11.45	17.45	3898	,,
8	,,	,,	,,	,,	11.46	17.51	3688	,,
9	,,	,,	,,	71	11.43	17.53	3527	69
10	,,	,,	,,	,,	11.41	17.58	3536	,,
11	,,	,,	,,	—	,,	,,	,,	,,
12	,,	,,	,,	72	,,	,,	,,	68
13	,,	,,	,,	71	,,	,,	,,	,,
14	,,	,,	,,	70	11.37	18.00	3612	,,
15	,,	,,	,,	,,	11.33[3]	18.06	3648	,,
16[1]	,,	,,	,,	—	,,	,,	,,	,,
17	12.18	17.02	4803	—	,,	,,	,,	,,
18	,,	,,	,,	69	,,	,,	,,	,,
19	,,	,,	,,	,,	,,	,,	,,	,,
20	,,	,,	,,	67	,,	,,	,,	,,
21	,,	,,	,,	69	,,	,,	,,	,,
22	,,	,,	,,	68	,,	,,	,,	,,
23	,,	,,	,,	,,	,,	,,	,,	,,
24	12.14	17.07	4113	—	,,	,,	,,	,,
25	12.09	17.14	4200	68	,,	,,	,,	,,
26	12.04	17.22	4494	,,	,,	,,	,,	,,
27	11.58	17.30	4029	,,	,,[4]	18.15	3902	,,
28[2]	11.53	17.38	3770	,,	,,	,,	,,	,,
29	,,	,,	,,	,,	,,	,,	,,	,,
30	,,	,,	,,	,,	,,	,,	,,	69
31	,,	,,	,,	,,	—	—	—	—

[1] On the journey.   [2] On the Cu-anza.   [3] Mongóa.   [4] Cha-N'ganji.

Days	July.				August.			
	Latitude S.	Longitude E. Greenwich	Altitudes	Temperature	Latitude S.	Longitude E. Greenwich	Altitudes	Temperature
	° ′	° ′	ft.		° ′	° ′	ft.	
1	11.33	18.15	3902	68	11.05	18.59	4396	70
2	,,	,,	,,	,,	,,	,,	,,	,,
3	,,	,,	,,	,,	,,	,,	,,	,,
4[1]	11.27	18.22	—	66	,,	,,	,,	,,
5	11.25	18.31	3839	,,	,,	,,	,,	,,
6	,,	,,	,,	64	,,	,,	,,	,,
7	11.24	18.39	4075	,,	,,	,,	,,	,,
8	11.22	18.46	4250	,,	,,	,,	,,	,,
9	,,	,,	,,	66	,,	,,	,,	,,
10[2]	11.21	18.50	4265	,,	11.00[1]	19.01	3893	,,
11	,,	,,	,,	65	10.54	19.02	—	—
12	,,	,,	,,	66	10.50	19.05	3821	—
13	,,	,,	,,	,,	10.46	19.06	,,	,,
14	,,	,,	,,	67	,,[4]	19.08	4022	,,
15	,,	,,	,,	,,	,,	,,	,,	,,
16	,,	,,	,,	,,	,,	,,	,,	72
17	,,	,,	,,	,,	,,	,,	,,	,,
18	,,	,,	,,	,,	,,	,,	,,	,,
19	,,	,,	,,	,,	,,	,,	,,	,,
20	,,	,,	,,	69	,,	,,	,,	,,
21	,,	,,	,,	,,	,,	,,	,,	,,
22[1]	11.15	18.52	4396	—	,,	,,	,,	,,
23	,,	,,	4390	—	,,	,,	,,	71
24	11.10	18.54	4396	—	,,	,,	,,	72
25[3]	11.05	18.59	,,	69	,,[1]	,,	,,	,,
26	,,	,,	,,	,,	10.40	19.07	3935	,,
27	,,	,,	,,	,,	10.36[5]	19.06	3743	,,
28	,,	,,	,,	,,	10.34	,,	3875	,,
29	,,	,,	,,	,,	,,	,,	,,	—
30	,,	,,	,,	70	,,	,,	,,	,,
31	,,	,,	,,	,,	,,	,,	,,	—

[1] On the journey. [2] N'Dumba Tembo. [3] Mughande. [4] Catuchi. [5] Muene T'chiquilla.

Great and rapid means of communication become therefore inevitable. None more than the African colonist will need the railway because none more than he will dread the littoral. From the sea-board, we repeat, he must fly, for if he attempt to settle there, he will fail to a dead certainty, and by that fact will help to condemn the great continent to the immobility in which we behold it to-day. Emigration, therefore, from the civilized nations of Europe should only be set on foot with a view to the colonization of Africa when the latter is in a position to offer the chief of guarantees—the means of transport to a healthy region.

Every attempt in this direction will foster such colonization; but simply to convey the colonist to the low-lying region, and compel him to set to work in the valleys where enormous rivers are ever flowing, and where marshy ground is permanent, is to consign him to destruction. The object should be to gain the interior with the least possible loss of time; to establish the European with the utmost amount of conveniences about him; to destroy, by means of a well-directed administration, the relative repugnance of the negro to anything in the shape of labour, by making such labour obligatory and rewarding him for the work done; to create vast centres of population, connected with each other by the regular navigation of the extensive watercourses of the interior, or properly arranged roads; to shun the fatal influence of the marshy ground by smothering it—in other words, by guiding on to it the nearest watercourses; for by means such as these, the great problem, of so much interest to Europe, will be finally solved.

Let such rivers as are navigable in the interior be turned to account; and from the extreme points of their navigableness let railways connect them with the coast so as to provide an economic and rapid means of transport.

To the railway, especially, that most precious resource of modern civilization—that powerful instrument of all progress—we must look as the greatest auxiliary in the gigantic work we contemplate.

The locomotive, whistling as it flies through the vast African forests, will doubtless produce the same magical effects as have hitherto accompanied its course. Traversing great distances with the velocity which is part of its nature, it will carry resources, life and labour, into places where, till that time, nature in her wildness alone reigned, transform desert tracts into habitable land, convert marshes into parks and gardens; in a word, it will raise Africa to the height occupied by the other continents of the world, and relieve humanity of one of her greatest stains, namely, the leaving so large a portion of her family still grovelling in a state of savagery.

Having thus put forward our facts and ventilated our opinions, we have only to exclaim with the fabulist:—

Nisi utile est quod facimus, stulta est gloria.

TABLE

OF

GEOGRAPHICAL OBSERVATIONS

MADE DURING THE

EXPEDITION OF 1877—1880.

278

GEOGRAPHICAL CO-ORDINATES.

Meridian Altitudes.		Hours.	Positions.		Altitudes.		Azimuth.	Latitude.	Longitude.
mer. ☉	106,85	—	—	—	—	—	—	8.47.56	—
"	98,40	—	—	—	—	—	—	8.47.57	—
"	102,49	—	—	—	—	—	—	12.34.17	13.22.30
"	100,45	7.07.22.00	Sub.	5.45.14.00	a.m.	147.20	—	12.55.11	13.07.44
"	100,04	7.22.15.00	Sub.	1.48.11.52	☉	147,20	280.50	12.55.30	13.07.44
	—	3.26.47.00	"	0.01.01.44	p.m. ☉	147,84	276,5	—	13.07.50
mer. ☉	91,63	1.51.34.00	"	—	☉	55,27	—	—	13.07.30
"	91,54	8.25.38.00	Sub.	0.05.12.56	☉	58,65	—	14.03.12	14.05.03
								14.03.10	
"	80.17.46	—	—	—	a.m.	73,35	—	11.16.46	15.02.35
"	91,40	6.08.08.30	—	3.24.45.30	p.m.	87,88	—	13.44.00	15.32.30
"	91,99	7.08.14.30	Add.	3.25.03.30	"	50,96	—	13.58.04	15.30.30
	—	4.41.00.00	"	3.25.12.30	☉	53.18.08	—	—	15.03.50
	—	20.50.21.00	Sub.	0.08.54.30	p.m.	51.57.34	—	13.44.00	15.00.11
	—	2.00.59.00	"	0.09.36.30	2 alt. ☽	92.03.40	—	13.44.00	15.19.10
2 alt. mer. ☽	101.16.10	7.32.12.30	"	0.09.47.30	2 alt. ☽	59.36.50	—	13.41.30	15.30.30
	—	8.00.26.00	"	0.00.58.30				13.28.30	
mer. ☉	96,54	—	—	—	☉	13,58	—	13.20.41	15.43.40
mer. ☽	83,19	6.03.08.00	Sub.	0.10.14.54	alt. ☽	79,71	—	13.00.00	16.01.30
mer. ☉	94,91	5.16.36.00	"	0.10.29.54	a.m.	92,62	—	12.57.10	16.13.20
	—	10.59.57.30	"	0.10.34.54	2 alt. ☉	101.15.20	—	12.57.10	16.13.20
mer. ☉	81.47.38	1.57.41.30	"	0.10.35.00	a.m.	76.17.24	—	12.21.49	16.42.30
	—	22.30.20.30	"	0.11.31.00	"	47.57.40	—	12.21.49	16.42.30
	—	20.31.02.00	"	0.13.08.30	"	46.30.50	—	—	16.46.37
	—	20.32.19.00	"	0.13.32.00	☽	19,89	—	—	—
	—	3.31.58.00	"	0.16.33.08	☉.	—	—	—	—
	—	—	"	0.18.24.00			73,10		
	—	8.06.06.30	"	0.18.06.09	☉	38,47	—	12.08.30	17.16.10
mer. ☽	116,91	—	"	0.18.16.00			—	12.08.30	17.06.10
	—	—	"	0.18.22.00	☉	186,21	71.15	11.54.50	17.34.30
mer. ☉	61,99	6.19.14.30	Sub.	0.18.55.40	"	86,52	71.00	—	17.34.30
	—	6.19.59.00	"	0.18.55.40	"	38,37			
	—	8.08.15.00			"	38,67			
	—	8.09.42.00		0.18.58.00					

279

June	5	Cu-anza		—	—	7.58.41.00	0.19.17.41	a.m.	35,79	71,40	—	17.34.30
„	6	Cu-anza		—	—	7.52.02.00	0.19.23.08	„	34,22	73,30 {ou 81,50}	—	17.34.30
„	7	Baudun		mer. ☉	61,37	9.56.20.30	0.19.28.41	„	56,79	51,80	11.47.30	17.46.30
„	9	Luanda[6]		mer. ♃	101,81	—	0.19.53.00	„	—	—	—	17.46.30
„	10	Cha-Calumbo		—	—	18.31.21.30	0.19.46.00	cor ☉	13.57.54	—	—	18.00.35
„	13	Cha-Calumbo		mer. ☉	60,925	8.15.11.30	0.20.03.19	a.m.	38,85	76,8	11.41.14	18.00.35
„	16	Mongôa[6]		2 alt. ☉	103.38.00	7.50.34.30	0.20.20.30	„	166,55	—	11.34.05	18.00.30
„	16	Mongôa[6]		—	—	—	0.20.23.00	„	—	—	—	18.08.30
„	17	Mongôn[6]		mer. ☉	60,88	—	0.20.27.30	„	—	—	—	18.08.30
„	21	Mongêa		„	—	8.52.39.30	0.20.46.30	„	40,01	76,2	11.34.02	18.09.00
„	22	Mongón		„	—	9.12.13.30	0.20.51.30	„	49,11	61,5	—	18.09.00
„	23	Mongôa		„	—	8.44.46.30	0.20.57.00	„	44,35	71,5	—	18.09.00
„	24	Mongôa		„	—	8.21.28.30	0.21.02.30	„	39,63	77,0	—	18.09.00
„	25	Cha-N'gauji		mer. ☉	60,80	—	—	„	—	—	—	—
„	26	Cha-N'gauji		„	—	20.24.38.30	0.21.12.30	„	36.10.10	—	11.32.43	18.23.00
„	28	Cha-N'gauji		„	—	7.52.57.00	0.21.20.44	a.m.	33,51	80,8	—	18.23.00
„	30	Cha-N'gauji		„	—	8.19.30.30	0.21.25.30	„	45,19	69,7	—	18.23.00
July	2	Cha-N'gauji		„	—	10.41.25.30	0.21.31.30	„	30,84	82,5	—	18.23.00
„	3	Cha-N'gauji[6]		—	—	—	0.21.33.00	„	—	—	—	—
„	5	Matari		mer. ☉	55.26.57	—	0.21.48.00	„	—	—	11.30.12	18.20.16
„	7	Cha-Cassingo[7]		mer. ♃	100,7	3.47.19.00	0.21.57.00	☉	16,03	—	11.23.30	18.38.10
„	11	Cangombe		mer. ☉	62,536	9.25.11.0	0.22.15.00	„	43.04.08	—	11.20.51	18.50.00
„	16	Muene Quibau		„	56.55 53	—	—	„	—	—	11.27.00	19.11.30
„	17	Cungombe		—	—	8 05 56.00	—	Sub.	—	—	—	18.50.00
„	22	Cangombe		mer. ☉	—	7.15.11.30	—	„	37,04	81,0	—	18.50.00
„	25	Muene C. je[8]		„	59.05.09	—	—	„	32,65	87,7	—	18.55.30
„	30	Chaufana		„	60 22.35	—	—	—	—	—	11.00.40	18.39.59
August	2	Muene Chicanji		„	61.25.15	—	—	—	—	—	10.32.01	18.37.05
„	2	N'Dumba Mughande		2 alt. mer. ☉	60.52.30	—	—	—	—	—	10.31.23	18.56.30
„	3	Cha-Calumbo		mer. ☉	61.45.13	—	—	—	—	—	11.07.02	18.39.51
„	4	Cu-ango		„	62.03.40	—	—	—	—	—	10.30.00	18.38.38
„	6	Cu-ango		„	62.45.30	—	—	—	—	—	10.27.22	18.32.38
„	7	Cu-ango		„	63 07.24	—	—	—	—	—	10.18.03	18.34.05
„	10	Cat-Louisa		„	64.05.35	—	—	—	—	—	10.12.50	18.43.30
„	12	Cu-ango		„	61.44.22	—	—	—	—	—	10.06.14	18.43.05
											10.03.05	

[1] The error of the *abba* was then 2,2 sub. The altitudes expressed in decimals and fractions represent the degrees into which Mr. d'Abbadie's instrument is divided; the others are degrees, minutes, seconds, and thirds of the sextant, or of the former instrument, already reduced.
[2] The error of the *abba* was 2,18 sub.
[3] The error of the *abba* was 0,06 sub, reduced thereafter to zero.

[4] The error of the sextant was 2′.
[5] Passage of Mercury over the face of the sun.
[6] Satellite of Jupiter.
[7] Error of *abba* 0,45 sub.
[8] The elements of calculation from 25th July to 18th November, mainly longitudes, were lost in the fire at the Duque de Bragança.

GEOGRAPHICAL CO-ORDINATES.

Date.	Stations.	Meridian Altitudes.	Hours.	Positions.	Altitudes.	Azimuth.	Latitude.	Longitude.
1877.								
October 5	Loanda [1]	mer. ☉	106,85	—	—	—	8.47.56	—
„ 7	Loanda	„	98,40	—	—	—	8.47.57	—
„ 26	Benguella	„	102,49	—	—	—	12.34.17	13.22.10
„ 31	Dombe	„	100,45	7.07.22.00	Sub. 5.45.14.00	a.m. 147.20	12.55.11	13.07.44
November 1	Dombe	„	100,04	7.22.15.00	—	☉ 147.20	12.55.30	13.07.44
„ 8	Dombe	—	—	3.26.47.00	—	p.m. 147.84	—	13.07.50
„ 25	Dombe [2]	—	—	1.51.34.00	Sub. 1.48.14.52	☉ 55.27	280.50	13.07.50
December 14	Quillengues	mer. ☉	91,63	—	0.01.01.44	„ 58,55	270,5	13.07.30
„ 16	Quillengues	„	91,54	8.25.38.00	Sub. 0.05.12.56	☉ 58,55	14.03.12	—
1878.							14.03.10	14.05.03
January 4	N'Gola	„	80.17.46	—	—	—	—	—
„ 14	Cacouda [3]	„	91,40	6.08.08.30	—	a.m. 73,35	11.16.46	—
„ 16	Lagoa Tchicoudi	„	91,99	7.08.14.30	Add. 3.25.03.30	p.m. 87,88	13.41.00	15.02.35
„ 17	Cu-nene	—	—	4.41.00.00	„ 3.25.12.30	a.m. 50,06	13.58.04	15.32.30
„ 30	Cacouda	—	—	20.50.21.00	Sub. 0.08.54.30	☉ 58.18.08	—	15.30.30
February 11	Cacouda	—	—	2.00.59.00	„ 0.09.36.30	p.m. 51.57.34	—	13.44.00	15.03.50
„ 14	Cu-se [4]	2 alt. mer. ☉	101.18.10	7.32.12.30	„ 0.09.47.30	2 alt. ☾ 92.03.40	—	13.44.00	15.00.11
„ 17	Calu'la	—	—	8.00.26.00	„ 0.09.58.30	2 alt. ☾ 50.36.50	—	13.41.30	15.19.10
„ 21	Cu-nene	mer. ☉	96,54	—	—	—	—	13.28.30	15.30.30
„ 23	Cu-nene	—	—	6.03.08.00	Sub. 0.10.14.54	☉ 13,58	—	13.20.41	—
„ 25	Otoari	mer. ☾	83,19	5.16.36.00	„ 0.10.29.54	alt. ☾ 79,71	—	—	15.43.40
„ 26	Cu-bango	mer. ☉	94,01	10.59.57.30	„ 0.10.34.54	„ 92.02	—	13.00.00	16.01.30
„ 26	Cu-bango	—	—	1.57.41.30	„ 0.10.35.00	2 alt. ☉ 101.15.20	—	12.57.10	16.13.20
March 9	Belmonte	—	—	22.30.20.30	„ 0.11.31.00	a.m. 76.17.24	—	12.57.10	16.13.20
„ 30	Belmonte	mer. ☉	61.47.38	20.31.02.00	„ 0.13.08.30	„ 47.57.40	—	13.21.40	16.42.30
April 6	Quilombe	—	—	20.32.19.00	„ 0.13.32.00	„ 46.30.50	—	12.21.49	16.42.30
May 6	Bihé [5]	—	—	3.31.58.00	„ 0.16.33.08	☉ 19,89	—	—	16.43.37
„ 22	Quieque [6]	—	—	—	„ 0.18.24.00	—	—	—	—
„ 23	Quieque	—	—	8.00.06.30	„ 0.18.06.00	☉ 38,47	73,10	—	—
„ 24	Numda [5]	—	—	—	„ 0.18.10.00	—	—	—	—
„ 26	Catongo	mer. ☽	110,91	6.19.14.30	„ 0.18.22.00	☉ 186,21	—	12.08.30	17.16.10
„ 26	Calungo	—	—	6.19.50.00	—	„ 86,52	—	12.08.30	17.06.10
June 1	Cu-anza	mer. ☉	61,00	8.05.15.00	Sub. 0.18.55.40	„ 38.37	71.15	11.54.50	17.34.30
„ 1	Cu-anza	—	—	8.05.42.00	„ 0.18.55.40	„ 38,67	71.00	—	17.34.30
„ 2	Cu-anza [5]	—	—	—	„ 0.18.58.00	—	—	—	17.34.30

June 5	Cu-anza	—	—	7.58.41.00	Sub. 0.10.17.41	a.m. 35,70	71,40	—	17.34.30
„ 6	Cu-anza	—	—	7.52.02.00	„ 0.19.33.08	☉ 34,22	{ 79.30 Lou 81,505 }	—	17.34.30
„ 7	Bandua	mer. ☉	61,37	9.66.20.30	„ 0.19.28.41	„ 56,70	51,50	11.47.30	17.46.30
„ 9	Luanda [6]	mer. ☾	104,81	—	„ 0.19.53.00	—	—	—	17.46.30
„ 10	Cha-Calumbo	—	—	18.31.21.30	„ 0.19.46.00	cor ☉ 13.57.54	—	—	18.00.35
„ 13	Cha-Calumbo	mer. ☉	60,925	8.15.11.30	„ 0.20.03.19	a.m. 38,85	76,8	11.41.14	18.00.35
„ 16	Mongôa	2 alt. ☉	109.38.00	7.50.34.30	„ 0.20.20.30	☉ 100,55	—	11.34.05	18.00.30
„ 16	Mongôa	—	—	—	„ 0.20.23.00	—	—	—	18.08.30
„ 17	Mongôa [6]	mer. ☉	60,88	—	„ 0.20.27.00	—	—	11.34.02	18.08.30
„ 21	Mongôa	—	—	8.52.30.30	„ 0.20.46.30	„ 40,01	76,2	—	18.00.00
„ 22	Mongôa	—	—	9.12.13.30	„ 0.20.51.30	„ 40,41	64,5	—	18.00.00
„ 23	Mongôa	—	—	8.44.46.30	„ 0.20.57.00	„ 44,35	71,5	—	18.00.00
„ 24	Mongôa	—	—	8.21.28.30	„ 0.21.02.30	„ 39,03	77,0	—	18.00.00
„ 25	Cha-N'ganji	mer. ☉	60,59	—	—	—	—	—	11.32.43	—
„ 26	Cha-N'ganji	—	—	20.24.38.30	„ 0.21.12.30	a.m. 36.10.10	—	—	18.23.00
„ 28	Cha-N'ganji	—	—	7.52.57.00	„ 0.21.20.44	☉ 33,51	80,8	—	18.23.00
„ 30	Cha-N'ganji	—	—	8.49 30.00	„ 0.21.25.30	„ 45,19	69,7	—	18.23.00
July 2	Cha-N'ganji	—	—	10.41.25.30	„ 0.21.31.30	„ 30,84	82,5	—	18.23.00
„ 3	Cha-N'ganji [6]	—	—	—	„ 0.21.13.00	—	—	—	—
„ 5	Matari	mer. ☉	55.26.57	—	„ 0.21.48.00	—	—	11.30.12	18.20.16
„ 7	Cha-Cussingo [7]	mer. ☽	100,7	3.47.10.00	„ 0.21.57.00	☉ 10,03	—	11.23.30	18.38.10
„ 11	Cangombe	mer. ☉	62,536	9.25.11.00	„ 0.22.15.00	„ 43.04.08	—	11.20.51	18.50.00
„ 16	Muene Quibau	„	56.55 53	—	—	—	—	11.27.00	19.11.30
„ 17	Cangomba	—	—	8.05.56.00	Sub. —	☉ 37,04	81,0	—	18.50.00
„ 22	Cangombe	—	—	7.45.11.30	—	„ 32,65	87,7	—	18.50.00
„ 25	Muene C-je [6]	mer. ☉	59.05.00	—	—	—	—	11.00.40	18.55.30
„ 30	Chanfana	„	60 22.35	—	—	—	—	10.52.04	18.39.59
August 2	Muene Chicanji	„	61.25.15	—	—	—	—	10.34.23	18.37.05
„ 2	N'Dumba Mughonde	2 alt. mer. ☉	60.52.30	—	—	—	—	11.07.02	18.56.30
„ 3	Cha-Calumbo	mer. ☉	61.15.13	—	—	—	—	10.30.00	18.39.51
„ 4	Cu-ango	„	62.03.40	—	—	—	—	10.27.22	18.38.38
„ 6	Cu-ango	„	62.45.30	—	—	—	—	10.18.05	18.32.38
„ 7	Cu-ango	„	63 07.24	—	—	—	—	10.12.50	18.34.05
„ 10	Cat-Jamisa	„	64.05.35	—	—	—	—	10.06.14	18.13.30
„ 12	Cu-ango	„	64.14.22	—	—	—	—	10.03.05	18.43.05

[1] The error of the *obba* was then 2,3 sub. The altitudes expressed in decimals and fractions represent the degrees into which Mr. d'Abbadie's instrument is divided; the others are degrees, minutes, seconds, and thirds of the sextant, or of the former instrument already reduced.
[2] The error of the *obba* was 2,18 sub.
[3] The error of the *obba* was 0,66 sub., reduced thereafter to zero.
[4] The error of the sextant was 2′.
[5] Passage of Mercury over the face of the sun.
[6] Satellite of Jupiter.
[7] Error of *obba* 0,05 sub.
[8] The elements of calculation from 25th July to 18th November, mainly longitudes, were lost in the arc at the Duque de Bragança.

280

Date.		Stations.	Meridian Altitudes.		Hours.	Positions.		Altitudes.		Azimuth.	Latitude.	Longitude
August	13	Cu-ango	mer. ☉	65.06.41	—	—		—		—	09.50.56	18.45.42
,,	15	Luali	,,	65.48.21	—	—		—		—	09.51.19	18.35.39
,,	17	Fumbejo	,,	66.34.50	—	—		—		—	09.45.48	18.23.52
,,	19	Cassanza	,,	67.21.18	—	—		—		—	09.38.08	18.10.39
,,	21	Cassanje	,,	68.03.58	—	—		—		—	09.35.06	17.51.30
,,	25	Catuchi	,,	68.11.05	—	—		—		—	10.46.30	19.01.30
,,	27	N'Dumba Tchiquilla	,,	70.12.05	—	—		—		—	10.34.30	19.01.00
November	9	Cassanjo	,,	82.24.13	—	—		—		—	09.35.20	17.56.30
,,	18	Cassanje		—	—	—		—		—	09.35.20	17.56.00
December	3	Cassanjo		—	01.27.46.00	0.57.35.30	Sub.	66,83	☉ p.m.	291,5	09.35.20	17.56.00
,,	15	Cassanje		—	02.18.39.40	—		50,62	,, ,,	—	09.35.20	17.56.00
,,	17	Cassanje		—	02.40.30.30	—		45,12	? ☉	—	09.35.20	17.56.00
,,	28	Banza e Lunda	mer. ☉	84,40	02.18.12.30	—		52,29		295,0	09.30.30	18.17.00
1879.												
February	18	Cassanje	,,	99,42	02 49.49.30	—		50,28	☉ p.m.	—	09.22.10	17.16.30
,,	25	Rio Lu-i	,,	72.45.57	—	—		—		—	08.59.00	17.12.30
,,	28	N'Gui	,,	73.18.54	—	—		—		—	08.27.34	16.50.30
March	4	N'Dala Samba		—	21.26.13.00	—		59,39	☉ a.m.	117,8	08.27.34	16.50.30
,,	5	N'Dala Samba		—	01.39.44.00	0.48.53.10	Sub.	69,66	☉ p.m.	333,7	09.27.43	16.22.50
,,	11	Calandula	mer. ☉	93,35	01.57.12.00	0.49.09.19		64,50	,, ,,	331,6	08.25.30	16.23.00
,,	13	Quesso	,,	91,95	23.02.56.30	—		81,42	☉ a.m.	73,3	09.22.30	16.07.30
,,	25	Banza Tango	mer. ☉	82.08.34	01.29.56.30	0.50.15.30	Sub.	87,60	☉ p.m.	318,3	09.12.00	16.00.40
,,	26	Banza Quiluanje	,,	87.60	—	—		—		—	08.55.36	16.00.40
April	8	Duque de Bragança	,,	81,82	21.44.59.00	0.51.14.10	,,	61,67	☉ a.m.	95,4	08.55.36	16.10.00
,,	2	Duque de Bragança	,,	84.36	—	0.53.54.39	Sub.	—		—	08.55.36	16.10.00
,,	29	Dumba-ia-Furmuosso	mer. ☉	73,84	02.47.53.00	0.54.48.45	,, ,,	53,07	☉ p.m.	360,4	08.41.30	16.27.00
May	2	Cauda-ia-Massango		8,00								
,,	5	Quimbaxo	,,	{72,25 / 127,75}	02.59.15.00	—	Sub	40,00	☉ p.m.	352,2	08.25.51	16.28.00
,,	6	Quimbaxe	,,	72,06	03.28 10.00	0.55.49.29	,, ,,	32,81	,, a.m.	349,1	08.22.36	16.28.42
,,	10	N'Bondo N'Gunza	,,	71,03	10.22.52.00	0.56.11.15	,, ,,	63,03	—	262,5	8.13.00	16.32.42
,,	12	N'Bondo N'Gunza		—	—	0.56.23.00	,, ,,	—		—		
,,	13	Calunga-N'Gangá	mer. ☉	70,34	1.19.31.00	0.56.09.45	,, ,,	60,66	☉ p.m.	376,4	8.04.00	16.48.19
,,	16	Cafuchila	,,	63,75	2.11.27.30	0.56.32.15	,, ,,	49,65	,, a.m.	—	7.53.14	16.50.28
,,	21	Quipanzo	,,	68,72	21.01.40.00	0.57.09.45	,, ,,	45,07	,, a.m.	—	7.43.32	16.55.06
,,	26	N'Guijo	,,	67,97	1.50.28.30	0.57.47.15	,, ,,	53,31	,, p.m.	369,9	7.27.18	17.11.08
,,	27	Cu-ango		—	3.58.08.30	0.57.54.45	,, ,,	24,17		—		

May	28	Mafargo	mor. ☉	67,75	—	Sub.	0.58.39.45	☉ p.m.	52,11	—	7.19.03	17.11.00
June	2	Mussengue	"	60,21.0¼	—	"	22.00.53.00	☉ a.m.	55,65	370,4	7.12.40	17.05.30
"	4	Macolo	"	66,9	—	"	—	—	—	163,5	7.06.16	17.05.31
"	6	Deserted Senzala	"	60,30.35	—	—	—	—	—	—	6.35.00	—
"	11	Cu-gho	"	65,88	—	Sub.	0.59.47.15	☉ a.m.	52,97	—	7.21.49	16.50.02
"	14	Muçanza	"	65,45	—	"	1.00.09.45	"	58,61	255,5	—	—
"	18	Sauganhe	"	65,1	—	"	1.01.39.35	☉ p.m.	53,34	375,7	7.44.15	16.16.33
"	21	Lu-embe	"	61,73	—	"	—	—	—	—	8.02.00	—
"	23	Lu-calla	"	61,58	—	"	1.01.17.15	☉ p.m.	51,21	374,5	8.10.40	16.18.10
"	27	Vunda-ia-Ebo	"	57.54.55	—	"	1.01.47.15	☉ a.m.	49,82	265,7	8.29.09	16.12.34
"	30	Duque de Bragança[2]		—	—	"	3.27.01.00	☉ p.m.	33,43	359,5	—	—
July	19	Duque de Bragança	mor. ☉	66,65	—	"	23.11.25.00	☉ p.m.	63,69	214,9	8.55.16	16.10.00
"	31	Duque de Bragança	"	—	—	Sub.	2.01.42.00	☉ p.m.	56,20	363,0	—	—
August	3	Samba Canço	"	70,13	—	"	22.28.07.00	☉ a.m.	59,12	69,35	9.03.39	16.51.00
"	5	Bondo-ia-Quilesso	"	70,55	—	"	2.01.56.00	☉ p.m.	56,91	369,3	9.12.51	15.26.13
"	6	Praça Velha	"	70,79	—	—	—	—	—	—	9.16.14	—
"	7	Ambaca	mor. ☉	71,11	—	Sub.	1.06.40.00	☉ a.m.	60,45	69,25	9.15.35	15.19.48
"	9	Rio Catombe[3]	"	71,46	—	"	—	—	—	—	9.30.30	15.32.30
"	12	Pungo N'Dongo	"	72,27	—	"	1.07.15.46	☉ a.m.	55,61	78,7	9.39.52	15.42.16
"	15	Pungo N'Dongo	"	72,27	—	"	1.07.40.00	☉ p.m.	53,78	360,1	9.39.52	15.42.16
"	27	Porto Xunga[4]	"	77,59	—	"	1.09.08.48	"	53,02	89,5	9.50.01	15.46.10
"	28	N'Gola Quitucho	"	78,02	—	—	—	—	—	—	9.47.55	15.57.20
"	29	Caquili	"	78,11	—	Sub.	1.09.23.36	☉ p.m.	53,29	350,1	9.46.29	16.03.30
"	30	Lombe do Pires	"	78,87	—	—	—	—	—	—	9.44.40	16.07.30
"	31	Quilinda	"	{79,26; 120,79}	—	Sub.	21.44.50.00	☉ a.m.	55,89	91,4	9.43.16	16.20.18
September	1	Lombe	"	79,81	—	—	—	—	—	—	9.35.19	16.10.30
"	2	Lombe do Motta	"	80.33	—	Sub.	2.38.41.00	☉ p.m.	52,91	—	9.28.58	16.12.58
"	5	Pungo N'Dongo	"	—	—	"	2.25.16.00	"	57,12	350,2	9.40.30	15.42.16
"	6	Pungo N'Dongo[5]	"	—	—	Sub.	—	—	—	—	9.40.30	15.42.16
"	12	Pungo N'Dongo	"	—	—	"	1.10.30.05	☉ a.m.	45,20	106,4	9.40.30	15.42.16
"	14	Ca-anza	"	84,58	—	"	1.11.10.00	"	—	—	9.46.35	—
"	16	Cachongun	"	85,95	—	Sub.	1.11.18.12	☉ p.m.	26,36	331,8	9.40.06	15.20.05
"	17	Nhanguo	"	86,38	—	—	—	—	—	—	9.40.24	15.11.30
"	29	Dondo a E.[6]	"	91,6	—	—	—	—	—	—	9.39.52	14.31.54
"	30	Dondo	"	92,01	—	—	—	—	—	—	9.41.00	14.31.54
"	22	Dondo	"	—	—	Sub.	1.12.50.34	☉ a.m.	71,81	96,4	9.41.00	14.31.51
October	10	Dondo	"	—	—	"	1.15.00.10	☉ p.m.	55,13	323,6	9.41.00	14.31.00
"	15	Loanda arrival	"	—	—	"	1.15.14.00	"	60,70	319,75	8.47.56	13.07.20
"	15	Loanda arrival[7]	"	—	—	"	1.15.24.00	"	60,33	319,8	8.47.56	13.07.30

[1] Satellite of Jupiter.
[2] Movement of the chronometer from 25th April to 30th June, 7,5.
[3] Error of abba 0,0"1.
[4] Error of abba 0,003.

[5] Satellite of Jupiter.
[6] Error of abba 0,02.
[7] In Loanda, on the 26th October, by observatory ball, obtained position for chronometer = 1h. 15'.24" longitude 13°.07'.30".

Date.	Stations.	Meridian Altitudes.	Hours.	Positions.	Altitudes.	Azimuth.	Latitude.	Longitude
August 13	Cu-ango	mer. ☉	65.06.41	—	—	—	—	09.59.56	18.45.42
„ 15	Luali	„	65.48.24	—	—	—	—	09.51.19	18.35.30
„ 17	Fumbejo	„	66.34.50	—	—	—	—	09.15.18	18.23.52
„ 19	Cassanza	„	67.21.18	—	—	—	—	09.38.08	18.10.52
„ 21	Cassanje	„	68.03.58	—	—	—	—	09.33.06	17.51.30
„ 25	Catuchi	„	68.14.05	—	—	—	—	10.46.30	19.01.30
„ 27	N'Dumba Tchiquilla	„	70.12.05	—	—	—	—	10.31.30	19.04.00
November 9	Cassanje	„	82.24.13	—	—	—	—	09.35.30	17.56.30
„ 18	Cassanje	—	—	—	—	—	—	09.35.30	17.56.30
December 3	Cassanje	—	—	01.27.16.03	Sub.	0.57.35.30	☉ p.m.	66,83	291,5	09.35.20	17.56.30
„ 15	Cassanje	—	—	02.18.39.00	„	—	„	50,82	—	09.35.20	17.56.00
„ 17	Cassanje	—	—	02.40.30.30	„	—	„	45,42	295,0	09.35.20	17.56.00
„ 28	Banza e Lunda	mer. ☉	84,40	02.18.12.30	„	—	☉	52,29	—	09.30.30	18.17.00
1870. February 18	Cassanje	„	—	02.49.49.30	—	—	☉ p.m.	50,28	—	—	—
„ 25	Rio Lu-i	„	99,42	—	—	—	—	—	—	09.22.10	17.16.30
„ 28	N'Guri	„	72.45.57	—	—	—	—	—	—	08.59.00	17.12.30
March 4	N'Dala Samba	„	73.18.54	—	—	—	—	—	—	09.27.34	16.50.30
„ 5	N'Dala Samba	„	—	21.26.13.00	—	—	☉ a.m.	59,29	117,8	09.27.34	16.50.30
„ 11	Cahundua	mer. ☉	93,35	01.30.44.00	Sub.	0.48.53.10	☉	69,66	393,7	09.27.43	16.22.50
„ 13	Queoso	„	91,95	01.57.12.00	„	0.49.09.19	☉	61,50	331,6	09.25.30	16.23.00
„ 25	Banza Tango	mer. ☉	82.08.34	23.02.56.30	—	—	☉ a.m.	81,12	73,3	09.22.30	16.07.30
„ 26	Banza Quilunje	„	87.60	01.29.56.30	Sub.	0.50.15.30	☉ p.m.	87,00	348,3	09.12.00	16.00.40
April 5	Duque de Bragança	„	81.82	—	—	—	—	—	—	08.55.36	16.00.10
„ 2	Duque de Bragança	„	84.36	21.44.59.00	Sub.	0.51.14.10	☉ a.m.	61,67	95,4	08.55.36	16.10.00
„ 25	Duque de Bragança	„	—	—	0.53.54.39	„	—	—	—	08.55.36	16.10.00
„ 29	Dumba-in-Funnuesso	mer. ☉	73,64	02.47.58.00	„	0.54.48.45	☉ p.m.	53,07	360,4	08.51.38	16.10.00
May 2	Canda-in-Massangu	„	8,00	—	—	—	—	—	—	08.41.30	16.27.00
„ 5	Quimbaxe	„	{72,25 / 127,75}	02.59.15.00	—	—	☉ p.m.	40,00	352,2	08.25.51	16.28.00
„ 6	Quimbaxe	„	72,06	03.28.10.00	Sub	0.55.49.29	„	32,81	340,1	08.22.36	16.28.42
„ 10	N'Bondo N'Gnuza	„	71,93	10.22.52.00	„	0.56.11.15	☉ a.m.	63,00	262,5	8.13.00	16.32.42
„ 12	N'Bondo N'Gnuza	„	—	—	0.56.23.00	—	—	—	—	—	—
„ 13	Calunga-N'Gangá	mer. ☉	70,34	1.19.31.00	—	0.56.09.45	☉ p.m.	60,66	376,4	8.04.00	16.18.19
„ 16	Cafuchia	„	69,75	2.11.27.30	„	0.56.32.15	„	49,65	—	7.53.14	16.50.28
„ 21	Quinanzo	„	68,72	21.01.40.00	„	0.57.40.45	☉ a.m.	45,07	—	7.43.52	16.55.00
„ 26	N'Guju	„	67,97	1.50.28.30	„	0.57.47.15	„	53,31	369,0	7.27.18	17.11.08
„ 27	Cu-ango	„	—	3.58.08.30	„	0.57.54.45	„	24,17	—	—	—

May 28	Mafurgo	mer. ☉	67,75	—	—	—	—	—	—	7.19.03	17.11 00
June 2	Mussenguo	„	60.21.04	1.56.33.00	Sub.	0.58.30.45	☉ p.m.	52,11	370,4	7.12.40	17.05 30
„ 3	Muenlo	„	66,0	23.00.53.00	„	0.58.54.45	☉ a.m.	55,05	163,5	7.08.16	17.05 30
„ 6	Deserted Sonzala	„	60.30.36	—	—	—	—	—	—	6.35.00	—
„ 11	Cu-gho	„	65,88	21.53.26.30	Sub.	0.60.47.15	☉ a.m.	52,97	—	7.21.40	16.50.02
„ 14	Mupauga	„	65,45	22.30.09.00	„	1.00.09.45	„	58,61	255,5	—	—
„ 18	Sanganhe	„	65.1	1.50.29.00	„	1.01.39.45	„	53,34	375,7	7.44.15	16.10.33
„ 24	Lu-ombe	„	64,73	—	—	—	—	—	—	8.02.00	—
„ 26	Lu-colla	„	61,58	2.01.30.30	Sub.	1.01.17.15	☉ p.m.	51,21	374,5	8.10.40	16.18.10
„ 27	Viunda-in-Ebo	„	57.54.55	21.50.28.00	„	1.01.47.15	☉ a.m.	49,82	205,7	8.29.00	16.12.34
„ 30	Duque de Bragança	„	—	3.27.01.00	„	1.02.09.45	„	33,43	359,5	—	—
July 19	Duque de Bragança	mer. ☉	66,05	23.14.25.00	—	—	☉ a.m.	63.69	244,9	8.55.16	16.10.00
„ 31	Duque de Bragança	„	—	2.01.42.00	Sub.	1.06.10.36	☉ p.m.	56,20	369,0	—	—
August 3	Samba Caugo	„	70,13	22.28.07.00	„	1.06.32.05	☉ a.m.	59,12	69,35	9.03.30	16.51.00
„ 5	Bondo-in-Quileuse	„	70,55	2.01.56.00	—	—	☉ p.m.	56,91	369,3	9.12.51	15.26.13
„ 6	Praça Velha	„	70,79	—	—	—	—	—	—	9.16.14	—
„ 7	Ambaca	mer. ☉	71,11	22.33.29.00	Sub.	1.06.40.00	☉ a.m.	60,45	69,25	9.15.35	15.19.18
„ 9	Rio Cutembe [3]	„	71,40	—	—	—	—	—	—	9.30.30	15.32.30
„ 12	Pungo N'Dongo	„	72,27	22.11.16.00	Sub.	1.07.15.46	☉ a.m.	55,61	78,7	9.39.52	15.42.16
„ 15	Pungo N'Dongo	„	72,27	2.25.58.30	„	1.07.40.00	☉ p.m.	53,78	360,1	9.39.32	15.42.16
„ 27	Porto Xunga [4]	„	77,50	21.38.50.30	„	1.09.08.48	☉ a.m.	53,02	89,5	9.50.01	15.16.10
„ 28	N'Gola Quituchó	„	78,0(3	—	—	—	—	—	—	9.47.55	15.57.20
„ 29	Caquili	„	78,44	2.35.40.00	Sub.	1.09.23.36	☉ p.m.	53,29	350,1	9.46.29	16.00.30
„ 30	Lombe do Pires	„	78,87	—	—	—	—	—	—	9.44.40	16.07.30
„ 31	Quibinda	„	{79,26 / 120,75}	21.44.59.00	Sub.	1.09.38.24	☉ a.m.	55,89	91,4	9.43.16	16.20.18
September 1	Lombe	„	79,81	—	—	—	—	—	—	9.35.19	16.10.30
„ 2	Lombe do Motta	„	80 43	2.38.41.00	Sub.	1.09.54.00	„	52,91	—	9.28.58	16.12.58
„ 5	Pungo N'Dongo	„	—	2.25.16.00	„	—	„	57,12	350,2	9.40.30	15.42.16
„ 6	Pungo N'Dongo [5]	„	—	—	Sub.	1.10.30.05	„	—	—	9.40.30	15.42.16
„ 12	Pungo N'Dongo	„	—	20.56.04.00	„	1.11.10.00	☉ a.m.	45,20	106,4	9.40.30	15.42.16
„ 14	Cu-anza	„	81,58	—	—	—	—	—	—	9.46.35	—
„ 15	Cachongua	„	85,95	4.26.02.00	Sub.	1.11.48.12	☉ p.m.	26,36	331,8	9.40 00	15.20.05
„ 17	Nhungue	„	86,38	—	—	—	—	—	—	9.40.24	15.11.30
„ 20	Dondo a E.[6]	„	91,6	—	—	—	—	—	—	9.30.52	14.31.54
„ 30	Dondo	„	92,01	—	—	—	—	—	—	9.41.00	14.31.51
„ 22	Dondo	„	—	22.34.45.00	Sub.	1.12 50.34	☉ a.m.	71,81	96,4	9.41.00	14.31.51
October 10	Dondo	„	—	2.15.50.00	„	1.15.00.10	☉ p.m.	55,13	321,6	9.41.00	14.31.00
„ 15	Loanda arrival	„	—	2.30.44.30	„	1.15.14.00	„	60,70	319,75	8.47.56	13.07.50
„ 15	Loanda arrival [7]	„	—	2.32.04.30	„	1.15.24.00	„	60,33	319,8	8.47.56	13.07.30

[1] Satellite of Jupiter.
[2] Movement of the chronometer from 24th April to 30th June, 7,5.
[3] Error of abba 0,04.
[4] Error of abba 0,003.
[5] Satellite of Jupiter.
[6] Error of abba 0,02.
[7] In Loanda, on the 26th October, by observatory Lell, obtained position for chronometer = 1h. 15′.24″ longitude 13°.07′.30″.

HEIGHTS ABOVE THE SEA-LEVEL
OF THE MOST IMPORTANT POSITIONS,
CALCULATED AT THE INFANTE D. LUIZ OBSERVATORY.

The measurements are given in metres. The boiling-point and temperature are expressed in degrees of the centigrade thermometers.

Places.	Boiling Points. Baudin's Hypsometers.				Mean.	Temperature.	Altitude.
	Nº.108.	Nº.109.	Nº.110	Nº.112.			
Quillengues . . .	97,12	97,14	97,13	97,17	97,140	25,0	869,1
Caconda . . . . {	94,73	94,75	94,73	94,77	94,745	25,0	} 1612,5
	94,83	94,86	94,83	94,88	94,850	24,5	
	94,70	94,78	94,75	94,83	94,729	24,0	
T'chimbuioca . . .	94,68	94,70	94,65	94,73	94,690	18,0	1697,3
Bihó . . . . . {	94,85	94,88	94,86	94,93	94,880	20,5	} 1572,7
	94,79	94,84	94,81	94,88	94,830	24,0	
	94,94	94,97	94,94	95.01	94,965	16,0	
Mongôa	96,50	96,54	96,51	96,55	96,525	26,0	1112,3
Cha N'ganji . . .	96,27	96,30	96,28	96,35	96,300	27,5	1188,7
N'Dumba Mughande	95,81	95,86	95,82	95,88	95,842	27,2	1340,1
Catuchi	96,17	96,23	96,20	96,26	96,215	29,0	1226,2
T'chiquilla	96,25	96,31	96,28	96,35	96,297	29,0	1180,3
Cassanje . . . {	96,89	96,91	96,89	—	96,896	26,0	} 945,3
	96,90	96,95	96,92	96,97	96,935	24,0	
	97,00	97,03	97,00	97,07	97,100	23,0	
Quesso	96,57	—	26,55	96,64	96,586	25,0	1040,6
Duque de Bragança . {	96,55	96,60	96,54	96,65	96,585	25,0	} 1060,1
	96,55	96,60	96,55	96,62	96,580	23,0	
N'guna Vunda . .	98,31	98,35	98,12	98,65	98,375	28,0	499,0
Rio Cugho	98,39	98,53	98,39	98,42	98,430	31,0	497,5
Pungo N'Dongo . .	96,70	96,71	96,74	96,80	96,74	26,0	1020,5
Nhanguo	97,75	97,77	97,80	97,85	97,79	22,0	691,1
Dondo	99,69	99,70	99,72	99,72	99,707	24,5	93,7
Mossamedes . . .	99,95	99,97	99,97	99,97	99,965	27,0	8m

CORRECTIONS IN THE INFANTE D. LUIZ OBSERVATORY.

	Hypsometers.			
	Nº. 108.	Nº. 109.	Nº. 110.	Nº. 112.
Before setting out	+ 0,34	+ 0,34	+ 0,31	+ 0,34
After arrival	+ 0,35	+ 0,31	+ 0,27	+ 0,32

ADDITIONS TO THE FAUNA

OF

CENTRAL AND WEST AFRICA.

FAUNA.

FROM BENGUELLA TO THE BIHÉ—FROM THE BIHÉ TO CASSANGE.[1]

MAMMIFERI.

1. SOREX, sp. (?)

    Obtained in the proximity of the River Cu-bango. Common name *Onkunga*.

2. HELIOPHOBIUS ARGENTEO-CINEREUS, Peters.

    Two specimens, one from Caconda, the other from the Bihé. The natives of the former call it *Oneta*, and those of the latter *Oguim*. It lives under ground, where it feeds on the roots of trees; it is eaten by the natives.

3. GALAGO MONTEIRI, Bartlett; *Proc. Z. S.*, London, 1868, p. 231, pl. 28.

    In the collection forwarded by our explorers, Capello and Ivens, we find a specimen of this species, which was already represented in the Museum at Lisbon by various specimens obtained from other parts of the interior of Angola. They do not all exactly agree in colour with the model exemplar sent by Mr. Monteiro alive to London in 1863, and there described by Mr. Bartlett; two Caconda specimens, which we owe to Mr. Anchieta, have hair of the purest ash colour; the others are more yellow in tint, especially at the extremities of the hair. The Caconda natives give to this species the name of *Bobo*, as we learn from Mr. Anchieta; on the label of the sample sent by Messrs. Capello and Ivens appears the native name of *Tchicafo*.

---

[1] Extract of the *Jornal de Sciencias Mathematicas, Physicas e Naturaes*, No. XXVI., Lisbon, 1879. The zoological products here described were classified by Dr. Barbosa du Bocage, the illustrious Director of the Museum of Lisbon. The first lot was collected on the way to the Bihé; and the second between the Bihé and Cassange.

4. GALAGO SENEGALENSIS, Geoff. Saint-Hillaire.

A male specimen. The native name is *Catoto*.

This and the preceding are the only Lemurideos we have hitherto received from Angola. The other specimens in our possession of *G. Senegalensis* are all from Caconda, where they bestow on it the name of *Nóno*.

5. VESPERUS MINUTUS, Temm. (?)

A specimen in spirit, and in a bad state of preservation.

6. KERIVOULA ARGENTATA, Tomes; *Proc. Z. S.*, London, 1861, p. 32.

A female, whose characteristics appear to agree with those which Mr. Tomes attributes to this species, saving in the dimensions, which are smaller than those mentioned by that gentleman. In his excellent Catalogue of the Chiroptera of the British Museum, Mr. Dobson inclines to the opinion that the *K. argentata* may be simply an adult individual or a local race of larger size than the *K. lanosa*, living on the S.E. coast of Africa, from the Zambesi to the Cape. Its native name in the interior of Angola is *Cafuenfuco*.

7. HERPESTES MELANURUS, Fraser. (?)

H. fulvescente-rufus nigro punctulatus, capite supra, dorso media caudaque rubiginosis, abdomine et artubus unicoloribus ochraceo-rufis; cauda fere corporis longitudinem æquante, apice late nigro. L. t. 530 m.; corporis cum capite 280 m.; caudæ 250 m.

It assimilates in general conformation, and somewhat in the colours, to the *Cynictis melanura*, Martin, represented in plate 9 of the *Zoologia typica* of Fraser, which is now considered as a true *Herpestes* with five toes to the fore and hind feet; but as we have no authentic exemplar of this species wherewith to compare our own, we cannot affirm that it is identical. In the latter, the upper part of the head, the back, and tail, more especially from the middle to the extreme end (which is black), are of a bright red, which I do not see indicated in the descriptions I was able to consult of the *H. melanurus*, and whereof the said plate of Fraser does not give the slightest idea. Some years ago Mr. Anchieta sent us from the river *Chimba*, in the territory of Mossamedes, another specimen of *Herpestes*, and which also, to our mind, approximates to the *H. melanurus* and the present specimen; but it differs from both in that the tail is sensibly much longer than the body (trunk and head together), and by the much greater extension of the black colour at the end of the tail; besides this, its colour is of a much duller red, and in this particular agrees better with the figure published by Fraser of the *H. melanurus*.

8. MYOXUS (GRAPHIURUS) MURINUS, Desm.

A single specimen, identical with others already in our possession from

Duque de Bragança and *Caconda*, determined by Professor Peters, of Berlin. V. *Jorn. Acad. Sc.*, Lisbon, No. x., 1870, p. 126.

We are informed by Messrs. Capello and Ivens that this species is found in the cavities of old trees, and is known to the natives by the name of *Cufuenho*.

BIRDS.

1. SCOPS CAPENSIS, Smith.

   "Native name *Cuculo*. Yellow eyes. Eats rats and other small animals."

   Accords perfectly in its characteristics with the specimens we have from other parts of Angola. V. *Orn. de Angola*, p. 60.

2. PIONIAS FUSCICOLLIS, Kuhl.

   "Native name *T'chicangue*. Yellow eyes. Feeds on seeds."

   Of this species, met with by Anderson to the north of the Damaras territory, we have specimens obtained by Mr. Anchieta in Quillengues and in the Humbe.

3. PIONIAS MEYERII, Rüpp.

   "Native name *Cuique*."

   Of the two exemplars we received, one came marked as from Cassange. It appears that this spot of West Africa is the nearest to the Equator where, up to the present, this species has been observed.

4. DENDROBATES NAMAQUUS, Licht.

   "Native name *Mangula*. Red eyes."

   The specimens of this species, which Mr. Anchieta has sent us from other parts of the Angola interior, bear on the labels a native name somewhat differing from the above, i.e. *Bangula* instead of *Mangula*, which is indistinctly applied to other species of woodpeckers.

5. MEROPS HIRUNDINACEUS, Vieill.

   "Native name *Mutico*. Red eyes. Lives near rivers, and feeds on insects and other smaller animals."

   This species, which Monteiro encountered in Benguella, was observed in the *Humbe* by Mr. Anchieta.

6. CENTROPUS MONACHUS, Rüpp.

   "Native name *Mucouco*."

7. CAPRIMULGUS SHELLEYI, Bocage.

   "Native name *Huicumbamba*. Black eyes. Feeds on insects."

   The collection of Messrs. Capello and Ivens contains but one specimen of this interesting species. Although its state of preservation leaves much to be desired, we have not the slightest doubt concerning its identity with the exemplars of *Caconda*, which we consider to be the representatives of an inedited species. V. *Jorn. Acad. Sc.*, Lisbon, No. XXIV., 1878, p. 266.

8. BRADYORNYS MURINUS, Hartl.
"Native name *Césso*. Black eyes."

9. BRADYORNIS DIABOLICUS, Sharpe.
"Native name *Mungange*."

10. DICRURUS DIVARICATUS.
"Native name *Mungange*. Light brown eyes."

11. FISCUS CAPELLI, new. sp.
F. collari simillimus, vix minor, spatio ante-oculari albo. L. t. 220 m.; alæ 92 m.; caudæ 118 m.; rostri 16 m.; tarsi 25 m.

Only two exemplars of this species came over, one full-grown with the tail incomplete, being reduced to the two intermediate feathers, and the other complete without indication of sex like the former one, with young plumage. In this, in lieu of the white mesh between the base of the beak and the eye, on each side of the head there is apparent a very distinct mesh of a yellowish grey.

We dedicate this species to one of the intrepid explorers to whom we owe this valuable consignment, Mr. Hermenegildo Capello.

These two specimens were obtained in *Cassange*, and bear different names, the young one *Quiquecuria*, the adult *Quimbimbe*.

12. PRIONOPS RETZII, Wahlb.
Native name *Céella*. Eyes canary colour."

13. MERISTES OLIVACEUS, Vieill.
"Native name *Muango*. Yellow eyes."

14. PICNONOTUS TRICOLOR, Hartl.
"Native name *Tumba-cambungo*."

15. CRATEROPUS HARTLAUBI, Bocage.
"Native name *Ceque*. Red eyes."

16. TURDUS STREPITANS, Smith. (?)
"Native name *Quissocola-lôa*. Eyes chestnut. Feeds on insects."
An adult specimen. Compared with other ensamples of the *T. strepitans*, from various places, we noted the following divergencies:—It is sensibly smaller; the lower portion is pure white, without the slightest tinge of red or buff; the meshes which cover the neck, breast, and part of the abdomen are larger than those of the *T. strepitans*, more confluent, and extend more to the lower part of the abdomen.

17. TURDUS LYBONIANUS, Smith.
"Native name *Quissomda*. Black eyes."

18. MONTICOLA BREVIPES, Waterh.

"Native name *Tchicamba*. Chestnut eyes. Feeds on fruit and insects."

19. MYRMECOCICHLA NIGRA, Vieill.

Two specimens, male and female; the latter coffee colour and without white epaulets.

"Native name *Munhamba*."

20. PHOLIDAUGES VERREAUXI, Bocage.

"Native name *Quicé*."

21. LAMPROCOLIUS ACUTICAUDUS, Bocage.

"Native name *Gonre*. Red eyes. Feeds on fruit."

22. PASSER DIFFUSUS, Smith.

"Native name *Mussuesso*."

23. TRERON CALVA, Temm.

"Native name *Bunzo*. Grey eyes. Feeds on fruit."

24. FRANCOLINUS SCHLEGELI, Heugl.

"Native name *Cambango*. Eyes chestnut. Lives in the woods."

It is the first time we have received this species, which is at this date rare among European collections; it is also the first instance of its capture so near the western coast. It was hitherto considered as confined to a rather restricted region of Central Africa, where it was discovered by the celebrated naturalist Von Heuglin. The first description of it was published by that gentleman in 1863 in the *Jornal de Cabanis*. (V. *Jornal f. Ornith.*, 1863, p. 275; and Heugl., *Orn. N. O. Afr.*, p. 898, plate xxx.)

25. ARDEA RUFIVENTRIS, Sundev.

"Native name *Bouda*. Iris with two concentric circles, one internal yellow, another external red. It lives on rivers, and feeds on fish."

26. ARDEOLA MINUTA.

"Native name *Cassoucua*. Iris canary colour."

27. EODIVANELLUS LATERALIS, Smith.

"Native name *Macó*. Iris light yellow, eyelids canary colour, the membrane in front of the eyes, upper third red and the rest yellow. Found in marshy places, where it feeds on the animals proper to such soil."

REPTILES AND AMPHIBIOUS CREATURES.

1. CHAMELEO DILEPIS, Hall.
   A sample from Caconda, where it is common.

2. AGAMA ARMATA, Peters.
   Two specimens also from Caconda.

3. AGAMA PLANICEPS, Peters.
   An exemplar from the vicinity of the river Calae.

4. EUMECES RETICULATUS, Peters.
   A specimen without indication of origin.

5. EUPREPES BINOTATUS, Bocage.
   An exemplar of large dimensions from Caconda.

6. BOEDON QUADRILINEATUM, Dum. and Bibr.
   Caught in the Bihé.

7. NAJA ANCHIETÆ, nov. sp.
   ? *Naja haje*, L. v *viridis*, Peters, *Monatsb. k. Akad.*, Berlin, Mai, 1873, p. 411, tab. I. fig. 1.
   Tête courte ; rostrale triangulaire fortement rabattue sur le devant du museau et séparant presque entièrement les naso-frontales ; un cercle complet autour de l'œil formé par une sus-orbitaire, une pré-orbitaire, deux post-orbitaires et trois ou quatre sous-orbitaires ; sept labiales supérieures, dont la troisième s'articule par son bord supérieur à la pré-orbitaire ; temporales 1 + 2. Dix-sept rangées d'écailles lisses sur le milieu du tronc. Plaques abdominales cent quatre-vingt-onze ; anale simple ; cinquante-quatre paires de souscaudales.
   Dimensions.—Longueur totale 80 centimètres ; queue 14 centimètres.
   Coloration.—En dessus d'une teinte brun-olivâtre, plus foncée sur les bords des écailles ; en dessous jaunâtre, varié de taches brunes. Un large collier noir ou brun-foncé sur le cou à une petite distance de la tête.
   M. Anchieta nous envoya de *Caconda*, il y a quelque temps, deux individus de cette curieuse espèce, qui nous semble bien distincte de la *Naja haje* d'après l'écaillure de la tête. Les indigènes de Caconda l'appellent *Turulangila*.

8. ECHIDNA ARIETANS, Merr.
   Two specimens, one from the River Calae, the other caught on an island of the River Cabindango. The natives call it *Buta*.

9. MONITOR SAURUS, Laurenti.
   "Native name *Sango*, River Lu-ando."

10. STELLIO ATRICOLLIS, Smith.

"Native name *T'chico*. Lives in the trees. Feeds on insects."

11. EUPREPES IVENSI, new sp.

Corps à forme cyclotetragone, allongé ; membres relativement courts ; queue très longue. Tête petite, à museau court et conique. Nasales en contact, triangulaires, la narine s'ouvrant près de l'angle supérieur; supéro-nasales étroites, également en contact et s'articulant par l'extrémité opposée à une freno-nasale, qui vient s'appuyer sur la première labiale ; deux frénales, l'antérieure carrée, la postérieure pentagonale et plus grande ; internasale triangulaire à bord antérieur arrondi, en contact par ses bords postérieurs avec les freno-nasales ; celles-ci de forme pentagonale et s'articulant à la frontale, qui est de forme hexagonale et bien développée ; deux fronto-pariétales distinctes, à peu près de la forme et de la grandeur des fronto-nasales ; inter-pariétale en forme de fer de lance, séparant complètement les deux pariétales. Rostrale emboitant l'extrémité du museau et présentant en dessus deux bords concaves qui reçoivent les nasales ; sept eabiales supérieures, les quatre premières quadrangulaires, la cinquième située au dessous de l'œil, plus haute et plus allongée que les précédentes et superposée à la quatrième par un court prolongement de son bord antérieur, les sixième et septième de forme plus irrégulière. Ouverture auriculaire garnie à son bord antérieur de trois lobules pointus. Paupière inférieure écailleuse, présentant au centre un petit disque transparent. Scutelles digitales carénées, les écailles des paumes et des plantes des pieds légèrement tuberculeuses. Trente-deux rangs d'écailles sur le tronc ; celles du dos à trois carènes très distinctes et rapprochées, celles des flancs lisses.

Dimensions.—Le plus grand de nos individus porte une queue de nouvelle formation assez court ; deux autres plus jeunes l'ont, au contraire, assez longue. Voici les dimensions d'un de ces individus :

Longueur totale 290 millim.; queue 200 m.; tête 15 m.; memb. ant. 21 m.; memb. post. 30 m.

Coloration.—En dessus et sur les côtés d'un noir-olivâtre, marqué de cinq raies longitudinales jaunes ; l'une plus large, occupant le milieu du dos, de la nuque à la base de la queue, et deux de chaque côté, dont la supérieure suit la ligne qui sépare le dos des flancs, et l'inférieure s'étend de l'ouverture auriculaire au tiers postérieur de la queue. En dessous d'un bleu clair uniforme.

Habitat.—Nos trois individus nous ont été envoyés du *Bié*, dans l'intérieur de Benguella par MM. Capello et Ivens pendant le cours de leur voyage d'exploration du Cu-ango. D'après nos hardis voyageurs, l'espèce y est connue sous le nom de *Muntambandonga*.

12. EUPREPES BAYONII, Bocage.

"District of Cassange."

13. ONYCHOCEPHALUS ANGOLENSIS, Bocage.
   "Native name *Chico-chico*. District of Cassange. Lives on the ground."

14. LIMNOPHIS BICOLOR, Günther.
   "Native name *Muzuzo*. River Lu-ando."

15. LEPTODIRA RUFESCENS, Günther.
   "Native name *Quintadagila*. District of Cassange."

16. RHAGERRHIS TRITÆNIATUS, Günther.
   "Native name *Calombolo*. Said to be venomous."

17. PHILOTHAMNUS HETEROLEPIDOTA, Günther.
   "Native name *Calumberembe*."

18. BUCEPHALUS TYPUS, Smith. Var. D. Smith, *H. S. Af. Zool.*, Reptiles, tab. XI.
   "Native name *Quilengo-lengo*. Held to be venomous."

19. CAUSUS RHOMBEATUS, Dum. and Bibr.
   "Native name *Quibolo-bolo*. Venomous."

20. DACTYLETHRA MULLERI, Peters.
   "Native name *T'chiula*."

21. DACTYLETHRA MULLERI, Peters.
   A specimen of the Dombe. Native name *Chimboto*.

22. RANA ORNATISSIMA, Bocage, new sp.

De la grandeur à peu-près de notre *R. temporaria* d'Europe. Tête aussi longue que large, à museau légèrement prominent; langue large, échancrée en arrière; deux groups de dents vomériennes situés à l'angle interne des ouvertures postérieures des narines et séparés par un intervalle; narines à égale distance de l'extrémité du museau et de l'œil; tympan distinct, inférieur en diamètre à l'ouverture oculaire; pas de parotides ni de plis glanduleux sur le dos; peau finement granuleuse en dessus et en dessous; membres postérieurs et orteils modérément longs, ceux-ci réunis à la base par une petite palmure; le quatrième orteil beaucoup plus long que le troisième et le cinquième, qui sont égaux; un tubercule saillant et aplati au bord interne du métatarse.

Dimensions.—Longueur de la tête 23 millim.; du tronc 45 m.; du memb. ant. 33 m.; du memb. post. 98 m.

Coloration.—Il est difficile de bien faire saisir, autrement que par une figure, le système de coloration, assez compliqué, de cette belle espèce. Sur la tête, le dos, la partie moyenne des flancs et la face supérieure des jambes règne une teinte d'un vert-clair que le séjour dans l'alcool tend à changer en gris de plomb; les flancs, une partie de la face latérale de la tête et le bord externe des extrémités sont d'un rose-lilas; les régions inférieures sont d'un jaune-verdâtre, qui prend sur l'anus, la face postérieure des cuisses et la face interne des jambes un ton plus vif et ocracé. Des taches nombreuses, variées et symétriques, d'un noir profond se montrent sur le dos et les flancs, à la face dorsale des membres et sur la gorge; telles sont : une large bande partant de l'extrémité du museau, traversant l'œil et terminant sur l'angle de la machoire après avoir contourné le tympan, qui est aussi noir : deux taches allongées formant chevron sur le milieu du dos derrière la tête, suivies plus en arrière d'une autre paire de taches allongées; des taches variées sur les flancs; des taches et des bandes transversales sur les membres; enfin sur la gorge une tache allongée, au centre, et deux de chaque côté forment un dessin très caractéristique. Les paumes et les plantes des pieds noirâtres.

Habitat.—L'individu unique que nous possédons de cette espèce a été recueilli au *Bié* par MM. Capello et Ivens.

23. PHRYNOBATRACHUS NATALENSIS, Smith.
    Two specimens from the Bihé.

24. HYPEROLIUS CITRINUS, Günther.
    From the Bihé.

25. HYPEROLIUS HUILLENSIS, Bocage.
    From the Bihé.

26. BUFO GUINEENSIS, Schleg. (?)
    A new specimen from the Bihé.

FISH.[2]

Fam. LABYRINTHICI—Genus *Ctenopoma*, Peters.

1. CTENOPOMA MULTISPINIS, Peters; Gthr., *Cat. Fishes Brit. Mus.*, vol. III. p. 373; Peters, *Mossamb. Flussfische*, p. 16; Gthr., *Ann. E. Mag. Nat. Hist.*, vol. XX. p. 110.

    Two specimens : *a.* Total length 100 millim.; *b.* Total length 78 millim.

[2] Extract of the *Jornal de Sciencias Mathematicas, Physicas e Naturaes*, No. XXX., Lisbon, 1881. They were classified in the Museum of Lisbon by Sr. Antonio Roberto Pereira Guimarães, Assistant Naturalist.

Fam. CHROMIDÆ—Genus *Chromis*, Cuv.

2. CROMIS MOSSAMBICUS, Peters; Gthr., *Cat. Fishes Brit. Mus.*, vol. IV. p. 268.

    Two specimens: *a.* Total length 80 millim; *b.* Total length 88 millim.

3. CHROMIS SPARRMANNI, Smith; Gthr., *Cat. Fishes Brit. Mus.*, vol. IV. p. 269.

    Complete accordance with the description of Dr. Günther, saving in the number of dorsal fins, which in this specimen is 15 instead of 13 or 14.
    One specimen, total length 88 millim.

Genus *Hemichromis*, Peters.

4. HEMICROMIS ROBUSTUS, Gthr.; *Proc. Z. S.*, London, 1864, p. 312.
    One specimen, total length 82 millim.

5. HEMICROMIS ANGOLENSIS, Steind., *Mem. Ac. Sc.*, Lisbon, 1865.
    One specimen, total length 90 millim.
    Habitat.—River Cu-anza. Common name, *Moaca*.

Fam. SILURIDÆ—Genus *Clarias*, Gronov.

6. CLARIA ANGUILLARIS, Linn.; Gthr., *Cat. Fishes Brit. Mus.*, vol. V. p. 14.

    Two specimens: *a.* Total length 20 cent.; *b.* Total length 12·5 cent.
    Habitat.—River Cuito. Common name *Ébande*.

Fam. MORMYRIDÆ—*Mormyrus*, Gthr.

7. MORMYRUS LHUYSI, Steind.; Steindachner, *SB. Ak. Wien*, 1870, LXI. p. 553, tab. 2, fig. 3, Senegal.

    The only specimen we have before us greatly resembles the *Mormyrus Lhuysi*, Steind., not only in the general shape of the body and its relative dimensions, but likewise in the system of colouring; it differs, however, in the number of fins and scales.
    Thus, Dr. Steindachner, in a Senegal specimen, found the following numbers:—
    P—14, D—20, A—28, L. lat. 48;
    whilst the formula of the specimen deposited in the Lisbon Museum is—
    P—10, D—25, A—33, L. lat. 53.
    One specimen, total length 85 millim.
    Habitat.—River Lu-ando. Common name *Dembe*.

Fam. CYPRINDÆ—Genus *Barbus*, Gthr.

8. BARBUS KESSLERI, Steind.; Gthr., *Cat. Fishes Brit. Mus.*, vol. VII. p. 107.

One specimen, total length to root of tail 97 millim.

We have still remaining four specimens to describe, one of the genus *Ctenopoma*, and three of the genus *Barbus*, but the elements of comparison for their study are wanting.

INSECTS.[3]

HYMENOPTERA.

APIDÆ.

1. APIS ADANSONII, Latr.
    Apis Adansonii, Latr., *Ann. du Mus. d'Hist. Nat.*, v. p. 172, No. 6.
    Apis scutellata, Lep., *Hist. Nat. d. Hym.*, I. p. 404.
    Apis mellifica, var. Gerst., *Insekt. v. Mossamb.*, p. 439.
    a.—c.

2. ANTHOPHORA FLAVICOLLIS, Gerst.
    Anthophora flavicollis, Gerst., *Insekt. v. Mossamb.*, p. 445, pl. XXIX, fig. 5.
    a. ♀ long. corp. 15 millim.

3. ANTHOPHORA ATROCINCTA, Lep.
    Anthophora atrocincta, Lep., *Hist. Nat. d. Hym.*, II. p. 35.
    a.

4. XYLOCOPA NIGRITA, Fab.
    Xylocopa nigrita, Lep., *Hist. Nat. d. Hym.*, II. p. 179; (♀) Gerst., *Reis. in Ost-Afr.*, p. 314.
    a.— ♀

5. XYLOCOPA COMBUSTA, Smith.
    Xylocopa combusta, Smith, *Nat. Hym. Ins.*, p. 350.
    a.

6. XYLOCOPA INCONSTANS, Smith.
    We refer to this species a specimen collected by Messrs. Capello and Ivens, because, besides not knowing the distinction, we compared it with

---

[3] We are indebted for the study we present upon insects to Sr. Alberto Girard' Assistant Naturalist at the Lisbon Museum.

another, sent to the Lisbon Museum by Mr. Anchieta, and classified under this name, and observed that it differed solely in having yellow bristles on the back part and sides of the thorax, as also in the first abdominal segment; whilst in Mr. Anchieta's specimen those bristles are white.

a.— ♀ long. corp. 33 millim.

7. XYLOCOPA CALENS, Lep.

Xylocopa calens, Lep., *Hist. Nat. d. Hym.*, II. p. 196, ♀.
a.— ♀

VESPIDÆ.

8. EUMENES TINCTOR, Christ.

Eumenes Savignyi, Guérin, *Icon. Rég. Anim. Ins.*, pl. 72, fig. 4.
Eumenes tinctor, Gerst., *Reis. in Ost-Afr.*, p. 321.
a.

9. BELONOGASTER, sp. (?)
a.

CRABRONIDÆ.

10. HEMIPEPSIS VINDEX, Smith.

Mignimia vindex, Smith, *Cat. Hym. Ins.*, III. p. 186 (♀).
Hemipepsis vindex, Gerst., *Reis. in. Ost-Afr.*, p. 327.
a.— ♀ long. corps. 37 millim.

11. PRIOCNEMIS, sp. (?)
a.— ♀

12. AMMOPHILA FERRUGINEIPES, Lep.

Ammophila ferrugineipes, Lep., *Hist. Nat. d. Hym.*, III. p. 383 (♀).
a. (♀)

13. SCOLIA CYANEA, Lep.

Scolia cyanea, Lep., *Hist. Nat. d. Hym.*, III. p. 525 (♂); Gerst., *Insekt. v. Mossamb.*, p. 494.
a.— ♀

FORMICIDÆ.

14. PALTOTHYREUS PESTILENTIA, Smith.
a.

15. PONERA, sp. (?)
a.

16. FORMICA MACULATA, Fabr.

Formica maculata, Lep., *Hist. Nat. d. Hym.*, I. p. 2, 15; Gerst., *Insekt. v. Mossamb.*, p. 509.
a.

CHRYSIDIDÆ.

17. Stilbum splendidum, Fab.

Stilbum splendidum, Lep., *Hist. Nat. d. Hym.*, IV. p. 15; Gerst., *Insekt. v. Mossamb.*, p. 519.

a.— ♀. Long. corp. 11 millim.

DIPTERA.

TABANIDÆ.

1. Tabanus exclamationis, new sp.

Approximates closely to the *Tabanus longitudinalis*, Loew. (*Insekt. v. Mossamb.*, p. 2). Head white, eyes bronzed, with very small facets, interval between them wide, with two red callosities arranged *en face*, furnished with white hairs beneath, trunk of dark grey, feelers white, antennæ pink, first and second article furnished with white hairs, and elongating upwards to a black point (the third is wanting in all the specimens); thorax pinky above, being four black stripes close together, which almost conceal the blue colour below; abdomen conical, beginning to narrow in the third segment, as long as the head and thorax together, yellow, without hair, having a brown dorsal line, occupying one-third of the breadth, having in the middle and at each segment a white triangular mark, with an angle turned to the base, furnished with black in the second segment, and not in the first and last, and (the abdomen) having also a narrow lateral stripe of the same colour as the dorsal, beginning at the second or third segment. It must be noted that as regards the colour of the *ground*, it is lighter towards the extremity of the abdomen, which the stripes darken, so that the last segment is almost black; belly yellow, with the lateral margins whitened, middle of the last two segments black; thighs grey, with some white hairs, abundant at the base; tibia red; tarsus black above, red below; wings transparent; costal frame black, the others chestnut.

Long. corp. 16 to 17 millim. Exp. al. 34 millim.

a.—c. ♀.

We imagined at first that our specimens referred to the *T. longitudinalis*, Loew; but on attentively reading the description, it appears to us, if we understand it properly, that the drawing of the thorax and abdomen is completely different, as well as the general colour, which we consider sufficient to separate the two species.

The Lepidoptera are represented by some "fourreaure" of Leyortas, of the Psychidæ family. They are formed by a collection of dry and thin branches, disposed longitudinally, and which cover and protect a silk cocoon wherein the worm is found. Monteiro, in his work upon Angola, gives an exact representation of these cocoons. (V. *Angola and the River Congo*, by J. J. Monteiro, London, 1875, vol. II. p. 295, pl. XVI.).

NEUROPTERA.

MYRMÉLÉONIDÆ.

1. PALPARES CAFFER (?), Burm.
   One sole exemplar spoiled.

ORTHOPTERA.

Dr. Ignacio Bolivar published, a short time ago, a remarkable study upon the Orthoptera of Angola existing in the Lisbon Museum, and at the same time studied the specimens of Messrs. Capello and Ivens.

It is this study which we transcribe here, and to which, as will be seen, we contribute no part.[4]

1. CAMOENSIA INSIGNIS, Bolivar., new sp.
   Jorn. Sc. Math. Phys. Nat., No. xxx., p. 3, No. 18.
   Cu-ango (Capello and Ivens).

2. ACRIDIUM TARTARICUM, Lin.
   Acridium tartaricum, Bolivar, loc. cit., p. 112, No. 22.

HEMIPTERA.

HETEROPTERA.

1. SPHÆROCORIS PÆCILUS, Dallas.
   Sphærocoris pæcilus, Dallas, *List of Hemip. Insect. in the Coll. of the Brit. Mus.*, I. p. 9.
   a. b.

2. CŒNOMORPHA NERVOSA, Dallas.
   Cœnomorpha nervosa, Dallas, loc. cit., I. p. 192.
   a. d.

3. PHILLOCEPHALA PLICATA, Reiche et Fairm.
   Phillocephala plicata, Reiche et Fairm., *Voy. en Abyss.*, III. p. 447; *At. Zool.*, pl. 29, fig. 2.
   a.— ♀

4. PETASCELIS, sp. (?)
   a.— ♂

---

[4] See *Jornal das Sciencias Mathematicas, Physicas e Naturaes*, No. xxx. p. 107.

5. MICTIS HETEROPUS, Latr.
   Mictis heteropus, Schaum., *Insekt. v. Mossamb.*, p. 41.
   a.— ♂
   b.— ♀

6. PLATIMERIS GUTTATIPENNIS, Stal.
   Platimeris guttatipennis, Stal., *Ofvers. Velensk Akad. Fürrhanell*, XVI. p. 188.
   a.

7. ACANTASPIS, sp. (?)
   a.

8. APPASUS, sp. (?)
   a.

9. LACCOTREPHES GROSSUS, Fab.
   Nepa grossa, Amyot. et Serv., *Hist. Nat. d. Hém.*, p. 440.
   a.

10. LACCOTREPHES BRACHIALIS, Gerst.
    Laccotrephes brachialis, Gerst., *Reis. in Ost-Afr.*, p. 422.
    a.—c.

11. BELOSTOMA ALGERIENSE, Duf.
    Belostoma Algeriense, Duf., *Mém. Soc. Roy. d. Sc. de Liége*, v. p. 186, pl. 1.
    Hydrocyrius herculeus, Gerst., *Reis. in Ost-Afr.*, p. 423.
    a.—c. Long. total. 65 millim. Larg. 27 millim.

HOMOPTERA.

1. PLATYPLEURA CAPENSIS, Lin.
   Platypleura Capensis, Amyot. et Serv., *Hist. Nat. d. Hém.*, p. 466, No. 2; Walker, *List of Homopt. Ins. Brit. Mus.*, I. p. 3.
   a.— ♂
   b.— ♀

2. PLATYPLEURA, sp. (?)
   a.—c. ♂
   d.— ♀

FLORA.

Messrs. Capello and Ivens collected on their journey a certain number of plants, which, having been forwarded to the botanical section of the National Museum, were incorporated in the herbaria. The whole of these plants, saving a small number gathered in the low lands of the Dombe, were taken from the elevated region of the high table-land of South Africa, from Caconda, the Bihé, and the country lying between those two points.

Dr. Welwitsch had already penetrated into that region, and explored a part of the high ground of the Huilla, and from his mature investigation, made from an exclusively botanical point of view, resulted a magnificent collection of specimens, which are at the present date for the most part studied and determined. The two recent explorers could not devote their entire attention to botany; occupied as they were with many and important matters, it was only incidentally that they gathered a few plants. Nevertheless the collection they formed is very interesting. Penetrating into the lofty central region, more to the north and much more deeply than Welwitsch had done, they had an opportunity of visiting lands whose flora was till then absolutely unknown.

If to this collection we unite the important parcels sent over from Caconda by Mr. Anchieta (who, already known as an admirable zoological collector, has proved himself to be a no less zealous and intelligent collector of botanical specimens), and a few exemplars furnished by Major Serpa Pinto on the banks of the river Nindu, we must admit that the recent journeys made by the Portuguese, important as they are from other points of view, have furnished a valuable contingent towards a knowledge of African vegetation.

The whole of these plants will be successively studied and described in special reports, I having had great assistance in the work from Mr. W. P. Hiern, a botanist of repute and particularly well versed in the tropical African flora.

A definitive examination of these plants has necessarily been delayed, as it was necessary to compare them with the specimens preserved in various museums of Europe, and I can therefore only furnish here a few notes, the result of a first survey made by Mr. Hiern and myself, and which are of a nature to give a merely cursory idea of the importance of the collection made by Messrs. Capello and Ivens.

That collection contains approximately 140 different species, represented mostly by examples susceptible of rigorous determination, and which, apart from certain corrections that a more careful examination will entail, may be distributed by their natural families in the following manner :—

RANUNCULACEÆ—A few species of the genus *Clematio*, one of which is probably new.

MENISPERMACEÆ—A species of the genus *Stephania*.

NYMPHÆACEÆ—A species of the *Nymphœa* genus, obtained from the Cubanzo.

CAPPARIDACEÆ—A species of *Cleome*.

POLYGALEÆ—A species of the genus *Polygala* and one of the *Securidœa*.

MALVACEÆ—Species of the *Sùla* and *Hibiscus*. The large malvaceæ, as for instance the *imbondeiro*, do not exist at great altitudes. From Quilengues upwards it is very rare, and at 3200 feet it disappears completely, according to a note of the explorers.

FILIACEÆ—A species of *Triumfetta*.

MALPIGHIACEÆ—A species of *Sphedamnocarpus*.

OCHNACEÆ—A species of *Ochna*, probably undescribed.

MELIACEÆ—A species of *Ekebergia*.

AMPELIDEÆ—Species of *Vitis*. One of them, met with pretty frequently, and to which the natives give the name of *Quinjuanjua*, produces an edible fruit, and is used in the preparation of a fermented liquor.

ANACARDIACEÆ—A species of *Rhus*.

LEGUMINOSÆ—Species of the genus *Crotalaria*, *Indigofera*, *Tephrosia*, *Sesbania*, *Herminiera*, *Æschynomene*, *Erythrina*, *Eriosema*, *Sivartzia*, *Cassia*, *Banhinia*, *Brachystegia*, and *Acasia*. The species of Brachystegia come from the Dombe, where they form the staple of the forests traversed by the explorers. The *Herminiera* was gathered in the same region, and no doubt on the bank of some river.

ROSACEÆ—A species of *Parinarium*.

MELASTOMACEÆ—Species of the *Dissotis* and *Antherotoma*.

SAMYDEÆ—A species probably belonging to the *Homalueno* genus.

PASSIFLOREÆ—A species of *Paropsia*, probably new.

CUCURBITACEÆ—A species probably appertaining to the genus *Zehneria*—a very imperfect specimen.

UMBELLIFERÆ—Incomplete specimens, apparently belonging to the *Fœniculum* and *Caruno*.

RUBIACEÆ—Species of the genuses, *Mussaenda, Oxyanthus, Tricalysia, Vangueria, Fadogia, Ancylanthos, Grumilea,* and *Spermacoce;* some of these species being very interesting, and undoubtedly new.

COMPOSITÆ—Species of the genuses *Vernonia, Conyza, Helichrysum, Aspilia, Coreopsio, Bidens, Emilia, Berkheya, Peiotaris,* and *Dicoma,* some of which are undescribed.

EBENACEÆ—A species of *Diospyros,* and one of *Euclea.*

ASCLEPIADEÆ—Species of the genus *Asclepias.*

GENTIANEÆ—A species of the genus *Chironia.*

SOLANACEÆ—A species of *Datura.*

SCROPHULARINEÆ—Species which seem to belong to the genuses *Striga* and *Sopubia.*

PEDALINEÆ—A species of *Sesamothamnus.*

ACANTHACEÆ—Species of *Barleria.*

VERBENACEÆ—Species of the *Lantana, Vitea,* and *Clerodendron.*

LABIUTÆ—A species of *Tinnea.*

POLYGONACEÆ—A species of *Polygonum.*

PROTEACEÆ—Imperfect specimens, apparently belonging to this family.

THYMÆLEACEÆ—Species of *Guidia* and *Lasiosiphon;* probably new.

EUPHORBIACEÆ—Species of *Bridelia, Phyllanthera, Manihot, Acalypha,* and *Ricinus.*

ORCHIDEÆ—A species probably of the genus *Habenaria.*

IRIDEÆ—Species of *Gladiolus* and *Morœa,* some of which are probably new.

SMILACEÆ—A species of *Smilase.*

LILIACEÆ—Species of *Asparagus* and *Bulbine.*

CYPERACEÆ—Species of *Cyperus.*

GRAMINEÆ—Species, among others, of the genuses *Panicum, Andropagon,* and *Elensine.*

Filices—Species in small number, about four.

This list, the result of a first and very rapid review, is subject to various corrections and alterations; it will suffice, however, to give an idea of the value and interest of the collection. In a subsequent and closer description we shall avail ourselves of the notes upon the common names and uses of some of those plants which accompanied the specimens, and that will be found of considerable interest to science.

COUNT DE FICALHO.

LISBON, *June,* 1881.

BRIEF SUMMARY OF A FEW OF THE AFRICAN DIALECTS.

English.	N'bunda.	Bihé or lunbundo.	Cabinda.	D'jenji or Baróze.	Garanganja.	Quioco.	Lunda.	Lun'cumbi.
One	Mochi	Unámoe	Bossi	Ussumué	Solo	Caxi	Cámo	Mochi.
Two	Quiali	Bivari	Inali	Babéle	Beri	Cari	Car	Bari.
Three	Quitato	Bitatu	Tatu	Balálo	Iatu	Tatu	Cassuto	Táto.
Four	Quinana	Biquana	Ñá	Banom	Oiné	Unna	Canlim	Quana.
Five	Quitano	Bitano	Tano	Liquitalizó	Tano	M'tano	Catano	Tano.
Six	Quissamana	Eyando	Samlano	Liquitalizó-immmué	Mussanyo	M'sambano	Sambano	Pando.
Seven	Samboari	Spando-vari	Samboali	Liquitalizó-nibaéle	—	T'chimbiari	T'chimbiari	Pando-bari.
Eight	Naque	Equiála	Náua	Liquitalizó-nibalálo	—	Nóque	T'chinana	T'chinae.
Nine	Ivóa	Equeila	Vóa	Liquitalizó-nibanem	Sciênda	Ivóa	Divôa	T'chivôa.
Ten	Liquinhe	Equin	Ciume	Lissumué	Lissume	Cúmo	Dicume	Ecumi.
Eleven	Quiuhe-mochi	Baquin-lumué	Ciume-tchimoćca	Lissume-inmumoé	—	Cume-caxi	—	E-cume-mochi.
Twelve	Quinhe-quiali	Baquin-bivari	Cóume-uali	Lissume-nibaéle	—	Cume-cari	—	E-cume-bari.
Thirteen	Quinhe-quitato	Baquin-bitatu	Cúume tatu	Lissume-nibalálo	—	Cume-tatu	—	
Twenty	Macoinhi-niali	Baquin-avari	Macume-uali	Massume-amaéle	Massume-beri	Macume-ácari	—	
Thirty	Macoinhi-atato	Baquin-atatu	Macume-matatu	Massume-amararo	Massume-iatu	Macume-átatu	—	
Forty	Macoinhi-amana	Baquin-aquana	Macume matuá	Massume-ananem	Massume-oiné	Macume-aúana	—	
Sixty	Macoinhi-as-sanana	Baquin - epau-do	Macume-massam-bano	Massume - liquitalizó-immumué	Massume m-ussanvo	Macume-inassambano	—	
Eighty	Macoinhi-naque	Baquin-equiála / Otchita-	Lu-nána	Massume - liqui-talizó-nibalálo	—	Macume-nóque	—	
One hundred	Hama	Otchita	Cáma	Massume-lia-massume	—	—	Quitóta	Tchita.
Two hundred	Hama iali	Otchita-bivari / Otchita-	Oama-uali	Massume lia-baéle	—	—	—	
Three hundred	Hama-iutato	bita-bilatu / Otchita-bi-	Cama-atatu	Massume-lia-balálo	—	—	—	
Four hundred	Hama-inana	ta-biquana	Cama-ñá	Massume-lia-banem	—	—	—	
One thousand	—	Culocai	Vere tchoucama	—	—	—	—	

PRONOUNS IN SIX AFRICAN DIALECTS.

English.	N'bunda.	Bihé or Iuu-bundo.	Cabinda.	Djenji or Baróze	Garan-ganja.	Quioco.	Ca-luiana.
I	Emú	Amè	Mino	Na	Oanè	Jamè	Menè
Thou	Eiè	Obè	Jeei	Oena	Guiobè	Baia	Oène
He	Iana	Eiè	N'andi	Iena	—	—	—
We	Etu	Etú	Befo	Runa	Vona-Ina	Anasso	—
You	Enn	Ené	Behenn	Quimina	—	—	—
They	Ené	Obo, Bi-ossi	Báo, Ba-bouse	Quibona	Obone	—	—

DECLENSION OF THE PRONOUNS OF THE N'BUNDA TONGUE.[1]

Singular. *Plural.*

First Person.
- Nom. —emè.
- Gen. —ia-mè.
- Dat. —cu-mè.
- Abl. —mè.

- Nom. —ètu.
- Gen. —i-ètu.
- Dat. —cu-ètu.
- Abl. —ètu.

Second Person.
- Nom. —eiè.
- Gen. —i-è or ri-è.
- Dat. —cu-i-è.
- Voc. —eiè!
- Abl. —è, iè.

- Nom. —enu.
- Gen. —i-ènu.
- Dat. cu-èuu
- Voc. —enuè!
- Abl. —ènu.

Third Person.
- Nom. —enè or munèe.
- Gen. —oè or iè.
- Dat. —cu-ène or cu-muène.
- Abl. —oè or iè.

- Nom. —ène.
- Gen. —iène.
- Dat. —cu-ène.
- Abl. —cue.

CONJUNCTIONS.

And—Né. That—Na. Also—Oé.

INTERJECTIONS.

Of pain	Ai!	Of grief, terror	Mamè!
Of wonder	Ao-ah! É-o-ah! O-ah!	Of silence	T'chibia!
Of affliction	Ai-o-è!	Of applause	Qui-o-ah!
Of fear	He!	By way of call	Chè!

---

[1] The greater part of the elements constituting the vocabulary of the N'Bunda tongue were supplied us by our distinguished and intelligent friend Sr. A. Urbano Monteiro de Castro.

N'BUNDA VOCABULARY.

Portuguese.	N'Bunda.	English.
Abaixar	Cu-butalala, Cu-butama	To lower
Abalar	Cu-cumuna	To decamp
Abalroar	Cu-balacanha	To contend
Abanar	Cu-buquirila	To fan
Abcesso	Qui-jimbo	An abscess
Abelha	N'hique	A bee
Abelhas	Ji-nhique	Bees
Abobora	Ri-nhango	A gourd
Aborrecer	Cu-zemba	To hate
Abortar	Cu-secula	To miscarry
Abraçar	Cu-zibubala	To embrace
Abraço	N'dando	An embrace
Acabar	Cu-azuba, cu-assuca, cu-bua	To finish
Acabou-se	Iabo, *masc.* and *fem.*	
Acabou-se	Cu-abo, *neut.*	It was finished
Accender	Cu-bia, Cu-uica	To kindle
Achar	Cu-quimona, Cu-sanja	To find
Acompanhar	Cu-batessa	To accompany
Acordar	Cu-toma	To awake
Acostumar-se	Cu-irila	To inure oneself to
Adiantar-se	Cu-rianga	To hasten
Adivinhar	Cu-suma	To foretell
Adoecer	Cu-cata	To sicken
Afastar	Cu-songoloca	To drive away
Afogar-se	Cu-fua-mu-menha	To drown
Agradecer	Cu-tondela	To thank
Agua	Menha	Water
Agua doce	Menha-matome	Fresh water
Agua salgada	Menha-malula	Salt water
Aguia	N'jinji	An eagle
Ajudar	Cu-cuatessa	To help
Ajuntar	Cu-cucula, Cu-bongolola	To assemble
Alegre	Lela	Gay
Aleijado de nascença	N'gonga	Crippled, from birth
Aleijado por molestia	N'mana	Crippled by a hurt
Aleijão	Qui-nema	Lameness
Algodão	Mujinha	Cotton
Aloès	Quicalango	Aloes
Altercar	Cu-richinga	To dispute
Alto	Leba, Zangura	High
Alumiar	Cu-muica	To light
Amadurecer	Cu-bia	To ripen
Amamentar	Cu-amuissa	To suckle

N'Bunda Vocabulary.

Portuguese.	N'Bunda.	English.
Amanhecer	Cu-cuaque	To dawn
Amante	N'bassa	A lover
Amargo	Lula	Bitter
Amigo	Ri-camba	A friend
Ancião	Qui-culacaje	An elder
Andar	Cu-enda	To go, to walk
Andar de pressa	Cu-longa	To make haste
Andar de vagar	Cu-riomba	To walk slowly
Andorinha	Piápia	A swallow
Animal	Qui-ama	An animal
Anno	Muvo (?)	A year
Anoitecer	Cu-lembeca	To become night
Apagar	Cu-jima	To put out a light
Apalpar	Cu-babata	To feel, to touch
Apanhar	Cu-bonga	To take, to catch
Apertado	Colo	Tight, urgent
Apertar	Cu-colessa	To bind, to press
Apontar	Cu-riquiza	To point at, to note
Approximar-se	Cu-sueta e Cu-zucama	To draw near
Aprender	Cu rilonga	To learn
Aquecer	Cu-temessa	To grow hot
Ar	Mulenghe	The air
Aranha	Qui-jandanda	A spider
Arco-iris	Congolo	A rainbow
Arder	Cu-t'chichima	To burn
Areia	Qui-sequele	Sand
Arma	Uta	A weapon
Arrancar	Cu-catula	To pull, to root up
Arrecadar	Cu-luca	To collect (taxes)
Arregaçar	Cu-zacular	To tuck up
Arriar	Cu-tuluca	To slacken (a rope)
Arvore	Mu lemba (?)	A tree
Aspirar	Cu-feuta	To breathe
Assar	Cu-ribia, Cu-zuza	To roast
Assentar-se	Cu-t'chicama	To sit down
Assoar-se	Cu-bemba	To blow the nose
Assustar	Cu-atucumuca	To frighten
Atar	Cu-cuta	To tie
Atirar	Cu-tacula	To shoot, to throw
Atmosphera	Cu-cama (?)	The atmosphere
Atravessar	Cu-cangalala	To cross
Atrazar-se	Cu-n'guenica	To linger
Atrever-se	Cu-buma	To dare, to venture
Atrevido	Mucu-an'ganje.	Daring, inconsiderate
Atrevimento	N'ganje	Boldness, effrontery
Aturar	Cu-amburila	To suffer, to bear
Aurora	Cú-guia	Dawn of day
Avarento	Ca-coria	Covetous
Ave	N'jila	A bird
Avistar	Cu-amutala	To descry, to see afar off
Avô ou Avó	Cuco	Grandfather, or grandmother
Aza	Ri-zaza	A wing
Azas	Ma-zaza	Wings
Azedo	N'gangama	Sour, harsh

Portuguese.	N'Bunda.	English.
Azeite	Maji	Oil
Azeite de dendem	Maji-ma-dendé	Cocoa oil
Azeite doce	Maji-ia-puto	Sweet oil
Azeite de ricino	Maji-ma-mono	Castor oil
Baba	Zeza	Foam, saliva
Babar	Cu-riuzila	To foam, to drivel
Bacia	Ri-longa	Basin
Baço	Candjila	Brown, swarthy
Baile	N'goma	A dance
Baixa ou varzea	Honga	A fall, or low ground
Baixo (adjectivo)	Abuto	Low (adjective)
Banana	Ri-conjo	Banana
Bananeira	Ma-conjo (?)	Banana-tree
Banhar-se	Cu-rissulula	To bathe
Banquete de carne humana	Congo, ou Di-congo	A banquet of human flesh
Bao-bab	Imbondo	Bao-bab
Barba	Muezo, ou olongeri (?)	The beard
Barrete	Cajinga	A cap
Barriga	Ri-vumo	The belly
Barroca	Ri-cungo	A gutter made by floods
Basso	Mu-toto	Spleen
Bastão	M'bassa, ou M'bassi	A stick
Bater	Cu-bunda	To beat
Bebado	Colua	Drunken
Beber	Cu-nua	To drink
Beiço	Mu-zumbo	A lip
Beliscão	Qui-n'jonjo	A pinch or nip
Beliscar	Cu-jangona	To pinch or nip
Bello	Euába, Uába	Fair, beautiful
Bexiga	Qui-sut'chino	A bladder
Bexigas (variolo)	Quin'gongo	Pits of smallpox
Bezerro	Mona-ia-n'gombe	A bullock
Bico	Mu-sungo	The beak of a bird
Bobo	Qui-tanga	A buffoon
Boca	Ri-cano	The mouth
Boçal	Mu-zenza	Rude, ignorant
Bofes	N'zalazala	The lungs
Bofetão	Hutche	A slap in the face
Bofetões	Ji-hutche	Blows
Boi	N'gombe	An ox
Bom	M'bote	Good
Borboleta	Qui-m'biámbia	A butterfly
Borbulha	Bulo	A pimple
Borrifar	Cu-sassa	To sprinkle
Bosque	Mu-chito	A wood
Bracelete	Ma-lunga	A bracelet
Braço	Qui-cuaco	The arm
Branco (adjectivo)	Izela	White
Branco (homen)	Mu-n'dele	A white man
Branco (pleben)	Ca-n'gundo	White people
Brando	Lenduca	Soft, gentle
Bravo	Tema	Wild
Braza	Ri-cala, Ri-tubia	Live charcoal

N'Bunda Vocabulary.

Portuguese.	N'Bunda.	English.
Brazas	Ma-cala, Ma-tubia	Live charcoal (plur.)
Brigar	Cu-zoca	To fight
Brincar	Cu-toneca	To frisk
Brinco (adorno)	Qui-n'guerenguéle	An ornament
Buraco	Ri-zungo	A gap, a hole
Buscar	Cu-tocana	To seek, to search
Cabaça	Ca-binda	A gourd
Cabeça	Mú-tue	The head, a chief
Cabello	N'demba	Hair
Cabo	M'binhe	An end, a handle
Cabra	N'combo	A she-goat
Caça	N'hanga	Chase, game
Caçador	Ri-nhangá, Ri-congo	A hunter
Caçar	Cu-losa, Cu-nhanga	To chase, to hunt
Cadeado	Ri-cumba	A padlock
Cadeia ou Corrente	Ri-bambo	A chain
Cadeira	Qui-alo	A chair, a seat
Cadeira de bambu	N'benza	A bamboo seat
Cair	Cu-ribala, Cu-noca	To fall
Calar a boca	Cu-richiba	To hold the tongue
Calcar	Cu-bata, Cu banda	To tread upon
Calcular	Cu-ricanda	To reckon
Caldo	Mu-zongué	Broth
Calor	N'bema	Heat
Calva	Ri-bala	Baldness
Cama	Ri-londe	A bed
Camaleão	Ri-muguena	A chameleon
Caminho	N'jila, Coca	A way, a road
Campo	Ri-canga	A field
Canhamo	Ri-ambu, ou Li-amba	Hemp
Canoa grande	Dongo	A large canoe
Canoa pequena	Qui-m'bola	A small ditto.
Cansado	N'buila	Tired
Cansar-se	Cu-buila	To tire oneself
Cantar	Cu-imba	To sing
Cantiga	Mu-imbo	A song
Cão	Imboa	A dog
Capim	Iango	Tall grass
Capinar	Cu-combela	To mow the "capim"
Capital	N'banza	Capital
Cara	N'polo	The face
Caranguejo	Qui-ala	A crab-fish
Caravana	Qui-buca	A caravan
Careca	Ri bala	Scurfy
Carga	M'bamba	A load, a burden
Carne	T'chito	Flesh, meat
Carneiro	M'buri	Sheep, mutton
Caroço	N'tendo	Stone (of fruit)
Carrapato	Ri-bata	A tick
Carregar	Cu-ambata, Cu-loga Cu-tuta	To load, to burden
Carvão	Ri-cala	Coal
Casa de palha	Cubata	Straw hut

Portuguese.	N'Bunda.	English.
Casa de pedra	Lumbo	Stone house
Casar	Cu-socana (?)	To marry
Casca de arvcor	Qui-bato	Bark of trees
Casca de frutoe	Qui-ango	Rind of fruit
Caspa	Qui-biache	Scurf
Castigar	Cu-beta, Cu-muba	To chastise
Cauda	Mu-quila	A tail
Cavacos	Jibato	Chips
Cavar	Cu-canda	To dig, to hollow
Caximbo	M'peiche	A pipe
Cego de nascença	Qui-lembo	Blind from birth
Cego por molestia	Qui-fofo	Blind through accident
Ceremonia	N'sonhe	Ceremony
Certo	Teno	Certain, sure
Cesto	Qui-nda	A basket
Céu	Iulo	The sky
Chamar	Cu-ambela, Cu-cola	To call
Chamma	Qui-lecuca	Flame
Chegar	Cu-bichila, Cu-zucuma	To draw near, to arrive
Cheia	Izala	An overflow
Cheirar	Cu-fenha	To smell, to scent
Cheiro	Ri-zumba	Scent
Chibo (cabrito)	N'combo	A kid
Chorar	Cu-rila	To cry
Chover	Cu-noca	To rain
Choviscar	Cu-sucomuca	To mizzle
Chovisco	Suco-suco	Light rain
Chuco	Mu-songo	A spear
Chupar	Cu-t'chiba	To suck
Chuva	N'vula	Rain
Cigarra	M'bangarala	A cicada
Cinto	N'ponda	A belt
Cintura	Canhonga	The waist
Cinza	Otucua	Ashes
Circumcisão	Saia	Circumcision
Circumcisar	Cu-saia	To circumcise
Ciume	Iti-fuba	Envy, jealousy
Clarear	Cu-n'zela	To dawn
Claro	N'zela	Clear, bright
Cobra	Nhoca	A snake
Cobre	Londo	Copper
Cobrir	Cu-futa	To cover
Cocar	Cu-asa	To scratch
Cocega	Hugota	Tickling, longing
Cola (fructo)	Ri-queso	Cola (fruit)
Colher	N'guto	To gather
Começar	Cu-mateca	To begin
Começou o luar	M'begeia tetama	The moon shone out
Comer	Cu-ria	To eat
Comilão	Qui-riacaje	A glutton
Commercio	Uendji	Trade, traffic
Compatriota	Mu-cuache	A fellow-countryman
Compor-se	Cu-ricoteca	To agree with
Comprar	Cu-sumba, Cu-senga	To buy
Comprido	Seba	Long

Portuguese.	N'Bunda.	English.
Comprimentar	Cu-monequena	To compliment
Comprimento (medida)	Cu-leba	Length
Concha	Qui-quesse	A shell
Concha (moeda do Congo)	N'jimbo	A cowry
Conhecer	Cu-ijia	To know
Conselheiro	N'punga	A counsellor
Consentir	Cu-amburila	To consent
Consorte (f.)	Mu-caje	Wife
Consorte (m.)	Mu-lume	Husband
Contar	Cu-tangar	To count, to relate
Copado	N'zanda	Tufted, bushy
Coração	N'zundo	Heart, spirit
Corda	Mu-cólo	A cord, rope
Cordão	Qui-bo	A lace, a string
Coroa	Qui-landa	A crown
Corpo	Mu-cuto	A body
Correr	Cu-lenga, Cu-songuela	To run, to flow
Cortar	Cu-batula	To cut
Coruja	Ca-coco	A screech owl
Corvo	Qui-lombe-lombe.	A crow
Coser	Cu-tunga	To sew
Costas	Ri-cunda	The back
Costellas	M'banje	The ribs
Costume	Quifa	A custom
Cotovello	Qui-pomuna	The elbow
Couro	Qui-ba	A hide, skin
Cousa	Qui-ma	A thing
Cova	Ri-cungo	A pit, ditch
Coxa	Ri-catacata	The thigh
Coxear	Cu-tengunha	To limp
Coxo	Qui-nema	Lame
Cozinhar	Cu-ulamba	To cook
Creança	N'dengué	An infant
Crear	Cu-sassa	To produce, to bring up
Creoulo	Buchilo	A home-born slave
Crepusculo	N'goióche	Twilight
Crer	Cu-t'chicana	To believe
Crescer	Cu-cula	To increase
Crime	Qui-tuche	A crime
Crista	Qui-coacoa	A cock's comb, a crest
Criticar	Cu-longolola	To criticize
Crocodilo	N'gando	A crocodile
Cuidar	Cu-fica	To think of, care for
Cultivar	Cu-rima	To till the ground
Cunhado	N'uere	Brother-in-law
Cunhados	Ji-uere	Brothers and sisters-in-law
Curandeiro	Qui-n'banda	The medicine-man
Curar	Cu-vissaca	To cure, heal
Curral	Qui-banga	A cattle enclosure
Curto	Buto	Short
Curvar-se	Cu-bolama	To bow down
Cuspir	Cu-tamate	To spit
Dansa	Qui-na	A dance
Dansar	Cu-quina, Cu-belela	To dance

Portuguese.	N'Bunda.	English.
Dansar (batuque)	Cu-semba	To dance (*batuque*)
Dar	Cu-ubana	To give
Dar nó	Cu-ta-ribumbo	To tie a knot
Dedo	Mu-lembo	A finger
Deitar-se	Cu-zeca, Cu-zendalala	To lie down
Deixar	Cu-ambula, Cu-rechissa	To leave, to let
Deixar passar	Cu-bitessa	To let pass
Dente	Ri-jo	A tooth
Dentes	Ma-jo	The teeth
Depositar	Cu-tutula	To deposit, to set down
Derradeiro	Suquinina	The last
Desagradar	Cu-ibila	To displease
Desatar	Cu-jituna	To untie
Desbocado	Qui-sebuisso	Hard mouthed, unruly
Descansar	Cu-nboca	To rest
Descansar a carga	Cu-tula	To set down a load
Descarregar	Cu-longorala, Cu-tu-turula	To unload, to discharge
Descascar	Cu-tela	To strip off bark
Descer	Cu-tuluca	To descend, to come down
Descobrir	Cu-rifolumuna	To uncover, to discover
Desdobrar	Cu-futumuna	To unfold
Desfazer	Cu-sangunuma	To undo, to loosen
Desgostar	Cu-zemba	To dislike, to disgust
Desgraça	Cu-t'chichima-lamba	Misfortune
Desmanchar	Cu-bula, Cu-sangumuna	To take to pieces
Despedir	Cu-zula	To dismiss
Despedir-se	Cu-t'chalessa	To take leave
Despejar	Cu-lundulula	To clear away
Desperto	Chiche	Awake
Desprender-se	Cu-sutumuca	To detach oneself
Destinar	Cu-t'chinda	To devote, to design
Destruir	Cu-jimonuna	To destroy
Deus	N'zambi	God
Devastar	Cu-bunda	To lay waste
Dever	Cu-levala	To owe
Dia	Qui-zúa	The day
Diarrhea	Mala-Manhinga	Diarrhœa
Dinheiro	Qui-tare	Money
Dinheiro de conchas	N'jimbo	Cowry money
Direcção	Muchinda	Direction
Direito	Lulama	Right, straight
Distrahir-se	Cu-laleca	To amuse oneself
Diurno	Ia-luanha	Daily
Dividir	Cu-uana	To part, to share
Dizer	Cu-amba	To say, to speak
Dobrar	Cu-bunjica	To fold, to bend
Doce	Tola, Toalela	Sweet
Docil	Lenduca	Docile
Doença	Cu-cata	Sickness
Doende	Cu-zumbi	Sickening
Doente	Ache, Ucate	Sick, ill
Doer	Cu-cata	To ache, suffer
Dono	Mu-áre	A gift
Dor	N'gongo	Grief, pain

N'Bunda Vocabulary.

Portuguese.	N'Bunda.	English.
Dormir	Cu-zeca, Cu-lambarala	To sleep
Duro	Colo, Colocota	Hard, harsh
Duvida	Pata	Doubt
Duvidar	Cu-cachicana	To doubt
Dysenteria	Mala	Dysentery
Echo	Cu-dumina	Echo
Elephante	N'zamba	An elephant
Elogiar	Cu-chimana	To praise
Embora	Maie, Mê	It is well
Emprenhar (v. n.)	Cu-emita	To conceive
Emprenhar (v. a.)	Cu-emetina	To impregnate
Empurrar	Cu-t'chinguice	To thrust
Encalhar	Cu cuáca	To run aground
Encantamento	Qui buisa	An enchantment
Encher	Cu-izalessa [cunana]	To fill
Encolher	Cu-riconha, Cu-coteca, Cu-	To shrink, shrivel
Encontrar	Cu-tacana	To meet, to encounter
Encontrar-se	Cu-t'chamenena	To meet one another
Endireitar	Cu-rinica	To straighten, take a direct
Enfeitado	Quembo	Adorned [road
Enfeitar	Cu-quemba	To dress, deck out
Enfeite	Cuquemba	Dress, ornaments
Enganar	Cu-fumba	To deceive, to cheat
Engasgar-se	Cu-vimenha	To get the throat stopped
Engordar	Cu-netessa	To fatten, grow fat
Engulir	Cu-minha	To swallow
Enrolar	Cu-burica	To roll, to roll up
Ensinar	Cu-longa	To teach
Entender	Cu-irna	To understand
Enterrar	Cu-funda	To bury
Entornar	Cu-t'chamuna	To pour out, spill
Entrar	Cu-bocola	To enter
Envenenar	Cu-loa	To poison
Enxada	Ri-temo	A mattock, a hoe
Enxadas	Ma-temo	Tools
Enxugar	Cu-cuta	To dry
Errar	Cu-tundala	To miss, to wander
Escama	Qui-beretete	Scale of a fish
Escamar o peixe	Cu-banga-m'biji	To scale fish
Escapar	Cu-laia	To escape
Escapar-se	Cu-sentemuca	To run away
Escarnecer	Cu-seba, Cu-muclela	To scoff, to rail at
Escolher	Cu-nona, Cu-sola	To choose
Esconder	Cu-suana	To hide
Escorregadico	T'chanana	Slippery
Escorregar	Cu-t'chanana	To slip, slide
Escorrer	Cu-sonsumuna	To drop
Escravo	M'bica	A slave
Escrever	Cu-soneca	To write
Escripto	Mu-canda	A writing, written
Escuridão	Cumuda	Darkness
Escuro	N'vundo	Dark
Escutar	Cu-bulacana, Cu-iverila	To listen

Portuguese.	N'Bunda.	English.
Esfolar	Cu-tala	To flay
Esfregar	Cu-t'chissa	To rub, scour
Esfriar	Cu-talala	To cool
Esmagar	Cu-bonda	To crush, bruise
Esmigalhar	Cu-tutula	To crumble
Espaço	Bulubo	Space
Espada	Mu-cuáli	A sword
Espalhar	Cu-muanga	To scatter
Espancar	Cu-beta, Cu-muba	To cudgel
Espantar	Cu-atucumuca	To frighten, astonish
Esperar	Cu-quinga	To await, to expect
Espernear	Cu-ribonda	To kick
Esperteza	Qui-muca	Alacrity
Esperto	Muca	Brisk, active
Espetar	Cu-sona, Cu-soneca	To put on a spit
Espinheiro	Mu-banga	A thorn-tree
Espinho	Manha	A thorn
Espirrar	Cu-gachacha	To sneeze, crackle
Esposa	Mu-caje	A bride
Esposo	Mu-lume	A bridegroom
Espraiada	Quin'zenza	A beach, strand
Espreguiçar-se	Cu-visonuna	To stretch oneself
Espremer	Cu-t'china	To squeeze, to wring
Espuma	Quifulo	Froth, foam
Esquecer	Cu-jamba	To forget
Esquentar	Cu-temessa	To heat
Esquerdo	Quiasso	The left
Estaca	Ri-taca	A stake, palisade
Estar	Cu-a, Cu-ala, Cu-cala	To be
Esteira	Richissa, Luaudo, Gaudo	A mat
Estender	Cu-sonuna	To spread
Estender a seccar	Cu-aneca	To spread out to dry
Esteril	M'baco, Cavale	Barren
Estiar	Cunana	To cease (rain)
Estimar	Cu-sola	To value, esteem
Estomago	Mu-t'china	The stomach
Estourar	Cu-baza	To burst with a noise
Estrada	N'jila	A highway
Estranho (forasteiro)	Qui-n'guanji	A foreigner
Estreito	Sossa	Narrow, a strait
Estrella	Tetémboa	A star
Estremecer	Cu-tequéta	To tremble, shudder
Estupido	T'chimba	Stupid
Excellente	Poena	Excellent
Expulsar	Cu-lundumuna	To drive out
Extinguir	Cu-lijimonuna	To extinguish
Faca	N'poco	A knife
Fado (sorte)	Mut'chinda	Fate
Faisca	Sosso	A spark
Falcão	Olococo	A hawk
Faltar	Cu-burica	To mistake
Fallador	Asueri	A talkative person
Fallar	Cu-zuela	To speak

N'Bunda Vocabulary.

Portuguese.	N'Bunda.	English.
Fallar em segredo	Cu-feta	To whisper
Faltar (não aparecer)	Cu-monequó	To be missing
Faltar (ter falta de qual-quer cosa)	Cu-camba	To want (something)
Fardo	Ri-cuba	A bale, a pack
Farinha	Fuba	Flour, meal
Farrapos	Ma-nhango	Rags
Fatigar-se	Cu-builla	To fatigue oneself
Fazer	Cu-banga	To do, to make
Fazer queixa	Cu-funda	To make a complaint
Fazer-se tolo	Cu-ritobessa	To make a fool of oneself
Fealdade	Cu-iba	Deformity
Fechar	Cu-jica	To shut
Feio	Iba	Ugly
Feiticeiro	Mu-roje	A fetish-man
Feitiço	Uanga, Izango	Fetish
Feixe	Qui-ta	A faggot
Feliz	Zelúa	Happy
Femea	Mu-hato	A female
Ferir	Cu-tua, Cu-cuama	To strike, wound
Fermentar	Cu-bota	To ferment
Ferro	Itari	Iron
Ficar	Cu-it'chala, Cu-cala	To remain, to be
Figado	Izavo	The liver
Filho	Mona	A son
Filho ultimo	Ca-súla	The younger son
Filhos	A-ana	Sons, children
Fino	Atolo (?)	Fine, thin
Flexivel	Lenduca	Flexible
Fogão	Ri-jico	A stove
Fogo	Túbia	Fire
Folhas	Ma-fo	Leaves
Fome	N'zála	Hunger
Fomentar	Cu-jola	To foment
Força	N'guzo	Force, strength
Formiga	Qui-t'chiquinha	An ant
Formiga branca	Ri-talamena	White ant
Formiga grande	Qui-sonde	Great ant
Formiga preta	Findja-songo	Black ant
Fortaleza	Qui-m'baca	A fortress, fortitude
Forte	Colo-suina	Strong
Fraco	Berequete	Weak
Frente	Pólo	The front
Fresco	Talala	Fresh, cool
Frigir	Cu-canga, Cu-canghala	To fry
Frio (adjectivo)	Talala	Cold
Frio (substantivo)	N'bambe	Cold
Frondoso	N'zanda	Leafy
Froxo	N'zoza	Slack, remiss
Fugir	Cu-alenga, Cu-toleca	To flee, to run away
Fumar	Cu-nua	To smoke
Fumo	Ri-t'chi	Smoke
Funeral	Itame	A burial
Furoar	Cu-tubula	To bore, pierce
Furoo	Ri-zungo	A hole, gap

Portuguese.	N'Bunda.	English.
Furtar	Cu-n'hana	To steal, thieve
Furunculo	Cazangambo	A boil, tubercle
Fuso	N'zelele	A spindle
Gabar	Cu-t'chimana	To praise
Gafanhoto	Qui-n'jongo	A locust
Gallinha	Sanji	A hen, fowl
Gallo	Corombolo	A cock
Ganhar	Cu-vua	To gain, get
Ganho	N'gamba	Gain
Garbo	Tolomba	Gallantry, grace
Garça	N'dele	A heron
Garganta	Qui-quelengo, Mu-ino	The throat
Gargantas	Mino	Trills
Gato do mato	T'chimba	Wild cat
Gemer	Cu-quema	To groan, to cry
Gemeo	N'gongo	A twin
Gemeo que nasce primeiro	Ca-culo	First-born twin
Gemeo que nasce segundo	Ca-baça	Second-born twin
Gengiva	Cufufunha	The gums
Genro	Olome	A son-in-law
Gente	Mun-tu	People
Giboia	Mu-ma	Large snake
Gomma	Oasso	Gum
Gordo	Neta	Fat
Gostar	Cu-nabela	To taste, to like
Governar	Cu-tumina	To rule, direct
Grande	Ouêne	Large, grand
Grandeza	Mutala	Largeness, grandeur
Grelo	Ri-esso	A sprout, a shoot
Grelôs	M'esso	Grelôts
Grelo de aboboza	Mu-engueleca	Gourd-sprout
Grelo de mandioca	Qui-zaca	Manioc-sprout
Grillo	Ri-zenze	A cricket
Gritar	Cu-ricola	To shout, cry out
Gresso	N'jimba	Big, coarse
Guardar	Cu-lunda	To keep, to watch
Guela	Qui-quelengo	The throat
Guerra	N'jita	War
Guloso	Benga, Labuve	Greedy, nice
Habilidade	N'dungue	Skill, dexterity
Habitar	Cu-cala	To inhabit
Habituar-se	Cu-ijirila	To accustom oneself
Herva	M'boa	Grass, herb
Hervas	Ji-m'boa	Herbs
Hiena	Qui-malanca	Hyena
Hippopotamo	N'guvo	Hippopotamus
Hombro	Qui-suche	Shoulder
Homem	Ri-ala	A man
Hospede	Mu-sonhe	A host, a guest
Idolo	Qui-teque	An idol
Igual	Suquela	Equal, even

N'Bunda Vocabulary. 315

Portuguese.	N'Bunda.	English.
Igualar	Cu-suquela	To level, to equal
Ilba	Qui-sanga	An island
Ilharga	Miocoto	The side, flank
Immundicie	Cut'chila	Filth
Impertinente	Temanana	Troublesome, exacting
Incendiar	Cu-bambuca	To set on fire
Inchado	N'jimba	Swollen, inflated
Inchar	Cu-jimba	To swell, to inflate
Inclinar-se	Cu-betama	To bend the head or body
Incommodar	Cu-temanana	To molest
Infeliz	Mundama	Unhappy
Ingrato	N'gulá	Ungrateful
Inhame	Qui-ringo, Quia, N'zamba	Inhame (yam)
Inimigo	N'guma	Enemy
Insultar, com palavras,	Cu-rit'chinga	To insult
Inteiro	N'vimba	Entire, complete
Inveja	Lungué	Envy
Ir	Cu-enda, Cu-á	To go
Ir-se	Cu-iamage-ia-mé	To go away, leak
Ir-se para sempre	Cu-endezela	To depart finally
Ira	N'jenda	Anger
Iras	J-n'jenda	Outburst of anger
Irmão, ã	Pangué	Brother, sister
Isca (engodo)	Qui-t'chica	A bait
Isolado	Ubeca	Isolated
Jangada	M'bimba	A raft
Joelho	Qui-pomuna	The knee
Jogo	M'bamba	Play, a game
Joven	N'zanga, N'zangala	A youth
Juramento	Loca	An oath
Jurar	Cu-ricuba, Cu-loca	To take an oath
Justo (certo)	Tena, Suquela	Right, exact
Kagado	M'bache	Tortoise
Labio	Mu-zumbo	A lip
Labios	Ri-zumbo	Lips
Laço	Ri-bumbo	A snare
Lacraia	N'gueinga	Scorpion
Lado	M'banji	Side
Ladrão	Mu-ije	A thief
Ladrar	Cu-boza	To bark
Lagarta	M'bamba	Palmer-worm
Lagartixa	Ri-tende	A water-lizard
Lagarto	Sengué	A lizard
Lago	Ri-zanga	A lake
Lagosta	Qui-ala	A lobster
Lagrima	Ri-soche	A tear
Lama	Ri-cua	Mud, mire
Largar	Cu-ambula	To let go, loose
Largo	Sancomuca	Broad
Largura	Cu-sanzamuca	Breadth
Lavar	Cu-sucula	To wash

Portuguese.	N'Bunda.	English.
Leão	Hoje	A lion
Lebre	Cabulo	A hare
Lembrar	Cu-t'chinguenca	To remind
Lenha	Ji-ninhe	Wood, fire-wood
Levantar	Cu-balamuca, Cu-betula	To raise, to lift
Levantar-se	Cu-fundumoca	To rise
Levar	Cu-beca	To carry away
Leve (ligeiro)	Lenguluca	Light, slight
Limpar	Cu-conda, Cu-sucula	To clean
Limpo	N'zela, N'conda	Clean
Lingua	Ri-mi	A tongue
Linguas	Ma-rimi	Tongues
Lobo	Qui-n'bungo	A wolf
Lodo	Iti-lua	Clay, loam
Lombriga	Ri-buca	A mawworm
Louco	Lage	Mad
Louva-adeus	Capopolo, Mucondo	Insect so called
Louvar	Cu-t'chimana	To praise
Lua [nuveus]	Ri-ége	The moon [from the clouds
Lua (a) mostra-se sem	Ri-ege iato	The moon appears or breaks
Luz	Luanha	Light, brightness
Maca	Oanda	A hammock
Macaco	Ima	A monkey
Machado	N'guimbo, Guitchalo	A hatchet
Macho	Ri-ala	Male
Macio	Lenducatete	Smooth, sleek
Madrugar	Cu-rimeneca	To rise early
Maduro	Iabi	Ripe
Mãe	Máma	A mother
Magia	Qui-lemba	Magic
Magro	N'bela	Lean
Maior (em idade)	Ri-cota	Older
Mal	Iba	Evil, mischief
Maldizer	Cu-longolóla	To curse, to defame
Mamar	Cu-ámoa	To suck
Mandar	Cu-'tuma, Cu-zuela	To order, send
Mandioca	Qui-ringo	Manioc
Manhã	Qui-menemene	The morning
Manilhas	Malunga	Bracelets
Mão	Maco	A hand
Mão direita	Maco-mu-curia	The right hand
Mao esquerda	Maco-ma-quiasso	The left hand
Mar	Lunga	The sea
Marca	M'bica	A mark, a token
Maré	N'vula	The tide
Maré cheia	N'vula iata	High tide
Maré vasia	N'vula iabo	Low tide
Marrar	Cu-luica	To butt with the head
Mastigar	Cu-janguta	To chew
Matar	Cu-jiba	To kill
Mato	Mu-chito	A wood, thicket
Mau	Tema	Bad, wicked
Medir	Cu-zonga	To measure, survey

N'Bunda Vocabulary.

Portuguese.	N'Bunda.	English.
Medo	Móma	Fear
Meio	Machache	The middle, half
Mel	Mique	Honey
Menina	Ca-quiáto	A little girl
Menino	Ca-iala	An infant
Mentir	Cu-tamacuto	To lie
Mentira	Macuto	A lie
Mercado	Qui-tanda	A market
Mergulhar	Cu-ta-m'fimba	To dip, to dive
Mergulho	M'fimba	A dip, a dive
Mestre	Messéne	A master
Metade	Cachache	Half
Metter	Cu-ta	To put. to place
Mez	M'beje	A mouth
Miar	Cu-rila	To mew
Mijar	Cu-sassa	To make water
Mijo	Masso	Urine
Milho	Ri-sa	Maize
Milho miudo	Massa-m'bala	Millet
Miolo	Hongo	Pith
Misturar	Cu-funga	To mix, to blend
Mó	Muisso	A mill-stone
Moeda	M'bongo	Money, coin
Moedas	Jim-bongo	Coins
Moer	Cu-nocuna	To grind
Molhado	N'zula	Wet, moist
Molhar	Cu-zula	To wet, moisten
Molle	Nengana	Soft
Mondar	Cu-sonzuela	To weed
Monte	Mu-lundo	A hill, mountain
Monturo	Ri-chita	A dung-hill
Morar	Cu-cala	To dwell, inhabit
Morcego	Qui-m'biambire	A bat
Morder	Cu-lumata	To bite
Morno	Lubuca	Lukewarm
Morrer	Cu-fua	To die
Morte	Cúfua	Death
Morto (fem.)	Iato	A corpse (fem.)
Morto (masc.)	Uafo	A corpse (masc.)
Mosca	N'je	A fly
Moscas	Jin-je	Flies
Mostrar	Cu-riquiza	To show, point out
Mover	Cu-tengueita	To move
Mudo	Ri-bubú	Dumb
Mugir	Cu-zila	To low
Muito	Dumba	Much, very
Mulher	Mu-hato, N'cási	A woman
Mulher casada	Mu-hato	A married woman
Mulher que trabalha	Mu-ocana	A work woman
Multidao	Qui-puche	A multitude
Mundo	Mugongo	The world
Muro	Lumbo	A wall
Nadar	Cu-coqueá	To swim

Portuguese.	N'Bunda.	English.
Nadega	Ri-taco	The buttock
Nadegas	Ma-taco	Haunches
Namorar	Cu-ta-ribassa	To woo, court
Numoro	Ri-bassa	Courtship
Nariz	Ri-suno	The nose
Nascer a planta	Cu-sabuca	To grow, to spring
Nascer o homem	Cu-rivala	To be born
Negar	Cu-rituna	To deny, refuse
Negocio	Uenje	Trade, business
Negro (adject.)	Itchi-querela	Black
Negro (subst.)	M'bundo	A black
Nevoa	Ri-mume	A fog, mist
Ninho	Qui-anzo	A nest
Nó	Ri-bumbo	A knot
Noite	O-suco	Night
Nome	Ri-jina	A name
Nora	Bal'acaje	A water-wheel
Novo	Iobe	New
Nú	Uazula	Naked
Nua	Iazula	Naked (fem.)
Nuca	Ri-cuche	The nape of the neck
Numeroso	Dumba	Numerous
Nuvem	Ri-tula	A cloud
Obrigado	Saquirila	Obliged
Obscenidade	N'daca	Obscenity
Obscenidades	Jin-daca	Obscenities
Obsceno	N'daca	Obscene
Observar	Cu-tongueinica	To observe
Offensa	Malebo	An offence
Officio	Mufumo	An office
Officios	Mifumo (?)	Offices
Oiro	Ulo	Gold
Olhar	Cu-tala, Cu-tongueinina	To look at
Olho	N'isso	An eye
Olho do pé	Qui-nama	Plant of the foot
Olhos	Ma-isso	Eyes
Onça	Hingo	A panther
Orelha	Ri-tue	An ear
Osso	Qui-fuba	A bone
Outono	Cu-samano	The autumn
Ouvir	Cu-ivua	To hear
Ovo	Ri-caque	An egg
Ovos	Má-iaque	Eggs
Pae	Tata	Father
Pagar	Cu-futa	To pay
Paiz	Coche	A country
Palavra	Mu-longa	A word
Palha	T'chita	Straw
Palma	Mu-soco	The palm
Palma da mao	Ri-cunda-ria-macu	Palm of the hand
Palmas	Mi-soco	Palms (of the hands)
Palmeira	Dende, Rić	Palm-tree

N'Bunda Vocabulary.

Portuguese.	N'Bunda.	English.
Panella	Imbia	A pipkin
Panno	Mulele	Cloth
Panno tecido de vegetaes	Mabella	Vegetable cloth
Pão	M'bolo	Bread
Papagaio	N'cusso	A parrot
Papo	Ri-colocumba	Maw (of a bird)
Papyro	Mabu	Papyrus
Parar	Cu-imara	To stop, to hinder
Parasita	Lua	A parasite
Parir	Cu-avala	To bring forth young
Partir (ausentar-se)	Cu-catuca	To depart, go away
Partir (dividir)	Cu-uana	To divide, to sever
Partir de noite	Cu-lembaca	To flit
Passar	Cu-hila	To pass, to carry over
Patria	Coche	Native country
Pau	Mu-chi	Wood
Paus	Mi-che	Sticks
Pé	Qui-nama	A foot
Pedaco	Qui-chinhe	A bit, a piece
Pedir	Cu-binga, Cu-bomba	To ask
Pedra	Ri-tave	A stone
Pegada	Ri-canda	A footstep
Pegar	Cu-cuata	To take hold of, to stick
Peito	N'tulo	The breast
Peito (seio de mulher)	Ri-ele	The bosom
Peixe	M'bije	A fish
Peixe fresco	M'bije-ia-lelo	Fresh fish
Peixe mulher	Qui-anda	A mermaid
Pellado	Cunuca	Without hair
Pelle	Qui-conda	Skin
Pendurar	Cu-nhingue éneca	To hang
Peneira	Qui-sessalo	A sieve
Peneirar	Cu-sessa	To sift
Penna	Qui-sala	A feather
Pensar	Cu-banza, Cu-fica	To attend on, to think
Pequeno	Ofele, Tete	Small, little
Perder	Cu-jimberila, Cu-fula	To lose
Perdiz	N'guáre	A partridge
Perguntar	Cu-ibula	To ask
Perna	Qui-nama	The leg
Persevejo	Qui-isso	Bug
Pesado	Eneme	Heavy
Pesar	Cu-eneme	To weigh
Pescar com anzol	Cu-lóa	To fish, with a hook
Pescar com rede	Cu-tamba	To fish, with a net
Pescoço	Ri-t'chingo	The neck
Pessoa	Mun-tu	A person
Pessoas	A-to ou Bantu	Persons
Pezar	Mahulo	Grief, repentance
Pilão	Qui-no	A mortar for pounding
Pimenta	N'dungo	Pepper
Pingar	Cu-buba	To drip
Pintar	Cu-t'chissa	To paint
Piolho	Ina	A louse

Portuguese	N'Bunda.	English.
Pisar com o pé	Cu-riata	To tread, to bruise
Plantar	Cu-cuna	To plant
Pobre	Ri-ama	Poor
Poço	I-t'chima	A well
Póde ser (talvez)	T'chila, Cu-cala, N'go	Perhaps
Poder	Cu-atena	To be able
Podre	N'bolo	Rotten
Polvora	Fundanga	Gunpowder
Pomba	Ri-embe	A female dove
Ponta	Ri-sun	A point
Pôr	Cuta, Cutula-cu-ata	To place, put
Pôr de parte	Cu-mughenga	To put aside
Pôr fóra	Cu-teche	To put out
Porco	N'gulo	A pig
Porco espinho	Qui-saca	A porcupine
Porco montez	Ianvo	A wild pig
Porrinho	N'ghimbo	Wart
Porta	Ri-bito	A door
Portas	Ma-bito	Doors
Possuir	Cu-ava	To possess
Posta de peixe	Tumba	A slice of fish
Pote	Ri-sanga	A pitcher
Pouso (de viagem)	Hundo	A halting-place
Povo	Mun-tu	The people
Povoção	Sanza, Banza	A town, village
Prato	Ri-longa	A plate, dish
Preceder	Cu-rianga	To go before
Precipitar (depositar)	Cu-quenzama	To precipitate
Precisar	Cu-messena	To want
Preguiça	Usuri	Laziness
Preguiçoso	Suri	Lazy
Prender	Cu-Cuica	To take hold of, seize
Prensa	Calaquelle	A press
Preparar	Cu-banga	To prepare
Presença	Polo	Presence
Precença (na) de alquem.	Mu-polo-ia-muntu	In some one's presence
Preso	Cuica	A prisoner
Pretender	Cu-acana	To claim
Primavera	Cu-tano	Spring
Primeiro	Ri-anga	First
Primo	Panghé	A cousin
Principe	Mani, Muene	A prince
Principiar	Cu-mateca	To begin
Privação	Obunga	Privation
Privado	Quibunji	A favourite
Procurar	Cu-sota	To search, ask for
Produzir	Cu-ima	To produce
Prompto	Longo	Ready
Provar	Cu-lóla	To prove, taste
Proximo	Zacama	Next
Publicar	Cu-fumanena	To publish
Pular	Cu-tumbuca, Cu-subuca	To leap, bound
Pulga	Ina-ia-imboa	A flea
Puro	Cu-cuto	Pure, untainted

N'Bunda Vocabulary.

Portuguese.	N'Bunda.	English.
Puxar	Cu-sunga, Cu-mana	To draw, to pull
Quarto	Inzo, Monzo	A room
Quarto de dormir	Monzo-ia-quile	A sleeping-room
Quebrar	Cu-burica, Cu-bula, Cu-tulola	To break
Queda	Cu-ribala	A fall, declivity
Queimar	Cu-bia, Cu-sumica	To burn
Queixada	N'gandelo	The jaw-bone
Queixo	Mu-ezo	The jaw
Quente	Temo	Warm
Querer	Cu-andala, Cu-t'chicana, Cu-Messeua	To will, to like
Quiabo	Qui-n'gombo	Quiabo (a plant)
Quitandeira	Mubare	A market-woman
Quitandeiras	A-bare	Market-women
Rã	Qui-n'gololo	A frog
Rachar	Cu-bassa	To cleave, crack
Raia (peixe)	Papa	A ray (fish)
Raio	N'zaje	A ray (of light)
Raiva	N'jenda	Rage, fury
Raivas	Ji-n'jenda	Rabies
Raiz	N'danje	A root
Ralhar	Cu-basela	To bluster, to scold
Ramo	N'tango	A branch, bough
Rapariga	Qui-lnemba	A girl
Rapaz	N'zanga, N'zingala	A boy
Rapido	Mulgengo	Rapid
Raposa	M'bulo	A fox
Rasgar	Cu-tandula	To tear, to rend
Raspar	Cu-colola	To scrape
Rato grande	Ri-bengo	A rat
Rato pequeno	Mundougo, Ca-mundongo	A mouse
Rato do mato	N'puco	Field-mouse
Rato de palmeira	Chit-n'janghele	Tree-mouse
Rebentar	Cu-basa	To burst
Receber	Cu-tambulula	To receive
Recontar	Ca-tangulula	To tell, relate
Recostar-se	Cu-sendalala	To lie down
Rede (maca)	Panda	A net
Relampago	Cuteluca	Lightning
Remedio	Milongo	Remedy, cure
Remelia	Qui-póta	Rheum of the eyes
Repugnancia	N'ghenghe	Reluctance
Resina	Cocoto	Resin
Respirar	Cu-buima	To breathe
Responder	Cu-cumbulula.	To answer
Revirar	Cu-bilula	To turn again
Revistar	Cu-ongola	To review
Ribombar	Cu-cumina	To resound, re-echo
Ribombo	Cumina	Re-echo
Rico	N'vama	Rich
Rio	Mu-guije	A river

Portuguese.	N'Bunda.	English.
Riqueza	Cu-vúa	Riches
Rir	Cu-elela	To laugh
Riscar	Cu-canda	To stripe
Risco	Mu-canda	A stripe
Risonho	Mu-ema	Gay
Rivaes	A-cajina	Rivals
Rival	Mu-cajina	A rival
Roca	Qui-fuco	A rock
Roçar mato	Cu-sola	To fell timber
Roças	A-rimo	A clearing
Roda	Conda	A wheel
Roer	Cu-cunha	To gnaw, to nibble
Rogar	Cu-bomba	To intreat
Rola	Ri-embe	A turtle-dove
Rolar	Cu-cundumuna	To coo
Roncar	Cu-cona, Cu-mucona	To snore
Rua	N'zunga	A street
Rugir (o leão)	Cu-rila	To roar
Saber	Cu-ijia	To know
Sacerdote	N'ganga	A priest
Sacudir	Cu-cumuna	To shake
Sair	Cu-tunda	To go out
Sal	Múngua	Salt
Saltar	Cu-tumbuca, Cu-somboca	To jump, spring
Sangue	Manhinga	Blood
Sanguesuga	Ri-zaie	A leech
Sanguesugas	Ma-zaie	Leeches
Sapo	Ri-sundo	A toad
Sarampo	Cafife	The measles
Sarna	Cáhana, Ji-cahana	The itch
Saudar	Cu-menequena	To salute
Seccar	Cu-cucuta	To dry
Secco	Cucuta	Dry
Sêde	Rinhota	Thirst
Segredar	Cu-cufeta	To secrete
Segredo	Feta	Secret
Segurar	Cu-ouata	To secure
Semente	M'buto	Seed
Sementes	Ji-mbuto	Seeds
Senhor	N'gana, Fumo, Muave	Master, Sir
Senhora	N'ga-munto	Mistress, Madam
Sentar-se	Cu-t'chicama	To sit down
Sentar-se de pernas cruzadas	Cu-tchicama macáta	To sit cross-legged
Sentir	Cu-rinsa	To feel
Separar	Cu-mughenga	To separate
Sepultar	Cu-funda	To bury
Sequestrar	Cu-bunda	To attach
Sertanejo	Mucu-ia-tunda	An inhabitant of the woods
Sertão	Tunda	Back-woods
Silencio	Rit'chibiena	Silence
Sino	N'gunga	A bell
Soebrbo	Ri-tula	Proud

Portuguese.	N'Bunda.	English.
Sobrar	Cu-subuca	To overflow
Sobrinho	Muebo	A nephew
Socar, pilar	Cu-sula	To cram, to bruise
Soffrer	Cu-n'gonga	To suffer
Soffrimento	N'gongo	Suffering, patience
Sogro	Ocué	A father-in-law
Sol	Ricumbe	The sun
Sol (o) poz-se	Ricumbe-riafo	The sun sets
Soltar	Cu-jituna	To set free
Soltereio	Ri-cure	A bachelor
Soluçar	Cu-t'chucomuca	To sob, hiccup
Soluço	Qui-t'chuco-t'chuco	A sob, hiccup
Sombra	Qui-lumbequeta	Shade
Somno	Quilo	Sleep
Sonhar	Cu-anda-n'zoje	To dream
Sonho	N'zoje	A dream
Soprar	Cu-bussa	To blow, to puff
Sorte	Muchinda	A lot, chance
Sovaco	Mu-cábia	Arm-pit
Subir	Cu-banda	To mount, to go up
Suja	Iat'chire	Dirt
Sujar	Cu-chiriosa	To befoul, to stain
Sujo	Uat'chire	Dirty, impure
Sumir-se	Cu-jiquinina	To disappear
Surdo	Mu-chilo	Deaf
Surra	Muchinga	A whipping, beating
Surrar	Cu-chinga	To whip, beat
Suspender	Cu-betula	To hang up
Susto	Uoma	Fright
Tabaco	Macanha	Tobacco
Taboleiro	Qui-tanda	A board, plank
Tábua	Ri-baia	A plank
Tamarindeiro	Mu-tamba	A tamarind-tree
Tamarindo	Ri-tamba	Tamarinds
Tambor	N'goma	A drum
Tanque	It'chima	A tank
Tapar	Cu-futa	To cover, to stop a hole
Tartaruga	Qui-covo	A tortoise
Tecer	Cu-leca	To weave
Tecto	Hongo, Ianzo	The ceiling, roof
Teimar	Cu-n'jiza	To be obstinate
Teimoso	N'jisa	Obstinate
Tempo	Ri-cumbe	Time
Tenda ou barraca	Casassamba	Tent or hut
Tenro	N'yeta, Tete	Tender, soft
Terminar	Cu-assuca	To finish
Terra	Mapo, Dunda	Earth
Tigela	Ri-tamina	Porringer
Tingir	Cu-teca	To dye
Tio, tia	Século	Uncle, aunt
Tirar	Cu-catula	To draw, pull
Tirar do solo	Cu-lola	To dig up
Tocar	Cu-t'chica	To touch

Portuguese.	N'Bunda.	English.
Tolice	Cu-toba	Folly
Tolo	Toba	Foolish
Tomar	Cu-tambula, Cu-zama	To take
Tomar sentido	Cu-aluca	To take care
Tomate	Mate	Tomato
Tomates	Ji-mate	Tomatoes
Tornozelo	Risso-ria	The ankle
Torrar	Cu-canda	To toast
Torto	N'hunga	Hurt, wrong
Tossir	Cu-cocôna	To cough
Tosse	Qu-chinda	Cough
Trabalhar	Cu-calacala, Cu-socana	To work
Trapo	N'bomba	A clout, rag
Trapo de "toilette"	N'zumbi	Cloth, dress
Travesseiro	N'peto	A bolster
Trazer	Cu-beca, Cu-tema	To fetch, bring
Tremer	Cu-tequéta	To tremble
Trilho	Pambo (?)	Track, path
Tripa	Mu-ria	Tripe
Tripas	Mi-ria	Intestines
Tronco	Muche	Trunk
Tropeçar	Cu-ribucana	To stumble
Trovão	N'vula	Thunder
Trovejar	Cu-tonóca	To thunder
Tubarão	Mu-ando	A shark
Tumulo	Qui-bila	Tomb
Ubre (de vacca)	Qui-ele	Udder (of a cow)
Ultimo	Su-quinina, Quinguinina	Last
Umbigo	N'gombo	Navel
Unha	Qui-ala	Nail, claw
Universo	Mugongo	Universe
Untar	Cu-t'chissa	To grease
Utero	Qui-saje	Uterus
Vaccinar	Cuta qui n'gongo	To vaccinate
Vadiar	Cu-laleca	To loiter
Vadio	Qui-lalo	A vagrant
Vagaroso	Qui-muanho	Lingering
Vallada	N'bamba	Intrenched
Valente	Qui-n'danda	Vigorous
Vara	Ri-bamba	Rod, yard
Varrer	Cu-comba	To sweep
Vasar	Cu-baba	To empty
Vasio	Cucuto	Empty
Vassoura	Qui-ezo	A broom
Vela	Mu-tchiba	A candle
Velho (adj.)	Ocúlo	Old
Velho (subst.)	Qui-culacaje	Old man
Vender	Cu-sumbissa	To sell
Veneno	Oanga	Poison
Vento	Qui-tembo	Wind
Ventosa	N'zungo	A cupping-glass
Ventre	Ri-vumo	Belly

N'Jenji Vocabulary.

Portuguese.	N'Bunda.	English.
Ver	Cu-mona, Cu-tanghlila	To see
Verdade	Qui-ri	Truth
Verde	Uisso, Acansa	Green
Vergonha	Sonhe, Ri-jino	Shame
Verme	M'bamba	Worm
Verruga	T'chimbolocoto	Wart
Vestir	Cu-zuata	To dress
Vida	Muenho	Life
Vinho de milho	U-ala	Maize wine
Vinho de palmeira	Maruvo	Palm wine
Vingar-se	Cu-rifuta	To avenge oneself
Vir	Cu-iza	To come
Virar	Cu-biluca	To turn
Viscosidade	N-zeza	Stickiness
Visitar	Cu-acumunequena	To visit
Viuvo	Mu-ture	Widower
Viuvos	A-ture	Widowers and widows
Viver	Cu-muenha	To live
Voar	Cu-luca, Cu-nhunga	To fly
Voltar	Cu-vutuca	To turn
Vomitar	Cu-lussa	To vomit
Vou por terra	N'ghia-cu-tunda	I am going by land
Voz	Ri'zue.	Voice

N'JENJI.[1]

Portuguese.	N'Jenji.	English.
Apodrecer	Cu-porire	To rot
Apparecer	Cu-támobona	To appear
Aprender	Cu-liluta	To learn
Arder	Cu-t'chiza	To burn
Areia	Messeque	Sand
Arma [latra]	Toboro	Arm (weapon)
Arma de carregar pela cu-	Toboro-iá-cutoani	Breech-loader
Arvore (pau)	Cota	Tree
Assar	Cu-bessa	To roast
Assentar	Cu-na	To seat
Atar	Cu-tama	To tie, to bind
Avarento	Afani	Avaricious
Azeite	Mafura	Oil
Beber	Cu-nôa	To drink
Comer	Cu-t'chia	To eat
Correr	Cu-titama	To run
Dormir	Cu-lubala	To sleep
Elephante	Li-tou	Elephant

[1] The N'jenji and Ca-luiana dialects are those spoken, as far as we could judge, in the vast region of the Baróze, the latter being probably used by the ancient Mu-cololo.

Portuguese.	N'Jenji.	English.
Fugir	Cu-saba	To fly, to run
Fumar	Cu-zuba	To smoke
Haver	Cu-tabona	To have
Ir ou andar	Cu-zamaia	To go
Parar	Cu-luquema	To stop
Querer	Cu-abata	To wish
Saltar	Cu-tura	To jump
Vestir	Cu-apára	To dress

GARANGANJA.

Portuguese.	Garanganja.	English.
Alegre	Liatócu	Gay, lively
Algodão	Mulecana	Cotton
Alma	Va-mufo	Soul
Alto	Cu-leha	High
Alumiar	Cu-minica	To light
Amanhecer	Uaqueré'ōa	To break (day)
Amante	Mu-cut'chia	Lover
Amargo	Ussoca	Bitter
Amarrar	Mu-uba	To fasten
Amigo (meu)	Cuno-oame	Friend (my)
Andorinha	Cafifa	Swallow (bird)
Anno	Muaca	Year
Anoitecer	Lili-cu-fucula	To grow right
•Apagar	Cu-zima	To extinguish
Apanhar	Cu-tola	To handle, touch
Apartar	Ulaja-niculitulila	To divide
Apertado	Liacossa	Narrow
Apodrecer	Cu-iabóra	To rot
Apontar	Cu-inica	To point out
Apparecer	Cu-mobona	To appear
Aprender	Cu-libula	To learn
Aquecer	Cu-tumessa	To heat
Arco (setta)	Cu-cassa	Bow (weapon)
Arder	Cu-ratema	To burn
Areia	Masseque	Sand
Arma	Tobola	Arm (weapon)
Arranhar	Cu-suenha	To scratch
Arremessar	Cu-ela	To throw away
Arrependido	Nalipupa	Penitent
Arvore (pau)	Qui-ti	Tree
Assar	Cu-sóca	To roast
Assentar	Cu-icara	To seat

Quioco Vocabulary.

Portuguese.	Garanganja.	English.
Atirar	Cu-era	To shoot
Avarento	U-latana	Avaricious
Azas	Ma-cara	Handles
Azeite	Ma-futo	Oil
Beber	Cu-toma	To drink
Comer	Cu-viriôa	To eat
Despir	Cu-rula	To strip
Dormir	Cu-lala	To sleep
Fugir	Cu-fiuca	To fly, to run
Fumar	Cu-péha	To smoke
Haver	Cu-lobassi	To have
Ir ou andar	Cu-jia	To go
Saltar	Cu-zomboca	To jump
Ver	Cu-lola	To see
Vestir	Cu-apàra	To dress

QUIOCO.

Portuguese.	Quioco.	English.
Abelhas	Ma-puca	Bees
Agua	Meia	Water
Alma	Uafa	Soul
Arco-iris	Congólo	Rainbow
Arma	Uta	Arm (weapon)
Arvore (pau)	Mi-tondo	Tree
Assentar	Cu-tuama	To sit
Avô	Caca	Grandfather
Avó	Cuco-mama	Grandmother
Banco	Mu	Bench
Barbas	Uenvo	Beard
Barriga	D'jimo	Belly
Beber	Cu-nôa	To drink
Beiços	Ni-vumbo	Lips
Bôca	Canôa	Mouth
Boi	N'gombe	Ox
Bonito	M'pema	Nice
Branco (côr)	T'chitoma	White
Branco (homem)	D'jungo	White man
Braços	Móce	Arms
Cabeça	Mutoè	Head

Portuguese.	Quioco.	English.
Cabellos	N'cambo	Hair
Cabra	M'pembe	Goat
Cachimbo	M'peixe	Pipe
Cadella	Boloa-cáôa	Bitch
Calor	Matocota	Heat
Cama	Mu-ghele	Bed
Cão	Cáôa	Dog
Capim	Muhando	High grass
Cara	Maquille	Face
Carneiro	M'panga	Sheep
Casas	Mu-n'zuo	House
Cavallo (marinho)	N'guvo	Horse (sea)
Chapéu de sol	Cafuanda	Hat
Chuva	N'vula	Rain
Cobra	Lulóca	Snake
Comer	Cu-ria	To eat
Coracão	Bungué	Heart
Deus	N'zambi (?)	God
Dentes	Ma-se	Teeth
Dia	Tangua	Day
Doente	Canaíndje	Ill, sick
Dormir	Cu-pomba	To sleep
Elephante	N'djamba	Elephant
Estrellas	Tugonoche	Stars
Farinha	Lupa	Floor
Feio	Mupi	Ugly
Filha	Cuemba	Daughter
Filho	Camique	Son
Fogo	Caghia	Fire
Formiga	Tunguenha-guenba	Ant
Frio	T'chica	Cold
Fumar	Cu-ma	To smoke
Gallinha	Cassumbi	Hen, fowl
Gallo	Demba-cassumbi	Cock
Homem	Sunga	Man
Ir ou andar	Cu-enda	To go
Irmã	Dum-boame	Sister
Irmão	Pueto	Brother
Lado direito	Cut'chi-zume	Right
Lado esquerdo	Cut'chi-meso	Left
Leão	Tamboć ou Temboć	Lion
Lua	Cacuje	Moon
Luz	Deia	Light
Mãe	Má-ma	Mother
Mandioca	Mucamba	Manioc
Mão direita	Zumé	Right hand

Lunda Vocabulary.

Portuguese.	Quioco.	English.
Mão esquerda	Messi	Left hand
Mãos	Minue	Hands
Mar	Calunga	Sea
Meio dia	Nonga-eimoala	Midday, noon
Mel	Uit'chi	Honey
Mulher	Po	Woman, wife
Nariz	N'zulo	Nose
Olhos	Messo	Eyes
Orelhas	Ma-t'chi	Ears
Pae	Tala	Father
Peito	Pambo	Breast
Pernas	Mólo	Legs
Pés	Mi-uoé	Feet
Pescoço	Cóta	Neck
Rio	N'guije	River
Rôla	Catelia	Turtle-dove
Sal	Múngua	Salt
Sangue	Manhenga	Blood
Sova	Muene-n'gana	Petty king
Sol	Muálua	Sun
Sul	Culuanda	South
Tabaco	Macanha	Tobacco
Terra	Mutifut'chi	Earth
Tia	Tata-pó	Aunt
Tio	Mat'cho	Uncle
Tipoia	Unda	Palanquin
Trovão	Djoji	Thunder
Trovoada	Fundji	Thunder-clap
Unhas	Djala	Nails, claws
Vacca	N'bôlo	Calf
Veias	Ma-chahá	
Verdade (É)	T'chaquêne	True (It is)

LUNDA.

Portuguese.	Lunda.	English.
Agua	Meme	Water
Agulha	Catumo	Needle
Amanhã	Diamachica	To-morrow
Amante	Mucaje (plu) Acaje	Lover
Amigo (meu)	Mu-run'ame	Friend (my)
Amigo (teu)	Mu-run'ei	Friend (thy)

Portuguese.	Lunda.	English.
Amigos (meus)	Arun'ame	Friends (my)
Amigos (teus)	A-run'ei	Friends (thy)
Anoitecer	Cu-t'chuco	To grow night
Arco (seta)	Djirian	Bow (weapon)
Arma	Uta (pl. Muta)	Arm (weapon)
Arvore	Mu-tondo	Tree
Arvore (pau)	Mi-tondo	Pole
Boi	N'gombe	Ox
Boi (silvestre)	M'bau	Buffalo
Branco (homem)	Mona-Cu-meme	White (man)
Cabellos	D'ji-n'suque	Hair
Cabra	M'pembé	Goat
Caça (empostas)	Dji-riama	Chase, hunting
Caça	Nama	Game, venison
Cama	Ulálo	Bed
Camas	Ma-lálo	Beds
Caneca	Lu-passa	Jug
Canecas	Dji-en'passa	Jugs
Canoas	Ma-oato	Canoes
Cão	Cabo (pl. A-tubua)	Dog
Capim	Massuco	High grass
Carneiro	Mu-cóco	Sheep
Carneiros	Ama-coco	Sheep (pl.)
Carregador (tipoias)	T'chimangata	Carrier
Casa	T'chi'cumbo	House
Casas	I'cumbo	Houses
Cavallo (marinho)	N'guvo	Horse (sea)
Copo	Lu-sumo	Cup, glass
Copos	Dji-sumo	Cups, glasses
Corça	N'cai	Doe
Corpo	Mu-djumba	Body
Coser (com agulha)	Cu-t'chima	To sew
Cosido (está)	Uássuca	Sewed
Cozinhar	Cu-suca	To cook
Dia	Dichuco	Day
Dias	Ma-chuco	Days
Dormir	Cu-langala	To sleep
Elephantes	N'zovo	Elephants
Euxada	Lu-casso	Hoe
Euxadas	Djincasso	Hoes
Faca	N'passa	Knife
Facas	Djin'passa	Knives
Fazendas	Ma-suma	Goods
Feijão	N'zengo	Bean
Feiticeiro	Mu-ladji	Fetish-man
Fogo	N'casso	Fire
Folhas	Ma-iji	Leaves
Fumo	Cunanga	Smoke
Gallinhas	A-n'zollo	Fowls

Ca-Luiana Vocabulary.

Portuguese.	Lunda.	English.
Homem	Icunguè	Man
Homems	Ama-cunguè	Men
Hontem	N'galoche	Yesterday
Infundi	Ruco	Dish so called
Lenha	N'cunhe	Wood
Longe (É)	Palepe	Far (it is)
Machado	Ca-sau	Hatchet
Machados	Tu-sau ?)	Hatchets
Mandioca	Candinga	Manioc
Mão	T'chi-cassa	Hand
Mãos	Ma-cassa	Hands
Mulher	Mi-n'banda	Woman, wife
Mulheres	N'banda	Women, wives
Nuima (oryx)	M'chilla	Numia (oryx)
Nuimas	Ama'chilla	Nuimas
Nuima gazella	M'ceifo	Gazelle
Nuimas	Ama'ceifo	Gazelles
Olho	Di-ce	Eye
Olhos	Mè-ce	Eyes
Orelha	Di-to	Ear
Orelhas	Ma-to	Ears
Palanca antelope	T'chi-fembe	Palanca
Palancas	I-fembe	Palancas
Pé	Mu-nto	Foot
Pés	Mi-ento	Feet
Rio	U-ita	River
Rios	Ma-uita	Rivers
Setas	Dji-ineu	Arrows
Sim, senhor	Muán-ini	Yes, sir
Sol	Mutenhe	Sun
Tabaco	Ruanda	Tobacco
Terra	Divo	Earth
Tipoia	Moa	Palanquin

CA-LUIANA.

Portuguese.	Ca-Luiana.	English.
Cavallo (marinho)	N'gufo	Horse (sea)
Dormir	Cu-langana	To sleep
Feio	Ontama	Ugly

Portuguese.	Ca-luana.	English.
Feiticeiro	Urot'chi	Fetish-man
Feitico	N'ganga	Fetish
Feixe	Icundi	Faggot, bundle
Femea	M'banda	Female
Filho	Moana	Son
Flor	Li-cumbi	Flower
Flores	Mia-cumbi	Flowers
Fogo	Quesse	Fire
Folha	Li-fo	Leaf
Folhas	Ma-fo	Leaves
Folles	Miniba	Bellows
Fome	N'dala	Hunger
Força	N'gofo	Force, strength
Formiga	Tumôe-môe	Ant
Fraco	Gufone	Weak
Fresco	T'chassosoma	Fresh
Frio	T'chissica	Cold
Fugir	Cu-temoca	To fly, to run
Fumar	Cu-féba	To smoke
Fumo	T'chisse	Smoke
Furar	Cu-furula	To bore
Furtar	Cu-combe	To rob
Fuzo	T'chitina	Spindle
Gafanhoto	Bimba	Locust
Gallinha	N'zolo	Fowl, hen
Gallo	Li-corombollo	Cock
Gallos	Ma-corombollo	Cocks
Gato do mato	Caronzo	Wild cat
Gemeos (primeiro)	Nhana-ca-cu-sema	Twin (first)
Gemeos (segundo)	Nhana-ca-cu-atame	Twin (second)
Gemer	Cu-ima	To groan
Gengiva	Caluvira	Gum
Giboia	Boma	Boa
Gordo	Oanuna	Fat
Grande	Oénene	Great, large
Grilo	Canzenzi	Cricket
Gritar	Cu-moanga	To cry out
Grosso	Chacatambi	Thick
Guardar	Cu-succa	To keep, guard
Guella	Caraca	Throat
Guloso	Oassupa	Gluttonous
Guerra	N'jita	War
Herva	T'chicoco	Herb, grass
Hombro	T'chi-peoca	Shoulder
Homem	N'jára	Man
Hyena	N'ganga	Hyena
Ilha	Li-seque-iatunda	Island
Ilhas	Ma-seque-iatunda	Islands
Inchado	T'chanana	Swollen
Infeliz	Oabindamoa	Unhappy, unlucky
Inimigo	Oatama	Enemy

Ca-Luiana Vocabulary. 333

Portuguese.	Ca-luiana.	English.
Inveja	Ulinoa-ca-noquenje	Envy
Ir ou andar	Cu-enda	To go
Irmã	Mana-oaiala	Sister
Irmão	Mana-cueto	Brother
Joelho	Mendo	Knee
Labio	Cano	Lip
Laço	Luobi	Noose
Lacraia	Carique	Scorpion
Lado direito	Sinarui	Right
Lado esquerdo	Cambau	Left
Ladrão	U-combe	Thief
Lagartas	Ma-cubi	Caterpillar
Lagurto	Cambo	Lizard
Lago	Cana-ca-calunga	Lake
Lagrimas	Ma-zossi	Tears
Lama	Iloba	Mud, mire
Largo	Clucatambe	Broad
Lavar	Cu-cussa	To wash
Leão	Mu-nhime	Lion
Lebre	Calumba	Hare
Leite	Maiére	Milk
Lenha	Itiabo	Wood
Leve	T'chapepera	Light (not heavy)
Limpar	Cu-combora	To clean
Lingua	Lilaca	Tongue, language
Lobo	Quimbo	Wolf
Lodo	Iloba	Mud, loam
Lombriga	Caboba	Worm
Louco	Oassaluca-coloba	Mad
Lua	N'zoro	Moon
Luz	Moera-cuessi	Light
Macaco	Buia	Monkey
Machado	Sirepe	Hatchet
Macho	Jára	Male
Macio	T'chassenena	Smooth
Maduro	Cuiá	Mature, ripe
Mãe	Ma-mãe	Mother
Magro	Oago-cama	Thin
Maior	T'chicatampe	Elder
Mamar	Cu-atama	To suck
Mandioca	Macamba	Manioc
Manhã	Tete-mena	To-morrow
Manilha	M'buro	Handle
Mão direita	T'chaculida	Right hand
Mão esquerda	Quimosso	Left hand
Mãos	Ma-cassa	Hands
Mar	Calunga-munéne	Sea
Massar	Cu-cassa	To beat
Mastigar	Cu-polocot	To chew
Matar	Cu-t'cha	To kill
Mato	Micula	Wood (thicket)

Portuguese.	Ca-luiana.	English.
Medir	Cu-esseca	To measure
Medo	Uoma	Fear
Mel	Ut'chi	Honey
Menino	Cauzi	Little child
Mentira	Oalimba	Lie
Mestre	Gangura	Master
Metade	Cat'chibele	Half
Mez	N'zolo	Month
Milho	Cabaça	Maize
Miolos	Quipuji	Brains
Molhado	Chazula	Wet
Monte	Pide	Hill, mount
Morcego	Capapa	Bat
Morto	Mufo	Dead
Mosca	Cadeane	Fly
Mosquito	Camama	Mosquito
Querer	Cu-t'chinga	To wish
Ver	Cu-bona	To see

INDEX.

Abba-Alta-Azimuth, i. 84, ii. 26, 189.
Abelmoschus esculentos, i. 358, 367.
Acacia furnesiana albida, i. 253, 281.
Acacias, i. 45, 49, 224, 281 ; ii. 22.
A-cajes, i. 387.
Acantaceas in Quicongo, ii. 89.
Adansonia (genus), i. 16 ; ii. 88. *A. digitata* i. 278, 367 ; inner bark of, i. 16, 278, ii. 266.
Africa, difficulty of studying, xxii.; nations labouring in, xxv; considerations respecting slavery in, i. 165.
Almandrilha, i. 8.
Aloes, *Liliacea*, i. 103 ; ii. 266.
Ambaca, ii. 187 ; productions of, ii. 189.
Ambaquistas, remarks upon, i. 194, ii. 39, 188.
Ambassi, Ambaca guide, i. 123, 132.
Ambris, ii. 82, 147.
Ambrizette, ii. 149.
Ambuella country, i. 93.
Angola, province of, i. 59.
Anha, district of, i. 60.
Anona muricata, i. 371.
Antelopes, varieties of, i. 67.
Ant-hills, i. 51, 81, 329.
Anthropophagy, fears that it inspires, i. 248; where exercised, i. 81, 165, 248; ii. 125, 217.
Ants, *bi-sondes*, i. 82, 95, 118, 241 ; red, 284 ; stinking, ii. 19.
Apocinaceas, i. 223, 303.
Aquilonda (Lake), remarks upon, ii. 145.
Arabs, their influence in Central Africa, ii. 262.
Arachis hypogea, i. 74, 366.
Arachnidios, ii. 30.
Arms, native names, i. 166.
Arundo phragmites, on the Lui, ii. 11.
Assagais, i. 53, 94.
Asses, i. 49, 58, 85, 124.
Asphalt, ii. 233.

A-topa, pipe, i. 393.
Athene perlata, owl, ii. 187.
Authors, general idea concerning the, i. xxiv ; become explorers, i. xxvi ; tributes of gratitude, xxxi ; speech made by them to the Ma-hungo, ii.76.
Avelino Fernandez, ii. 229.

Ba-bihé people, i. 108.
Baboons (*Galago Senigalensis*) (*galago monteiri*) nat. *t'chicafo*, i. 241.
Ba-cano, among the Bangala, i. 324.
Baccari river, ii. 125.
Ba-congo, tribes of the. ii. 88, 135.
Ba-cuando tribes, i. 108.
Ba-cuisso tribes, i. 108.
Ba-cundi tribes, ii. 125.
Ba-ganguella people, i. 108.
Bagre, *clarias anguillaris*, i. 253, 301, 358 ; ii. 107.
Bai-lundo, district of, i. 42, 102 ; people, i. 13, 191.
Baker, Sir S., i. 113.
Bale, dangerous rivulet, ii. 13.
Balearia regulorum, i. 67.
Ba-lunda people, i. 385.
Banana, *Musacea*, i. 25, 103 ; ii. 255.
Ba-nanos people, i. 80, 81 ; incursions of, i. 39, 80.
Ban-bonda, territory of, i. 108.
Ban-cumbi tribes, i. 81.
Ban-dombe tribes, i. 10, 25.
Bandua, lofty barrier in Luimbi, i. 145.
Ban-gala tribes, i. 263 ; general features of, i. 323 ; wars, adultery among them, i. 324 ; their drunkenness, i. 325 ; ambition, dwellings, their construction, i. 326; industry, wives, &c. i, 327; their establishment in the territory of Cassange, chronological data, i. 333 ; trouble caused by, i. 346; meeting a caravan of, ii. 217.

Bangaloango, nat. *Erythrina, h* (?), i. 146.
Bango, i. 38, 167.
Bango, mountain of Cassange, ii. 11; ascent of, ii. 42.
Bangueolo, i. 17, 102.
Ba-nhaneca tribes, i. 112.
Ban-sumbi, Otubo chief of the, i. 76; their sufferings, ii. 111.
Banximba territory, i. 66.
Banza, village and sova, i. 314.
Banza e Lunda, i. 344; tempest in, i. 346; disputes with, i. 347; aspect of the sova, interview with him, i. 349.
Banza Dalango, ii. 233.
Banza N'Borungo, territory of, i. 247.
Bao-babs, *Malvacea*, nat. *Imbundeiro*, i. 35, 47; ii. 12, 185, 190, 195, 214, 225.
Barraguenho, rivulet of, i. 215.
Barros, guide, i. 20, 70; dismissal of, in Bihé, i. 131.
Basalts in the Serra Hengue, ii. 190.
Ba-songo people, i. 108.
Battue, grand, i. 245.
Batuque (dance), description of, i. 70.
Beards, of the authors, sensation caused by, i. 83, 114, 169.
Bees, i. 95, 197, 214, 230, 359.
Beisas, antelopes, i. 67.
Belmonte, description of, i. 98.
Bembe, road to Encoge, ii. 149.
Bengo, valley of, ii. 226.
Benguella, city of, i. 10; description of, i. 11; salubrity, i. 14; population, i. 14; trade, i. 16; departure from, i. 20; southern track, i. 21.
Berengella, mad apples (*Solanum melongena* or *ovigeram*), i. 366.
Bernardino Antonio Gomes, his influence in this mission, i. xxv.
Bi-cumbi, wooden shackles, i. 143.
Bihé, general description, i. 102; district connected with, i. 102; population of 102; productions, i. 103; wonderful development of vegetation, i. 104; inhabitants, i. 106; traditions, i. 107; people settled in, i. 108; women of, i. 110; religion, i. 112; native industry, i. 115; capital and sova of, i. 116; people, i. 103, 191.
Bihénos people, i. 103, 195; iron trade of, i. 115; mode of making war, i. 142.
Bin-bonzo, sweet potatoes, i. 74.
Bin-bundo people, i. 108; ii. 17; fetishism among, i. 112.
Binda, calabash, i. 83; ii. 107.

Bin-delle, white men, i. 83; strange stories of, i. 168, 181.
Birds of ill-augury, i. 234; in the N'guri, ii. 214.
Bi-sonde ant, i. 82; attack of, in the Bihé, i. 118.
Boar, wild, i. 274 302.
Boat, *Halket*, i. 312, 345; human, i. 332.
Boceta, native box, ii. 23.
Boerhavia sp. (?), i. 371.
Bombax, i. 243.
Bombó, process of obtaining it, i. 364.
Bondo-ia-quilesso, site of, ii. 185.
Bondos, tobacco of, ii. 27; entomology of, ii. 28.
Bongo serra, ii. 22.
Bonze, i. 167.
Borassus, in Quioco, i. 224; in the Hungo, ii. 88.
Borbulo, Mount, i. 38.
Brachystegia tamarindoide, nat. *ossasa* and *ucuba*, i. 82.
Brazza, M. de, ii. 142.
Bread, nat. *jimbolo*, i. 365.
Brigham Young, African, i. 265.
Bucorax caffer (?) in the N'guri, ii. 214.
Bucephalus typus, quilengo-lengo, i. 357.
Buchner, Dr. Max, i. 395; ii. 43.
Bucusso, district of, i. 93, 102.
Bucusso, sova of the Cubango, i. 93.
Buffalo, *Bubalus caffer*, nat. *m'pacaça*, i. 48, 59, 67, 127, 312; ii. 132.
Bulimus rucifex, nat. *t'chiquecula*, i. 284.
Bulo Jango, site of, ii. 185.
Bumba, *Jagga* of Cassange, i. 329; ii. 11.
Bumbo, musical instrument, i. 62, 88, 94, 138.
Bundo serra, i. 66.
Bungo, ii. 223.
Buphaga erythrorrhyncha, ii. 215.
Burseraceas, i. 45; in Quioco, i. 223; in Quicongo, ii. 89.
Burton (F. R.), Captain, ii. 247.
Buta, Echdina arietans, i. 357.
Butessa, i. 167, 171.
Butterflies, i. 95.

Cababa, rivulet, i. 59.
Cabaje Mutomba, vassal of the Yanvo, i. 380.
Caballo, cascade, ii. 199.
Cabbage, i. 103, 358.
Cabeba, supreme chief of the Lunda, 385; mode of punishing his subjects, i. 390.
Cabenda-Candambo, village of, ii. 152.

Cabeto, site of, ii. 212.
Cabindas, i. 25.
Cabindondo, river of, i. 30.
Cabulo, cataract, ii. 225.
Cachellangues people, i. 317.
Cachinge, serras of, ii. 192.
Cacol-Calombo, grottoes in. ii. 207
Caconda, district of, i. 10, 59.
Caculo-Cabaça, ii, 164.
Cadoche, river in Quioco, i. 229.
Cadotcha, sova of Quiteque, i. 137.
Caembe-Camungu, cataract of the Cassai, i. 247.
Caembo Muculo, sova, i. 389.
Caengue (Muene) lands belonging to that sova, journeys to, i. 247, 308.
Caffres, i. 109.
Cafuchila, first sova of the Hungo, ii. 69; confusion respecting, ii. 70.
Ca-jagga, title of chief, i. 134.
Cujinga, i. 53, 331; ii. 54.
Calachingo, family of i. 329.
Calne, river, i. 85.
Calahari, desert of, i. 109.
Calala, i. 387.
Calumus, florus, ii. 86.
Calandula, sova, i. 345; ii. 45.
Calaei, title in Quioco, i. 174.
Calfelé, title in Quioco, i. 174.
Caluculla, i. 33.
Calundo, track of, ii. 191, 207.
Calunga, family of the, i. 329.
Calunga, or great water, the sea, i. 113. ii. 162, 196.
Calunga, river, i. 34, 38.
Calunga-Canjimbo, sova, ii. 153.
Calunga N'bando, compulsory present of, ii. 66.
Calunga (N'dombo Acambo), king of Jinga, ii. 52.
Caluquembe, district of, i. 48.
Camassa, sova of the Quembo, i. 311.
Camassamba, senzala, road from Cha-Quilembi, i. 197.
Camaxe, rivulet, a terrible mishap at, ii. 154.
Camba, territory of, i. 66.
Cumba, rivulet, ii. 141.
Cambamba, sova, i. 314; redemption of a prisoner, i. 315.
Cambamba, libata of, ii. 89.
Cambambe, ii. 225, 223.
Cambaxe, sova, ii. 64.
Cambo, river, its source, its course, ii. 27, 61.
Cambollo, *banza* of Cassange, i. 316, 335, ii. 7.

Cambolla (Cangonga), *jagga*, ii. 9; *banza* of, description of his residence, remarks upon the jagga, presents, ii. 10.
Cambundi Catembo, the senzala of, i. 331.
Cameron, i. 130; ii. 250, 261.
Camicungo, river of, ii. 38.
Camoaxi, river of, ii. 38.
Camp, *v.* Encampment.
Campanjili (Muata), vassal of the Yauvo, i. 389.
Canda-ia-Cunzella, dispute at, ii. 58.
Canda-ia-Legho, ii. 50.
Canda-ia-Lumbombo in the Jinga. ii. 60.
Candanje, river, ii. 65.
Canda-ria-Massango in the Jinga, ii. 58.
Cundas in the Jinga, ii. 53.
Candeeira, sova, i. 155.
Candimba, merchant, i. 16.
Candumbo, lands of, sources of the Cunene, i. 90; senzala of, ii. 199.
Cane (sugar), *Saccharium officinalis*, i. 22, 58, 60, 366; ii. 149,
Canena Steatomys edulis, i. 68.
Cangombe, capital of the Bihé, i. 116, 118; description of the *m'balla* and *mu-icanzo*, i. 120.
Canguanda, senzala on the Lu-lua, i. 247.
Cangumbe, Ganguella libata, i. 126.
Canbica (Muene), i. 390.
Canhumgamua, river, i. 86.
Canica, site of, i. 196.
Cunis aureus in the Minungo, i. 271.
Canis mesomelus (?), i. 369.
Canjamba serra, i 301, 308.
Cannabis sativa, i. 334; its effect, ii. 28.
Cannibalism, *v.* Anthropophagy.
Canoes in Porto Real, ii. 185.
Cantalla (Muene), sova, i. 187, 191, 311.
Canunguessa, market, i. 17, 102.
Capaimbo, senzala of Quioco, i. 160.
Capambo (Tabanus), ii. 19.
Capanda track, *vid*, ii. 211.
Capangombe, i. 81.
Caparanga, cataract, of the Cuango (Louisa falls), i. 274.
Capata-iéu, nests of the, ii. 29.
Capelles in the Jinga, ii. 53.
Capitango in Quioco, i. 190.
Capricornios, ii. 29.
Caprimulgidæ, family of the, ii. 183.
Caprimulgos Shelleyi, ii. 183.

Capulca, the cook, i. 34. 75, 90, 173, 308, 347, 351; ii. 30, 55, 80, 180.
Capullo Dionzo, river, i. 33.
Caputo, libata, i. 87; dispute with the natives, i. 87.
Caquilla, island of, ii. 199.
Caquinda, war in, i. 95.
Caravans, their mode of marching, i. 77; *quibucas* and *n'bucas* i. 37; meeting with, i. 369; ii. 207, 222.
Carica papaya, fruit, ii. 257.
Carimba, senzala, energetic protest, i. 282.
Cariombo, river, ii. 185.
Carriers, difficulties in engaging, i. 3; contracted at Novo Redondo, i. 9, 24; death of one i. 240; ii. 154; number who died on the journey, ii. 157; list of, ii. 160.
Cassai, river, i. 102, 191, 197, 247.
Cassai, the faithful bitch, i. 175; her pups, crime committed by, i. 342.
Cassalla, mount, ii. 11.
Cassange, i. 200, district and subdivisions, i. 320; fair, decline and panorama, i. 321; commercial activity, i. 322; interior territories with which it is connected, i. 322; climate, i. 328; form of termite hills therein, i. 329; *jaggado*, reigning families, i. 329; indecision at, i. 335; fever, i. 336; definite project, i. 337; return to, i. 373; troubles with the men at, i. 375; last day of residence in, ii. 3.
Cassango, senzala, i. 197.
Cassanhe, senzala, i. 91.
Cassanje, cambambu, diviner, i. 383.
Cassanje, hamlet, ii. 181.
Cassanza, river of the Quembo, i. 286.
Cassasio, serra, ii. 220.
Cassia occidentalis, nat. "stinking," i. 275.
Cassongo-Calombo, territory of that sova, i. 18, 102.
Cassoque, village of, ii. 222.
Cassungo of various colours, i. 8, 393.
Castor-oil plant, *Ricinus communis*, i. 28.
Catalla Canjinga, lands of, ii. 27.
Catanga, important market of, i. 17, 102, 138; copper-mine at, ii. 233.
Catanha, territory of, ii. 15.
Catanha, serra, i. 49; ii. 15, 27, 55.
Catão, chief of the ban-sumbi, treachery and dishonesty, protests and flight, i. 130, 131.

Catape, river, i. 59.
Cateco, the guide, ii. 50; in the Jinga, ii. 64; disputes with, ii. 66, 75.
Catenda, serras of, ii. 192.
Catende, district of, i. 180, 191, 197.
Catenha, mount. ii. 201.
Catete, lake, Songo, i. 154.
Catonga, site of, i. 58.
Catoplebas taurina, antelope, i. 43.
Catraio, the assistant, i. 192; flight of his wife, ii. 4; his forgetfulness, ii. 19; carelessness, ii. 177.
Catuchi (Muene), sova, i. 297; aspect of the inhabitants, i. 299; tobacco and salt, want of, i. 300; sport, i. 302.
Catucua, serra, ii. 64.
Catuma Caimba, sova, ii, 152:
Catuma Cangando, sova, ii. 149; reception and an amusing incident, ii. 150.
Catumbella, district of, i. 10.
Catunga, senzala, abundance in, i, 257.
Catupo, serra, i. 129.
Cauali, river, ii. 146; basin of, ii. 153.
Caughi, villa of, ii. 212.
Cauandas, people of, i. 165.
Canéu, rivulet, i. 196.
Caueu, son of the sova of the Bihé, i. 126; nephew of the sova of Quioco. i. 176; ballet-dancer, i. 176, 226, 292.
Cauris, Cypréa moneta, cowries, i. 198.
Causus rhombeatus, nat. *quibolobolo*, i. 357.
Cavunje, river, vegetation on the banks of, i. 338.
Caxita, rocks of, ii. 141.
Cazangaralla, *mu-sumba* of, i. 388.
Cazembe, *caquinhata* of, i. 199, 389.
Cazembe, origin of, i. 386.
Cazengo, ii. 208.
Celli or Celi, men of. i. 24, 248, 337.
Cemeteries, i. 160, 211; in Cassange, ii. 7, 37.
Cephalobus mergens, antelope, i. 43, 274.
Cervicapra bohor, antelope, i. 43.
Cha-cala, senzala of, ii. 128.
Cha-Calumbo, senzala of, i. 147, 243.
Cha-Cassingo, sova of Quioco, i. 160.
Cha-Cupinga, cemetery in Quioco, i. 160.
Chaduiji, river, affluent of the Cuango. i. 252.
Cha-Landa, sova, ii. 38.
Chalucinga, i. 33.
Cha-Massango, track of, ii. 92.

Chamærops, fan-palm, ii. 88.
Cha-Nama, successor to the State in Lunda, i. 180, 386.
Cha-Nende, sova of Quioco, i. 160.
Chanfana, sova, his residence &c, i. 238; presents, i. 239; death of a carrier there, i. 240.
Chu-N'ganji, complications, i. 155, 156; pretensions, i. 157; his genealogic tree, i. 158; visit to N'Damba Tembo, i. 205; his reception, i. 297; flight, i. 208.
Cha-Quessi, Muata of N'Dumba, i. 160; guide, i. 163.
Cha-Quicala, a traveller, i. 247.
Cha-Quicumbe, senzala, i. 292.
Cha-Quilembe, senzala in Quioco, i. 197.
Cha-Tumba, sova, i. 247.
Chella, serra of, i. 33; cataract of the Cunene, i. 66.
Chenopodium ambrosioides, i. 284, 371.
Chiboco. *v.* T'chiboco.
Chicondi, *v.* T'chicondi
Circumlocution, native, i. 377; ii. 25.
Chicupa, *v.* T'chicapa.
Children, reflections upon African, ii. 167.
Chili pepper, i. 364; ii. 9.
Chimbarandungo, sova, i. 53—57.
Chimbuioca, i. 94.
Chingolo, falls of the Cubango, i. 93.
Chromis mossambicus, ii. 201.
Chromis Sparmanni, ii. 201.
Chronometers, remarks upon, ii 205; immense value of, ii. 206.
Chinje, territory, *v.* Xinge.
Churasco, i. 88, 367.
Cicadas, nat. *m'banzarala*, ii. 30.
Citrons, i. 103.
Clarias anguillaris, bagre, i. 301.
Clematis, i. 82.
Climatology of the flora, ii. 146.
Cloth (trade), (coast), i. 7; wholesale, i. 325.
Coal, ii. 233, 266.
Cochlospermum angolensis, ii. 214.
Cocoons, silk, ii. 192.
Coffee, i. 60; ii. 266.
Coje (Muene), i. 229; his exigencies, i. 230; *itambi*, i. 231; batuques, i. 231.
Colobus angolensis, doubts as to its origin, i. 258.
Colobus palliatus, i. 369.
Colombolo, Rhagerrhis tritœniatus, i. 357.
Colonization of Central Africa, ii. 268.
Compana (Muata), sova, i. 309.

Condo, cataract of, remarks upon, ii. 203.
Conga, i. 169.
Conflagrations, ii. 136.
Congo, king of the, ii. 74.
Congo, system of the, i. 102.
Convolvulaceas in Quioco, i. 224.
Copal gum, ii. 266.
Cope, Mount, i. 38.
Copororo, river of S. Francisco, Dombe, i. 21, 22.
Copper, i. 22, 223; ii. 233, 266.
Cork, i. 224.
Corythaix paulina, ii. 30.
Cosmetornis rexillarius, ii. 183.
Cosmogony (native), ii. 158.
Cotton, i. 23, 60; ii. 149, 164, 266.
Cowries, *Cypréa moneta*, i. 198.
Crane, i. 67.
Crocodiles, i. 67; ii. 157, 186.
Cryptogamicaso in Cassange, ii. 7.
Cuafo, river in Quioco, i. 229.
Cu-amato, territory of, i. 66.
Cu-ando, river, i. 61, 102; stepping-stones or *mupas* of, i. 63.
Cuango, river, i. 102, 190; sources in the territory of Muene Quibau, i. 196; vegetation on its borders, i. 243; sinuous course, i. 243, 253, 263, thorny banks, i. 276; cataracts, ii. 141.
Cuango *pequeno*, or little Cuango river, i. 299, 304.
Cuanja, cataract of the Cubango, i. 93.
Cuanza, i. 102, 122; origin, i. 128, description of, in N'jamba, i. 144, 145; considerations respecting, ii. 199; fauna of, ii. 202; the basin of the, a few remarks upon, ii. 226.
Cubango, river, course of the, i. 93; cataracts, i. 93.
Cubunje, rivulet, i. 58.
Cucumbi, river, affluent of the Cuango, i. 312.
Cucus indicator, or honey-bird, i. 281.
Cu-engo, river, ii. 126.
Cuenguare, stepping-stones (*mupas*) of, i. 66.
Cugho, river, discovery of, and source, ii. 88; dispute on crossing, ii. 90.
Cugho, watermen, ii. 89.
Cuiji, river, southern limit of the Songo, i. 191.
Cuji, river, ii. 35.
Cuilo, river, ii. 69; disemboguement into the Cuango, ii. 134.
Cuilo munêne, river, i. 309.
Cuimé, river in Quioco, i. 229.

Cuio, town of, i. 22.
Cuiques, *Pionias Meyerii*, i. 358.
Cuito, river, i. 99, 102, 123; sacrifice at, i. 131.
Cumaghia (senzala), i. 238.
Cunene, river, i. 47, 66; fauna, i. 67; bridge over, i. 90.
Cunga, journey to, ii. 227.
Cunga-ria-Cunga, cascade of, ii. 141.
Cuqueima, river, i. 119, 123; bridge over, i. 125.
Cuso, river, i. 61.
Cussique, affluent of the Luando, i. 160.
Cutapa (Muene), i. 387, 392; ii. 248.
Cutato, river, i. 95.
Cutieques, dwarfs in the north of the Lunda, i. 248, 317.
Cutota, rivulet, i. 51.
Cuverai, rivulet, i. 47.
Cuviji, river, ii. 94.
Cynocephalus sp. ?, in Luimbe, i. 146.
Cynocephalus porcarius, ii. 86.
Cyprèa moneta, shells, i. 198.
Cyrena fluminalis, i. 24.

Dambis in the Jinga, ii. 53.
Dances, i. 70, 226, 258, 331; ii. 130.
Danguena, territory of, i. 66.
Danje, district of, subdivision of Jinga, ii. 52; sources of the Canali, Sussa, and Luando in, ii. 146, 153.
Danje-ia-menba, site of, ii. 221.
Decamera-tonantis, ii. 213.
Deer, i. 67, 241.
Dembe (*Mormyrus Lhuisi*), ii. 204.
Dembei, river, i. 140; a funeral near, i. 140.
Dembo (Naboangongo), ii. 82.
Dembos, lands of the, ii. 154.
Dendrobates namaquus, i. 358.
Desertions, i. 24, 131, 144, 292; ii. 61.
Diary, extracts of, i. 123, 247; ii. 65, 66, 103, 123, 136.
Discongo, banquet, i. 332.
Discorea alata (?) inhame, i. 58, 366.
Discoreas, i. 366.
Disnas (huts), i. 238.
Ditenda Yanvo, i. 388.
D'jango, i. 238, 300.
D'jengi, i. 17.
D'jindungo pepper, i. 364.
Dombe Grande, district of, i. 10, 80; mineralogy, i. 22; aguardente in, i. 23; geographical position, i. 24.
Dombe Pequeno, district of, i. 10.
Domingos (N'jinji carrier), ii. 3.

Dondo, ii. 208; arrival at, ii. 225.
Dongo, subdivision of Jinga, ii. 52.
Dongolo, falls of the Cubango, i. 93.
Doti, i. 7.
Dove, i. 67.
Duque de Bragança, district of, ii. 46; arrival at, ii. 161; position and establishment, ii. 163; fertility and climate, ii. 164; departure from, ii. 180.
Drunkenness, ii. 256.
Dysentery, ii. 129, 136.

Ebande, Clarias anguillaris, i. 301.
Echdina arietans, nat. *buta*, i. 357.
Edemonas on the Lui, ii. 11.
Egito, district, i. 10.
Eh! Eh! Oah! exclamation, i. 55, 164.
Elais, palm, ii. 88, 144.
Elemi, nat. *m'pafu*, i. 223; ii. 86, 89, 267.
Eleotragus reduncus, antelope, i. 314.
Elephants, nat. *n'jamba*, i. 107, 193.
Elotarsus, i. 358.
Empacaceiros, ii. 215.
Encampment the first, i. 30; awakening of, i. 172; ii. 31; construction of, ii. 8; breaking up of, ii. 31, 32; destroyed by fire, ii. 173.
Encoge, *pambo* of, ii. 149.
Endoa, rivulet, i. 216.
Entozoario, noteworthy specimen, ii. 209.
Eonga in the Bihé, i. 167.
Eriodendron anf., in Quicongo, ii. 89, 145, 214.
Erythrina, i. 45; *E. huillensis*, nat. *ofuanganga*, i. 82, 146; *E. chrisocarpa*, nat. *n'gombe*, i. 82; in Quioco, i. 224; ii. 214.
Erythrophlœum guincense, i. 382.
Eschinomenes on the Lui, ii. 11.
Esponjeira, Acacia farnesiana in the Quembo, i. 281.
Ethnography, ii. 234.
Euphorbiaceas in Quicongo, ii. 89.
Euphorbias, i. 49, 82, 103, 224.
Euprepes Ivensi, ii. 201.
Euryotis Anchieta, nat. *Unberi*, i. 68.
Expedition, remarks upon its organization, &c., xxiv—xxvi.
Explorers, early days in Africa, difficulties and troubles of, i. 1, 2; recent works deficient in information, i. 6.
Extracts of the diary, *v.* Diary.

Faba, rapids, ii. 45.

Index. 341

Fair, of Cassange, i. 286, 321.
Farofia, i. 364.
Fauna, African, ii. 283.
Feathers, ostrich and marabout, ii. 266.
Fendi, district, i. 60 ; mountains, i. 66.
Ferns, i. 105 ; ii, 5, 11.
Fetish, tortoise-shell, i. 90; against musket-balls, i. 246; against rain, i. 251.
Fetishism, i. 112, 324; ii. 243.
Fevers, i. 99, 336, 342, 356, 359; ii. 132, 223.
Ficus elastica, i. 339.
Figueiredo (Antonio de), ii. 58.
Filippe, i. 192, 230, 240.
Finde, *pluteau* of, ii. 147.
Firing the Forest, i. 277.
Fiscus capelli, i, 358.
Fish of the Calae, i. 84; of the Luando, i. 154; of the Cuango, i. 301, 339 ; of the Cuanza, ii. 200, 204.
Flea, Brazilian (*pulex penetrans*), ii. 209.
Flies, honey-making, attacks of, ii. 198, 212.
Flora, climatologic zones in the Hungo, ii. 146; African, its wealth, ii. 265.
Fly (ox), ii. 19.
Food in West and Central Africa, ii. 254.
Forked log, punishment, i. 362.
Fortuna, mu-sumbi, i. 151 ; ii. 98, 103.
Fortuna, river, discovery of, ii. 98; lost on the banks of, ii. 99, 100.
Francisco, the model *muzumbo*, v. *Muzumbo*.
Frogs, *Rana ornatissima*, (highly ornamented), ii. 205 ; strange noise made by, ii. 5.
Fruit, native, danger of, ii. 35.
Fuba, manioc flour, i. 180; making of, i. 239; mode of obtaining, i. 364.
Fuche-ia-Cacalla, site of, i. 341, 358; payment of a *mu-cuno* at, i. 342.
Fugeras, in Quicongo, ii. 89.
Fuma in Quioco, i. 174.
Fumaranga, sova, i. 248.
Fumbezo, small river, i. 284.
Funantes, i. 16.
Funda, libata on the Cu-bango, i. 92.
Funda-Imbi, senzala, ii. 152.
Funeral, ceremonies, i. 140, 379.
Fungo, fruit, i. 224.
Futa, territory of, ii. 88, 124.

Galangue, district, i. 60, 102.
Galengue, Oryx gazella, i. 67.

Gamba, rivulet, ii. 19.
Gandeeira, sova of Huamba, i. 169.
Ganga, rivulet, i. 33.
Gangas, Balearia regulorum, i. 67.
Ganguellas, i. 93, 102 ; industry of the people, i. 93.
Garanganja, i. 17, 102 ; copper-mine at ii. 233.
Garanhi, river, i. 388.
Garapa, native beer, i. 35, 58.
Gazelles, i. 67, 302, 355.
Gengi, i. 102.
Geology, i. 21 ; ii. 231.
Ginguba, Anachis hypogea, i. 58 ; ii. 163, 254, 266.
Gnats, i. 95.
Goîtres, i, 148, 232.
Gold, ii. 266.
Golungo, ii. 208.
Gongó, fruit, i. 39.
Gongólo (myriapodes), i. 329.
Goods, values and qualities of, in the interior, i. 322.
Goose, i. 67.
Gramineous plants, i. 354.
Granite, i. 32, 43, 217 ; ii. 214, 231.
Grasses, *Capim, Panicum* and *Andropogon*, i. 224; ii. 13; firing of, i. 277.
Grave, a hunter's, i. 215.
Greenwich meridian adopted, ii. 271.
Grus carunculata, crane, nat. *panda*, i. 67.
Guingas, rocks of, ii. 194.
Gums, i. 16, 369.

Hacca, game, i. 375.
Halket-boat, Macintosh, native description of, i. 312, 345.
Hallucination, strange, i. 374.
Hamba, river, ii. 61, 65.
Hango, territory of the, ii. 184.
Hartmann, R., ii. 250.
Head-dresses, i. 80, 111, 369 ; ii. 54, 71, 120, 123, 130, 219.
Heleji, river, ii. 191.
Hemichromis angolensis, ii. 204.
Hemp, ii. 266.
Hengue, serra, basalts in, ii. 190.
Herminieras in Quioco, i. 224.
Herminiera E., ii. 14.
Hippopotamus, nat. *n'guvo*, i. 67, 274 ; snares for, i. 69 ; death of one, i. 249 ; in Yacca, ii. 129, 199.
Hippotragus equinus, i. 221.
Hippotragus niger, antelope, i. 67.
Hives (bee) in Quioco, i. 197, 281, 359.

Index

Holo, subdivision of the district of Cassange, i. 320 ; track of, ii. 81, 149.
Honey, nat. *uitchi*, in Quioco, i. 197 ; fondness of the natives for, i. 281.
Honey-bird. *Cucus indicator*, i. 281.
Honey-combs, i. 281.
Horary in Duque de Bragança, ii. 162.
Hottentot, natives, i. xxi.
Huambo, district of, i. 79, 81.
Huicumbamba (*Caprimulgo Shelleyi*), ii. 183.
Huilla, district, i. 49, 81.
Hunga, port, ii. 196.
Hungo, territory of the, ii. 71 ; inhabitants, colour, head-dresses, ii. 71, 72 ; women, ii. 73 ; dwellings, &c., ii. 74.
Hunters in Quioco, i. 214 ; visit to encampment, i. 217 ; distrustful, ii. 108.
Huts, i. 96, 198.
Huta, bow of the Quiocos, i. 166.
Hydromel, *v.* Mead.
Hyenas, i. 21 ; *H. fusca*, i. 271, 358.
Hyphœne, i. 358 ; ii. 88.
Hypnosis, disease, native names and remarks upon, i. 136.
Hyppotragus equinus, Ma-lanca, i. 274.
Hyppotragus niger? nat. *palanca*, i. 274.

Ibari N'Kutu, ii. 141.
Ica, i. 167.
Icollo, ii. 208.
Imbarri, i. 18.
Imbia, i. 167.
Imboa, boggy land in Cassange, i. 355.
Imbundeiro, *v.* Baobab.
India-rubber, i. 197, 303, 322, 369, 394 ; ii. 16, 89, 215, 266.
Infundi of maize flour or manioc root, i. 31, 61, 75, 339, 363.
Inga, territory of, i. 66.
Inhame, Discorea, i. 58 ; 366 ; ii. 255.
Instructions, first paragraph of, i. xxviii.
Inundated plateau, nat. *anharas, anhanas*, i. 85, 93 ; ii. 11.
Iron (magnetic) i. 47 ; oligist, i. 223 ; ii. 233, 266.
Itambi, i. 26 ; among the Bau-gala, i. 378
Ivory, i. 16, 322, 369, 394 ; ii. 215, 266.

Jackals, *Canis aureus*, i. 271, 358, 372.
Jaggado, i. 320.
Jaggas of Cassange, i. 320 ; disputes and effects upon the fair at Cassange, i. 321 ; their tyrannies, i. 330 ; ceremonies of investiture, &c., i. 331.

Jatropha manihot, manioc, i. 82.
Jau, district of, i. 36.
Jimbolamento, in Africa, i. 179.
Jimbolo, bread, i. 365.
Jinga, project to cross the, ii. 49 ; the road to, ii. 51 ; description of, ii. 52 ; population, monarch and aristocracy, ii. 52, 53.
Jingas, pockets, ii. 54 ; habitations, ii. 60.
Jinguengue, fruit, i. 366.
Jinguiji, river, affluent of the Cassai, i. 247.
Jinvunji, fetish influence, i. 380.
João de Andrade Corvo, i. xxvi.
João Baptista Ferreira, i. 18. .
José de Anchieta, i. 60, 67.
José de Senbra da Silva, ii. 195.
José, the guide, ii. 3, 83 ; his system of charming a snake, ii. 14 ; his uncles, ii. 35, 183 ; his valuable service, ii. 106.

Kete, i. 7.
Kitchen, novel, i. 35.

Lakes, i. 23, 66, 248 ; salt, ii. 15 ; 88, 126, 137, 145.
Landolphias in Qu'congo, ii. 89.
Languages and dialects, ii. 248.
Laula, rivulet, i. 126.
Lazarinos, fire-arm, i. 8.
Lemba (Mutu's wife), ii. 118.
Lemons, i. 103.
Leopard, *Lepardus jubatos*, i. 67.
Leucoryx, antelope, nat. *nuima*, i. 67.
Leva, river, i. 58.
Lhinica (Muene), i. 232 ; dangers and disputes, i. 233.
Liamba, smoking, i. 393 ; ii. 27.
Lianzundo, cataract of, ii. 45.
Liba, river, i. 102.
Libata, *v.* Senzala ; description, i. 61 ; of the sova of Quingolo, i. 85.
Licomte, i. 16 ; ii. 266.
Limes, i. 103.
Limestone, ii. 231.
Liniani, i. 17.
Lion, *ossi*, i. 58, 47.
Livingstone, i. 18, 130 ; ii. 190.
Loanda (St. Paul da Assumpoño de), capital of Angola, seat of the government, arrival at, ii. 227 ; reception there, ii. 228.
Lobenda, senzala, ii. 129.
Locusts, i. 95.

Lombe, river, point of affluence in the Cuanza, ii. 194; at Caballo, ii. 207; do Motta, ii. 207.
Londimba, river, i. 58.
Louisa falls, i. 273.
Lu-ache, river, ii. 65.
Lu-ajimo, river, i. 200, 322.
Lu-alaba, river, i. 102, 199.
Lu-ali, river in Quioco, i. 232.
Luamba, territory of, ii, 153.
Luando, affluent of the Cuanza, i. 145; 146; description and source, i. 153; ii. 157.
Luandos, i. 197.
Luango, senzala, ii. 11.
Luangue, river, i. 309.
Luba, i. 322; ii. 217.
Lu-bilachi, river, i. 218.
Lubiza, i. 102.
Lubbock (Sir John), ii. 213, 246.
Lubuco territory, i. 369; 217.
Lu-buri, river, i. 248.
Lu-calla, river, affluent of the Cuanza, ii. 45; banks of the, ii. 49; source of the, ii. 153, 184.
Lucano, i. 393.
Luce, river, eastern limit of Quioco, i. 191.
Luceque, district, i. 66.
Lu-chilo, river, ii. 181.
Luco, plant, employment of root in making beer, i. 58, 365.
Lucoquessa, her importance in the Lunda, i. 190, 386.
Lu-culla, river, limit of the Songo, i. 160, 229.
Lu-ejime, i. 247.
Lu-embe, river, i. 200.
Luena, serra, ii. 225.
Lughias, ii. 33.
Luimbe, territory of, i. 144.
Lu-ioto, salt river, affluent of the Cuango, i, 271, 283.
Lui, river, ii. 5. 11.
Lu-iza, river in the Lunda, i. 388.
Lu-lua, river, i. 247.
Lu-undo, i. 15.
Lu-me, river, i. 196.
Lu-nano, i. 15.
Lunda, of the Muata Yanvo, i. 18, 317; difficulty of the Bihénos in crossing, i. 394; natives of, i. 394.
Lungue, division of the, ii. 191.
Lu-oje, river, ii. 147.
Lu-quengue, river, affluent of the Cassia, i. 217.
Lu-quiche, river, ii. 126.

Ma-becos, *Canis mesomelus* (?), i. 369.
Mabella, *Hyphæne guinensis*, i. 53, 197, 239, 369, 394.
Mabu, *Papyrus antiq.*, mats of, i. 197.
Macaca Acatumbo, sources of the Culango, i. 93.
Macalungo, road to, i. 211.
Ma-colla, fruit, i. 224.
Macolo, river, ii. 132.
Ma-cosa, tribes of the, i. 187, 191, 390.
Macotas, i. 53, 116, 119. 174.
Maculo, disease, treatment of, i. 371.
Macume-N'jimbo, territory of, source of the Cugho, ii. 88, 224.
Macundi, bean, i. 366.
Ma-cunhapamba, ii. 28.
Mafungo, senzala, ii. 129.
Mad-apples, i. 366.
Mayhia, arrows in Quioco, i. 169.
Mahabo, senzala, ii. 67.
Mahungo, *jagga* of Cassange, i. 329.
Mahungo people, ii. 72; surrounded by, ii. 75; discourse of, ii. 76; exigencies of, ii. 82; discussions with, ii. 83.
Maize, i. 103; ii. 149, 254, 266.
Malange, district of, i. 323; ii. 38, 191; return to, ii. 207.
Malavo, name given to aguardente, i, 135.
Ma-libundo, ii. 30.
Ma-lunga, i. 167; in the Jinga; ii. 54.
Maluvo, palm wine, i. 366; ii. 88; process of extracting it, ii. 144.
Malvaceas, i. 367; ii 89.
Manatus senegalensis, mermaid, ii. 202.
Ma-n'cuba (ticks), i. 127.
Manioc, *Jatropha manihot*, i. 37, 103; taste of, ii. 26, 254.
Mangongo, libata of, ii 89.
Mangos, i. 77, 348.
Ma-n'gula, *Dendrobates namaquus*, i. 358.
Ma-numa, i. 330.
Mantis, grass, ii. 28.
Maoanda, libata in Quioco, i. 232.
Maoungo, river, i. 247.
Mapemba, river, ii. 108.
Ma-pura, bee country, i. 197.
Ma-quioco, eastern designation, i. 191; tribes of, i. 224; uses, customs, &c. in Catuchi, i. 299.
March in the dark, i. 271.
Marianga, *Pensetum* (?) on the banks of Cuango, i. 213; in Cassange, ii. 5, 124.

Maria segunda, beads, i. 8.
Market, nat. *T'chituca*, i. 84, 197, 389.
Marimba, musical instrument, i. 62, 94, 139.
Marriage on the journey, ii. 118.
Marshes, in the Cuango, ii. 13.
Ma-shinge people, i. 345.
Ma-songo, principal carriers at the fair, i. 322; caravan of, ii. 16.
Ma-sosso, ii. 124.
Massambala, Sorghum, i. 37, 103; ii. 254.
Massango, Penisetum typhoideum, i. 103; ii. 254.
Matamba, subdivision of the Jinga, ii. 52, 71.
Matchimbo, rivulet, i. 247.
Ma-t'chobo, shaggy, amphibious goat, i. 129.
Mateba, Hyphæne guinensis, i. 358.
Matete, i. 365.
Matheus Gomes Pereira, i. 61.
Mu-tomuzumos in the Jinga, ii. 53.
Ma-vuvi, silk-weaving spider, ii. 30.
Maxim, i. 339.
Ma-yacca people, ii. 119; description of, ii. 123.
Mazal (Muene), i. 229.
M'bacas, caravans in Africa, ii. 18.
M'bala, i. 187, 209.
M'bambu, Erythroplæum guineense, i. 228, 382.
M'bangarala (*Cicadas*), ii. 30.
M'boellas people, i. 390.
M'briche, river, ii. 149.
M'chiri, sova of the Garanganja, musical tendencies, i. 138; Quioco road, i. 197.
Mead, hydromel, nat. *quingundo*, in Quioco, i. 186.
Mechow, Von, meeting with, ii. 223.
Merionis, Afric. rat, i. 68.
Mermaid (*Manatus senegalensis*), ii. 202.
Metroxilon, poles of, ii. 93.
Mica, i. 21, 43; ii. 233.
Micendeiras, sycamores in Belmonte, i. 98.
Mieji, river, northern limit of the Quioco, i. 191.
Mienguelecas, description of, i. 367.
Milongo, i. 73, 286.
Minungo, lands of, i. 262.
Missalo, sieve, i. 327.
Missions, ii. 262.
Moaza-n'gombe, river, i. 248.

Mocambe, serra, ii. 232.
Moenga, serras of the, i. 162, 243, 308.
Moi-Chandalla-Dicoata, female sova, startling declaration, i. 237.
Moles, i. 68.
Moma, libata, i. 95, 128.
Mona-N'gola, denomination of the Jingas, ii. 54.
Mongôa, sova of the Songo, i. 148; complications, i. 149; nocturnal expedition, i. 150.
Monkeys, i. 146. 241; ii. 86.
Mornyrus Lhuisi, ii. 204.
Mortality in Malange and Cassange, ii. 37.
Mossamedes, i. 81; ii. 229.
Mosquitoes, attacks of, i. 96, 270, 372; mode of dispersing them, i. 270.
Moteba, ancient Yanvo, i. 338.
M'pacaça (*Bubulus caffer*), v. Buffalo.
M'pafu in Quioco, i. 228; in the Hungo, ii. 86.
M'peixe, i. 167.
M'pembas in the Jinga, ii. 54.
M'puca, Quioco, i. 174; his discourse, i. 178.
Muaca (*Hemichromis angolensis*), ii. 204.
Muaji, oath, i. 382.
Mu-anza, ii. 33.
Muata-Cha-Munji, vassal of King N'Dumba, i. 160.
Muata-Yanvo, i. 18, 289, 385.
Muata, title in Quioco, i. 160.
Muavi, oath, 382.
Mu-caje, i. 364.
Mu-canda, i. 166.
Mu-cano, fine, i. 333; ii. 7.
Mucari, river, ii. 38.
Mucete, huts, i. 238.
Mu-cha, of salt, i. 285, 369.
Muchi, small sticks to guide cattle, i. 39.
Muchila, i. 14.
Muchito in the Hungo, ii. 87; in Quicongo, ii. 94.
Mu-chinga, i. 102, 167.
Muco N'gola, denomination of the Jingas, ii. 54.
Mu-coali, axe, i. 392.
Mucole-Maiale, senzala, ii. 152.
Mucole-Quipanzo, senzala, ii. 87.
Mucuna pruriens, i. 274.
Mucuna, river, almost lost in, ii. 67.
Mucunha, sova in the Bihé, i. 126.
Mu-curulumbia mantis, ii. 27.
Muene, lord in the Bihé, i. 160.

Muene Cantalla, sova, i. 187, 191.
Muene Caria, dignity in Quioco, i. 147, 190.
Muene Congo Tubinge, ii. 125.
Muene Puto, name of the Portuguese monarch, i. 133.
Muene Puto Cassongo, (Quianvo), ii. 120.
Muene-Songo, ii. 141.
Muen'iche in the Jinga, ii. 54.
Mu-ghande, for fishing, i. 154.
Mu-hamba, i. 10, 74, 369; of the Ambaquista, ii. 40.
Muhamba, river, ii. 12.
Muhungo in Quioco, i. 228; ii. 141.
Muhungo, *Jagga* of Cassange, i. 329.
Muhunzo serra, ii. 42.
Muiji, river in Quioco, i. 229.
Mulondo, lands of, i. 66.
Muluia, river, ii. 125.
Munda, serra, i. 33, 38.
Munda, senzala, ii. 153.
Mundambala, hatchet in Quioco, i. 167.
Muntalandonga (Euprepes Ivensi), ii. 201.
Muntimbo, village, i. 283.
Mupas, rapids of the Cuando, i. 63; of the Cunene, i. 66; of the Cubango, i. 92; of the Cutato, i. 95; of the Cuanza, ii. 45, 220; of the Cuango, ii. 141.
Mussala, rivulet, ii. 123.
Muquiche in Quioco, dress, dances, i. 294; objects, i. 296.
Muquisse, powder, i. 318.
Muropöe, empire of the, i. 386.
Mus ratus, dorsalis, and *pumilio*, nat. *onguero*, i. 67.
Mu-sumba in the Lunda, residence of the *cabeba*, and position, i. 385; mode of constructing, i. 389.
Mussombo, lake, sources of the Cuanza, i. 122.
Muta, site of, ii. 220.
Mu-tala, bedstead, i. 327.
Mutemo-Ambuilla, ii. 153.
Mutia, i. 387.
Mutombo Muculi, sova, i. 389.
Mutopa, i, 166.
Mutu, carrier, fall into the river, i. 254; his marriage, ii. 118.
Mutula, rapids of, ii. 198.
Mu-topa, pipe, for the *Liamba*, ii. 27.
Muzumbo, interpreter, i. 188; aptitude i. 211; flight and robbery, i. 212.
Mu-zumbo Tembo, first monarch of the Songo, i. 107, 191.
Myriapodes, Spirostreptus gongólo, i.

241; new species found in Cassange, i. 329.
Naja negricolis, remarks respecting the, i. 65.
Nama-Muene, i. 267.
Nanja, sova, i. 35.
Nanos, v. Bananos.
Naoeji, Yanvo, i. 388.
N'baca, caravan, i. 37.
N'bije, i. 166.
N'bonzo, i. 58.
N'bunda, language spoken in Loanda, i. 15.
N'bundo, dialect of the Lu-nano, i. 15.
N'bungo, wolf, i. 21.
N'burututo, ii, 214.
N'cunha, i. 167.
N'cusso, ii. 126.
N'Dala Quissua, *Jagga* of the Bondos, ii. 25.
N'Dala Samba, ii. 35; divisional line of waters, ii. 38.
N'Damba, sova, i. 58.
N'dengue, ii. 4.
N'djabite, hatchet, i. 115, 147; in Quioco, i. 167.
N'dua, oath among the Ban-bondo, i. 382,
N'dui (Decamera-tonantis), as used by the natives, ii. 213.
N'dulo, i. 102.
N'Dumba Cachilo-chilo, sova, i. 292.
N'Dumba Mughande, sova, i. 292.
N'Dumba T'chiquilla, sova, i. 211; description, i. 304; his drunkenness and pretensions, i. 306.
N'Dumba Tembo, king of the Quioco, i. 174; first visit, i. 175; description, i. 177; his discourse, i. 179; strange pretension, i. 180; present sent, i. 181; return visit, i. 187: a narrative, i. 190; journey made in his company, i. 214.
N'dundje (Muene), sova of the Missungo, i. 257, 332.
Nenuphares in Cassange, ii. 5.
Nephila bragantina, ii. 30.
Nests, ii. 29, 214.
N'gace, oath, i. 382.
N'gami, inundated plains of, i. 93.
N'gana, lord, i. 160.
N'gana, n'zambi, fetish in Quioco, i. 113.
N'gana, N'zendo, sova, ii 153.
N'gando, sova, i. 127.
N'ganga-ia-puto, ii. 45.
N'ganga n'zumba, sova, ii. 15.
N'ganga, rivulet, ii. 124.

N'gola, village, i. 51.
N'gola n'boles in the Jinga, ii. 53.
N'gola, Quituche, sova, ii. 198.
N'golas (Quilluanjes Quiassambas), ii. 52.
N'gombe, Erythrina chrisecarpa, i. 82.
N'gonga, family of the, i. 329.
N'guengue, libata, i. 58.
N'guenzi, i. 102.
N'gumbe, ii. 30.
N'yunguachito, ii. 214.
N'guri, district of, ii. 13; journey to, and difficulties on the road, ii. 14.
N'guri, serra, ii. 11.
N'guvo, sova of the Cassai, i. 247.
N'guvo, v. Hippopotamus.
N'hangue-ia-Pepe, ii. 220.
N'hembas people, i. 91.
N'hongos, district of the, ii. 220.
Niangué, i. 18.
Nicotiana tabacum rustica, ii. 72.
Niger, basin of the, ii. 238.
Nimia, Luco-em (?), ii. 236.
N'jamba, elephant, i. 107.
N'jamba, libata in the Cuanza, i. 142.
N'jombo, river, abundance of fish in, i. 229.
Nogueira (A. F.), ii. 245.
Nourse, river, i. 67.
Novo Redondo, district, i. 9, 10.
N'poco coculula, i. 167.
Nu-cele, falls of the Cu-lato, i. 95.
Nunha, Bihé village so called, i. 123.
Nymphaceas in Quicongo, numerous species of, ii. 89.
Nymphea stellata, nat. *ebangue,* i. 92.
N'zamba, falls of the Cuango, i. 345.
N'zare, designation of the Cassai, i. 247.

Oath, among the Ban-gala, i. 382; mode of administering, i. 383; final result, i. 385.
Obaba-Tenda, rivulet, i. 47.
Obongo, natives, i. 112.
Odonata, ii. 28.
Oca, a hundred men in the Bihé, i. 134.
Oeiras, ii. 233.
Ofuanganga, Erythrina huillensis, i. 82.
Olimbinda, libata, i. 144.
Olococos, Elotarsus, i. 358.
Olumupa, i. 95; greatest altitude attained, i. 98.
Ongue, panther, i. 21, 214.
Onguero, Mus ratus, dorsalis, and *pumilio,* i. 67.

Opabanganda, falls of the Cubango, i. 93.
Oranges, i. 60, 103; ii. 195, 198.
Orchideas epidendres, ii. 89.
Oreas canna, antelope, i. 43.
Oriungo, Rubiacea, i. 45.
Oryx capensis, gemsbok, i. 129.
Oryx gazella, nat. *golengue,* i. 67.
Ossassa, Brachystegia tamar, i. 82.
Ossi, lion, i. 48.
Otubo, chief of the *Ban-sumbi,* i. 76, 263; thievery, ii. 174; attempted evasion, ii. 180.
Ovampo, district of, i. 93.
Oxen (saddle), i. 78, 84.
Ox-fly, ii. 19.

Pacaça Aquibonda, division of the Jinga, district of, ii. 153.
Painting, i. 318.
Palança, Rocks of, ii. 220.
Palanca, Hyppotragus n. (?), or *equinus,* i. 274.
—— in Quicongo, ii. 110.
Palm oil, i. 394; ii. 266.
Palm-trees, ii. 88.
Palma christi, i. 103, 366; ii. 266.
Pamba (Ambaca), visit to, ii. 187.
Pambo of Encoge, ii. 149.
Pambos in the Dondo, ii. 225.
Panda, Grus carunculata, i. 67.
Panicum, variety of *capim,* grass, i. 224.
Panthers, i. 21, 67, 275.
Papa, serras of, ii. 184.
Papaeira, *Carrica Papaya,* ii, 257.
Papyrus antiquorum, nat. *mabu,* i. 93. 243, 354; in Cassange, ii. 5.
Partridges, ii. 38, 192.
Paschoal (Narciso Antonio), ii. 3.
Patrulhas, ii. 181.
Pedras negras, the Black Rocks, ii. 193.
Peinde, district, parrots of, i. 258; backwoods, i. 322; lands of, ii. 22.
Pelomys fallax, rat, i. 68.
Pelopæus spirifex, nat. *maribundo,* ii. 30.
Penisetum hyphoideum, i. 224.
Pepper (chili), i. 364; ii. 9, 266.
Pereira de Mello, governor of Benguella, i. 20.
Pest of the woods, fly, ii. 19.
Petro, senzala, ii. 152.
Pezo (Muene), amusing intimation, i. 243.
Phacochærus ethiop, wild boar, i. 274.

Pharmacies, allopathic, dosimetric, and phenic, i. 73.
Phasianella Heddingtonensis, i. 24.
Picapus, *Dendrobates namaquus*, woodpecker, i. 358.
Pigeons, wood, ii. 38, 192.
Pine-apples, i. 44, 103.
Pionias Meyerii, i. 355.
Pipes, nat. *quixibo*, i. 74.
Pirão, i. 258; making of, i. 364.
Plantations, i. 58; ii. 78.
Plateaux (inundated), i. 85.
Populo, Diptero, fly, i. 52.
Potatoes, *Solanum tuberosum*, nat. *n'bonzo*, i. 37.
Potatoes, sweet, *Convolvulus batatas*, i. 58, 74.
Porto Real, ii. 185.
Praça Velha, ii, 187.
Ptyelus olvaceus, i. 146; ii. 181.
Pulex Penetrans, v. Flea.
Pumpkins, i. 358.
Pungo N'Dongo, rocks of, ii. 190; geological formation, ii. 194; noteworthy impressions upon, ii. 194, 195; town of, ii. 195; return to, ii. 208; winds at, ii. 210.
Puva, Mount, i. 58.

Quartz, i. 21, 22, 43, 135, 217.
Que, river, i. 51, 58.
Quembo, district of, i. 191, 313; fauna, i. 313; Portuguese fair, i. 321.
Quendengongo, sova, i. 37,
Quiabos, Abelmoschus esculentos, i. 358, 367.
Quiambella, serra, ii. 200.
Quingala in the interior, i. 373.
Quiangolo, island of, ii. 199.
Quianvo (Muene Puto Cassango), ii. 120.
Quibau (Muene), his letter, i. 193.
Quibinda, village of, ii. 203.
Quibulo-bolo, Causus rhombeatus, i. 357.
Quibonde, lake in the Songo, i. 154.
Quibucas, organized in Cassange, i. 37; in Africa, ii. 18.
Quibundo, senzala, i. 197.
Quicalla, site in the Bihé, i. 126.
Quicanga, senzala of, ii. 152.
Qui co'os, ii. 199.
Quicongo, district of, ii. 88; aspect and vegetation, ii. 88.
Quicuba, ganguella sova, i. 126.
Quicué, rivulet, i. 49.

Quicunji, falls of the Cuango, ii. 126.
Quifanjimbo, river, i. 388.
Quifanjimbo, internal lake, i. 248; ii. 218.
Quifucussa, sova, ii. 27.
Qui-jinga in the Jinga, ii. 54.
Quilau, Monnt, in the Sambo, i. 86.
Quilemba, i. 18.
Quilemo, sova of the Bihé, i. 116, 120; present, i. 121; visit and reception, i. 121, 124.
Quilengo-lengo, Bucephalus typus, i. 357.
Quileba serra, i. 66; divisional line of the waters of the Atlantic and Indian oceans, i. 81.
Quillengues, district of, i. 10, 36; geographical position, mountains, &c., i. 36, 37, 38, 39.
Quillengues, people, i. 80; valley of, i. 46.
Quilluanjes in the Jinga, ii. 53.
Quilolos, i. 390; ii. 123.
Quilombo, v. Encampment; of the Bihé wars, i. 142.
Quilulo, serras of, ii. 192.
Quilulo-n'sandi, Bihé, fetish, i. 112.
Quimalanca, hyena, i. 21.
Quimana, village of, ii. 149.
Quimangata, i. 374.
Quimbamba (Cosmetornis vexillarius), ii. 183.
Quimbaxe, river, ii. 64.
Quimbimbe, Fiscus capelli, i. 358.
Quimbombo, beer, i. 365.
Quimbundo, i. 308.
Quin-bundo, erroneous designation, i. 108; idiom of the Bihé, i. 108.
Quinbandi, lands of, i. 121.
Quinbungo Quiassama, ii. 51.
Quinbanda, medicine-man, i. 26, 380.
Quindas, i. 63, 180, 364.
Quingolo, district of, i. 79. 81, 85.
Quingunde, mead of the Quioco, i. 198, 366.
Quinguri, banquet of, i. 332.
Quini, i. 167.
Quioco (T'chiboco), notes upon the, i. 223; flora, fruits, i. 224; inhabitants, i. 224.
Quionja, dwelling of the Coimbras in the Bihé, i. 138.
Quioza, prisoners of war, i. 97; senzala in the Cuanza, i. 97.
Quipangula, site of, i. 44.
Quipundi, i. 167.

Quipungo, district, i. 48, 49.
Quipungos, natives, i. 52; thugs, i. 52.
Quipupa, chalybeate water in, i. 20; geology, i. 21.
Quiquanga, confection of, i. 364.
Quissama, ii. 215.
Quissangua, beverage, i. 65, 185, 365.
Quissanja, small marimba, i. 173, 189.
Quissaquina Caboco, falls of, ii. 220.
Quissongo, military commander in the Bihé, i. 142, 174, 206.
Quissongo, chief of the caravan, i. 132, 147; (old) of the Bihé, ii. 154.
Quitamba, Caquigungo, i. 335, 355.
Quitandas, i. 197; ii. 225.
Quitanguca, village of, ii. 152.
Quitaxe, falls of, ii. 203.
Quiteca N'bungo, lands of, i. xxix; ii. 124.
Quiteque, site in the Bihé, i. 136.
Quitoché, rocks of, ii. 194.
Quitoeta, mountains of, ii. 201.
Quituche, i. 183; ii. 7.
Quitumba Caquipungo, banza, ii. 12.
Quitumba, sova, i. 317.
Qui-vuvi, silk spider, ii. 27, 192.
Quizau Malunga, senzala of, ii. 88.
Quizengamo, quilolo of the Quianvo, ii. 123.
Quizumene, *mu-sumba* of, i. 388.
Quizunguelle, senzala of Quioco, i. 160.

Rafts at Porto Real, ii. 186.
Railway (Ambaca) projected, ii. 189.
Rainy season, i. 104.
Rauinas, fire-arms, i. 8.
Raphael Gorjão (Manuel), ii. 228.
Raphia vinifera, i. 21, 146.
Raphias, in the Hungo, ii. 88; zones where it exists, ii. 144, 146.
Rapids, *v. Mupas*.
Rats, i. 67.
Resins, i. 223; ii. 89.
Religion, i. 112; ii. 243.
Rhagerrhis tritæniatus, colombolo, i. 357.
Rhinoceros, i. 218; horn, i. 221, 394; varieties of, i. 222.
Rice, ii. 266.
Ricinus communis, i. 82.
Roberto Franco (José), ii. 230.
Rubiaceas, in Quioco, i. 224; in Quicongo, ii. 89.

Sá da Bandeira, his map, ii. 203.
Saccharium officinalis, sugar cane, i. 23.

Saccostomus lapidarius, rat, i. 68.
Sala-lé, termites, i. 95.
Salt in the Quembo, deficiency of, i. 285; its value in the interior, i. 285, 300; ii. 266.
St. Salvador, ii. 74, 126.
Samba, backwoods of, i. 199, 389.
Samba Cango, ii. 183.
Sambo, district of, i. 79, 91.
Santa Maria, herb, *Chenopodium ambrosioides*, i. 284, 371.
Sanza Manda, site of, ii. 38, 213.
Scarabeus, Cleopteros, ii. 29.
Schutt (Otto), ii. 12.
Schweinfurth, i. 112; ii. 186.
Scops capensis, i. 236.
Scops leucotis, ii. 187.
Scopus umbretta, ii. 214.
Scorpion, sting of, i. 352.
Scurvy, first symptoms of, i. 360; ii. 221.
Secula Binza, rivulet, i. 59.
Seculo of the sova of Bihé, i. 174.
Senegambia, country of, i. xxii.
Sengue, site of, ii. 220.
Senzala, village, i. 34; description of interior, i. 362; deserted, ii. 78.
Serpa Pinto (Major Alexandre A. d a Rocha), i. 73; first news of his return, ii. 196; his opinion on missionary labour, ii. 261.
Sharpia angolensis, i. 358.
Shells, cowries, i. 198; ii. 80.
Shinge, *v.* Xinge.
Silk in Africa, ii. 192, 266.
Silk-weaving spider, ii. 27, 192.
Silva Americano, steamer, ii. 227.
Silva Porto, i. 17, 98.
Silver in the Jinga, ii, 58, 233, 266.
Silverio (Captain A.), chefe of Duque de Bragança, his residence, ii. 46; dinner with, ii. 165; his pets, ii. 181; adieu to, ii. 212.
Siminophis bicolor, nat. *mu-zuzo*, i. 357.
Slavery, ii. 260.
Snakes, i. 65; attack of, i. 357; meeting with, fright caused by, ii, 14.
Soana Molopo, i. 386.
Snuff among the Hungos, ii. 72.
Social relations of the natives of West and Central Africa, ii. 240, 258.
Socobala, site of, i. 38.
Solanum melongena, sp., i. 366.
Soma-catito, subalterns, i. 142.
Soma-ia-can-djambu, sort of general in the Bihé, i. 142.

Sombrero, Mount, i. 11.
Songo, lands of, i. 191, 201.
Sorgho, Sorghum, nat. *massambala*, i. 37, 103.
Sovas, ceremonies at decease, i. 92; godfathers, ii. 166; blind, ii. 197, 198.
Sovetas, disputes with, ii. 38.
Songanhe, village of, ii. 149.
Songo, territory of the, i. 160.
Sosso, natives of the, ii. 125, *v.* Ma-Sosso.
Sousa (Antonio de), ii. 227.
Spathodea campanulata, ii. 148.
Speke, i. 113; ii. 259.
Spirostreptus gougólo, ii. 29.
Spittle, i. 178; ii. 152.
Spittoon (royal) i. 178; ii. 152.
Stanley (Henry M.), communications with, i. xxx; i. 130; ii. 229.
Stanley Pool, ii. 141.
Steatomys edulis, nat. *Canena*, i. 68.
Steel, native, i. 115.
Stork, i. 67.
Storms, i. 96, 298, 346, 359; ii. 62, 63.
Stramonium, Solanea, i. 36, 103.
Strepsiceros cudu, antelope, i. 43.
Suco-ia-muquita, cataract of the Cuango, ii. 27, 141.
Suco-ia-n'bundi, cataract of the Cuango, ii. 27, 141.
Suele, river, i. 389.
Sulphur, i. 22; ii. 266.
Su-la Tebeles, i. 93.
Sumbo, Mount, i. 38.
Supa, pass of the, i. 37.
Sussa, province of the Jinga, ii 52.
Sussa, river, ii. 147.
Sycamores, *micendeiras*, i. 98, 118, 146; in Cassange, ii. 2.
Synagris cornuta, fly, its sting, ii. 19, 28.

Tacúla, i. 13; ii. 22, 163; in the Jinga, uses of, ii. 59, 266.
Taculas, bees in the, i. 359.
Tala-Mogongo, serras of, i. 191; northwestern edge, i. 261; elevation, i. 262; ravine of, ii. 5; grand view from, and vegetation of, ii. 22.
Tama, serra, i. 33, 38.
Tamarinds, ii. 22.
Tamega, gun-boat, i. 9.
Tanagra erythrorrhyncha, ii. 215.
Tango, river affluent of the Cassai, i. 247.
Taramanjamba, i. 33.

Tattooing (?), branding, i. 317; ii. 219
T'chabicua, lands of, i. 66.
T'chiboco, native pronunciation of Quioco, i. 113, 160.
T'chibungo, mountains of, i. 196.
T'chica, tombs at, ii. 37.
T'chicanji (Muene), curiosity of the chief, i, 241.
T'chicapa, or chicapa, river, i, 102, 196, 247.
T'chicondi, or Chicondi, lake, i. 66, 68.
T'chigundo, small river in Quioco, i. 229
T'chimbarandungo, sova, *v.* Chimbarandungo.
T'chimbolo, bread, i. 63.
T'chinbondi, lake, in the Quembo, i. 285.
T'chinbungo, wolf, i. 107.
T'chingando, leguminous plant, used for fishing, i. 154.
T'chingolo, *mupas* of the Cubango, i. 92.
T'chinguri, minister of the sova T'chiquilla, i. 306.
T'chininga, or Chinhinga, serra, i. 48.
T'chiòrola, river, i. 81.
T'chipocama, or chipocama, senzala in the Bihé, i. 126.
T'chiquecua, i. 167.
T'chiquecula, Bulimus rucifex, in Cassange, i. 284.
T'chiquilla, sova, *v.* N'Dumba T'chiquilla.
T'chisanga, marimba, i. 77.
T'chita territory, i. 301.
T'chitaca, market in Quioco, articles met with, i. 184; general description, i. 185.
Telphusa Anchietæ, ii. 200.
Telphusa Bayoniana, ii. 200.
Tembo in Quioco, i. 177; N'Dumba, Muzumbo, Cassange, limits of the state, i. 191.
Tembo Aluma, sova, ii. 27.
Temo, i. 167; ii. 65.
Temperature, equable, ii. 270.
Tenga territory, i. 386.
Termites, *Nevropteros, fam. Planipennos*, i. 95, 51, 81, 329; ii. 30.
Thugs (African), i. 52.
Tiber, lake in the Hungo, ii. 78; meditations on its banks, ii. 80; persecuted by thieves at, ii. 81.
Tibesti, country of, i. xxii.
Tibu Tib, Arab of Imbarri, i. 18, 318.
Tiger Bay, ii. 232.

Tipoia, palanquin, i. 21; ii. 178; danger in using, ii. 191.
Tito (Pedro de Almeida), ii. 229.
Tiué, i. 33.
Toads, noise made by, ii. 6.
Toaza or Tuaza, falls of the Cuango, i. 345; ii. 141.
Tobacco, i. 103, 300, 358; ii. 27, 149, 164, 266.
Toccus elegans, i. 236.
Tomatoes, i. 358.
Tongo, fruit, i. 224.
Trade, tendency of the natives to, ii. 17.
Transvaal, country of the, i. xxii.
Tribes, migration of, ii. 236.
Tui, rivulet, i. 34.
Tumba, lake, i. 23.
Tunda, backwoods of, i. 337.
Tundo, fruit, i. 224.
Tundo, sova, i. 247.
Tungo N'Dongo, mountain, ii, 42.
Typhus in Quioco, i. 224; on the Cuango, i. 243; in Cassange, ii. 5.

Uálua, beer, mode of manufacturing, i. 365.
Ucha, fruit, i. 49.
Ucuba, Brachystegia tamar, i. 82.
Uitchi, honey, i. 197.
Ulemba, Urticacea, i. 49.
Ulondo, serra, of the Huambo, i. 79, 85.
Ulua, territory of, i. 18.
Umba (Domingos' innamorata), ii. 4.
Umenganga, fruit, i. 49.
Unberi, Eurotys Anchieta, i. 68.
Undado in the Jinga, ii. 54.
Unga, flour in Quioco, i. 309.
Unguiji, river, ii. 108.
Unicorn, *abbuda*, i. 16.
Uondé, hive, i, 197.
Upanda, i. 7.
Urginea sp. (?) i. 283.
Ussamba, acacia, i. 49.
Usserem, river, i. 58.
Ussolo, Urticacea, i. 49.
Uta, ii. 14.
Utumba, immense bog, a fall into, ii. 34.

Vasco Guedes de Carvalho e Menezes, ii. 227.
Veado, Cephalobus mergens (?), i. 43, 274.
Vegetation, rapid development, i. 104.
Venus, African, i. 147.

Victorias in Cassange, ii. 5.
Viduas paradiseas, ii. 183.
Vine, wild, *Vitis heraclifolia*, i. 82; ii. 255.
Vissecua, serra, i. 34, 38, 42.
Von Mechow, *v.* Mechow.
Vunda-ia-Buta, in the Jinga, ii. 64; sova, ii. 154; value of human life there, ii. 156.
Vunda-ia-Cassanda, ii. 167.
Vunda-ia-Ebo, burial at, ii. 157.
Vunda-ia-Mequenna in the Jinga, ii. 74.
Vunda-ia-N'gola Quilluanje in the Jinga, ii. 64.
Vunda-ia-T'chirimbimbe, ii. 166
Vunda-ia-Vunda-N'gola, important sova, ii. 153.
Vundas in the Jinga, ii. 53.
Vunji, serra, ii. 185.

Walrus' teeth, i. 16.
Water, ferruginous, Quipupa, i. 20.
Wolves, i. 21, 107, 340, 358,
Wax (bees), i. 16, 197, 224, 322, 369; ii 255.
Woodpecker (*Dendrobates namaques*), nat. *Ma-ngula*, i. 358.
Women of the caravan, ii. 81, 116.

Xylophages, ii. 30.
Xinge (Shinge), territory of, ii. 22.

Yacca, territory of, limits of exploration, i. xxix; information respecting its people, customs, &c., ii. 131.
Yanvos, their states, dynasty, i, 386; ceremonies, i. 318.
Yondo, district and subdivision of the territory of Cassange, i. 320; mountains, i. 313.
Yula, rivulet, i. 304, 308.

Zamba, cataract, ii. 141.
Zambese, valley of the, i. 91, 102.
Zebras, i. 67.
Zombo, serras of, ii. 126.
Zuala-mavuno, tribes, i. 218.
Zuarte, cloth, i. 7.
Zumbi, i. 26.
Zundo-ia-Cassungo in the Jinga, ii. 60.
Zundo-ia-Faco, ii. 49.
Zundos in the Jinga, ii. 53.

FINIS.

www.ingramcontent.com/pod-product-compliance
Lightning Source LLC
Chambersburg PA
CBHW020104020526
44112CB00033B/838